Behavior Management

Behavior Management

From Theoretical Implications to Practical Applications

Second Edition

JOHN W. MAAG
University of Nebraska–Lincoln

WADSWORTH
CENGAGE Learning™

Australia • Brazil • Japan • Korea • Mexico • Singapore • Spain • United Kingdom • United States

WADSWORTH
CENGAGE Learning

Behavior Management: From Theoretical Implications to Practical Applications, Second Edition
John W. Maag

Publisher: Edith Beard Brady

Education Editor: Dan Alpert

Development Editor: Tangelique Williams

Technology Project Manager: Barry Connolly

Editorial Assistant: Heather Kazakoff

Marketing Manager: Dory Schaeffer

Marketing Assistant: Neena Chandra

Advertising Project Manager: Shemika Britt

Project Manager, Editorial Production: Trudy Brown

Print/Media Buyer: Doreen Suruki

Permissions Editor: Kiely Sexton

Production Service: Strawberry Field Publishing

Text Designer: Adriane Bosworth

Copy Editor: Tom Briggs

Cover Designer: Gopa & Ted2

Cover Image: "Weather Change" (detail) by Gopa & Ted2

Compositor: Newgen

For product information and technology assistance, contact us at
Cengage Learning Customer & Sales Support, 1-800-354-9706

For permission to use material from this text or product, submit all requests online at **cengage.com/permissions**
Further permissions questions can be emailed to
permissionrequest@cengage.com

Library of Congress Control Number: 2002117700

Student Edition with InfoTrac College Edition
ISBN-13: 978-0-534-60885-9
ISBN-10: 0-534-60885-X

Student Edition without InfoTrac College Edition
ISBN-13: 978-0-534-60887-3
ISBN-10: 0-534-60887-6

Wadsworth
10 Davis Drive
Belmont, CA 94002-3098
USA

Cengage Learning is a leading provider of customized learning solutions with office locations around the globe, including Singapore, the United Kingdom, Australia, Mexico, Brazil, and Japan. Locate your local office at: **international.cengage.com/region**

Cengage Learning products are represented in Canada by Nelson Education, Ltd.

For your course and learning solutions, visit **academic.cengage.com**

Purchase any of our products at your local college store or at our preferred online store **www.ichapters.com**

Printed in the U.S.A.
6 7 8 9 10 11 10

I would like to dedicate this book to all the students who have taken courses from me in behavior management. They have constantly challenged me to make the information practical and relevant to real life. Without these students, there would be no book. I am indebted to them.

Contents

Preface   xiii
About the Author   xix

Chapter 1

Introduction to Behavior Management   1

Behavior Modification   2
Defining Behavior   4
Three-Term Contingency   8
Important Terms   12
Applied Behavior Analysis   15
Bringing It All Together   17

Summary   17

Activities   18

Review Questions   18

References   19

Chapter 2

Impediments to Managing Behavior   21

The Medical Model   23
Academic and Social Behavior   26
Contextual Variation   27
Personal Standards and Social Behavior   31
The Concept of Control   32

Summary   34

Activities   34

Review Questions   35

References   35

Chapter 3

Theories of Behavior   37

Biophysical Explanations   40
Psychodynamic Theory   41
Behavioral Approaches   45
Social Learning Theory   51
The Ecological/Sociological Model   54

Summary   60

Activities   60

Review Questions   61

References   61

Chapter 4

Basic Principles of Behavior   65

Principles Related to Increasing Behavior   66
Schedules of Reinforcement   77
Principles Related to Decreasing Behavior   82
Stimulus Control and Related Terms   86
Response Class and Related Terms   89

Summary   90

Activities   91

Review Questions   91

References   92

Chapter 5

Counting and Recording Behavior   93

Reasons Counting Behavior Is Important   94
Considerations Prior to Recording Behavior   100
Factors to Consider When Pinpointing a Target Behavior   101
Techniques for Recording Behavior   104
Methods for Calculating Interobserver Reliability   115

Summary   120

Activities   120

Review Questions   121

References   121

Chapter 6
Graphing Behavior   125

Benefits of Graphing Behavioral Observations   126
Elements of a Graph   128
Collecting Baseline Data   130
Designs for Graphing Behavior   132
Summary   *147*
Activities   *147*
Review Questions   *148*
References   *148*

Chapter 7
Functional Assessment of Behavior Problems   151

An Overview of Functional Assessment   153
Stages of Functional Assessment   160
Writing Behavioral Support Plans   175
Issues in Functional Assessment   179
Summary   *191*
Activities   *192*
Review Questions   *192*
References   *193*

Chapter 8
Preventative Approaches   199

Curricular Considerations   201
Direct Instruction   211
Environmental Accommodations   223
Summary   *232*
Activities   *233*
Review Questions   *233*
References   *234*

Chapter 9
Reinforcement Techniques for Increasing Behavior   237

Token Economies   239
Behavioral Contracts   251
Group-Oriented Contingencies   260
Novel Applications of Positive Reinforcement   268

Summary 275

Activities 276

Review Questions 276

References 277

Chapter 10
Differential Reinforcement for Decreasing Behavior 279

Types of Differential Reinforcement 280
Schedules of DRO and DRL 283
Considerations When Using Differential Reinforcement 292

Summary 293

Activities 293

Review Questions 294

References 294

Chapter 11
Punishment 295

Undesirable Side Effects of Punishment 297
Limitations of Punishment 301
Types of Punishment 304

Summary 319

Activities 319

Review Questions 319

References 320

Chapter 12
Teaching Self-Management 323

Theoretical Underpinnings of Self-Management 324
Self-Monitoring 327
Self-Evaluation 339
Self-Reinforcement 344

Summary 347

Activities 347

Review Questions 348

References 348

Chapter 13

Cognitive-Behavior Modification   351

An Overview of Cognitive-Behavior Modification   352
Methods of Cognitive-Behavioral Assessment   357
Cognitive-Behavior Modification Intervention Techniques   361

Summary   375
Activities   375
Review Questions   376
References   376

Chapter 14

Promoting Generalization   381

An Overview of Generalization   382
Tactics for Promoting Generalization   387
Recommendations for Applying Generalization Tactics   394
Issues in Promoting Generalization   395

Summary   398
Activities   398
Review Questions   398
References   399

Glossary   401

Index   421

Preface

Welcome to the wonderful world of behavior management. You are about to enter a realm about which few teachers have a solid working knowledge but many possess broad misconceptions. For instance, too many teachers think that behavior management consists of providing students with M & Ms or stickers when they exhibit appropriate behaviors. Behavior management entails much more—analyzing behavior, deciding what to change, collecting information on the behaviors of concern, using schedules of reinforcement, and monitoring progress—not to mention the variety of techniques for promoting students' appropriate behaviors. Some teachers may not be competent in behavior management because it is much more than simply giving a reward to children for "being good" or punishing them for "being bad." It should come as no surprise, therefore, that behavior management is probably one of the most misunderstood concepts in education today. It never ceases to amaze me that so many people can have such strong feelings concerning a topic about which they know so little.

What will become readily apparent to you is that behavior management is not easy—it is a time-consuming and difficult endeavor. Consequently, teachers need to ask themselves if students' inappropriate behavior is worth the time and effort required to develop and implement behavior management techniques. Sometimes the answer will be "no," and that is okay—not every behavior requires intervention. However, students with challenging behaviors can benefit most from the techniques presented in this book.

STUDENTS WITH CHALLENGING BEHAVIORS

About 90–95 percent of students who attend public school are well behaved, and most of these students respond to mild, traditional forms of discipline. Who cannot remember receiving a verbal reprimand from a teacher along the lines of "Stop talking and get to work!" Other traditional approaches that work for these students include having them stay after class or school to complete work, having them sit in the hall for a time-out, sending them to the principal's office, or conferencing with their parents. These students are, for the most part, internally motivated, do not require many tangible rewards, and have parents who tell them, "I don't care what Billy does in class; you will follow the teacher's directions." These students also aren't the ones who have substantial learning problems and who are acting out so that they don't appear to be stupid to their peers. Therefore, making small curricular modifications will eliminate many of their behavior problems. However, about 5–10 percent of students don't respond to these approaches. Managing their noncompliance is a formidable task—a challenge! We don't know what to do with them. Therefore, students with challenging behaviors are simply ones for whom our traditional techniques have failed.

When teachers are asked about student behaviors that cause them the most concern, the preponderance of behaviors named are those that fit into the disruptive and oppositional categories. These behaviors include fighting, teasing, leaving seats, and talking out of turn. These students can arouse negative feelings and induce negative behavior in others. Often, they are not popular among their peers, and they typically experience academic failure in addition to social rejection or alienation. Most teachers choose to avoid them as much as possible. Their behaviors are so persistently irritating to authority figures that these students seem to be asking for punishment or rebuke. It should come as no surprise, therefore, that teachers spend an inordinate amount of time trying to decrease the frequency of inappropriate behaviors these students exhibit in their classrooms.

THE FOCUS OF BEHAVIOR MANAGEMENT

Although it is often desirable to reduce disruptive behaviors, reduction is only one small part of a program for effectively managing students' challenging behaviors. The major goal of behavior management—the one that is emphasized in this book—involves increasing desirable student behaviors. To be effective behavior managers, teachers need specialized information and skills. Unfortunately, the needed information and skills are often inaccessible or unavailable to teachers. One of the main reasons I wrote this book was so that teachers at all career levels, ranging from teachers-in-training to seasoned veterans, can become better managers of student behavior. Acquiring these skills is essential because many more students than before are displaying an increasingly broad range of challenging behaviors in classrooms around the country.

THINGS TO KEEP IN MIND

One of my major goals in writing this book was to ensure, to the greatest extent possible, that it be "user-friendly." This commitment has sometimes been a challenge. For example, it is important for any textbook on behavior management to include discussions of principles of behavior, techniques for recording behavior, and methods for graphing behavior (which appear in Chapters 4, 5, and 6, respectively). In many textbooks, this information comes across as highly technical. To combat this problem, I fused many real-life examples and tried to keep the text as free of technical jargon as possible while preserving the theoretical and empirical foundations on which the book is based. That is one reason the subtitle is *From Theoretical Implications to Practical Applications.*

Unlike in other books on behavior management, you will find that the chapters containing specific interventions techniques (such as Chapters 8–14) go into considerable detail. I have included "how-to" lists, charts, graphs, and illustrations. My goal is for you to be able to implement the techniques successfully, rather than simply read a one- or two-page condensed description of them, as is typical of other behavior management books. Therefore, I hope you will keep this book handy and refer to it often during your teaching career. If you find this book helpful as you begin to teach, please tell a colleague about it. If you do not like it, please let me know why, and I will try to make it better.

As you read this book, always keep in mind that developing and implementing behavior management techniques are difficult! There are no quick fixes to students' challenging behaviors. In addition, behavior management is no substitute for teaching. That is, behavior management does not teach students new behaviors; teachers do. Rather, behavior management techniques are helpful in getting students to use behaviors and skills they already know but are not currently exhibiting. To accomplish this goal, you must systematically analyze and modify the antecedents (events that occur before a behavior) and consequences (events that occur after a behavior) that surround behavior. You should always start by analyzing and modifying the antecedents. This places you in a better position to prevent future episodes of misbehavior from occurring. It is important to maintain a preventative mindset.

Although behavior management is not easy, there is a great payoff for taking the time and effort to learn and implement the techniques described in this book. You will run more effective classrooms with students who treat each other, and you, with respect and who complete their work in a timely fashion. Not coincidentally, learning and implementing these techniques represents one of the best ways to preserve your own sanity in those occasionally insane moments that occur in every classroom.

THE APPROACH OF THIS BOOK

This book focuses primarily on students' observable behavior and the environmental factors that affect its expression—unlike many other books, which assume that behavior can be explained and manipulated through medical, pharmacological, or genetic treatments. Consequently, this book avoids labels that have little or no relevance to managing students' behaviors. Regardless of the labels students receive, they still engage in behavior whose expression is shaped by the environment.

One thing that will become clear is that developing and implementing behavior management interventions require considerable attention to detail—in identifying behaviors of concern, recording their occurrence precisely, and following detailed intervention plans. Although this approach may seem rigid or overly structured, there is one key rule to follow as you develop behavior management interventions: Take what students give you. In other words, do not be afraid to be flexible. Good behavior management interventions are constantly evolving to meet the ever-changing aspects of students' behaviors.

To meet this challenge, this book is organized into 14 chapters. Chapter 1 presents an introduction to behavior management and the basic tenets of behavior modification and applied behavior analysis on which it is based. Chapter 2 describes impediments to managing behavior that can interfere with our ability to deal with students' inappropriate behaviors. Chapter 3 provides an overview of the origins of behavior management by presenting various theories of human behavior. Chapter 4 focuses on the basic principles of behavior modification that form the foundation for all the subsequent interventions described in the book. Chapter 5 discusses the importance of targeting, counting, and recording behavior as it occurs in natural settings. Chapter 6 describes methods for taking the information collected from counting and recording behavior and graphing it to provide a visual representation of whether an intervention is working. Knowledge of the material presented in Chapters 5 and 6 is necessary to engage in one of the most important aspects of behavior management—conducting functional assessment—the focus of Chapter 7. Through functional assessment, we can analyze contextual and curricular variables and teach students replacement behaviors. Chapter 8 focuses on preventing behavior problems by describing techniques for making curricular modifications, applying effective instructional strategies, and making environmental accommodations. Chapter 9 describes techniques for increasing behavior, including token economies, behavioral contracts, group-oriented contingencies, and novel approaches. Chapter 10 examines ways to use differential reinforcement for decreasing behavior. By using the information presented in Chapters 9 and 10, we can eliminate about 95 percent of all behavior problems. The remaining 5 percent are usually modifiable using punishment—the focus of Chapter 11. Chapter 12 discusses how to teach students self-management—the ultimate goal of any behavior management intervention. Chapter 13 gives an overview of cognitive-behavior modification. These techniques center on the role our beliefs about, or interpretations of, events play in our emotional reactions and behavioral responses. Finally, Chapter 14 discusses how to promote generalization from the settings in which intervention took place to other settings.

New to this Edition

There are several new features to the second edition of this book. First, there are activities at the end of each chapter that reinforce information presented in the chapters. Chapter 5 on functional assessment has been expanded and includes a discussion of developing behavioral support plans. More practice examples have also been incorporated throughout the text to illustrate key concepts and ideas.

Finally, a companion Web site has been developed to support the text. This Web site includes an array of valuable resources for educators to refer to throughout this course and into their teaching practices.

AN EXAMPLE FOR THOUGHT

You are busily circulating around the room helping individual students who are working on their arithmetic assignment. You ignore the sounds of students talking and laughing behind you. Then Mike knocks several books to the floor getting out of his chair and saunters over, asking you for permission to go to the bathroom. When you deny his request, he sighs loudly and takes the long route back to his desk. As he swerves between the rows of desks, he kicks several students' feet, knocks the books off the desk of another student, and tweaks the ear of the boy sitting in front of him. Finally, he sits down and dramatically gets out his worksheet—only to break his pencil before completing the first problem. He then sits back, flipping his broken pencil in the air. When you ask him what he's doing, he replies, "Nothing." The other students in the class now have stopped working and are alternately staring at you and at Mike. You give him permission to sharpen his pencil.

The giggles begin and grow louder as Mike sharpens his pencil down to a stub. He then opens the compartment containing the pencil shavings, only to spill them on the floor. He apologizes insincerely as he bends down to clean up the mess, nonchalantly stepping on a classmate's foot. As he begins to stand, he purposely bumps his head on another student's desk. The entire class is now laughing.

Although Mike's antics are not severe, your class routine has been disrupted, and you are angry and frustrated. This scenario, and many like it, occur daily in the lives of teachers. How do you handle Mike and others like him? *Read on and find out!*

ACKNOWLEDGMENTS

I would like to thank the following reviewers for their helpful comments and suggestions for improving the manuscript: Lewis Browning, University of Southern Indiana; Sumita Chakraborti-Ghosh, Tennessee State University; Mary Ann Nelson, Georgia Southern University; Mary Newell, Florida A & M University; Aleck Peck, Boston College; and Marshall Zumberg, Wayne State University.

About the Author

Dr. John W. Maag is a professor at the University of Nebraska–Lincoln, where he specializes in the education and treatment of children and adolescents with emotional and behavioral disorders. His research interests include functional assessment, self-management training, and the assessment and treatment of depression and attention-deficit/hyperactivity disorder. Dr. Maag is a nationally recognized behavioral consultant on best practices for managing resistance and improving relationships with others. He has published over 80 articles and book chapters, as well as authoring three books—one of which, *Parenting Without Punishment,* won a Parents' Choice Award. He was also the recipient of the University of Nebraska–Lincoln Distinguished Teaching Award. A licensed psychotherapist, Dr. Maag is a frequent public speaker and consulting editor to numerous journals.

Behavior Management

*From Theoretical
Implications to
Practical Applications*

INTRODUCTION TO BEHAVIOR MANAGEMENT

CHAPTER OVERVIEW

- Behavior Modification
- Defining Behavior
- Three-Term Contingency
- Important Terms
- Applied Behavior Analysis
- Putting It All Together

CHAPTER OBJECTIVES

After completing this chapter, you will be able to do the following:

1. Describe the attributes of and misconceptions about behavior modification.

2. Explain the difference between traits and objectively defined behavior.

3. Explain the difference between overt and covert behavior.

4. Recognize that functional relations exist between behavior and environmental variables (antecedents and consequences).

5. Conduct an A-B-C analysis.

6. Define reinforcement, punishment, discipline, and consistence, and explain the misconceptions surrounding these terms.

7. Define applied behavior analysis (ABA) and describe its attributes.

Behavior management is a familiar, albeit misunderstood, term that many teachers evoke when confronted with students displaying challenging behaviors. Like many often-heard terms, it triggers reactions that range from complete rejection to total acceptance of it as an educational change approach. Perhaps some of the strong attitudes people have toward behavior management stems from its reliance on principles of *behavior modification*—a term that conjures strong images. Therefore, this chapter begins with a discussion of behavior modification. Second, both overt and covert behaviors are defined and differentiated from subjective occurrences that people frequently mistake for behavior. Third, the three-term contingency is described as a way to better understand factors that prompt and maintain behaviors. Fourth, several terms important to behavior management are introduced and reconceptualized in ways different from those in which society traditionally views them. Finally, the discipline of applied behavior analysis (ABA) is described as a model for integrating the techniques presented in much of this text.

BEHAVIOR MODIFICATION

The term of behavior modification elicits strong negative reactions because it is incorrectly associated with coercion and bribery.

The term **behavior modification** usually elicits strong reactions from people. At one extreme it is viewed as the answer to all of society's ills; at the other it is seen as a coercive and manipulative tool no better than the brainwashing techniques that captors often inflict on prisoners of war. The reality is that behavior modification is neither. Instead, behavior modification in the classroom involves identifying maladaptive behaviors that interfere with learning and assisting students in developing more adaptive behaviors.

Attributes of Behavior Modification

Martin and Pear (1999) described four attributes of behavior modification that have been derived from scientific study. These attributes demonstrate that behavior can be systematically modified in a desired direction.

The most important attribute is that behavior can be precisely defined and measured. Measuring allows us to assign numbers to behavior and to place the numbers on a graph before, during, and after implementing a particular behavior management intervention. Quantifying and graphing behavior in this fashion provides several useful pieces of information. First, it helps us determine whether the targeted behavior is severe enough to warrant intervention. Sometimes our perceptions of given behavior are different from the actual behavior. This discrepancy becomes apparent when we can see the behavior

Measuring, recording, and graphing behavior does not have to be a burdensome process, and it is appropriate for students who present the most challenging behaviors.

Although there are numerous theories regarding the nature of learning, the noted psychologist B. F. Skinner probably summed it up best by stating that "learning is not doing, it is changing what we do."

visually represented on a graph. Second, it enables us to determine whether the intervention was effective by comparing the counts of behavior before and after intervention. Third, seeing the results of measuring behavior makes us better teachers. Specifically, teachers who measure behavior make more frequent and appropriate decisions regarding the continuation, modification, or discontinuation of a particular intervention.

Second, behavioral principles form the basis for developing effective interventions. The work of B. F. Skinner, described in Chapter 3, has had the greatest impact on the development of effective interventions. These interventions are based on behavioral principles described in Chapter 4. Unfortunately, most teachers do not have a good working knowledge of principles of behavior. This ignorance often results in the misapplication of positive reinforcement techniques and overreliance on punishment—two principles that will be elaborated upon shortly.

Third, behavior modification is based on research. In fact, perhaps no other aspect of psychology and education has been as thoroughly investigated as have techniques of behavior modification. An unfortunate practice in which many educators engage is "jumping on the bandwagon" of any new technique reported in the media. Techniques such as facilitative communication, modality testing and teaching, applied kinesiology, optometric vision training, and neural repatterning have a pseudoscientific appeal—at some time they are chic. These fads seem to come and go like the tides. However, they have not withstood the rigors of scientific scrutiny. In contrast, techniques of behavior modification have been empirically tested and found to be effective for modifying students' behaviors.

Fourth, intervention techniques derived from the basic principles of behavior can be used to rearrange students' environments to promote appropriate behavior. This results in students who are more self-sufficient, independently functioning members of society—one of the ultimate goals of education. The environment can be rearranged in a variety of ways to promote appropriate behavior. For example, a teacher can move a student closer to or farther away from certain classmates. The environment includes classroom variables such as the teacher's and students' behaviors, the physical arrangement, tasks to be completed, and materials used to deliver instruction.

The four procedures described by Walker and Shea (1995) are discussed in detail in several chapters in this book.

Walker and Shea (1995) condensed the attributes of behavior modification into four procedures in which teachers can engage in the classroom:

1. Observe and clarify the behavior to be changed.
2. Select and present potent reinforcers at the appropriate time.
3. Design and impose, with consistency, an intervention technique based on the principles of reinforcement.
4. Monitor and evaluate the effectiveness of the intervention. (p. 43)

Misconceptions About Behavior Modification

Although these procedures, as well as attributes of behavior modification, reflect a systematic method of helping students perform more socially desirable behaviors, the term *behavior modification* still has negative connotations. Some of the negative reactions stem from the meaning of the word *modification,* which brings to mind images of inhumane and coercive attempts to control or change peoples' behavior (Alberto & Troutman, 1999). The mistaken use of the term is one reason this book is titled *Behavior Management.* Although the term *management* is not ideal—a point raised in the Preface—it nevertheless refers to the process of giving individuals direction, guidance, and training regarding their performance.

Another reason for public outcry is because behavior modification is often (and incorrectly) associated with procedures that cause pain or discomfort, such as the use of electroshock therapy or restraints to suppress aberrant behavior. Tragically, aversive procedures sometimes have been abused under the guise of behavior modification. For example, at an institution in Florida, one of the mildest punishments involved washing residents' mouths out with detergent when they spoke in what staff considered a verbally inappropriate fashion (Risley, 1975). This unfortunate situation only demonstrates that any technique can be misused by uncaring or illtrained personnel.

Unfortunately, the bad press behavior modification often receives detracts from its societal value and myriad practical applications, as described by Martin and Pear (1999) and listed in Table 1.1. As this table clearly shows, behavior modification can be used to solve a number of societal problems. Yet it can also be used by unscrupulous persons for unworthy ends. However, because behavior modification is simply the planned, systematic application of methods for teaching everyday behaviors, its use cannot be prohibited. Few teachers deliberately cause their students to engage in inappropriate behaviors, yet this may be the unintended outcome when they do not systematically evaluate the consequences of their interactions with students. This problem can be avoided by teachers who learn about behavior modification in an intelligent and responsible manner. This process begins with an exploration of what behavior actually is.

DEFINING BEHAVIOR

Behavior simply refers to what individuals do—their observable actions. Behavior can be verbal or nonverbal. The use of language is an important aspect of verbal behavior, involving asking or answering a question, commenting on something, telling a joke, and so forth. Nonverbal behaviors are physical actions. Some nonverbal behaviors serve a communicative function, such as

TABLE 1.1	CONTRIBUTIONS OF BEHAVIOR MODIFICATION

1. Improving education practices in every content area, from preschool to colleges and universities

2. Improving the behavior of individuals with developmental disabilities, autism, and schizophrenia

3. Treating clinical conditions such as anxiety, obsessions and compulsions, stress-related problems, depression, obesity, marital problems, sexual dysfunctions, and personality disorders

4. Treating medical problems such as seizure disorders, chronic pain, addictive disorders, and sleep disorders

5. Establishing treatment compliance, promoting healthy living, dealing with aging and chronic illness, and managing caregivers

6. Decreasing littering in public campgrounds

7. Increasing the recycling of soft drink containers

8. Helping community boards solve problems

9. Promoting energy conservation by increasing bus ridership

10. Encouraging welfare recipients to attend self-help meetings

11. Helping college students live together in a cooperative housing environment

12. Improving productivity, decreasing tardiness and absenteeism, increasing sales volume, creating new business, improving worker safety, reducing theft by employees, and improving management–employee relations

13. Improving the skills of athletes, motivating athletes to practice and to undergo endurance training, changing the behavior of coaches, and psyching up athletes for competition

Source: Martin and Pear (1999).

smiling, nodding one's head, or raising one's eyebrows in response to another person's gesture or comment. Other nonverbal behaviors entail more pronounced movements that serve functions other than communication, such as running, throwing a ball, or putting on shoes. Some activities, such as working on a crossword puzzle, require both verbal and nonverbal behavior (Sarafino, 1996). The key aspects of behavior are that it not only requires human action but also is performed as a way to interact with various elements of the environment. Consequently, being buffeted by a strong gust of wind is not an example of behavior because both living and nonliving organisms respond similarly to high winds (Cooper, Heron, & Heward, 1987).

The principles of behavior described in this chapter form the basis for many of the behavior change procedures discussed in this book.

Considering Covert Behavior

Behavior typically focuses on overt actions—either verbal or nonverbal—that are observable to others. However, some experts have suggested that not all behaviors can be directly observed, that they are covert. Interpretations of a situation or event are based on beliefs, perceptions, and expectations stored in memory (Howell & Nolet, 2000). For example, some college students dislike giving presentations to their classmates. They may worry that they will make a mistake and that their classmates will either laugh at them or become bored. These covert beliefs, or self-statements, can stimulate emotions such as anxiety or fear and physical sensations such as sweaty palms or rapid breathing and heart rate. These students may also exhibit overt behaviors such as nervous laughter, rigid body posture, and hand wringing, although these behaviors do not always accurately reflect their covert behaviors.

Covert behaviors and self-statements are not extensively covered in this text because they do not enjoy the empirical support that techniques based on the modification of overt behaviors have. Nevertheless, thoughts can influence the expression of behaviors, which is why a discussion of cognitive-behavior modification appears in Chapter 13. However, it is important to understand that the most effective way of managing students' challenging behaviors is by observing their overt expressions and differentiating them from subjective traits that teachers often incorrectly ascribe to behavior.

This book focuses on overt behavior because it can be observed objectively and its modification can be validated. Nevertheless, there is a growing body of literature focusing on the assessment and treatment of covert behavior. Consequently, Chapter 13 addresses the use of cognitive-behavior modification.

Things That Are Not Behavior

From our previous discussion, we know that actions produced by nonliving organisms, such as being buffeted by strong winds, do not constitute behavior. This may appear obvious. However, people make a subtler mistake in attributing actions to behavior—namely, the tendency to label subjective (biased, skewed) and global traits as behaviors. For example, teachers may label students' behaviors as "lazy," "honest," "friendly," "hard-working," "angry," "shy," and "inattentive." The basic problem in using words like these to describe behaviors is typified in the age-old saying "Beauty is in the eye of the beholder." Perceptions of reality are based on individuals' past experiences, which necessarily differ from person to person. For example, a common behavior for many elementary-age boys is to hit each other on the arm. One teacher may call this student "friendly" and another may call him "mean." Inevitably, the same student's behavior can appear both appropriate and inappropriate depending on the characteristics of the observer doing the labeling.

There are several other problems with using subjective terms to describe behavior. First, the use of such terms shifts the focus from the student's behavior to the student herself. If we use a term like "lazy" to describe a student's behavior, we are not really talking about her actions. Instead, we are using our subjective judgment to attribute a reason for her behaving in a certain way. For example, a student may be wandering around the room and talking to peers instead of doing her assignment of 10 math problems on a worksheet. The teacher may regard the student's behavior— her laziness—as the result of some personality trait. What does the student do? She fails to finish 10 math problems on a worksheet. Why? Because she is lazy. What is she? She is lazy. However, we do not know whether laziness is the real reson for the unfinished work or whether, for example, the student wants to avoid an assignment that she believes she cannot complete correctly.

The second problem with using subjective terms such as "lazy" is that a teacher may set in motion a self-fulfilling prophecy whereby the student comes to believe she is lazy and acts accordingly. The teacher who labeled her may then say "I told you so." The solution is to use more objective terms to describe the specific behaviors desired of the student and to determine what purpose not completing the work may have served. For example, the teacher might alter the assignment so that it is congruent with the student's skill level.

The third problem with describing behavior subjectively is that it hinders both teacher and student from detecting academic improvements. Describing a student as "lazy" does not help us to determine if the behavior of completing math problems is improving, staying the same, or getting worse. In contrast, saying that the student completed 4 out of 10 math problems permits us to set realistic goals for improvement. We can be confident that our efforts were successful if the student completes 7 problems on the subsequent assignment.

The fourth problem with describing behavior subjectively is that doing so may escalate a confrontation between teacher and student that could otherwise have been avoided. For example, a student may be told to stop being so "hostile" when he trips a classmate. Later, the student socks a peer in the arm in an age-appropriate expression of friendship. Nevertheless, the teacher views this new behavior as another example of being "hostile" and reprimands the student. The student, in turn, may think that this admonishment is unfair because, to his way of thinking, he was being friendly, not hostile. A power struggle may ensue (Maag, 2001a).

These problems can be avoided by describing students' behaviors in objective terms—but this is not as easy as it sounds. Seasoned teachers have just as much difficulty being objective as do novices. This is because we all like to condense our speech to convey the most meaning with the least number of words. Although this goal is noble, doing so makes it difficult to discuss students' behaviors objectively. Table 1.2 provides some common examples of subjective descriptions of inappropriate and appropriate behaviors and their objective counterparts. Although it takes some time to begin thinking in objective terms when describing behavior, the benefits to both teachers and students are considerable. Namely, it permits us to identify and analyze the factors that trigger and maintain behaviors.

TABLE 1.2   SUBJECTIVE AND OBJECTIVE DESCRIPTORS OF INAPPROPRIATE AND APPROPRIATE BEHAVIORS

Inappropriate Behaviors	
Subjective Description	**Objective Description**
Is lazy	Does not finish all 10 math problems
Uses bad language	Says "shut up" when asked to put books away
Is immature	Cries when doesn't get to be first in line
Is manipulative	Asks Ms. Jones to listen to music after Mr. Smith says "no"
Acts oppositional	Has to be told three times to stop talking to classmate

Appropriate Behaviors	
Subjective Description	**Objective Description**
Is polite	Says "thank you" after receiving a compliment
Acts friendly	Smiles when talking to others
Has good work habits	Sits up straight, keeps eyes on teacher, raises hand before talking
Gets along well with others	Asks classmates to play games at recess
Exercises self-control	Finishes work without being asked

THREE-TERM CONTINGENCY

Behavior was previously defined as students' overt and observable actions. It does not occur in a random or unorganized fashion. Rather, students behave purposely, and their behaviors attain meaning as a function of the context—situation or circumstances—that exists in a particular environment (Maag, 1999). The **environment** is the universe of events and objects, both animate and inanimate, that are part of our surroundings (Johnston & Pennypacker, 1993). For example, a classroom environment is composed of animate objects such as students and adults and a host of inanimate objects including (but not limited to) tables, chairs, chalkboards, materials, and tasks. The world is an orderly place in which each event happens in relation to other events. The relation between events is called a **contingency.** Contingencies are identified through the sequential relation between antecedents and consequences that prompt and maintain behaviors. This arrangement is depicted in Figure 1.1.

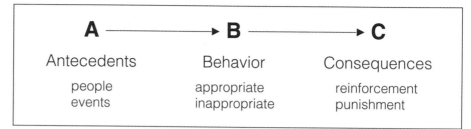

FIGURE 1.1

Three-Term Contingency

Antecedents

Antecedents are the circumstances that exist in the environment before a behavior is exhibited. Antecedents exist for all behaviors and serve as a cue or prompt for an individual to behave in a particular way. For example, a red traffic light is an antecedent that prompts the behavior of depressing the brake. Other examples of antecedents include a phone ringing as a cue to pick it up, a teacher asking a question as a cue to provide an answer, and someone smiling at another individual as a cue to smile back or say "hello."

It is important to understand that antecedents do not *cause* behavior—they only serve as cues. For example, there is no inherent biological predisposition for us to depress the brake when encountering a red traffic light—it is a learned behavior. The red light cue cannot prevent us from choosing to accelerate. Antecedents not only cue behavior but also can elicit specific behaviors that help us avoid punishment or obtain reinforcement. Most of us stop at a red light to avoid the potential punishing consequences of receiving a ticket, getting into an accident, or injuring another person. Therefore, although our behavior may be cued by antecedents, it is ultimately controlled by consequences.

Consequences

Consequences affect future behavior by serving to either increase, decrease, or maintain it. There are two forms of consequences: (1) A new stimulus is presented or added to the environment, or (2) an already-present stimulus is avoided, terminated, or removed from the environment. Both forms are illustrated in Table 1.3. In the first example, the teacher's question serves as a prompt or cue for Nancy to provide the answer. The verbal behavior of Nancy's giving the correct answer introduces a new stimulus into the environment— teacher praise. Assuming Nancy values teacher praise, that consequence will likely maintain or increase her behavior of answering questions. In the second

TABLE **1.3**   TWO FUNCTIONS OF CONSEQUENCES

Antecedents	Behavior	Consequences
Teacher asks Nancy a question.	Nancy gives correct answer.	Teacher tells Nancy she gave a great answer (stimulus presented).
Billy calls Jimmy a jerk.	Jimmy hits Billy.	Billy stops calling Jimmy a jerk (stimulus terminated).

example, Jimmy presumably finds it aversive for Billy to call him a jerk. This antecedent serves as a cue for Jimmy to hit Billy. Billy consequently stops calling Jimmy a jerk, and so an already-present stimulus is terminated.

A-B-C Analysis

As depicted in Figure 1.2, an **A-B-C Analysis** involves writing down a sequence of events beginning with antecedents, followed by behavior, and terminating with consequences. Levitt and Rutherford (1978) offered three reasons to conduct an A-B-C analysis:

1. To get a general feel for the behavior of the student in order to help target the specific behavior to work on.
2. To determine, in a generally disruptive classroom, during a certain time of day, which students are the main disrupters.
3. To get a fix on some environmental cues to disruptive behavior: Is it occurring at a certain time each day? Is the teacher setting the students off by some cue?

In an A-B-C analysis, a piece of paper is turned sideways and divided into three columns labeled "Antecedents," "Behavior," and "Consequences," as shown in Figure 1.2. Observations are then numbered and recorded according to whether they were seen as antecedents, behavior, or consequences. Alberto and Troutman (1999) recommended asking the following questions to assist in making sense of the A-B-C analysis:

1. What are the behaviors that can be described as inappropriate? The behavior analyst should be able to justify labeling the behaviors inappropriate given the setting and the activity taking place.
2. Is this behavior occurring frequently, or has a unique occurrence been identified?

Antecedents	Behavior	Consequences
1. Teacher: "Time for math worksheets." Teacher begins handing out sheets.	2. Kevin gets up from his desk and walks around the room.	3. Sally giggles when Kevin pushes her elbow as she writes her name on the worksheet.
4. Teacher tells Kevin to sit down.	5. Kevin raises his hand.	6. Teacher: "I'll be right with you, Kevin."
7. Kevin turns around to talk to Bill.	8. Teacher tells Kevin to stop talking and get to work.	9. Kevin drops his worksheet on the floor.
10. Teacher is looking for a pencil at her desk.	11. Kevin gets up from his seat and heads for the pencil sharpener.	12. Teacher: "Where's your worksheet, Kevin?"
13. Kevin: "I'm not sure."	14. Teacher: "Check under your desk."	15. Kevin: "I'll copy the problems from Bill."
16. Teacher: "Pick up your worksheet or you'll stay in for recess."	17. Kevin walks over to the worksheet.	18. Teacher ignores Kevin.
19. Kevin knocks Sally's book off her desk.	20. Teacher: "Kevin, pick up her book now."	21. Kevin smiles at Sally.

FIGURE **1.2**

Example of an A-B-C Analysis

3. Can reinforcement or punishment of the behavior be identified? The reinforcement may be delivered by the teacher, parent, another child, or some naturally occurring environmental consequence.
4. Is there a pattern to these consequences?
5. Can antecedents to the behavior(s) be identified?
6. Is there a pattern that can be identified for certain events or stimuli (antecedents) that consistently precede the behavior's occurrence?
7. Are there recurrent chains of certain antecedents, behaviors, and consequences?
8. Given the identified inappropriate behavior(s) of the student and the patterns of antecedents and consequences, what behavior really needs to be modified, and who is engaging in the behavior? (pp. 107–108)

Based on the way we conduct A-B-C analyses, it may seem that the relation between antecedents, behavior, and consequences is linear. However, this is not the case. Instead, the relations between antecedents, behavior, and consequences are reciprocal (Gable, Hendrickson, Warren, Evans, & Evans, 1988). At the simplest level, reciprocity means that the consequences of a given behavior can become the antecedents for a succeeding behavior. As an illustration, apply an A-B-C analysis to the following exchange between teacher and student:

TEACHER: *"Nancy, what is the capital of the United States?"*
NANCY: *"Washington, DC."*
TEACHER: *"Nice answer, Nancy."*
NANCY: *"Thank you, Ms. Anderson."*
TEACHER: *"You're welcome, Nancy."*

In this illustration, the first three exchanges should be obvious. The teacher's question is the antecedent for Nancy's verbal behavior of saying "Washington, DC." The consequence is the teacher's saying "Nice answer." However, this consequence then becomes the antecedent for Nancy's saying "Thank you," which is the next behavior in the sequence. And so it can go indefinitely.

The key task in conducting an A-B-C analysis is to identify patterns. It is less relevant whether a given response is viewed as an antecedent or a consequence. For example, in Figure 1.2, it is not particularly important to determine whether Sally's giggling is reinforcing Kevin's out-of-seat behavior (no. 3) or serving as an antecedent for the teacher's telling Kevin to sit down (no. 4). Rather, the crucial insight to be obtained from the A-B-C analysis is that Kevin's behavior is being reinforced through attention from both Sally and the teacher.

IMPORTANT TERMS

There are several terms that most laypersons and those new to behavior management misunderstand—terms many teachers and parents use on a regular basis. Yet few of them understand their true meaning or the ways in which they can be used (and misused) on behalf of behavior management.

The first two terms—discipline and consequence—are typically and incorrectly associated with punishment. The word *discipline* is found in every handbook on school policies and procedures. Disciplinary actions include expulsion, in-school and out-of-school suspensions, restitution, and detentions, to name but a few. Most of us would consider these actions punitive, applied only when a student misbehaves. Although that is most likely the intent of the authors of these handbooks, it nevertheless is an incorrect application of the term. According to the *American Heritage Dictionary*, **discipline** refers to "training that is expected to produce a specific character or pattern of behavior, especially training that produces moral or mental improvement." A key word in this definition is *improvement*. Improvement entails increasing skills or competence in a particular area. Yet in the schools, the goal is to eliminate inappropriate behaviors.

We know from our previous discussion of the three-term contingency that a consequence occurs after a behavior is performed. It can either increase or decrease the future likelihood of a behavior occurring. Therefore, the word *consequence* has neither positive nor negative connotations. Yet most teachers and parents use the word to describe the application of some form of punishment. All we have to do is think back to our childhoods and our parents' use of the word *consequence,* which most of us associated with punishment.

The consequences presented in Figure 1.1 are categorized as either reinforcement or punishment. They are the two most misunderstood terms associated with behavior management—and yet their definitions are simple. **Reinforcement** *increases* the probability that the behavior it follows will reoccur, whereas **punishment** *decreases* the probability that the behavior it follows will do so. The key concept in these two definitions is that reinforcement and punishment are not *things* but *effects.* If a consequence increases a behavior, then reinforcement took place; if it decreases the behavior, then punishment took place. Both reinforcement and punishment are naturally occurring phenomena.

In reality, anything can be either a reinforcer or punisher, depending on its effect on behavior. For example, even though teacher praise is typically thought of as being reinforcing, some students may find such praise embarrassing. Imagine a student who completes 10 math problems in 5 minutes. The teacher comes over and says "Nice job." The student then completes 3 math problems during the subsequent 5 minutes. In this scenario, the effect of the teacher praise is punishment because it decreases behavior. The opposite also can be true. For example, imagine a young child moving his hand close to a hot burner. The parent may issue a stern "No" and slap the back of his hand, an action that can cause pain and even temporary inflammation of the skin. Yet, if the child repeatedly places his hand by the burner, then, by effect, the slap is not punishment but rather reinforcement because the behavior increases.

We sometimes view students who seem to continue behaving poorly when confronted with punishment as disordered or even masochistic. What we fail to recognize is that the attention the student receives from us may be more reinforcing than the punishment inflicted may be punishing. Unless the punishment is severe, reinforcement will win out almost every time (Maag, 2001b).

It is ironic that such a simple and straightforward concept as positive reinforcement continues to generate controversy. Many people seem unable to get past the stereotypic notion that systematic or planned use of positive reinforcement is a manipulative tool wielded to make people engage in behaviors chosen by others (Alberto & Troutman, 1999). Consequently, positive reinforcement continues to be viewed by some as coercive and as undermining students' ability to become self-directed and intrinsically motivated. The statement some teachers make—that they do not believe in positive reinforcement—is analogous to their saying they do not believe in gravity. Just because someone may not like an effect does not negate its existence. Planned or unplanned positive reinforcement occurs in every classroom—all students' behaviors are followed by consequences from peers, adults, or both. Therefore, is it not better to preplan the use of reinforcement to increase appropriate student behaviors rather than letting it occur naturally and running the risk of reinforcing inappropriate behaviors?

There are numerous other examples of positive reinforcement at work in the natural environment. Alberto and Troutman (1999) provided the following examples of naturally occurring positive reinforcers:

1. An office worker goes to work each day expecting to receive a check at the end of the week. If the check is delivered on Friday in an amount that he finds satisfying, it increases the probability that he will return to work on Monday.
2. A [L]ittle [L]eaguer hits a double and is applauded by fans and teammates. This motivates her to play again next Saturday.
3. A baby coos at his mother's approach so she cuddles him and spends more time playing with him. The mother's response increases the frequency of the baby's cooing, which increases the time spent playing, which increases . . . .
4. A student spends 45 minutes each night for a week studying for a history exam. If the student makes an A on the exam, this consequence will motivate her to study just as hard for her next exam. (p. 208)

Few people dispute that positive reinforcement is an effective naturally occurring phenomenon, but as Axelrod (1983) suggested, they object to its planned use to elicit behaviors. This view is puzzling. It makes more sense for a teacher to plan the application of positive reinforcement for a student's behavior than to let it occur randomly and run the risk that it will increase inappropriate behaviors.

Kohn (1993) has been a vocal critic of positive reinforcement, claiming that it simply does not work (clearly an oxymoronic statement because, by definition, if something does not increase behavior then it is not a reinforcer). An articulate spokesperson, he has expressed his views in the popular media and in professional journals and books (e.g., Kohn, 1993, 1996). Kohn claimed that some 20 studies conducted over the past 30 years showed that positive reinforcement procedures produced only temporary improvements in behavior and that their removal lead to a return of the behavior problem, often at a worse level than before. In making his argument, Kohn ignored over 100 studies with results contrary to his claims. However, his biggest error was equating reward with reinforcement.

A **reward** (or prize) is something given to a person for an accomplishment. A reward may or may not be a positive reinforcer. For example, an athlete may begin training to compete in the discus throw several years before the next Olympics. During this time, his discus-throwing behavior will occur at a

There is much confusion about several terms associated with behavior management. Reinforcement and reward are not synonymous; nor are the terms punishment and discipline.

high rate as part of his training regime. Consequently, he wins the goal medal—certainly the ultimate reward—and decides to retire from competition. The subsequent frequency of discus-throwing behavior certainly will decrease compared to the level displayed prior to the Olympics. Therefore, the "reward" (i.e., a gold medal) functioned as punishment because its effect was to decrease future discus-throwing behavior. In contrast, if the athlete places a disappointing 10th and subsequently spends more time practicing throwing the discus to compete more effectively in the next Olympiad, then his poor showing functioned as reinforcement because it had the effect of increasing subsequent discus-throwing behavior.

Kohn is not the only person who has objected to the planned use of positive reinforcement—criticisms are broad based and ingrained in our society. Axelrod (1996) pointed out how certain individuals object to positive reinforcement on the grounds that appropriate behavior should be performed because it is the right and natural thing to do, and not because one expects to receive compensation or reward. But how effective can the technique of saying "should" or "expect" be for increasing a behavior that a student is not currently performing? Another question begs an answer: Are people who oppose the use of reinforcement also against the use of punishment? Probably not. Many schools that do not permit the use of positive reinforcement techniques, viewing them as a form of bribery, administer a variety of consequences designed to decrease behavior, such as suspension and corporal punishment. This double standard is apparent in many segments of our society—a point elaborated on in the next chapter.

The criticisms of the systematic use of positive reinforcement are not likely to cease even though empirical support for its effectiveness has been provided. Instead, only when teachers have enough courage and foresight to use positive reinforcement techniques in a preplanned, systematic, performance-based, and self-evaluative way will their effectiveness be acknowledged and their techniques implemented by other teachers.

APPLIED BEHAVIOR ANALYSIS

The application of principles of behavior modification as a systematic, performance-based, self-evaluative endeavor is called **applied behavior analysis** (ABA). It is based largely on the work of B. F. Skinnner, as described in Chapter 3. ABA explains the interaction between human behavior and environmental factors—antecedents and consequences—that affect behavior expression. Teachers apply the ABA approach to behavior management by studying students' behaviors and their functional relations to antecedents and consequences. The three-term (A-B-C) contingency schema is a key tool of ABA. Specifically, teachers use the model presented in Figure 1.1 to organize the observed antecedents and consequences of behavior in order to make predictions about factors that trigger and maintain its occurrence. Teachers then test these predictions by systematically altering or substituting antecedents and consequences and noting their effect on the behavior of concern. Through this approach, teachers design and test interventions to change behavior in a precisely measurable and accountable manner. Sulzer-Azaroff and Mayer (1977) described several important attributes of ABA.

First, ABA is **performance based**—it is concerned with students' behavior and the ways in which environmental factors affect its expression. As mentioned previously, terms such as "lazy," "shy," "assertive," or "lonely" are avoided because they have different meanings to different teachers. Once a behavior is defined precisely, its occurrence and nonoccurrence can be accurately measured so that a complete description can be obtained.

Second, ABA uses **principles of behavior** derived from both laboratory and field studies that have identified lawful relations between behavior and the environmental variables that affect its occurrence. Principles of behavior have been found to apply under many conditions and among many individuals with diverse characteristics. For example, positive reinforcement is a universal principle that is in effect regardless of the age, gender, culture, or disability of a child (Wielkiewicz, 1995). The same can be said for punishment (Maag, 2001b).

Third, ABA is **analytic** because functional relations between an intervention and a target behavior can be demonstrated. In other words, the idea is to systematically control the occurrence and nonoccurrence of the behavior by introducing and withdrawing an intervention. For example, a teacher may decide to write individual students' names on pieces of paper and place them in a jar whenever they provide a correct answer. At the end of the week, the teacher draws three names out of the jar, and those students get to eat pizza in the classroom during lunch while their classmates dine in the cafetaria. Through the use of an analytic system, the teacher counts the number of correct answers provided for several days prior to implementing the intervention and also while the intervention is in effect. In this way, she can compare the number of answers correct before and during intervention to determine whether it was effective, thereby helping her decide whether to continue or to try something else.

Fourth, ABA is **applied** because it is characterized by the social importance of the behavior to be changed. To meet this criterion, we must ask ourselves whether we are trying to change behaviors that will enhance the quality of students' lives. For example, a teacher may desperately want a student to sit quietly in his seat. However, is sitting quietly in a seat a socially important be-

Applied behavior analysis is a systematic, performance-based, self-evaluative method for changing behavior.

havior? We may be tempted to answer "Yes." However, if we think about it, what is the goal for having students remain in their seats? To complete more work, of course. Therefore, a more socially appropriate behavior to change is the amount of work the student completes at his desk. If his work completion rate dramatically improves, it is unlikely that he is spending an inordinate amount of time out of his seat. Besides, work completion is a behavior that all teachers (and all of society) value.

BRINGING IT ALL TOGETHER

The overriding assumption of behavior modification, as operationalized in ABA, is that almost all behaviors are learned. There are few human behaviors that are genetically preprogrammed. The notable exceptions are some reflexive behaviors (e.g., blowing air in a person's face, causing a blink reaction, and an infant's ability to cry, coo, and smile). But beyond these types of behaviors, students learn, for example, how to read, study, talk politely, cooperate or whine, fight, steal, and lie through their experiences and interaction with the environment. The good news about this model is that students, with our help, can unlearn inappropriate behaviors and learn appropriate ones. The bad news is that behavior management takes time and effort. The good and bad news is that anyone can use behavioral procedures. However, as Kerr and Nelson (2002) cautioned, under no circumstances should specific behavioral techniques be used by teachers who do not thoroughly understand the basic principles and assumptions of ABA. Although the techniques described in this text can be powerful, they also can be easily misapplied. Only when behavioral techniques are combined with systematic measurement and evaluation can we say that ABA is taking place. Therefore, the techniques presented in this book should be practiced initially under the supervision of competent applied behavior analysts. When ABA is used in an ethically responsible manner, it should help promote the betterment of both individuals and society (Sulzer-Azaroff & Mayer, 1977).

SUMMARY

This chapter introduced the basics of behavior management. Behavior modification has specific attributes, but people often have misconceptions about it. Behavior consists of observable actions. The three-term contingency involves analyzing the impact of antecedents and consequences on the occurrence of behavior. Antecedents are the events that come before behavior and that cue or prompt (but do not cause) its occurrence. Consequences occur after behavior and either maintain, increase, or decrease it. Reinforcement and punishment are defined based on their effects on behavior: Reinforcement increases behavior and punishment decreases it. A reward may be either a reinforcer or a punisher depending on its effect on behavior. Contrary to popular belief, discipline is not the same as punishment. Discipline is the process of imparting skills or knowledge and so has more in common with reinforcement than punishment. Finally, ABA is a systematic, performance-based, and self-evaluative method for changing behavior.

ACTIVITIES

1. Take a piece of paper, turn it sideways, draw three columns, and label them "Antecedents," "Behavior," and "Consequences." Keep this sheet of paper by your television set. When your favorite show comes on, spend 15 minutes conducting an A-B-C analysis. When you are finished, see if you can determine any patterns in the ways the characters behaved, as well as the antecedents that prompted their behaviors and the consequences that maintained them.
2. During a conversation with friends, note how many subjective words they use to describe things. Take a piece of paper, make two columns, and label them "Subjective" and "Objective." List the subjective terms you heard your friends use during the conversation. Then come up with objective counterparts for each subjective word, and record them in the "Objective" column. See if the objective terms clarify the topic of conversation or change it.

REVIEW QUESTIONS

1. What are the attributes of behavior modification, and why is it misunderstood?
2. What is the benefit of using objective rather than subjective terms to describe behavior?
3. How does covert behavior differ from overt behavior?
4. What is the best way to measure whether learning has occurred?
5. How does the three-term contingency help explain how people learn behaviors?
6. How do antecedents and consequences affect the types of behaviors that students exhibit?

7. What are the benefits of conducting an A-B-C analysis?
8. Define *reinforcement, punishment, discipline,* and *rewards.*
9. Why does society look so unfavorably on positive reinforcement?
10. What are the attributes of applied behavior analysis (ABA)?

REFERENCES

Alberto, P. A., & Troutman, A. C. (1999). *Applied behavior analysis for teachers* (5th ed.). Columbus, OH: Merrill.

Axelrod, S. (1983). *Behavior modification for the classroom teacher* (2nd ed.). New York: McGraw-Hill.

Axelrod, S. (1996). What's wrong with behavior analysis? *Journal of Behavioral Education, 6,* 247–256.

Cooper, J. O., Heron, T. E., & Heward, W. L. (1987). *Applied behavior analysis.* Columbus, OH: Merrill.

Gable, R. A., Hendrickson, J. M., Warren, S. F., Evans, W. H., & Evans, S. S. (1988). The promise and pitfalls of an ecological perspective on children's behavioral disorders. In R. B. Rutherford, Jr., & J. W. Maag (Eds.), *Severe behavior disorders of children and youth* (Vol. 11, pp. 156–166). Reston, VA: Council for Children with Behavioral Disorders.

Howell, K. W., & Nolet, V. (2000). *Curriculum-based evaluation* (3rd ed.). Belmont, CA: Wadsworth.

Johnston, J. M., & Pennypacker, H. S. (1993). *Strategies and tactics for human behavioral research* (2nd ed.). Hillsdale, NJ: Lawrence Erlbaum.

Kerr, M. M., & Nelson, C. M. (2002). *Strategies for managing behavior problems in the classroom* (4th ed.). Englewood Cliffs, NJ: Prentice-Hall.

Kohn, A. (1993). *Punished by rewards: The trouble with gold stars, incentive plans, A's, praise, and other bribes.* Boston: Houghton Mifflin.

Kohn, A. (1996). By all available means: Cameron and Pierce's defense of extrinsic motivators. *Review of Educational Research, 66,* 1–4.

Levitt, L. K., & Rutherford, R. B., Jr. (1978). *Strategies for handling the disruptive student.* Tempe: College of Education, Arizona State University.

Maag, J. W. (1999). Why they say no: Foundational premises and techniques for managing resistance. *Focus on Exceptional Children, 32*(1), 1–16.

Maag, J. W. (2001a). *Powerful struggles: Managing resistance, building rapport.* Longmont, CO: Sopris West.

Maag, J. W. (2001b). Rewarded by punishment: Reflections on the disuse of positive reinforcement in schools. *Exceptional Children, 67,* 173–186.

Martin, G., & Pear, J. (1999). *Behavior modification: What it is and how to do it* (6th ed.). Upper Saddle River, NJ: Prentice-Hall.

Risley, T. R. (1975). Certified procedures not people. In W. S. Wood (Ed.), *Issues in evaluating behavior modification* (pp. 159–181). Champaign, IL: Research Press.

Sarafino, E. P. (1996). *Principles of behavior change: Understanding behavior modification techniques.* New York: Wiley.

Sulzer-Azaroff, B., & Mayer, G. R. (1977). *Applying behavior-analysis procedures with children and youth.* New York: Holt, Rinehart & Winston.

Walker, J. E., & Shea, T. M. (1995). *Behavior management: A practical approach for educators* (6th ed.). Columbus, OH: Merrill.

Wielkiewicz, R. M. (1995). *Behavior management in the schools: Principles and procedures* (2nd ed.) Boston: Allyn & Bacon.

IMPEDIMENTS TO MANAGING BEHAVIOR

CHAPTER OVERVIEW

- The Medical Model
- Academic and Social Behavior
- Contextual Variation
- Personal Standards and Social Behavior
- The Concept of Control

CHAPTER OBJECTIVES

After completing this chapter, you will be able to do the following:

1. Understand why differential diagnosis, based on the medical model, hampers efforts to manage students' behaviors effectively.

2. Recognize that labels are socially defined and socially negotiated.

3. Recognize that academic and social behavior are governed by similar principles of learning and respond to similar interventions.

4. Understand that context determines whether a behavior is viewed as appropriate or inappropriate.

5. Describe how our culture accepts the use of punishment and disapproves of the use of reinforcement.

6. Understand that teachers' standards affect whether a behavior is viewed as appropriate or inappropriate.

"Each of us has our own reality of which we try to persuade others" (Scarr, 1985, p. 499). This quote by Scarr relates to the fact that information from the environment is filtered through our human senses and converted in our brains into perceptions and thoughts. The by-product of this process—knowledge—is influenced, in part, by social and cultural contexts. However, it is also true that we perceive and process knowledge within the constraints of our belief systems. One example of personal constraints on knowledge is found in eyewitness accounts of crimes (Loftus, 1979). Fleeting impressions of criminal behavior are elaborated by individuals into complete accounts that they believe to be "true." Innocent people may be identified as the criminals, and events may be construed in ways that are consistent with observers' emotions and prejudices. When such events are videotaped and viewed repeatedly by outside observers, a different consensus of the event emerges—one that is not consistent with eyewitness accounts from people at the scene. The problem is that the eyewitness to a crime, or some other emotional event, gleans only partial knowledge from the immediate experience. The eyewitness fills in the gaps in her or his knowledge by plausible constructions of what "must have" or "should have" happened to make sense of the scene. Unfortunately, this eyewitness account is often at variance with that of observers who can review the event more than once in the calm of a videotape viewing room.

Like the witnesses to a crime, each of us approaches problems with a unique theoretical viewpoint, whether explicit or implicit. The popular term for this theoretical viewpoint is **paradigm**—which simply means a "pattern" or "model." However, there is a more functional definition that relates to the present discussion. A paradigm is the set of rules and regulations that establish boundaries and explain how to solve problems within the given boundaries. To put it plainly, paradigms filter incoming experiences. We view the world through paradigms all the time, selecting from the world those data that best fit our rules and regulations while trying to ignore the rest. As a result, what may be perfectly obvious to the person adhering to one paradigm may be totally imperceptible to someone with a different paradigm.

We hold paradigms when it comes to managing students' challenging behaviors. A common paradigm for many of us is that behavior problems reside within students and that students must change their behaviors (rather than our changing our own behaviors). Another common paradigm is that we expect students to be good and react to them when they are bad. This paradigm places students at risk for receiving our attention only when they misbehave. Most importantly, our personal, paradigm-based rules and regulations blind us to creative solutions in managing students' behaviors. We look for solutions through old paradigms that keep us from viewing behavior problems and their treatment from alternate vantage points.

This chapter presents five impediments to effectively managing students' behaviors. They are considered impediments because we tend to view each from a similar point of view—one that inhibits our ability to effectively manage students' behaviors. Remember, managing students' challenging behaviors is difficult, and the job becomes even more difficult when we adhere to traditional conceptualizations regarding behavior problems. Therefore, changing our mindsets about the impediments discussed in this chapter will help us manage students' behaviors more effectively.

THE MEDICAL MODEL

Students who engage in inappropriate behaviors are likely to come in conflict with elements of their environment such as teachers, police, parents, and peers. Such students often receive a deviant label from the mental health and judicial communities. Diagnostic labels such as "conduct disorder," "antisocial personality," "attention deficit disorder," and "oppositional defiant disorder" reflect the medical orientation of psychiatry—that accurate diagnosis leads to effective interventions. Unfortunately, this process of **differential diagnosis** offers few practical solutions to our task of managing students' challenging behaviors.

Why Differential Diagnosis Is Ineffective

First, diagnosing a student with a medical "condition" either purposely or inadvertently places the blame for behaving poorly on the student. For example, some teachers may believe they cannot help a student with attention deficit/hyperactivity disorder (ADHD) because this condition is as innate as diabetes. The unintended result is that teachers have a built-in excuse not to take the time to develop and implement appropriate interventions for the specific behaviors causing problems in the classroom. Valuable time may be wasted waiting for these students to be placed on medication instead of conducting an A-B-C analysis and developing interventions to address the problem behaviors.

Second, medical diagnoses make it easy for students to "become" their behavior in the eyes of some teachers. For example, a student who repeatedly engages in aggressive behavior may eventually be viewed as an aggressive student. This process, which dehumanizes the student, would never be used for physical problems. Imagine a student with a broken arm being called a "broken-arm student" by a teacher. Yet teachers routinely "turn" students into their behavior. This phenomenon, like the first one, makes it easy for teachers to give up trying to change the behavior. After all, if a student has an internal condition, what can possibly be done to change it?

Third, and most dangerously, in framing behavior problems as internal conditions, we tend to think that all interventions must also be medical—if the only tool we have is a hammer, the whole world looks like a nail. Consequently, we are less likely to take the time to learn, develop, and implement the techniques described in this book. ADHD, which is conceptualized as a medical problem, provides a telling example. The most common treatment is medication, typically with the drug Ritalin. Although Ritalin can be a valuable component in treating ADHD, it creates a "paradigm blinder" such that intervention is conceptualized solely along medical lines. Consequently, teachers sometimes ask parents of students with ADHD who are engaging in inappropriate classroom behaviors to have their medication increased. The irony is that there are many classroom-based interventions for managing the behavior of students with ADHD (Reid & Maag, 1998). Not coincidentally, there are over 2000 studies examining the effects of Ritalin on the behavior of students with ADHD but less than 100 studies examining the effectiveness of behavior management techniques on the same behaviors. Why? Because our paradigms keep us from looking at alternative conceptualizations.

The Myth of Mental Illness

Over four decades ago, the psychiatrist Thomas Szasz (1960) wrote a controversial, yet influential, article titled "The Myth of Mental Illness." Szasz began by stating that the words *illness* and *disorder* suggest that a person is suffering from some internal (and perhaps as yet undetectable) neurological or biochemical deficit. If no physical problem could be found, the argument continued, it was only because current technology did not exist to identify it. Therefore, mental illness was no different than other physical diseases such as measles or hepatitis. However, Szasz then described several problems with this conceptualization of mental illness or disorder. His comments should help us look beyond a diagnosed disorder and focus on the observable behaviors students display.

The first problem is that deviant behaviors such as a schizophrenic person's bizarre statement that "bugs are crawling out of scabs on my body" cannot typically be explained by a defect or disease of the nervous system (although schizophrenia may have some as-yet-unknown biochemical cause). Nevertheless, it is only our societal values that make this type of statement to appear bizarre. For example, Laing (1969) analyzed the language of individuals with schizophrenia and found that even the most bizarre language had meaning for the person using it. Therefore, just because someone is saying or doing something that society believes to be out of the norm does not necessarily mean that the

Thomas Szasz was once considered a maverick psychiatrist whose writings cast bright lights on those areas where our knowledge shades over into opinion and moral judgment.

person suffers from a mental "illness" or "disorder." Rather, the behavior may serve a highly adaptive purpose for the individual—an idea that is essential to managing behaviors effectively, as elaborated on in Chapter 7.

The second problem Szasz described is that making a diagnosis requires a comparison of specific behavior to some societal standard. Standards, however, can vary from situation to situation within and across cultures. The judgment that students are exhibiting behaviors severe enough to receive diagnostic labels is based on evaluators' matching their past experiences to the society and culture in which they live. In other words, the concept of "disorder" implies a deviation from some clearly defined norms. In the case of physical illness, the norm is clearly indicated through a variety of means. For example, there is universal agreement that normal body temperature is 98.6 degrees. A temperature of 103 degrees indicates the presence of a fever. That diagnosis won't vary from physician to physician, or from one part of the country to another.

There are no similar markers for determining whether behaviors are appropriate or inappropriate because they are socially determined and negotiated, and they vary across time. For example, imagine watching the *Andy Griffith Show*—a sitcom from the 1950s and 1960s that still appears in reruns. Think of the types of situations Opie found himself in and the behaviors he exhibited. Now let's momentarily move to a sitcom from the 1980s and 1990s—*Roseanne*—and think about her three kids and the behaviors they exhibited. Imagine Opie behaving in a similar manner on the *Andy Griffith Show.* In that context, his behavior would have looked bizarre, and he would probably have been diagnosed with some behavior disorder. The irony is that Opie's problems have become nothing more than a case of bad timing—being four decades behind the now-accepted societal standards for child behavior—at least as television depicts them on sitcoms.

The third problem Szasz described with regard to mental illness is that, although a diagnosis is made based on the assumption that some neurological or biochemical deficit exists, treatment is usually nonmedical. The reason for making a diagnosis is to inform us about what treatments (interventions) may be effective. Otherwise, what good is a diagnosis? For example, if a diagnosis of oppositional-defiant disorder (ODD) is made, then, in theory, this label should provide us with information on how to treat the student. Yet there is no medical (or nonmedical) treatment that is specific to ODD. An examination of the "symptoms" appearing in Table 2.1 may lead us to wonder whether *all* students around the age of puberty have ODD. A diagnosis of ODD only serves to state the obvious: A student is demonstrating undesirable behaviors, and a robust intervention is required. Focusing on the diagnosis, rather than on the specific behaviors, is misleading and nonproductive.

To summarize, the medical model focuses on problems assumed to be inherent to individuals. However, this approach ignores how the concept of

TABLE 2.1   DIAGNOSTIC CRITERIA FOR OPPOSITIONAL-DEFIANT DISORDER

- Often loses temper
- Often argues with adults
- Often actively defies or refuses adult requests or rules, for example, refuses to do chores at home
- Often deliberately does things that annoy other people, for example, grabs other children's hats
- Often blames others for his or her own mistakes
- Is often touchy or easily annoyed by others
- Is often angry and resentful
- Is often spiteful or vindictive
- Often swears or uses obscene language

Source: Reprinted with permission from the *Diagnostic and Statistical Manual of Mental Disorders, Fourth Edition.* Copyright 1994 American Psychiatric Association.

disorder is a function of a particular social paradigm. ADHD again illustrates this point. It is 50 times more likely to be diagnosed in the United States than in Britain or France. American culture is preoccupied with treating all types of problems, including disruptive behaviors, with medication. Voluminous research reports on the effects of stimulant medication exist in the United States. The accessibility of this information to professionals (through journals) and the public (through popular media) may have oversensitized us to common behaviors now assumed to be symptoms of ADHD (Reid & Maag, 1997). In contrast, behaviors associated with ADHD in Britain and France are viewed as conduct problems, and so ADHD is rarely diagnosed, and medication infrequently prescribed. Instead, behavior management techniques tend to be employed.

The point is that labeling inappropriate behavior as a disorder is limiting. We will be better equipped to deal with students' difficult behaviors if we look beyond any particular label or diagnosis, analyze the conditions under which inappropriate behavior occurs, and rearrange the environment to make appropriate behavior more likely to occur.

ACADEMIC AND SOCIAL BEHAVIOR

Teachers often have been conditioned to view academic and social behavior differently. University and college teacher-training programs usually offer separate courses that deal with these topics. In public schools, the popular belief about special education teachers is that those working with students with learning disabilities focus on academics whereas those working with students with

Unfortunately, colleges and universities, public schools, and state departments of education are guilty of perpetuating the erroneous distinction between academic and social behavior.

behavior disorders focus on social skills. In reality, distinctions between academic and social behavior are arbitrary—both are governed by similar principles of learning and both respond to similar interventions (Howell & Nolet, 2000).

One of the goals of education is to teach students the values appropriate for life in a democracy (Sarason, 1982). These values, such as the importance of working cooperatively, require students to exhibit socially appropriate behaviors. In fact, some educators believe that the best way to teach academics is through social interaction. Although this may be philosophically appealing, it can be a hard concept for teachers to embrace.

The power of paradigms as mindsets should again be apparent in the present discussion. Teachers who believe their only job is to help students gain academic knowledge expect them to behave in a manner that promotes acquiring that knowledge. And if students don't behave appropriately, teachers may view this as someone else's problem. However, if teachers believe that social behaviors are acquired in the same way as academic behaviors, then they will be more likely to accept responsibility for helping students to acquire appropriate social behaviors. Teachers would then spend as much time developing interventions for promoting students' appropriate behaviors as they currently do preparing academic lessons.

CONTEXTUAL VARIATION

Not only does context give behavior its meaning, but when context is manipulated, a domino or chain reaction is created in which the meaning, purpose, and desire to perform a behavior is changed. Therefore, analyzing and manipulating context represent important steps in the behavior change process.

Behavior does not occur in a random or unorganized fashion. People behave purposely, and their behavior attains meaning as a function of the **context**—the situation or circumstances—that exists in a particular environment (Maag, 1999). As noted in Chapter 1, the environment is the universe of events and objects, both animate and inanimate, that are part of our surroundings (Johnston & Pennypacker, 1993). Some of these events are concrete and tangible. For example, a classroom environment is composed of animate objects such as students and adults and a host of inanimate objects including (but not limited to) tables, chairs, chalkboards, and materials. Other events are less visible and obvious. For example, Clinard and Meier (1995) stated that social norms (i.e., standard rules about how individuals should behave under given circumstances) and cultural mores (i.e., social manifestations of norms) have a profound effect on how behavior is expressed and interpreted—a point that is strikingly illustrated by the two following examples.

A widely held belief is that alcohol abuse is a major cause of family violence. In cases of spousal violence, both offender and victim have frequently been drinking before the incident. An often-cited explanation for this association is that alcohol disinhibits violent tendencies. However, Gelles and Cornell (1985) pointed to cross-cultural studies of drinking behavior as evidence against the "disinhibitor" theory. These studies found that how people react to drinking varies from culture to culture. In some cultures, people drink and become violent; in others, they drink and act passive. The researchers explained the difference in terms of what people in certain societies believe about alcohol. If they believe it is a disinhibitor, they become disinhibited; if they believe it is a depressant, they become depressed. Gelles and Cornell ended their discussion by stating that, because our society believes that alcohol consumption unleashes violent tendencies, people are given a "time-out" from normal rules of social behavior when they drink or when others believe they are drunk.

A second, and equally telling, example involves the sociocultural context of anorexia nervosa. The relentless pursuit of thinness that is typical of many anorexics is little more than a caricature of what American society considers beautiful. Schwartz, Thompson, and Johnson (1982) believed that the increase in anorexia nervosa reflects our cultural preoccupation with thinness in women and feelings of revulsion toward obesity and excessive eating. Most revealing was their comparison of anorexia nervosa and hysteria—both predominantly manifested in women—across cultures. Hysteria, now considered one of the somatoform (i.e., psychosomatic) disorders, is a condition in which emotional conflict is "converted" into physical symptoms (e.g., blindness, stomach aches, paralysis) as a means of masking some underlying disturbance. Although hysteria is quite rare among women in the United States, it is still experienced by women in Islamic countries where female sexuality is customarily repressed. But these latter women rarely manifest anorexia nervosa, presumably because their cultures do not sanction the display of scantily clad and thin females to the extent that exists in American culture.

Recognizing Context as a Determinant of Behavior

The meaning a given behavior has for people is a function of the context in which that behavior is displayed. For example, lifeguards have more meaning by the side of a pool than on a ski slope, and reading has more meaning in a library than it does at a soccer match. In addition, few behaviors are categorically inappropriate or appropriate without first considering the context in which they occur. Running and yelling provide obvious examples. Within the context of a math lesson, these behaviors would be considered inappropriate; in the context of playing basketball, they would be acceptable and even valued. A perhaps less apparent example, but one that makes the same point, involves cutting someone's throat with a knife—clearly a behavior most people would consider aberrant, especially within the context of a mugging. However, it would be quite appropriate if someone was performing an emergency tracheotomy to save a life. Virtually all behaviors are appropriate given some context or frame of reference.

Context also serves as a cue that influences whether certain behaviors are performed. Some cues exert powerful control over behavior whereas others have no appreciable effect (Cooper, Heron, & Heward, 1987). For example, a phone ringing almost always elicits the behaviors of picking up the receiver and saying "hello." In contrast, receiving a piece of junk mail rarely elicits the behavior of reading it. Limitless contextual variables may serve as cues for students engaging in any number of inappropriate behaviors. For example, a student may make animal noises as a way to avoid completing a math assignment or to obtain the attention of certain peers.

Effectively managing students' problem behaviors requires understanding the role of context. The more meaning students perceive in a given behavior, the more likely they are to perform it. For example, lessons that students find contextually relevant (i.e., that have personal meaning) will motivate them, activate their storage and retrieval in memory, and promote their early application of skills.

Appreciating Context

Students are more likely to display challenging behaviors when teachers fail to appreciate how context affects behavior. For example, one teacher may permit students to get out of their seats and talk quietly with their peers whereas a second may strictly forbid these behaviors. If a student gets out of her seat and talks to her peers in the second teacher's classroom, her behavior will be considered inappropriate. But the behavior, in and of itself, is not inappropriate; rather, it does not fit into the context of the second teacher.

The other side of this coin is that some students may not be very good at interpreting different contexts. These students yell and run around whether they are on the playground or taking a test. Not surprisingly, what often separates students with challenging behaviors from their classmates is not their behavior per se but their responses to adults when confronted. Normally behaving students may apologize and deescalate the situation. Students with challenging behaviors often fail to read context and instead become antagonistic, exacerbating the situation. Rather than viewing these students as disorderly, teachers need to teach them to recognize and perform the behaviors that are required for various contexts.

Teaching students to read context and adjust their behavior accordingly is not that difficult, but it does represent a major paradigm shift. It is easy for teachers to provide students with verbal and visual cues when a context changes and to model appropriate behaviors for them. It is far more difficult for teachers to shift paradigms. A major obstacle is that academic behaviors, which teachers spend so much time teaching, are less affected by context than are social behaviors. For example, two plus two equals four in any context. But with social behavior, unless contextual factors are acknowledged, appreciated, and analyzed, changing students' behaviors will be a difficult endeavor.

Facilitating Opportunities for Students to Interact

Behavior is interactive: It occurs relative to the context, students, and other persons (teachers and peers) involved in the interaction. Human interactions occur because individuals mutually reinforce each other (Strain, Odom, & McConnell, 1984). Interactions between teacher and student are metaphorically like a tennis match: The student serves (i.e., performs a behavior—either appropriate or inappropriate) and the teacher returns (i.e., responds with some consequence—either reinforcing or punishing). This process, called **social reciprocity,** provides a framework for examining and developing classroom contexts that are conducive for promoting students' appropriate behavior. Teachers who are effective behavior managers analyze the consequences for students' behavior and the context wherein it occurs. For example, a student may make animal noises during a math lesson because certain peers are verbally encouraging him to do so (obtaining reinforcement). In the context of a math lesson, animal noises are inappropriate. Therefore, the teacher may reinforce peers for ignoring the student making animal noises while encouraging him to make animal noises during a visit to the local zoo.

These goals are difficult to accomplish unless teachers create classroom environments that facilitate student interactions. The idea is to vary classroom contexts, provide students with rules for and examples of when certain behaviors are appropriate and inappropriate, and develop lessons for them to learn the differences. Unfortunately, teachers often implement classroom management systems that discourage student interaction (Neel, 1988). For example, it is difficult to have students discuss, negotiate, and compromise if the class is set up so that they are reinforced only for sitting quietly in their seats and talking when they raise their hands. Similarly, it is difficult to foster skills in solving problems, asking for help, or making do with what is available when all assignments are put in folders, materials are readily available, and teachers stand ready to eliminate all roadblocks.

To avoid falling into this trap, teachers are better served by evaluating contexts and interactions rather than presumed "disorders" or "deficits" inherent in students. As Howell and Nolet (2000) observed, Brunswick insightfully wrote that situations or tasks, and not students, should be the basic units of analysis. Behavior problems, then, are viewed as resulting from a "poor fit" be-

It is impossible to avoid reinforcement. The reciprocal nature of social interaction demonstrates that human communication is maintained through external reinforcement.

tween the student and the context, which typically includes peers, teachers, instructional tasks, classroom structure and activities, and the larger school community.

PERSONAL STANDARDS AND SOCIAL BEHAVIOR

Szasz (1960) pointed out how evaluators cannot make an unbiased diagnosis of mental illness because their social, ethnic, religious, cultural, legal, and personal beliefs unavoidably interfere. This problem is elaborated upon here with specific regard to how teachers appraise students' social behaviors. Although academic and social behavior are similar in many respects, there is one important difference: Academic behaviors have performance standards empirically derived from normative samples or preexisting sets of learning outcomes. No such criteria exist for social behaviors. Instead, as with mental illnesses, the criteria for judging students' behaviors to be either appropriate or inappropriate are left to the subjective and varied personal standards of teachers. For example, when Walker and Rankin (1983) gave teachers a list of maladaptive behaviors and asked them to note which ones they would not accept in their classrooms, one teacher marked 51 as unacceptable while another marked 8.

A related problem is that, because teachers do not have the same personal standards, not all classrooms require the same social behaviors for success. Furthermore, the behavioral requirements of classrooms are frequently quite different from those of the everyday world. For example, a classroom is probably the only setting in which individuals have to raise their hands to get a drink or use the bathroom. This variability introduces confusion as students try to match contexts and behavior. ADHD, again, provides a telling example.

ADHD is characterized by inattention, impulsivity, and hyperactivity. The last characteristic, hyperactivity, refers to the level of students' motor movement. This trait is probably evenly distributed throughout the population: Most people have some average level of motor movement; others have high levels of motor movement, called hyperactivity; and still others have low levels of motor movement, called hypoactivity. Figure 2.1 places high and low motor movement on a normal (or bell) curve along with high and low teacher tolerance levels.

For the pair to the right of average, motor movement is in the high range, a level typically associated with hyperactivity. The other trait—teacher tolerance—is also quite high, which means that the teacher can tolerate extreme displays of behavior. In this teacher's class, is a hyperactive student's motor movement likely to cause problems? This scenario is reversed for the pair of traits to the left of average. Here, although levels of motor movement are low,

Unreasonable teacher standards are often the reason students' behavior appears inappropriate. Unfortunately, it is much easier to intervene with students' behavior than with teachers'.

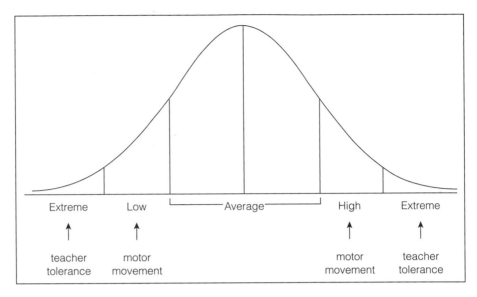

Extreme   Low   Average   High   Extreme

teacher   motor   motor   teacher
tolerance   movement   movement tolerance

FIGURE 2.1

Normal Curve

the teacher's tolerance level is even lower. This means that the teacher will not tolerate any displays of inappropriate behavior. If peers' motor movements are lower than those of a student to the left of average, does that student's motor movement constitute a problem? This scenario illustrates the importance of taking into account teacher factors when developing interventions for managing students' behaviors.

THE CONCEPT OF CONTROL

The popular and accepted view is that teachers' primary responsibility is to promote academic behavior through instruction and to control inappropriate behavior through punishment. Put another way, we expect students to be good (and ignore them when they are) and react to them when they are bad (by punishing them). We commonly ignore students when they are behaving in an acceptable manner such as reading a book and writing answers. However, if students are making noises, doodling, or walking around, we are quick to administer a verbal reprimand (i.e., punishment). Some students quickly learn that the only way to get attention from us is to misbehave—negative attention is better than no attention at all.

The Control Mentality

The view that good behavior should be ignored and bad behavior punished is pervasive. Skinner (1971) believed that our society embraces punishment much more than reinforcement because the former does not threaten our sense of freedom and dignity. We believe we are free to choose to behave in responsible ways to avoid punishment. Conversely, reinforcement is seen as externally applied, implying that people behave in certain ways, not because they are internally motivated, but because they are being coerced. Opponents of behavior modification often use this line of reasoning to discourage its use. Alberto and Troutman (1999) summed up their concerns:

> Other objections to operant procedures have come from those who feel that any systematic effort to change behavior is coercive and, thus, inhumane. Those who take this position often describe themselves as "humanists." Their objections are based on a rejection of a deterministic viewpoint and advocacy of free will and personal freedom. (p. 42)

Although punitive contingencies may be less noticeable than reinforcement (e.g., a student sits quietly to avoid a stern look from the teacher), the former is consistent with the concept of control and antithetical to the concept of conflict promoting socially appropriate student behaviors.

The control mentality is pervasive throughout education. Consequently, schools have developed elaborate management plans to decrease inappropriate student behaviors. Teachers will find behavior management difficult unless they view students' misbehaviors not simply as requiring punishment but rather as providing an opportunity for increasing their appropriate behaviors. Teachers readily understand this view for academic behaviors but not for social behaviors. For example, most teachers would agree that when students make mistakes in division the goal is not to "punish" or decrease their division behavior. Rather, the goal is to implement procedures to provide students with the correct strategy and practice to increase their competence in division. The same logic should apply to social behavior.

Punitive approaches are so widely embraced because they work so well for most of the students in public schools. Therefore, when teachers are confronted with the 1–2 percent of students who engage in strongly challenging behaviors, the response is to use more punishment. This approach is highly restrictive and ineffective.

Instruction Versus Correction

Another factor contributing to the control mentality is the erroneous belief that the correction of problem behaviors is effective instruction. Correction occurs after an incident and so is reactive; instruction is a planned event and so is proactive. Neel (1988) provided the following example:

> In a reading lesson, who schedules the time of instruction, selects the material, makes the presentation, looks for responses, and then provides correction? The

teacher does. When a behavior problem occurs, who schedules it, provides the materials, evaluates the response, and decides if the incident need go on? The student does. Who, then, is doing the learning? (p. 26)

Neel (1988) contended that the reason behavior problems are so difficult to address is that they place teachers in the role of student, a role they are not used to and find uncomfortable. Effective behavior management will be an elusive goal as long as teachers view inappropriate student behaviors as requiring only correction. The more we become aware of the limitations of the control mentality to solve behavior problems, the easier the management of these problems becomes.

SUMMARY

This chapter described five impediments to managing students' behaviors successfully. First, an overreliance on the medical model places the focus not on the student's behavior but on the student. Teachers then waste time trying to determine the cause of some behavior rather than analyzing the antecedents and consequences that prompt and maintain it. Second, academic and social behaviors are erroneously viewed as different. Instead, students' misbehaviors should be viewed as opportunities to teach appropriate social skills, and not simply something to be punished. Third, behaviors attain their meaning from the context—situation or circumstances—in which they occur. Therefore, effective behavior managers examine students' behavior in relation to the context. Fourth, teachers' personal standards may either increase or reduce the likelihood of students misbehaving. Teachers who set unrealistically high standards set up students to fail; those who set very low standards will have unstructured and inconsistent classrooms. Fifth, many teachers expect students to behave well and punish them when they behave poorly. This control mentality results in the use of ineffective reactive rather than effective proactive approaches to behavior management.

ACTIVITIES

1. Create a new mental disorder. Give your new "disorder" a label, description, and symptoms, using as many objective words as you can for each component. Is your disorder more objective than the oppositional-defiant disorder described in this chapter?
2. Check out from the library a copy of the *Diagnostic and Statistical Manual of Mental Disorders* and look up the criteria for oppositional-defiant

disorder, conduct disorder, and attention deficit / hyperactivity disorder. List all the similar and different symptoms for the three disorders. Are there more similarities or differences amoung the three disorders? What could account for any similarities?

REVIEW QUESTIONS

1. Why is the idea of differential diagnosis ineffective for developing behavior management interventions for students?
2. What are the four points Szasz makes in stating that mental illness is a myth?
3. What are several ways to convince a teacher that academic and social behavior should be viewed similarly?
4. Generate three examples of how context dictates whether a behavior is viewed as appropriate or inappropriate.
5. Give three examples of situations in which a teacher's personal standards might become the defining factor in a student's behavior appearing inappropriate.
6. How does the control mentality inhibit effective management of students' behaviors?

REFERENCES

Alberto, P. A., & Troutman, A. C. (1999). *Applied behavior analysis for teachers* (5th ed.). Columbus, OH: Merrill.

Clinard, M. B., & Meier, R. F. (1995). *Sociology of deviant behavior* (9th ed.). Fort Worth, TX: Harcourt Brace.

Cooper, J. O., Heron, T. E., & Heward, W. L. (1987). *Applied behavior analysis.* Columbus, OH: Merrill.

Gelles, R. J., & Cornell, C. P. (1985). *Intimate violence in families.* Beverly Hills, CA: Sage.

Howell, K. W., & Nolet, V. (2000). *Curriculum-based evaluation* (3rd ed.). Belmont, CA: Wadsworth.

Johnston, J. M., & Pennypacker, H. S. (1993). *Strategies and tactics for human behavioral research* (2nd ed.). Hillsdale, NJ: Lawrence Erlbaum.

Laing, R. D. (1969). *The divided self.* New York: Pantheon Books.

Loftus, E. F. (1979). *Eyewitness testimony.* Cambridge, MA: Harvard University Press.

Maag, J. W. (1992). Integrating consultation into social skills training: Implications for practice. *Journal of Educational and Psychological Consultation, 3,* 233–258.

Neel, R. S. (1988). Classroom conversion kit: A teacher's guide to teaching social competency. In R. B. Rutherford, Jr., & J. W. Maag (Eds.), *Severe behavior disorders of children and youth* (Vol. 11, pp. 25–31). Reston, VA: Council for Children with Behavioral Disorders.

Reid, R., & Maag, J. W. (1997). Attention deficit hyperactivity disorder: Over here and over there. *Educational and Child Psychology, 14,* 10–20.

Reid, R., & Maag, J. W. (1998). Functional assessment: A method for developing classroom-based accommodations and interventions for children with ADHD. *Reading & Writing Quarterly, 14,* 9–42.

Sarason, S. B. (1982). *The culture of the school and the problem of change* (2nd ed.). Boston: Allyn & Bacon.

Scarr, S. (1985). Constructing psychology: Making facts and fables for our times. *American Psychologist, 40,* 499–512.

Schwartz, D. M., Thompson, M. G., & Johnson, C. L. (1982). Anorexia nervosa and bulimia: The socio-cultural context. *International Journal of Eating Disorders, 1,* 20–36.

Skinner, B. F. (1971). *Beyond freedom and dignity.* New York: Bantam Books.

Strain, P. S., Odom, S. L., & McConnell, S. (1984). Promoting social reciprocity of exceptional children: Identification, target behavior selection, and intervention. *Remedial and Special Education, 5*(1), 21–28.

Szasz, T. S. (1960). The myth of mental illness. *American Psychologist, 15,* 113–118.

Walker, H. M., & Rankin, R. (1983). Assessing the behavioral expectations and demands of less restrictive settings. *School Psychology Review, 12,* 274–284.

THEORIES OF BEHAVIOR

CHAPTER OVERVIEW

- Biophysical Explanations
- Psychodynamic Theory
- Behavioral Approaches
- Social Learning Theory
- The Ecological/Sociological Model

CHAPTER OBJECTIVES

After completing this chapter, you will be able to do the following:

1. Understand the origin of the biophysical approach and the reasons it has limited utility for teachers.

2. Explain psychodynamic model, including parts of individuals' personality, psychosexual stages of development, and defense mechanisms.

3. Recognize the difference between respondent and operant conditioning.

4. Explain social learning theory and its implications for managing behavior.

5. Understand the basic concepts and tenets of the ecological model and the ways in which labeling theory contributes to how students' inappropriate behaviors are conceptualized.

Theories of behavior seek to answer this question: Why do students behave as they do? The answer to this question is elusive, yet it has important implications for managing students' behaviors. If we can determine the reasons students behave as they do, then we can tailor interventions accordingly. For example, if we believe that a student's hyperactive behavior results from a biochemical imbalance in the brain, then medication may be the treatment of choice. But if we believe that her behavior is caused by some emotional conflict, then psychotherapy may be recommended to alleviate the anxiety associated with the conflict. Or, if we believe that a student has learned that he can gain attention by engaging in hyperactive behavior, we may want to teach him more adaptive behaviors for getting attention. From a different perspective, if a student is labeled hyperactive because a certain teacher has an extremely low tolerance level, we may want to try to change that teacher's perceptions of what constitutes hyperactivity. The point is that how we conceptualize the reason a student misbehaves will have direct implications for the type of intervention.

Not all explanations for behavior are equally useful. Alberto and Troutman (1999) described four requirements for a theory of behavior to be useful. First, it should be **inclusive:** It should provide a reasonable explanation for almost all behavior in which students engage. A theory has limited usefulness if it explains only a small amount of human behavior. For example, some people believe that a full moon causes students to behave inappropriately. However, a full moon is unlikely to account for most students' inappropriate behaviors.

Second, a theory should be **verifiable**—that is, able to be scientifically tested. For example, the statement "Education is good" is not verifiable. We would have to deprive some students of education in order to verify whether they performed worse than students who received education. Depriving some students of an education is neither ethically nor legally acceptable.

Third, a theory should possess **predictive utility:** It should be able to predict the likelihood of students' behaviors occurring under certain circumstances. For example, a teacher might tell a class of second-graders that if they all finish their addition worksheets in 10 minutes they can have a popcorn party at the end of the day. We can predict, with some degree of accuracy and consistency, what the outcome of this stipulation will be. Most students like popcorn and so will work toward earning this reward.

Fourth, a theory should be **parsimonious**—that is, the simplest one that explains the majority of students' behaviors. For example, one neurobiological theory explains hyperactivity as resulting from a low level of cerebral glucose metabolism (Zametkin et al., 1990). Positron emission tomography (PET) scanning is required to analyze cerebral glucose metabolism. This involves injecting radioactive tracers into an individual's bloodstream and analyzing its effect on cerebral glucose metabolism rates. This theory is not parsimonious because it is highly complicated and explains only a small amount, if any, of students' behaviors. In contrast, we can confidently state that a student makes animal noises in class because he receives attention from other students in the form of smiles and giggles. This simple explanation accounts for a large amount of students' behaviors.

Five of the most popular and well-established theories that account for students' behaviors are presented in this chapter. However, just because a theory is popular or has appeared in the literature for many years does not necessarily mean it meets the four requirements described previously. Our task is to examine each theory in terms of its strengths and weaknesses. In addition, strict adherence to any one theory will result in **paradigm paralysis**—the inability to see alternative points of view. The negative by-product of paradigm paralysis is that we may become so consumed with a certain theory for students' behaviors that we are incapable of developing effective interventions that derive from other theories.

The first two theories described in this chapter are based on a medical-disease model of deviance, which regards behavior problems as internal to students, much like physical diseases. The **biophysical model** looks to neurological, biochemical, and physical defects or malfunctions, and to illnesses to explain students' inappropriate behaviors. **Psychodynamic theory** is loosely based on a medical-disease model because behavior problems are considered to be internal to students. According to this theory, deviant behaviors result from disharmony between parts of a student's personality and unresolved conflicts arising at different developmental stages. Conflicts generate anxiety that is manifested through students' displays of inappropriate behaviors. Although these two theories may seem peripheral to the orientation of this book, they nevertheless represent dominant points of view that continue to shape approaches to understanding and managing students' problematic behaviors.

The last three theories are based on various principles of learning and the social contexts in which behaviors occur. According to the **behavioral model,** students learn behaviors—both appropriate and inappropriate—by receiving either reinforcing or punishing consequences. **Social learning theory** takes this assumption several steps further. It suggests that not only do antecedents and consequences exert a powerful influence over behavior but, just as importantly, students learn through observation, imitation, and cognitive processes (perception, beliefs, problem solving). According to the **ecological/sociological model,** students' behaviors are not inherently inappropriate but acquire meaning only when examined in relation to the social and cultural contexts or situations in which they occur.

Behavioral and social learning theories probably best fit the four requirements for an explanation of behavior to be useful.

BIOPHYSICAL EXPLANATIONS

Scientists have been searching for biophysical explanations for human behavior ever since the ancient Greek physician Hippocrates proposed that bodily functioning is composed of four "humors"—blood, phlegm, yellow bile, and black bile. Proponents of biophysical explanations for behavior believe that physical defects, malfunctions, and illnesses directly affect students' behavior. Teachers who are influenced by the biophysical model are concerned primarily with changing or compensating for students' malfunctioning organic systems or processes, which presumably are causing the inappropriate behavior. If these changes are beyond the scope of the teachers' expertise, they may then suggest that the parents seek medical assistance. Several types of interventions are assumed to cure or lessen the effects of biophysical problems: prenatal and postnatal health care, proper nutrition and diet, megavitamin therapy, symptom control medications, and genetic counseling (Walker & Shea, 1995). The effectiveness of these interventions will vary depending on the specific condition and the time of detection.

However, biophysical explanations have limited usefulness (Alberto & Troutman, 1999). Technologies have been developed that prevent or lessen some serious problems. The best-known example of such technology is the routine testing of all infants for phenylketonuria (PKU), a hereditary disorder of the metabolism. Placing infants with PKU on special diets can prevent the mental retardation formerly associated with this disorder.

Some biophysical explanations are testable, thereby meeting the second of the four requirements for usefulness described previously. For example, scientists can establish the existence of Down syndrome by observing chromosomes. However, verifying that students' behavior problems result from some biophysical conditions based on "soft" neurological signs (e.g., hyperactivity, perceptual problems, or motor awkwardness) has been difficult. Werry (1986) stated that in most cases determining the presence of a biophysical problem is based on a series of medical, historical, and psychological measures that are unreliable and that discriminate poorly between students with and without mild brain damage. Under these circumstances, Werry believed that determining the presence of a biophysical problem involves nothing more than an enlightened guess. He ended his discussion by stating that, even when specific biophysical factors can be identified, there is no way of proving that they *caused* the behavior being observed. Most people fail to understand this crucial point. Here is the logical trap they may fall into: If one person has a biophysical defect and displays inappropriate behavior, then anyone who displays any inappropriate behavior must have some biophysical defect.

The logical pitfall results because we are observing an effect—the student's behavior—and ascribing to it a cause—a biophysical defect. This reasoning reflects a classical logical error known as **affirming the consequent.** It is easy to demonstrate this logical error using the example of epilepsy. It is correct to say that if a student has brain lesions he may exhibit seizures. However, it is not correct to assume that if the student exhibits seizures he automatically has brain lesions. Any number of other factors—such as lack of sleep, dietary changes, high fever, meningitis, carbon monoxide, lead poisoning, alcohol, medication, and allergic reactions—can also result in seizures (Chusid, 1982). Consequently, even with testable evidence for the existence of some biophysical defect, it does not follow that any specific behavior automatically results from the disorder.

Explanations based on presumed biophysical defects have little predictive utility for teachers. For example, to say that a student is inattentive, impulsive, or hyperactive as a result of a low level of cerebral glucose metabolism tells us nothing about the conditions under which she might learn to pay attention better, think before acting, or move slower.

The final criterion, parsimony, is also frequently violated when biophysical factors are said to cause students' inappropriate behaviors. Focusing on these causes, again, results in paradigm paralysis by distracting teachers from simpler, more immediate factors that may be controlling behaviors in the classroom. For example, a student may have difficulty paying attention because he lacks the necessary skills for performing the task at hand. Or a student may not pay attention to the teacher because she is receiving attention from a peer every time she looks around the room.

Perhaps the greatest danger of biophysical explanations is that some teachers may use them as excuses not to teach. For example, the student can't pay attention because he has an attention deficit disorder, not because the teacher hasn't modified her instruction or the environment. Or the student won't sit down because she's brain-damaged, not because the teacher hasn't found an effective behavior management intervention. Biophysical explanations may also cause teachers to have low expectations for some students—she can't learn because she has brain damage. When this happens, teachers may not even try to teach things students are capable of learning.

Although the biophysical model has received popular support as an explanation for such conditions as ADHD and depression, there is no compelling evidence that the behavior problems of students reflect internal disorders in the same way as do physical illnesses.

PSYCHODYNAMIC THEORY

Psychodynamic theory originated from Sigmund Freud's work applying the medical-disease model to the human personality (Freud, 1935). Freud was trained as a research physician, but finding his earnings inadequate to support his family, he began to practice medicine. From Jean Chariot, he learned hypnosis as a method for treating various mental disorders, particularly hysteria. He also learned the cathartic, or "talking out your problems," form of therapy from Joseph Brea. As Freud began to probe deeply into the minds of his patients, he developed the psychodynamic model of human behavior (Reinert & Huang, 1987).

Morton Hunt (1993), a historian of psychology, wrote that "more than any other figure in the annals of psychology, Sigmund Freud has been both extravagantly praised and savagely castigated for his theories, venerated and condemned as a person, and regarded as a great scientist, a cult leader, and a fraud" (p. 166). Regardless of the adulation and criticism Freud has received, few would deny the incredible impact his ideas have had on Western culture. For example, the common practice of calling a self-centered person "egocentric," or of describing unconscious and embarrassing utterances as "slips of the tongue," or of viewing men who carry a gun or drive fast cars as seeking to compensate for underlying sexual inadequacies all illustrate how psychodynamic theory has permeated everyday life. Even the popular media, both print and broadcast, have popularized Freud. For example, the term *anal retentive,* which is used to describe someone who is overly orderly, has become a common expression heard on numerous television shows.

According to Freud, our behavior is affected by three intrapsychic components: id, ego, and superego. In most of us, these three systems work in harmony and meet our basic needs and desires. However, if the three are in conflict, anxiety develops that is expressed in inappropriate behaviors. In addition to the three components of personality, Freud described five psychosexual stages of development: oral, anal, phallic, latency, and genital. At each stage, certain developmental tasks must be accomplished and certain conflicts resolved. If these tasks and conflicts are not successfully negotiated, anxiety develops that, again, is manifested in inappropriate behavior. Freud also described defense mechanisms that represent unconscious attempts to reduce anxiety. Everyone appears to engage in defense mechanisms at least occasionally. For example, few of us can deny that, at least once, we avoided studying for a test in favor of going out with friends by rationalizing that we already knew the material or that the test would be easy. However, with severe anxiety, the defense mechanisms become self-deceptive and distort reality. Although the mechanisms may temporarily reduce anxiety, inappropriate behavior persists. (Information on defense mechanisms appears in Table 3.1.)

There are several reasons for providing additional information on Freud's theory. First, his theory both made explicit and deepened our recognition of the importance of basic biological drives in early development (Rizzo & Zabel, 1988). Although most teachers do not have the time or expertise to extensively alter students' personality structures, understanding these factors provides us

It is important to interpret Freud's theory carefully. Some aspects of his theory make perfect sense, such as individuals' use of defense mechanisms. Other aspects, such as the Oedipal complex, do not hold up in today's society with its various family systems.

with an appreciation of the complexity of human behavior. Second, Freud's is probably the most comprehensive theory of why people behave the way they do that has evolved from the medical-disease model. Third, his theory resulted in the development of several educational approaches during the 1960s geared toward providing anxiety-free educational environments. Although many of these approaches failed, they did stress the importance of teachers understanding the meaning of students' inappropriate behaviors (Keith, 1991). The key question to ask as we explore Freud's theory is whether psychodynamic explanations for inappropriate behaviors have implications for behavior management.

Intrapsychic Components

The **id** is the biological component of personality and is present at birth. It supplies the total inherited instinctual energy for personality. The id operates on the pleasure principle—the reduction or elimination of tension. Tension is seen as painful or uncomfortable, and pleasure or satisfaction is achieved when this pain or discomfort is eased. The goal of the id is to avoid pain and attain pleasure.

The **ego** is the mediating system between the demands of the id and the constraints of the social world. The ego is the cognitive component that mediates the demands of the id. Conflict inevitably arises between these two components. In negotiating conflict, the ego follows a logical and rational process known as the reality principle.

The **superego,** or social conscience component, represents the norms and values of society that are taught to children by their parents and significant others. The superego can be thought of as punishing or controlling (conscience) or as acting as a mechanism of guilt control. The superego manipulates the ego by use of rewards and punishments. Appropriate responses to the demands of the id are rewarded by satisfied feelings, whereas inappropriate responses are followed by feelings of guilt.

Psychosexual Stages of Development

Freud conceptualized five psychosexual stages of development, all centered around three erogenous zones: mouth, anal area, and genital area. As a child passes through the various developmental stages, one of the three erotic zones becomes the focal point of gratification (Reinert & Huang, 1987).

The **oral stage** begins at birth and continues until about 2 years of age. During this stage, the mouth is the center of gratification, as the child begins to differentiate between the mother's breast and himself. This is the beginning of ego development, which will continue through the phallic stage. As anyone who has raised children knows, in the oral stage, nearly everything seems to enter the mouth. There are two substages in the oral stage. During the oral-dependent stage, which extends over the first few months of life, the child resembles a bird, swallowing whatever is presented. If the child becomes fixated at (attached to) this substage, she may become overly dependent on the world or overly optimistic. The oral-aggressive substage develops at the time that teeth become an effective tool. A child fixated at this substage may be orally and verbally aggressive.

The **anal stage** begins during the second year of life, when the anal area becomes the principal region for gratification. Two substages are again delineated: (1) the anal-expulsive, when a child derives much gratification from expelling feces, and (2) the anal-retentive, when gratification is obtained by holding in and controlling feces. The anal stage of development usually ends by the fourth year of life. Problems during the anal stage can lead to one of several conflicts. Students may become too orderly, with every pencil and every book in their desks having an exact spot, or the opposite behaviors might develop. Defiant, obstinate, cruel, and destructive behaviors may result from inappropriate progression through the anal stage of development.

The **phallic stage,** during which the superego emerges, becomes dominant in about the fourth year of life. During this stage, children are preoccupied with the genital area of the body. Masturbating, looking at the genitals (the child's own and others'), and engaging in sex play with other children are common behaviors. At this stage, children are interested in where babies come from and what the physical differences between boys and girls are. The Oedipus complex (i.e., attachment of the child to the parent of the opposite sex) was originally used to describe behaviors of both boys and girls. Unconsciously, boys are forced, through fears of castration, to repress their desires for their mothers and to identify with and model themselves after their fathers. Although a similar process is believed to occur in girls, its resolution is not as clear (Schwartz & Johnson, 1985). In any case, the outcome of this turmoil may have implications for subsequent behavior. Exaggerated masculinity, including boastfulness, extreme aggressiveness, and other behaviors that bring the child into conflict with peers and authority, may be the result of unresolved conflicts at the phallic stage (Reinert & Huang, 1987).

The **latency stage** is really not a stage of development, but rather a rest period between the turbulent phallic and genital stages. During this period, interest in sexual matters is dormant; the conflicts of the phallic stage have been resolved, and identification with the parent of the same sex has been accomplished. These years are relatively calm. Because of social and cultural influences, boys belong to boys' groups and play boys' games, whereas girls establish relationships with girls and pursue activities of a feminine nature. Learning

The term *anal retentive* has become so much of a colloquialism in our society that we have shortened it to the terse *anal* to describe someone who is detail-oriented.

seems to come quickly at this stage, because other conflicts have been put aside.

The **genital stage** begins with puberty and leads to mature adulthood. During this stage, the conflicts of the phallic stage reemerge. However, there are three basic differences between the phallic and genital stages. First, during the phallic stage, children's focus of sexual interest is within the family; during the genital stage, it is external to the family. Second, during the phallic stage, children seek satisfaction only for themselves; during the genital stage, they seek to bring satisfaction not only to themselves but to the persons of interest. Third, children now have the physiological capability to act out feelings toward the opposite sex.

Ego Defense Mechanisms

Ego defense mechanisms are unconscious devices that help minimize anxiety and maintain psychological equilibrium. They protect the ego from becoming overwhelmed by the demands of the id and superego. These mechanisms can be either realistic and helpful ways to assist individuals to make rational decisions, or they can be used to distort reality. For example, rationalizing the failure to obtain a desired new job by saying that it would have been too much work may not be considered unhealthy. In contrast, distorting or denying the actual occurrence of certain events is decidedly unhealthy. A summary of some of the more common defense mechanisms appears in Table 3.1.

BEHAVIORAL APPROACHES

The roots of behavioral approaches can be traced to a 19th-century philosophical movement known as **positivism.** Positivism emphasized that the only valid knowledge is that which is objectively observable. These behavioral approaches are distinctly different from both medical-disease models described previously, which focus on internal, largely unobservable factors. Behavioral approaches ushered in the era of examining individuals' observable behaviors instead of their presumed underlying biophysical defects or intrapsychic structures. Perhaps the greatest contribution of behavioral approaches rests in the concept of **functionalism.** Functionalism emphasized that individuals' behaviors serve a specific purpose or function. Most of the principles and techniques presented in the subsequent chapters of this book are rooted in the idea of functionalism—that all behavior is purposeful, and determining the function a behavior serves provides meaningful information for developing and implementing effective behavior management interventions. Behavioral

TABLE 3.1	COMMON DEFENSE MECHANISMS
Defense Mechanism	**Description**
Denial	Represents a way to avoid the reality of a situation. If a situation is too traumatic or threatening, temporary denial can be a healthy coping mechanism. For example, a person who sustains a severed spinal cord as a result of a motor vehicle accident may be helped initially by denying the reality of the paralysis, believing he will walk again. This coping mechanism can encourage participation in rehabilitation efforts. However, persistent denial is counterproductive.
Repression	Bans unacceptable ideas or impulses from consciousness, so that internal conflicts can be reasonably managed. An example of this might be admitting the death of a loved one but then forgetting the death ever occurred. "Freudian slips"—saying something out loud and wondering why we said such a thing—are examples of repressed material.
Suppression	Refers to the conscious or deliberate avoidance of ideas. It is different from repression, which is unconscious and automatic. Therefore, in the case of suppression, an individual may remember the death of a loved one but consciously try not to think about it by occupying her mind with other thoughts.
Negation	Represents a compromise between denial and repression. When using this defense mechanism, an individual is making a special point of saying that something isn't so. For example, a child may be constantly losing at a game but saying that he's not angry as a way of acknowledging his anger (relief from repression).
Projection	Consists of an individual's denial of some characteristic disliked in herself and assigning the undesired characteristic to another person. An example of this is when an individual claims another person doesn't like her when, in actuality, the individual is really stating that she does not like that person.
Displacement	Refers to the shifting of an emotion from an appropriate to an inappropriate object. An individual's feelings are taken out on someone or something else, rather than directing them to the person responsible for the feeling. A boss who blames a subordinate for his own mistake exhibits displacement.
Introjection	Involves the process of incorporating the values of others as one's own. It represents the process whereby cultural and generational values are transmitted and maintained. It becomes maladaptive when an individual incorporates others' values as a substitute for his own identity. Abandoning previously held values in favor of joining a cult would be an example of introjection.
Reaction formation	Occurs when an individual feels so uncomfortable with another person or situation that she acts in the exact opposite of the way she feels. For example, if a child is severely scolded for playing in the mud, she may become repulsed by dirt.
Undoing	Takes reaction formation one step further, neutralizing the offending impulse by engaging in some compulsive behavior. Therefore, a child who is repulsed by dirt may engage in compulsive hand washing.
Sublimation	Involves modifying an instinctual impulse into a socially appropriate and acceptable channel. Sublimation is thought to help the id gain external expression. For example, the workaholic may substitute work for sexual passion.

approaches—and their offshoot, social learning theory—meet all the criteria for usefulness described by Alberto and Troutman (1999).

This section focuses on two behavioral approaches: (1) Pavlov's respondent conditioning and (2) Skinner's operant conditioning. The physiologist Ivan Pavlov developed a behavioral theory that focused on pairing two stimuli, or events, together to elicit a response. The psychologist John B. Watson expanded Pavlov's conceptualizations to explain many behavior problems—most notably how phobias are developed. Skinner's operant theory forms the basis for many of the principles, techniques, and interventions presented in this book. Social learning theory, which emerged from behavioral approaches, has become a major influence in education and psychology and so will be addressed in a separate section.

Respondent Conditioning

Respondent conditioning is based on Pavlov's observations of dogs salivating. His classic experiment involved pairing meat powder (which elicits salivation—an automatic reflex) with a tone that would normally have no effect on dogs' salivation. The presentation of the tone preceded the presentation of the meat powder, and after repeated pairings, salivation occurred when only the tone was presented. The meat powder was labeled the unconditioned stimulus (UCS), and the tone was labeled the conditioned stimulus (CS). Salivation is an unconditioned response (UR) to meat powder and a conditioned response (CR) to the tone. The relation is depicted in Figure 3.1. The process of pairing stimuli so that an unconditioned stimulus elicits a response is known as Pavlovian, classical, or respondent conditioning.

Watson was the first psychologist to use the term *behaviorism*, in the early 1900s. Watson advocated the complete elimination of any data in psychology that did not result from direct observation. He used Pavlov's respondent conditioning approach to instill a phobia in a little boy named Albert by pairing the presentation of a white rat (CS) with a loud noise (UCS). Watson contended

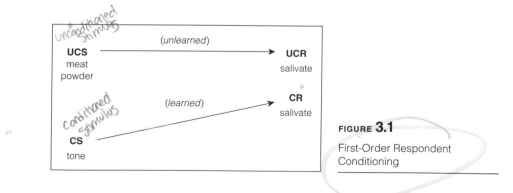

FIGURE 3.1

First-Order Respondent Conditioning

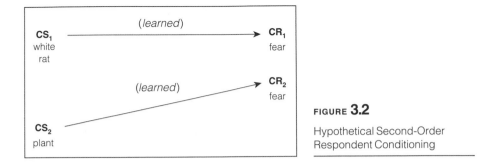

FIGURE 3.2

Hypothetical Second-Order Respondent Conditioning

that all emotional responses, such as fear, are conditioned in similar ways. This type of thinking is sometimes illustrated with second-order respondent conditioning. An example of second-order respondent conditioning, using Watson's initial experiment on Albert, is depicted in Figure 3.2.

In second-order respondent conditioning, the white rat becomes the conditioned stimulus (CS) that elicits fear—the conditioned response (CR). However, any other stimulus now may be paired with the CS, and the new stimulus may elicit fear. In Figure 3.2, the first CS (white rat) and CR (fear) are indicated with the subscript 1. The subscript 2 is used to indicate the new CS and CR. Hence, by repeatedly pairing a neutral stimulus, such as a houseplant, with the white rat, the houseplant may eventually elicit the fear CR.

First- and second-order respondent conditioning, which may be responsible for the development of many fears and phobias, forms the basis of a method of behavior change known as behavior therapy. Behavior therapists concentrate on breaking down maladaptive conditioned reflexes and building more adaptive responses. These therapists often work with people who have irrational fears or phobias or who want to modify habits like smoking, overeating, or drinking alcohol. Table 3.2 describes the three common behavior therapy interventions based on classical conditioning.

Fortunately for little Albert, a graduate student of Watson's was able to "decondition" the boy's fear of furry animals.

Operant Conditioning

As mentioned previously, many of the techniques presented in this book are based on principles of **operant conditioning.** Skinner (1938) distinguished operant from respondent conditioning. Respondent conditioning deals with behaviors elicited by stimuli that precede them. Most such behaviors are reflexive—that is, they are not under voluntary control. In contrast, operant conditioning—sometimes called **instrumental conditioning** because the organism's behavior is instrumental in its receiving reinforcement—deals with behaviors usually thought of as voluntary rather than reflexive. Operant conditioning is concerned primarily with the consequences of behavior and the establishment of functional relations between behavior and consequences.

TABLE	COMMON BEHAVIOR THERAPY INTERVENTIONS BASED ON CLASSICAL CONDITIONING
Intervention	**Description**
Systematic desensitization	Treats phobias based on the belief that, if a response incompatible with fear, such as relaxation, can be made to occur in the presence of a stimulus that normally produces fear, then the incompatible response will subsequently inhibit the occurrence of fear. Therefore, a reasonable treatment for phobias is to identify responses opposite to fear and to teach the individual to engage in those responses in situations that normally produce fear. The fear-antagonistic behavior most suitable is relaxation. In systematic desensitization, a physiological state inhibitory of anxiety is induced in a person by means of muscle relaxation, and then he is exposed to a weak anxiety-evoking stimulus for a few seconds. If the exposure is repeated several times, the stimulus progressively loses its ability to evoke anxiety. Successively "stronger" stimuli are then introduced and similarly treated.
Aversion therapy	Was developed to counteract the power of undesirable reinforcers (those that tend to be overused or that harm others). This method involves the repeated pairing (over a number of trials) of an undesirable reinforcer with an aversive event, such as electric shock. The rationale is that the undesirable reinforcer will then become less reinforcing, because it will come to elicit a response similar to that elicited by the aversive stimulus. For example, in the treatment of alcoholism, a person may be given a drug that will make her nauseous. Just before the drug takes effect, she is given a sip of an alcoholic beverage. Thus, the sight, smell, and taste of the drink is followed immediately by nausea. After repeated pairings, alcohol eventually itself should elicit nausea, which will tend to cause her to avoid alcohol.
Covert sensitization	Involves having the individual imagine both the undesirable reinforcer and the aversive stimulus. This procedure is so named because the pairing of the stimuli occurs only in the individual's imagination (i.e., it is "covert"), and the anticipated result of this covert pairing process is that the undesirable reinforcer becomes aversive (i.e., the individual becomes "sensitized" to it). One use of the procedure is with clients who wish to give up smoking. For example, the individual might be instructed to vividly imagine lighting a cigarette after dinner in a restaurant, inhaling, and then suddenly becoming so violently ill that he vomits all over his hands, his clothes, the table cloth, and other people at the table. He continues to vomit and, when his stomach is empty, to gag while the other people in the restaurant stare at him in amazement and disgust. When the maximum degree of aversiveness is felt, the individual is instructed to imagine turning away from his cigarette and immediately beginning to feel better. The scenario concludes with the individual washing up in the bathroom, without his cigarettes, and feeling tremendous relief.

Chapter 4 is devoted exclusively to describing the principles of operant theory. Therefore, only an overview of the theory is presented here.

Skinner's early work was with animals, primarily white rats. He developed a cage with a bar that, when pressed, automatically released a pellet of food (or a drop of water). This device has been dubbed a Skinner box after its inventor. When a rat was first placed in a Skinner box, it engaged in many kinds of spontaneous behaviors typical of rats—moving around, sniffing, putting its front paws on the sides of the cage, cleaning itself, and so on. Eventually, as the rat explored the cage, it accidentally pressed the bar, whereupon a pellet of food automatically dropped into the feeding tray beneath the bar. Nevertheless, no learning took place; in human terms, we might say that the animal did not even "notice" the food but merely continued its random movements. Eventually, it pressed the bar again and another pellet dropped. This time the animal "noticed" the food, and a connection was established between the pressing on the bar and the reinforcement of food. The rat began pressing the bar as fast as it could, eating the pellet, and then pressing the bar to produce another. What happened was that the rat, placed in the cage, operated on it in various ways. One particular kind of operant behavior, pressing the bar, had a satisfying result—it produced food. Therefore, it was repeated. The presentation of the food constituted a reinforcement of the bar-pressing behavior. The law of operant conditioning states that operant behavior that is reinforced tends to be repeated, whereas operant behavior that is not reinforced occurs only at random intervals or is abandoned.

An example of operant theory at work in humans can be seen in the behavior of children learning to eat independently. A common behavior of young children placed in a high chair is food throwing. When food is placed on the child's tray, she may either eat it or throw it—both behaviors are developmentally appropriate. However, if the child initially throws the food, she may receive attention from her parents. For example, a parent, with a smile on his face, perhaps happy that the child is showing independence, may say, "Now dear, we don't throw the food, we eat it." This remark is common and innocent; however, it has the effect of reinforcing food throwing. This is not to say that parents should never react to their children's food throwing. Nevertheless, the child in this example has learned that a certain response (food throwing) results in a pleasurable experience (attention from parent), in the same way that the rat in the Skinner box learned that lever pressing results in receiving food.

The previous example illustrates that, from the time children are born, they make a large number of random responses to their environment. Children literally "operate" on their environment through motor and verbal responses. Operant behaviors are conscious responses to their environment that are maintained through reinforcement (i.e., anything that serves to maintain or increase behavior). As such, operant behaviors are clearly a major concern for teachers who attempt to modify students' behaviors. Whether operant behaviors are modified depends on what happens immediately after each instance. If a student completes a good piece of work and is regularly complimented by his teacher, he is likely to do good work in the future. Whether the teacher's compliment "Good work" will increase the strength of the operant depends on whether the teacher's praise is a positive reinforcer or a punisher to the student. Operant conditioning, in simplest terms, means reinforcing desired behaviors in ways that will cause a student to repeat the desired behavior.

SOCIAL LEARNING THEORY

Social learning theory developed slowly, taking ideas from various approaches and intertwining them into an elaborate and lavishly detailed tapestry of concepts and notions (Rizzo & Zabel, 1988). It is difficult to trace the origins of social learning theory to any one person, although Albert Bandura and his colleagues synthesized previous ideas.

According to Bandura (1977), children learn many new social behaviors simply by observing the actions of important models around them—parents, siblings, teachers, playmates and peers, television heroes, and even storybook characters—and by storing these responses in memory in the form of mental images. Bandura called this process **observational learning** and believed that it is the major way children acquire new kinds of social behavior. However, children obviously do not imitate, or perform, everything they learn through observation. They know that some responses are appropriate for them to perform whereas others are not. For example, many boys know how to apply lipstick and put on a dress, presumably from observing female models, yet they rarely perform these behaviors. This distinction between observational learning (sometimes called acquisition) and performance is an important one.

Observational Learning and Performance

Some four decades ago, Bandura (1965) conducted what was to become a seminal study on the effects of modeling and imitation. Bandura showed three groups of young children a film in which a woman engaged in various acts of aggression toward an inflated clown doll called "Bobo." She hit Bobo with a wooden mallet, kicked him, and straddled him on the floor while punching him. But Bandura created three versions of the film, each of which had a different ending. One group of children saw the woman being praised and rewarded by another adult for her aggressive behavior; the second group saw her being scolded and punished for her aggression; the third group saw her receiving no feedback for her aggression. The children were later left with Bobo and other toys, told that they could do what they liked, and observed for imitative aggression. This "free play" period may be considered a test for imitative performance (Perry & Bussey, 1984). Not surprisingly, children who had seen the model punished displayed less aggression than did the children in the other groups.

Bandura then asked the children to display for him everything they had seen the woman do. He promised to give them small prizes for each of the woman's behaviors they could remember. This memory test with incentives offered for correct responses may be considered a test of observational learning (Perry & Bussey, 1984). Children in all three groups demonstrated superior and similar recall of the woman's behavior. According to Bandura, this indicated that the children in all three groups learned the woman's behavior equally well through observation but that the children in the model-punished group had simply chosen not to perform the aggression during the free-play period, perhaps because they feared punishment for doing so.

For Perry and Bussey (1984), Bandura's study clearly showed that observational learning (or original acquisition) can be differentiated from performance. They also suggested that the feedback children see a model receive for performing a behavior will influence their imitative performance. Many teachers take their cue from this last finding when they either praise or reprimand students in front of their classmates for performing certain behaviors in the hope that classmates will either engage in or avoid such behaviors.

Mechanisms of Observational Learning

Bandura believed that most observational learning occurs covertly through the use of cognitive processes. Specifically, children can learn and remember many new behaviors by observing and forming mental images of a model's behavior. But they must possess the cognitive skills to make sense of the model's behavior, be motivated to remember the behavior, and possess the motor skills to reproduce the behavior before acquisition can occur.

Bandura's conception is often called "no trial learning" because much observational learning occurs without the child overtly performing the modeled behavior at the time it is displayed by the model. This aspect of social learning theory differs from the ideas of behaviorists such as Skinner, who believed that children must both perform a behavior and be reinforced for performing it before learning can occur.

Cognitive Factors in Imitative Performance

Bandura suggested that imitative performance is largely under the control of cognitive factors because students perform only a small portion of a model's behavior. The specific cognitive factor Bandura described is **expectations.** There are two types of expectations: efficacy and outcome (Hughes, 1988). **Efficacy expectations** refer to a student's belief that she can, in fact, adequately perform the modeled behavior. **Outcome expectations** refer to a student's belief that, if he imitates certain behaviors, certain consequences will follow. Imitation is most likely to occur when a student expects that the outcome will be positive (i.e., receiving reinforcement). Hence, Bandura believed that both observational learning and performance are influenced by cognitive factors.

Cognitive aspects of learning, as well as specific cognitive interventions, are the focus of Chapter 13.

Bandura went on to suggest that students learn the outcomes they are likely to receive from performing various responses in three ways. First, they learn by receiving verbal instructions. For example, the teacher who says, "I'd sure like it if you'd keep your desk as neat as your classmates'!" or "Don't talk without first raising your hand!" is helping the student learn to expect certain social reactions to certain behaviors.

Second, and consistent with a behavioral approach, children learn expectations through past experiences of being either reinforced or punished for imitating certain behaviors. Perry and Bussey (1984) provided the following examples:

> Most children are rewarded for imitating their parents' altruism, but not their martini drinking; they are praised for imitating others of their own sex, but criticized for behaving like members of the opposite sex; and they are cheered for executing expert soccer plays in the field, but scolded for kicking balls in the house. (p. 123)

Third, and perhaps most importantly, students learn to anticipate consequences for imitation by observing the outcomes that others receive for performing certain behaviors. These consequences are vicarious and can be either reinforcing or punishing. For example, **vicarious reinforcement** occurs when a student sees a teacher praise a classmate for answering a question correctly. Conversely, **vicarious punishment** occurs when a student sees a classmate receive a verbal reprimand from a teacher for making animal noises.

Implications of Social Learning Theory

Bandura's social learning theory of imitative learning has led to a number of accurate, verifiable concepts. Perhaps the biggest contribution of social learning theory has been to approaches for teaching students social skills (Goldstein & McGinnis, 1997). Many social skills training programs have, at their core, a strong emphasis on the use of instruction, modeling, behavioral rehearsal, and social reinforcement (both vicarious and direct).

For students to learn prosocial skills, the desired behaviors must be repeatedly modeled by individuals who subsequently receive reinforcement. Students must then receive instruction and extensive chances to practice the modeled skills under favorable conditions until they can perform them skillfully and naturally. Finally, students should be positively reinforced for performing the newly acquired social skills. This approach may appear quite simple. However, as Kauffman (2001) noted, "The apparent simplicity is deceptive, because it is often necessary to make subtle adjustments in technique to make them work" (p. 352). Nevertheless, interventions based on social learning theory have been used to treat a wide variety of behavior problems including, but not limited to, aggression, phobias, anxiety, attentional deficits, stealing, and selective mutism.

THE ECOLOGICAL/SOCIOLOGICAL MODEL

The last section of this chapter focuses primarily on the ecological model but also includes a discussion of the sociological view that the labels students receive contribute to the behaviors they perform (Reinert & Huang, 1987). In reality, the ecological and sociological models are fairly similar (Kauffman, 2001).

The Influence of Environmental Factors and Labels

The ecological model takes the principles of Skinner's operant conditioning theory one step further by elaborating on the influence of environmental factors—some of which are sociological. Skinner's operant model acknowledges that environmental consequences—in terms of what students find either pleasurable or aversive—affects whether their behavior will be maintained, increase, or decrease. However, the ecological model also states that students' behavior is not inherently appropriate or inappropriate. Rather, a given behavior can appear inappropriate only when examined in the context in which it occurs. Context is partially shaped by the cultural norms of a particular society. Inappropriate behavior results from a mismatch between students and the contexts in which they operate. The ecological model sees behavior problems as encompassing both students and their environment, and not simply a condition inherent to the students. Consequently, an ecologically based teacher uses interventions that address the interaction between students and environment (Reinert & Huang, 1987). The focus of the ecological model is depicted in Figure 3.3.

As Figure 3.3 shows, students' behavior is not the only focus of intervention. Instead, it is the interaction between students' behavior and other elements of the environment including (but not limited to) the physical arrangement of the classroom, task demands and materials, and other students' and adults' behaviors. Therefore, from an ecological viewpoint, intervention may focus on changing the peers' or the teacher's behavior. The drawback of the

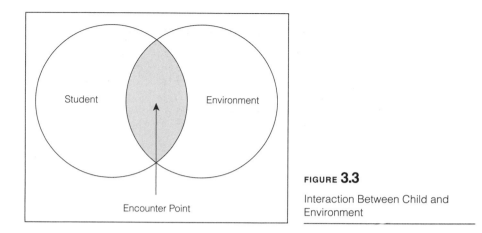

Student   Environment

Encounter Point

Interaction Between Child and Environment

ecological model is that teachers rarely want to examine their behaviors as a possible contributor to students' behavior problems. Yet, from an ecological perspective, teachers' behaviors should be examined just as much as students'.

The following example demonstrates the influence teachers exert on whether students' behavior is viewed as appropriate or inappropriate. A boy in the third-grade was having a difficult time due to his high activity levels and inability to remain in his chair. His teacher considered him to be hyperactive because he refused to follow her directions to remain seated. However, a different picture emerged in the next school year. His fourth-grade teacher's personal standards and tolerance levels were different from those of his third-grade teacher. Specifically, she did not try to stop him from getting out of his seat. Instead, she assigned him three desks—one in the middle of the room and one in each back corner. The boy could get up from one desk any time he wanted and move to one of his other desks. Regardless of where the boy was sitting, he was working and was not considered hyperactive. Providing the student with three desks is an example of an ecological intervention. It involved an encounter point between the student's behavior, the classroom arrangement, and the teacher's tolerance levels—not to mention her uncanny common sense.

Although his writings are quite old now, William Rhodes (1970) nevertheless has been the most eloquent spokesperson for the ecological model. He conceptualized behavior problems as **alien niches** (Rhodes & Paul, 1978). Students are ushered into, or find their way into, these niches. Deviant categories (i.e., labels), such as emotional disturbance, behavior disorder, or mental illness, provide society with ecological niches in which students can function without disturbing the mainstream of the school. It is at this point that the sociological perspective comes into play—all labels are not created equal. For example, society attributes problems associated with the label "emotional disturbance" to students' inability or unwillingness, which brings into question

Although it may be impossible to avoid labeling students, all labels are not equal. Some labels allow students to abdicate personal responsibility whereas others hold them immanently responsible.

their moral character (Noblit, Paul, & Schlechty, 1991). Conversely, society is more sympathetic to conditions believed to have a medical or physical origin (Sleeter, 1986), such as the labels "mental retardation" or "learning disability," and, so holds students who deal with or overcome such problems in high esteem.

These societal views often are transmitted through the media (Maag & Howell, 1992). For example, on the 1980s television show *Life Goes On,* one of the main characters was a likable adolescent with Down syndrome. There also have been many television documentaries on celebrities with learning disabilities. The media depicted these characters and individuals as survivors who overcame their limitations. In contrast, it would be difficult to imagine a person running for political office admitting on television that he was seriously emotionally disturbed. In fact, George McGovern was forced to replace Thomas Eagleton as his running mate during the 1972 presidential campaign after the media reported that Eagleton had once been hospitalized for depression. Although Eagleton "recovered," he was still viewed as weak for having had emotional problems in the first place. The point is that, from an ecological perspective, cultural factors have a substantial influence on whether behavior, and the person exhibiting it, is or is not viewed as deviant.

Basic Ecological Concepts

Many decades ago, Rhodes and Tracy (1972) described several concepts basic to an understanding of the ecological model. These concepts, which still stand up well, are summarized in Table 3.3. They help us understand the basis on which ecological theory was formulated.

Basic Tenets

The ecosystem is not something separate from students. Students do not exist within an ecosystem but rather they are part of the ecosystem. Each individual in a classroom—teachers and students—occupies a niche—a psychological place that gives meaning to the behaviors in which they engage. These behaviors provide predictability both to students and teachers and to the rest of the ecosystem. The ecological model can be summarized in terms of two basic principles: equilibrium and interrelatedness (Montgomery & Paul, 1982).

Ecosystems seek equilibrium—all elements in an ecosystem try to maintain consistency and predictability. For example, if a student receives negative attention from a teacher for making animal noises, he may continue to misbehave after the teacher begins ignoring him in order to get attention from an al-

TABLE 3.3   **BASIC CONCEPTS OF THE ECOLOGICAL MODEL**

Concept	Description
Ecosystem	Refers to the interaction of individuals and environment. It is the central concept in the ecological model. For human ecologists, the term refers to the community of people studied, together with their natural habitat.
Natural habitat	Refers to the place, or places (environments), in which a species lives. In ecology, the species is never studied outside this environment. Individuals isolated from their natural environment cannot be examined in detail, nor can they function adequately in isolation.
Ecological niche	Refers to the role individuals play in the ecosystem. This is to be distinguished from habitat, which refers to the places where individuals live.
Niche beadth	Refers to the range of roles that individuals are able to carry out. It also refers to the restraints that society places on individuals in certain niches such that they may or may not shift to various divergent niches.
Goodness of fit	Refers to the congruence between individuals' characteristics and the environments in which they are placed.
Adaptation	Refers to the rate of adjustment to a new niche, or habitat, and the range of environments to which the species can adjust. If a species is highly adaptable, it will be able to adjust to a variety of different environments and niches at a relatively rapid rate.

ternative source—peers. This example is illustrative but simplistic because ecosystems are composed of many sensitively organized elements. Therefore, permanent equilibrium is unlikely to occur although an ecosystem may achieve it temporarily. A "disturbance" occurs when various components of an ecosystem are so out of harmony that the stability of the environment is threatened.

Ecological disturbances can be resolved, and the various components brought into equilibrium, through four processes: adaptation, assimilation, expulsion, and succession (Montgomery & Paul, 1982). **Adaptation** occurs when one component changes, or is changed, so that it better fits the rest of the ecosystem. When adaptation does not occur and the disturbance continues, the ecosystem may either assimilate the disturbing element by establishing a new niche for it or expel it from the system altogether. Finally, if the disturbing element cannot be adapted, assimilated, or expelled, ecological succession takes place. Namely, the total ecosystem is altered in some basic way, with simultaneous changes in relationships and expectations. For example, if Lisa is a behavior problem in Ms. Robinson's room (e.g., refuses to sit in her seat), several strategies are available to Ms. Robinson. She may modify Lisa's behavior (adaptation), put her in the corner (assimilation), or send her to the principal's office (expulsion). Ms. Robinson could also create a classroom environment in which staying in one's seat is not necessary (succession).

The second principle is the interrelatedness of ecological components. Each component of the environment affects, and is affected by, every other component of that environment. Changes in one component necessitate changes in every other and, thus, in the ecosystem as a whole. For example, a mother and father may have a rebellious child who stays out after curfew. The child may be rebelling as a way to reduce marital strife, and so the parents may stop arguing between themselves to focus attention on their child's misbehavior. In essence, the child's inappropriate behavior serves the function of stopping spousal bickering. Consequently, an ecological approach would focus on helping the parents stop arguing—simply modifying the child's inappropriate behavior would be ineffective.

The Disturbing Environment

Several examples have been provided that illustrate how students' behavior problems may be the by-product rather than the cause of ecological disturbances. Montgomery and Paul (1982) identified three kinds of environmental disturbances that contribute to problem behavior.

Conditions Within Classrooms   Classrooms contain a variety of conditions that promote or maintain inappropriate behaviors: unfair competition, inappropriate or irrelevant academic requirements, autocratic or permissive teaching styles, excessive structure or lack of structure, and overstimulation or understimulation, to name but a few. Many students are able and willing to tolerate these conditions. However, some students who either are incapable or refuse to modify their behaviors to these ecological conditions may be labeled as emotionally disturbed or behaviorally disordered. These students require conditions within the classroom that minimize rather than promote behavior problems. The example of the teacher who provided the so-called hyperactive student with three desks illustrates classroom conditions that minimize the incidence of inappropriate behavior. Teachers who require students to complete an abundance of seatwork assignments are asking for behavior problems. The reason is that some students find worksheets boring or irrelevant, or lack the skills to complete them independently. Ironically, some students are punished for completing their work quickly by being assigned more work. Teachers can minimize behavior problems by using peer tutoring as an alternative to excessive seatwork assignments. Teachers should also establish rules for students during seat-work activities so that they know how to obtain assistance and what activities to engage in if they complete the assignment early.

Dissonance Between Environments   Any student who is expected to adapt to radically different demands in different settings is at risk for displaying behavior problems. Sometimes the conflicting demands of home and school or of general education classes and special education classes are too much for some students to handle. Here is a telling example involving the general education and special education classes. Prior to the age of inclusion, most students labeled as behaviorally disordered were removed from the general education classroom. Although the reasons for their removal varied, these students had two things in common: (1) Their behaviors were disruptive to others, and (2) they were not performing adequately academically. While receiving their education in a pull-out program (e.g., a resource or self-contained classroom), these students usually worked in a modified curriculum that included instruction in more real-life content than existed in the general education classroom. Real-life content included daily living skills, social skills, and survival math and reading. However, with inclusion, these students were returned to the general education classroom and expected to perform competently in the same environment and curriculum in which they had previously failed and that had contributed to their initial removal. These students again became frustrated and tended to misbehave—and the school's response was to punish them. This response is a classic example of the classroom ecosystem's failure to meet the needs of individual students.

Poorness of Fit Between the Behavior and the Environment   Students have their own sets of skills, attitudes, perceptions, and values. These qualities combine to produce characteristic ways of dealing with others, reacting to conflicts, and responding to environmental forces. As long as students are in an environment that is appropriate to their attributes and that tolerates their behavior, there is a goodness of fit, and disturbance is minimized. However, when an environment makes inappropriate demands on students, they are likely to react negatively and be viewed as behavior problems because a poorness of fit exists.

Sometimes a goodness of fit involves stress and conflict. The ultimate goal is not to eliminate all obstacles from students' environments. Chess and Thomas (1984) suggested that stress and conflict are essential ingredients of the developmental process. New demands and expectations help students enhance their levels of performance in a variety of academic and social skills. For example, a student may be uncomfortable giving a presentation in front of the class and so engage in inappropriate behaviors in an attempt to avoid the task. The student's inappropriate behavior should not be an automatic signal for the teacher to withdraw the demand in order to restore the student's level of comfort. Instead, the teacher should teach the student the best strategy for giving a presentation. The teacher must decide whether this strategy will increase the likelihood that the student can learn the skills for giving a presentation. However, if the student does not possess the prerequisite skills to make use of the strategy, then a poorness of fit exists, and another strategy should be selected. It is the excessive stress due to poorness of fit that results in behavior problems.

SUMMARY

This chapter focussed on five theories explaining the origins of behavior problems. The first two theories, biophysical and psychodynamic, follow a medical model orientation in that the source of the problem is believed to exist within the student. Although both theories are popular, they do not meet many of the four usefulness criteria of being inclusive, verifiable, predictive, or parsimonious. In contrast, behavioral theories—especially Skinner's operant conditioning model—meet all four criteria and form the basis for much of the information presented in the rest of this book. Social learning theory is a hybrid that combines many aspects of the operant conditioning model with observational learning and cognitive processes. It meets all four usefulness criteria and also forms the basis of much of the information presented in this book. The ecological/sociological model takes into account the context and social values of the culture when examining students' behaviors. Although this approach is not as verifiable through scientific experimentation, it nevertheless provides useful information that can be incorporated into interventions based on behavioral and social learning theories.

ACTIVITIES

1. List five common behavior problems teachers encounter in students. Next to each behavior, provide an explanation based on one or several of the five theories presented in this chapter. Which theory provides the most information that could help us develop and implement an intervention?
2. Try this experiment with your pet dog or cat. Obtain a bell. Then ring the bell at the same time you place its bowl of food on the floor. Pair the bell and food for one week. After one week, ring the bell without putting the food down and see if your pet comes for what it believes will be food. If it comes, you have used Pavlov's respondent conditioning theory to condition your pet.
3. The next time you're in a grocery store line behind a mother with a little child, make a funny face at the child. See if the child tries to make the same face back at you. If the child does, you have provided an example of social learning theory and the effects of modeling and imitation.

REVIEW QUESTIONS

1. Why does the biophysical model have so much appeal?
2. What are the limitations of the biophysical model?
3. Describe Freud's three components of personality and his five psycho-sexual stages of development.
4. Provide an example of each of Freud's defense mechanisms.
5. What are the relevance and limitations of Freud's theory to managing children's behavior?
6. Give three everyday examples of Pavlov's respondent conditioning in effect.
7. Describe Skinner's operant conditioning theory. How does it differ from Pavlov's respondent conditioning theory?
8. What are the basic tenets of social learning theory?
9. What are the implications of social learning theory for teaching students prosocial behavior?
10. What are the implications of the ecological/sociological perspective for managing students' behavior?

REFERENCES

Alberto, P. A., & Troutman, A. C. (1999). *Applied behavior analysis for teachers* (5th ed.). Columbus, OH: Merrill.

Bandura, A. (1965). Influence of models' reinforcement contingencies on the acquisition of imitative responses. *Journal of Personality and Social Psychology, 1,* 589–595.

Bandura, A. (1977). *Social learning theory.* Englewood Cliffs, NJ: Prentice-Hall.

Chess, S., & Thomas, A. (1984). *Origins and evolution of behavior disorders: From infancy to early adult life.* Cambridge, MA: Harvard University Press.

Chusid, J. G. (1982). *Correlative neuroanatomy and functional neurology* (18th ed.). Los Altos, CA: Lange Medical Publications.

Freud, S. (1935). *A general introduction to psychoanalysis.* New York: Liveright. (First German edition, 1917.)

Goldstein, A. P., & McGinnis, E. (1997). *Skillstreaming the adolescent: New strategies and perspectives for teaching prosocial skills.* Champaign, IL: Research Press.

Hughes, J. N. (1988). *Cognitive behavior therapy with children in schools.* New York: Pergamon.

Hunt, M. (1993). *The story of psychology.* New York: Anchor.

Kauffman, J. M. (2001). *Characteristics of emotional and behavioral disorders of children and youth* (7th ed.). Columbus, OH: Merrill.

Keith, C. (1991). Psychodynamic theory and practice. In J. L. Paul & B. C. Epanchin (Eds.), *Educating emotionally disturbed children and youth: Theories and practices for teachers* (pp. 116–147). Columbus, OH: Merrill.

Maag, J. W., & Howell, K. W. (1992). Special education and the exclusion of youth with social maladjustments: A cultural-organizational perspective. *Remedial and Special Education, 13*(1), 47–54.

Montgomery, M. D., & Paul, J. L. (1982). Ecological theory and practice. In J. L. Paul & B. C. Epanchin (Eds.), *Emotional disturbance in children: Theories and methods for teachers* (pp. 214–241). Columbus, OH: Merrill.

Noblit, G. W., Paul, J. L., & Schlechty, P. (1991). The social and cultural construction of emotional disturbance. In J. L. Paul & B. C. Epanchin (Eds.), *Educating emotionally disturbed children and youth: Theories and practices for teachers* (pp. 218–242). Columbus, OH: Merrill.

Perry, D. G., & Bussey, K. (1984). *Social development.* Englewood Cliffs, NJ: Prentice-Hall.

Reinert, H. R., & Huang, A. (1987). *Children in conflict* (3rd ed.). Columbus, OH: Merrill.

Rhodes, W. (1970). A community participation analysis of emotional disturbance. *Exceptional Children, 36,* 309–314.

Rhodes, W., & Paul, L. (1978). *Emotionally disturbed and deviant children: New views and approaches.* Englewood Cliffs, NJ: Prentice-Hall.

Rhodes, W. C., & Tracy, M. L. (1972). *A study of child variance.* Ann Arbor, MI: Institute for the Study of Mental Retardation and Related Disabilities.

Rizzo, J. V., & Zabel, R. H. (1988). *Educating children and adolescents with behavioral disorders: An integrative approach.* Boston: Allyn & Bacon.

Schwartz, S., & Johnson, J. H. (1985). *Psychopathology of childhood: A clinical-experimental approach* (2nd ed.). New York: Pergamon.

Skinner, B. F. (1938). *The behavior of organisms: An experimental analysis.* New York: Appleton-Century.

Sleeter, C. E. (1986). Learning disabilities: The social construction of a special education category. *Exceptional Children, 53,* 46–54.

Walker, J. E., & Shea, T. M. (1995). *Behavior management: A practical approach for educators* (6th ed.). New York: Macmillan.

Werry, J. S. (1986). Biological factors. In H. C. Quay & J. S. Werry (Eds.), *Psychopathological disorders of childhood* (3rd ed., pp. 294–331). New York: Wiley.

Zametkin, A. J., Nordahl, T. E., Gross, M., King, A. C., Semple, W. E., Rumsley, J., Hamburger, S., & Cohen, R. M. (1990). Cerebral glucose metabolism in adults with hyperactivity of childhood onset. *New England Journal of Medicine, 323,* 1361–1366.

Basic Principles
of Behavior

Chapter Overview

- Principles Related to Increasing Behavior
- Schedules of Reinforcement
- Principles Related to Decreasing Behavior
- Stimulus Control and Related Terms
- Response Class and Related Terms

Chapter Objectives

After completing this chapter, you will be able to do the following:

1. Understand principles and terms associated with reinforcement.

2. Identify the guidelines for using positive reinforcement.

3. Describe various schedules of reinforcement.

4. Understand principles and terms associated with decreasing behavior.

5. Explain the concept of stimulus control and related terms.

6. Understand response class and related principles.

A principle of behavior modification describes a basic functional relation between behavior and environmental variables (Cooper Heron, & Heward, 1987). As noted previously, basic principles of behavior and their accompanying change procedures have been demonstrated in thousands of experiments across various species, behaviors, and conditions. A behavior change procedure is a method of operationalizing, or putting into practice, a principle of behavior. And without knowledge of basic principles of behavior, it is impossible to develop effective interventions. Therefore, this chapter describes various principles of behavior. Many students for whom this information is new feel overwhelmed trying to remember all the terminology. However, this is not that daunting a task because most interventions derive from relatively few principles of behavior. For example, the principle of reinforcement has generated several intervention techniques including (but not limited to) token economies, behavioral contracts, and group-oriented contingencies—all of which are discussed in Chapter 9. Similarly, there are numerous intervention techniques based on the principle of punishment—time-out is probably the best known.

The behavioral terms and principles described in this chapter are organized under five general headings: (1) principles related to increasing behavior, (2) schedules of reinforcement, (3) principles related to decreasing behavior, (4) stimulus control and related terms, and (5) response class and related terms. There is some overlap among terms that are described under each heading. It is a good sign if you can spot similarities between terms because this means integration is taking place. The key to understanding these principles is to be able to generate your own examples rather than simply trying to commit them to memory. Other authors have also described these principles, and their positions have been incorporated into this chapter (Cooper, Heron, & Heward, 1987; Malott, Malott, & Trojan, 2000; Martin & Pear, 1999; Wielkiewicz, 1995). Table 4.1 summarizes many of the principles presented in this chapter according to whether they are associated with increasing or decreasing behavior.

PRINCIPLES RELATED TO INCREASING BEHAVIOR

As we learned in Chapter 1, reinforcement is one of the most misunderstood concepts in behavior modification, yet it represents the mechanism by which we increase students' appropriate behaviors. Recall from Chapter 1 that the terms *reinforcement* and *reward* are not synonymous. A student can earn a reward for performing a behavior or completing a task. However, what makes a reward reinforcing is its effect on behavior. By definition, something is a reinforcer if it has the effect of increasing behavior. Given this definition, it is impossible to determine whether something will be reinforcing until its effect on

TABLE 4.1	PRINCIPLES ASSOCIATED WITH INCREASING AND DECREASING BEHAVIOR
Increasing Behavior	**Decreasing Behavior**
Positive reinforcement	Application of contingent stimulation
Premack principle	Contingent withdrawal of a positive reinforcer
Shaping	Response cost
Stimulus–response chain	Conditioned punishment
Backward chaining	Extinction
Conditioned reinforcement	Extinction curve
Negative reinforcement	Spontaneous recovery
Avoidance conditioning	Forgetting
Schedules of reinforcement	

behavior is observed. Consequently, we should cringe when we hear a teacher say "I've tried reinforcement, and it doesn't work." That statement is an oxymoron. If something did not have the effect of increasing behavior, then it wasn't a reinforcer! This point will become clearer as the different types of reinforcement and related terms are described in this section.

Positive Reinforcement

Positive reinforcement is any stimulus, when presented after the occurrence of a behavior, that *increases* the future occurrence of that behavior. The principle of positive reinforcement has two parts: (1) If in a given situation someone does something that is followed immediately by a certain consequence, (2) then that person is more likely to do the same thing again when she or he next encounters a similar situation.

Here is an example that will help clarify the effect of positive reinforcement. After a student completes 5 math problems in 10 minutes, his teacher pats him on the back and says "Nice job." As a result of this social contact, he completes 10 math problems during the subsequent 10 minutes. We can say that the pat on the back and the verbal compliment are reinforcing because they have the effect of increasing the number of math problems completed. A different consequence can be applied to the same scenario. After the student completes 5 math problems, the teacher says to him, "What in the world is wrong with you? I know you aren't stupid. Get in gear and work harder!" Most of us will view these comments as representing a verbal reprimand—something aversive. However, if the student completes 10 math problems during the subsequent 10 minutes, then these apparently aversive comments are, in fact, a positive reinforcer because they have the effect of increasing the number of math problems completed. Finally, if, as a result of our original interaction of patting the student on the back and saying "Nice job," he completes only 5 problems during the subsequent 10 minutes, then this interaction cannot be considered a case of positive reinforcement. Remember, something is a positive reinforcer only if it has the effect of *increasing* behavior.

Positive reinforcement represents a powerful tool for increasing students' appropriate behaviors. However, its effectiveness depends on our following several guidelines.

Ignore Inappropriate Behavior   Some students try to get a reaction from a teacher when they are bored. To the teacher's way of thinking, a negative reaction, perhaps in the form of a verbal reprimand, should decrease the misbehavior. Instead, however, the teacher's negative reaction simply serves to positively reinforce the inappropriate behavior. Therefore, one important ingredient of positive reinforcement is consistently ignoring as many of students' undesirable behaviors as possible. Ignoring is based on the behavioral principle of extinction, described in detail in the section on decreasing behavior.

There are several considerations in ignoring inappropriate behavior. First, ignoring should not be used with behaviors that are dangerous to the offending student or others. For example, students who destroy property, hit or kick others, engage in racial slurs or other types of derogatory name-calling, or threaten themselves with bodily harm cannot be ignored. Second, for ignoring to be effective, peers must also ignore the inappropriate behavior. This goal can be accomplished by positively reinforcing peers who ignore a student's misbehavior. Third, if a student is preoccupied with the inappropriate behavior, he may not notice he is being ignored. In this instance, the very act of performing the behavior is reinforcing to the student—he is reinforcing himself.

Reinforce Immediately   A positive reinforcer strengthens any response that it immediately follows. The failure to reinforce immediately may result in inappropriate behavior inadvertently being reinforced. For example, a teacher may see a student who is usually "off task" working particularly hard on a given day. However, the teacher is too busy grading papers and answering other students' questions to go over and reinforce her. At the end of class, as the teacher is busily sorting papers at her desk, she remembers how well the student worked today. The teacher says "Nice job working today" as she looks up and sees her push another student. What behavior was just reinforced? Pushing—which highlights the importance of reinforcing immediately after the desirable behavior occurs.

From a practical standpoint, reinforcing students immediately helps them know exactly what they have done that is appropriate. For example, if a teacher smiles at a student when he is quietly working in his seat and also takes the time to tell him how pleased she is that he is quiet, he knows exactly what the teacher likes that he is doing. But if the teacher waits until the end of the day to tell the student he had a "good day," the reinforcement loses much of its punch. The student must sort out all of the things he did that day. He may not remember what he did that was considered "good."

Reinforcing students immediately also reduces the likelihood that a positive reinforcer and a nontargeted behavior will inadvertently be paired. When this condition occurs—usually because reinforcement was not delivered immediately—**superstitious behavior** is said to develop. It involves the accidental association of a response and a positive reinforcer. For example, recall the teacher who praised a student for earlier work just as the student shoved a peer in the back. In this example, the reinforcer (teacher praise) was inadvertently paired with an inappropriate behavior (shoving).

In one sense, superstitious behavior can be thought of as an example of respondent conditioning—two things are inadvertently paired together.

Reinforce Contingently   A contingency involves precisely defining the circumstances under which a behavior will produce a specific consequence (Cooper, Heron, & Heward, 1987). A contingency specifies an "if-then" relation: If a student finishes her math assignment in 10 minutes, then she can read a book.

Students should never be reinforced before the target behavior has been performed. Sometimes teachers provide reinforcers before students engage in the desired behavior in the hope that it will motivate them to begin working. But this practice rarely works. For example, a teacher wants to get a student to complete his math assignment independently. She knows that the student enjoys drawing and decides to use this activity to motivate him to complete the daily math assignments. The teacher tells the student that he can spend 10 minutes drawing if he will then finish his math assignment. The student readily agrees. But the teacher finds that it takes a great deal of effort to get the student to stop drawing and begin his math assignment. In this example, the reinforcer is not administered contingently. That is, the student does not have to earn it by first completing the assignment. A more effective approach would be for the teacher to let the student draw for 10 minutes *after* he completes the assignment.

By repeatedly receiving reinforcement after the desired behavior occurs, students can make the association that certain behavior results in reinforcement. Once this association is made, we can say that **conditioning** has taken place. Conditioning is most likely to occur when reinforcement is administered immediately.

Recognize That Reinforcement Is Individual   There are very few universal reinforcers—food and water are two that come to mind. Therefore, it is unfair and unwise to assume that all students will respond to a reinforcer, even food, in the same way. This means that it is important to take the time to find out what is reinforcing to different students. Walker and Shea (1995) described five ways for identifying reinforcers: (1) preference scales, (2) preference lists, (3) interviews with student, (4) interviews with parents or teachers, and (5) direct observation.

Many companies publish positive reinforcement preference scales such as the sample items appearing in Figure 4.1, which are from Cautela's (1981) Adolescent Reinforcement Survey Schedule (ARSS). The purpose of these scales is to help students identify their preferences. In most instances, teachers present students with a variety of objects and activities—both social and tangible. Through the use of questions and pictures, teachers systematically helps students select, compare, and rank order the objects and activities from most to least preferred. The advantage of preference scales is that they provide students with potential reinforcers that they may not have thought of. The disadvantages are that not all students will find the items and activities reinforcing, they may not be appropriate for a given student's age, and some students may not possess the language skills to describe what they like (Walker & Shea, 1995).

Unlike preference scales, in which students rate the degree to which they like or dislike something, preference lists simply provide a inventory of items such as those appearing in Table 4.2. From these lists students select preferred items that teachers can then use as reinforcers. The biggest advantage of preference lists is that they help both teachers and students expand their repertoire of possible reinforcers. The main disadvantage of such lists is that students may not find any of the listed items reinforcing. We can reduce that likelihood by interviewing students, teachers, and parents to get possible foods, toys, privileges, activities, and so on to add to the list. However, the most effective way to identify positive reinforcers is to observe what students like to do when they have free access to materials, activities, and people.

Direct observation makes use of the **Premack principle.** In 1963, Lloyd Homme (cited in Levitt & Rutherford, 1978) was confronted with the task of controlling the behavior of three preschool-aged children without using punishment or tangible reinforcers such as candy or trinkets. The first child was screaming and running around the room, the second child was pushing a chair noisily across the floor, and the third child was playing with a puzzle. Homme simply made participation in these behaviors contingent on the children first doing a small amount of what he wanted them to do. The first request was for them to sit quietly in chairs and look at the blackboard. This direction was followed by the command "Everybody run and scream now." This contingency, based on the Premack principle, gave him immediate control over the children's behavior.

The Premack principle states that a high-probability behavior is contingent on the occurrence of a low-probability behavior (Premack, 1959). A

Topic	Statement
Family members and the home	Going out to eat with my brother and/or sister Not at all ___ A little___ A fair amount ___ Much ___ Very much ___ Receiving compliments from my parents Not at all ___ A little___ A fair amount ___ Much ___ Very much ___
Friends	Talking on the phone with my friends Not at all ___ A little___ A fair amount ___ Much ___ Very much ___ Riding around in a car with my friends Not at all ___ A little___ A fair amount ___ Much ___ Very much ___
Preferred age groups	Interacting with people younger than I, of the opposite sex Not at all ___ A little___ A fair amount ___ Much ___ Very much ___ Interacting with people who are my own age and sex Not at all ___ A little___ A fair amount ___ Much ___ Very much ___
School and school-related activities	Going to the library Not at all ___ A little___ A fair amount ___ Much ___ Very much ___ Skipping classes Not at all ___ A little___ A fair amount ___ Much ___ Very much ___
Members of the opposite sex	Flirting with members of the opposite sex Not at all ___ A little___ A fair amount ___ Much ___ Very much ___ Kissing members of the opposite sex Not at all ___ A little___ A fair amount ___ Much ___ Very much ___
Free-time activities	Listening to music on the radio Not at all ___ A little___ A fair amount ___ Much ___ Very much ___ Going to concerts Not at all ___ A little___ A fair amount ___ Much ___ Very much ___
Appearance	Looking nice Not at all ___ A little___ A fair amount ___ Much ___ Very much ___ Buying clothes Not at all ___ A little___ A fair amount ___ Much ___ Very much ___
Eating, drinking, smoking, and taking drugs	Drinking nonalcoholic beverages Not at all ___ A little___ A fair amount ___ Much ___ Very much ___ Smoking cigarettes Not at all ___ A little___ A fair amount ___ Much ___ Very much ___

FIGURE 4.1

Sample Statements from the ARSS

From *Behavioral analysis forms for clinical intervention: Volume 2* (pp. 4–8) by J. R. Cautela, 1981, Champaign, IL: Research Press. Copyright 1981 by Research Press. Adapted with permission.

TABLE 4.2	SAMPLE PREFERENCE LIST		
	Type of Potential Reinforcers		
Food	**Toys and Objects**	**Activities**	**Privileges**
Gum	Pocket calculators	Play board games	Pass out papers
Raisins	Stamps and stickers	Finger paint	Decorate bulletin
Popcorn	Matchbox cars	Listen to music	board
Cookies	Squirt guns	Play basketball	Sharpen pencils
M & Ms	Yo-yos	Take trip to zoo	Take note to office
Candy kisses	Crossword puzzles	Display work	Help librarian
Potato chips	Pictures	Show and tell	Be lunch monitor
Juices	Posters	Read a book	Visit another class
Ice cream bars	Magazines	Do a puzzle	Move desk
Milk	Pens and pencils	Dress up in costumes	Be first in line
Peanuts	Airplane gliders	Use wood-burning kit	Empty wastebasket

In applying the Premack principle, teachers are using potential problem behaviors (e.g., students writing notes to friends) to reinforce desired behaviors (e.g., paying attention). By permitting students to engage in some potentially inappropriate behaviors contingently, teachers change the context surrounding the inappropriate behavior changes, which, in turn, changes the meaning and purpose of the behavior, and the desire students previously had to perform the behavior.

high-probability behavior is one that students have a greater likelihood of engaging in when they have free access to preferred activities. For example, if children have free access to eat whatever they want, some foods have a higher probability of being eaten (e.g., ice cream, candy, chips, soda pop, gum, chocolate) than others (e.g., spinach, Brussel sprouts, lima beans, liver, poached eggs). Sometimes the Premack principle is called "Mom's rule" because many parents use high-probability behaviors as reinforcers for the occurrence of low-probability behaviors. For example, a mother may tell her children, "After you finish your spinach you can have a bowl of ice cream."

Premack (1959) believed that the behaviors students engage in during free-access situations can become powerful reinforcers. For example, we might observe that many junior high school students spend an inordinate amount of class time writing notes to their friends. This suggests that note writing might be a powerful reinforcer. Thus, a student can be told that after she finishes her math assignment she can write a note to a friend. Furthermore, if her performance on the assignment reaches a specified criterion, she can deliver the note to the friend.

Restrict Access to Reinforcement Positive reinforcement is effective when students have access to it only *after* performing the desired behavior. This guideline makes use of the behavioral principles of satiation and deprivation.

Satiation occurs when students have experienced the reinforcer to such an extent that it is no longer reinforcing. For example, a teacher may decide to use candy, such as Star Bursts, as a reinforcer to increase the number of words a student spells correctly. After every word the student spells correctly, the teacher gives him one Star Burst. However, after about 15 words spelled correctly, the student no doubt will "burn out" (satiate) on the candy. Consequently, it will lose its reinforcing properties, and the student will cease to perform the desired behavior. To prevent satiation, it is important to give only a small amount of the reinforcer for each appropriate behavior performed. For example, instead of giving a Star Burst for each word spelled correctly, the teacher might give one after every five words spelled correctly. This represents a fixed-ratio schedule of reinforcement that will be described in more detail shortly.

The time prior to students' receiving positive reinforcement is called **deprivation.** Most reinforcers will not be effective unless students have been deprived of them for some period prior to their use. For example, Star Bursts will be ineffective if the student has just finished eating two packages of them before entering the classroom. In general, the longer the deprivation time, the more effective the reinforcer will be. Therefore, the goal is to ensure that only teachers control students' access to positive reinforcers. For example, giving a student 15 minutes of time on the Internet will be ineffective if she has Internet access at home because satiation may occur. Teachers can also create deprivation by applying the free-access rule. The **free-access rule** states that the maximum amount of a reinforcer available to students should be less than that which they would seek if they had free access to it. For example, a student may want to consume one package of Star Bursts a day. If each package contains of 10 Star Bursts, then the number of Star Bursts that the student can earn in a day should not exceed 10.

Reinforce Approximations of Behavior   Reinforcing approximations of a behavior is an application of the general behavioral principle of **shaping**—the process of reinforcing successively closer approximations of the target behavior. Shaping involves breaking down the desired behavior into its subcomponents and then reinforcing students as they perform each of the steps toward the final behavior. For example, we may have as a terminal behavior a student's accurate completion of a 25-problem multiplication worksheet. We may initially reinforce the student when she completes 5 of the problems, regardless of their correctness. Then we may reinforce the student for completing 5 problems correctly. This process can be repeated until eventually all 25 problems are completed correctly.

The process of successive approximations is most often used in conjunction with task analysis, which is described in Chapter 8.

Most new behaviors are not performed perfectly on the first attempt. Rather, students learn new behaviors through a step-by-step approach. Furthermore, many disruptive behaviors become habitual in students' lives and so are difficult to change immediately. It helps to give students time, appropriate attention, and praise to encourage them to keep on trying. For example, if a student is chronically late to class by 10 minutes or more, he should be praised when he makes it to class only 5 minutes late. Once he begins to make improvements in the desired direction, future behavior changes become much easier. Shaping sets up students for success. Sometimes shaping is called errorless learning because the initial behavior is so inconsequential that almost every student can perform it and receive reinforcement.

We can enhance the effectiveness of shaping when we teach students that the behavior they just performed is a cue or prompt (i.e., antecedent) to perform the next behavior in the sequence. For example, we may teach a student that when doing a long division problem the first step is to determine how many times the divisor goes into the dividend. This amount is then written above the dividend, with the remainder recorded below the dividend. Writing the remainder becomes a cue for the student to subtract. Subtracting then becomes a cue for the student to bring down the next number in the dividend, and so forth. This approaches develops a **stimulus–response chain** in which each response produces the discriminative stimulus (cue) for the next response (behavior). It is "discriminative" because the student can distinguish a stimulus that prompts a behavior from one that does not. It is a "chain" because multiple stimuli and responses exist before the terminal behavior is performed.

We can use shaping and stimulus–response chains in another way. Sometimes students learn behaviors better when they can see what the final product looks like. For example, some children learn to tie their shoes when a parent completes all but the final response in the chain—pulling the bows tight. Once a child can pull the bows tight, she is ready to perform the second-to-last behavior in the sequence as well (i.e., looping one bow under the other). This approach is called **backward chaining** because the terminal response in the chain is conditioned first. The response that precedes it is next conditioned— and so on until the initial response in the chain is performed.

Reinforce Continually at First   **Continuous reinforcement**—reinforcing every instance of the desirable behavior—is used to establish a new behavior. Through the use of shaping or a similar procedure, we may have gotten students to perform a desired behavior for the first time. At this point, they still do not have much experience in performing the behavior on a regular basis. In situations like this one, we want to reinforce continuously. For the moment, the need for frequent reinforcement outweighs concerns about satiation. We can postpone for a while the occurrence of satiation by having a large reserve of positive reinforcers. Nevertheless, it is helpful to move students to an intermittent schedule of reinforcement as soon as a behavior is being consistently performed.

Reinforce Intermittently After Behavior Is Established   Once a behavior has been established, we can move to one of the intermittent schedules of reinforcement, which are described shortly. Continuous reinforcement will get the behavior started, but an intermittent (sporadic) schedule is a more feasible and natural approach to maintaining it. We should continue to let students know that we are pleased with their performance but not try to provide reinforcement (praise) following each occurrence of the target behavior. After the entire set of interactions with students has become more positive, a smile or a few good words will keep it that way.

Primary and Secondary (Conditioned) Reinforcers

Any stimulus that is reinforcing in itself is a **primary reinforcer.** For example, food, drink, sleep, and shelter are inherently desirable—we can't live without them. In contrast, a stimulus is called a secondary or **conditioned reinforcer** if it is not originally reinforcing but acquires reinforcing power through association with a stimulus that is reinforcing. An example of a conditioned reinforcer is money. Money, in and of itself, is nothing more than paper. However, it acquires its reinforcing power because it can be exchanged for items that are reinforcing. Money is a special type of secondary reinforcer called a **generalized conditioned reinforcer** because it can be exchanged for a limitless number of things. If money could be exchanged only for socks and lamps, it would quickly lose its secondary reinforcing properties. A token economy is based on the reinforcing power of money. Students can be given tokens for performing appropriate behaviors that can be exchanged for presented reinforcers such as privileges and activities.

Negative Reinforcement (Escape Conditioning)

Perhaps no one behavior modification concept results in more confusion than negative reinforcement. Because the word *negative* appears before the word *reinforcement,* many people assume it is some type of punishment. But nothing could be further from the truth. The key to understanding the concept is to focus on the word *reinforcement.* We know that something is only considered a reinforcer based on its effect on behavior—when it increases a behavior. Therefore, whether the words *negative, bad, aversive, stimulating, sensual,* or *nasty* appear before the word *reinforcement,* we still know what the effect on behavior will be—to increase it! With this information in hand, we can now examine the definition of negative reinforcement.

The principle of **negative reinforcement** states that there are certain stimuli whose removal immediately after we perform a behavior will increase the likelihood that we will perform that behavior in the future. Basically, it feels good when we can perform a behavior to terminate an aversive stimulus. Therefore, we will perform that behavior in the future in the hopes that it will terminate the aversive stimulus as it did in the past.

Two everyday situations provide examples of negative reinforcement. When we get in a car and turn the ignition, an alarm sounds signifying that we should put on our seat belts. Most of us find the alarm aversive because we do not like hearing it. Therefore, we put on our seat belts to terminate the noise. The behavior of putting on our seat belts has been negatively reinforced because it terminated the obnoxious sound. As another example, let us assume we are in a hurry to get to work, so we rush out of the house without first checking the weather, only to find ourselves in a torrential downpour. The rain that falls on us is aversive—it feels bad. Therefore, we increase the occurrence of some behavior to terminate the aversive stimulus—we get an umbrella! These two examples illustrate why negative reinforcement is sometimes called escape conditioning—we are engaging in a behavior to escape some aversive stimulus.

There are numerous examples of negative reinforcement at work in the real world. If a mother nags a child long and loud enough, he may clean his room as a way to stop her nagging. Feeling guilty is another example of negative reinforcement. Suppose we are at a party and say something uncomplimentary to a friend about another person, only to turn around and see that person within earshot. Many of us will then feel guilty. Guilt feels bad—it's aversive. Therefore, to get rid of the bad feeling, we may apologize to that person. Apologizing has been negatively reinforced because it terminates the guilty feelings.

Negative reinforcement is the main reason some teachers continue to use time-out as a punishment even when it does not reduce students' inappropriate behaviors. For example, a student may be making animal noises in class—a behavior the teacher finds aversive. The teacher can terminate this behavior by sending the student to time-out. Therefore, the teacher's behavior of sending the student to time-out has been negatively reinforced and is likely to be performed more frequently in the future. This phenomenon leads to a risky condition called the negative reinforcement trap—a trap in which many teachers are caught without even realizing it.

Patterson (1975) coined the term **negative reinforcement trap** to explain the coercive relationships that often evolve between parents and children although such relationships can also be observed between teachers and students. Students learn to behave in ways that allow them to escape aversive stimuli. Returning to a familiar example, a student may be removed from class for making animal noises. If the student finds the academic lesson to be aversive, and if sitting in the hall or visiting the principal's office terminates this aversive stimulus, making animal noises has been negatively reinforced and will continue to be performed. The trap springs shut when the teacher terminates the perceived aversive stimulus (i.e., animal noises) by sending the student out of class. Therefore, the teacher's behavior of sending the student to the principal's office has been negatively reinforced. This trap perpetuates a cycle in which both teachers and students are negatively reinforced for engaging in counterproductive behaviors.

The negative reinforcement trap also can occur between couples. Spousal arguments often are perpetuated as a way to terminate the aversiveness of each partner's comments.

Avoidance Conditioning

In **avoidance conditioning,** a behavior is performed to prevent the occurrence of an aversive stimulus. Consequently, a behavior will increase in frequency if it prevents an aversive stimulus from occurring. Avoidance conditioning is similar to negative reinforcement (escape conditioning). However, as the term implies, in avoidance conditioning, we avoid being exposed to the aversive stimulus by first engaging in some behavior. The example of the seat belt alarm can be used to illustrate avoidance conditioning. In negative reinforcement (escape conditioning), the alarm is present until the behavior of putting on the seat belt increases. In avoidance conditioning, we would first put our seat belts on before starting the car to avoid hearing the alarm. Or a child may first clean his room to avoid hearing his parent nag.

SCHEDULES OF REINFORCEMENT

"Schedule of reinforcement" refers to the specific way reinforcement is programmed to occur as a result of the number of responses and the time between responses. Recall that continuous reinforcement is useful when teaching new behaviors. However, intermittent reinforcement helps avoid satiation and is more natural and powerful. Martin and Pear (1999) provided the following example, which illustrates the effects of intermittent versus continuous reinforcement:

> Suppose you are writing with a ballpoint pen that suddenly stops. What do you do? You probably shake it up and down a couple of times and try to write with it a few more times. If it still doesn't write, you throw it away and get another pen. Now suppose that you are writing with another ballpoint pen. This second pen occasionally skips. You shake it a few times and write some more, and then it misses some more. Each time you shake it, it writes a little more. Now comes the question: In which situation are you likely to persist longer in shaking and attempting to use the pen? Obviously, the second situation, because the pen occasionally quits but it usually writes again. When a behavior has always been reinforced and then is never rein-

forced (such as when a pen quits suddenly), behavior extinguishes fairly quickly. When intermittent reinforcement is involved in maintaining a behavior (such as a pen writing after shaking it), that behavior extinguishes more slowly. (p. 55)

Intermittent schedules of reinforcement not only help us avoid satiation but also allow us to reduce reinforcement and teach students to be more internally motivated. Several types of intermittent reinforcement are described in this section.

Fixed-Ratio Schedule of Reinforcement

On a **fixed-ratio (FR) schedule,** reinforcement occurs each time a set number of behaviors of a particular type are performed. For example, if a teacher wants a student to complete 10 math problems before receiving reinforcement, the student is on an FR-10 schedule. If the amount of behavior required for reinforcement is increased gradually, the characteristic effect of an FR schedule is a high rate of responding followed by a pause (a period of no responding) after each reinforcement and before the student starts working toward the next reinforcement. However, if too much responding is required, or if the amount of responding required to receive reinforcement is increased too rapidly, **ratio strain** occurs. In these cases, the pause between responding will be so great that little or no subsequent responding occurs. For example, a teacher may require a student to complete 50 math problems before receiving reinforcement. The student works very hard to complete the problems and receive reinforcement. However, by the time she completes the 50 problems, she will be too tired to want to immediately begin tackling another 50 problems even to obtain further reinforcement.

Variable-Ratio Schedule of Reinforcement

A **variable-ratio (VR) schedule** resembles an FR schedule except that the number of responses required to receive reinforcement changes unpredictably from one reinforcement to the next. The number of responses required varies around some average. For example, if a teacher wants a student to complete an average of 35 math problems, then 15 completed problems may be required to produce the first reinforcement, 40 to produce the second, 20 to produce the third, 5 to produce the fourth, and so on. If an average of 35 responses is required for reinforcement, this schedule is a VR-35. Provided that the average amount of behavior required per reinforcement is increased gradually, the characteristic effect of a VR schedule is a high rate of responding. Slot machines in gambling casinos operate on a VR schedule of reinforcement, and, as most of us know, slot machines can produce a large amount of coin-dropping and lever-pulling behaviors.

Fixed-Interval Schedule of Reinforcement

Some behaviors that occur at a low rate but continue for a long time, such as students completing math word problems, are not appropriate for a ratio schedule of reinforcement. Most such problems take a while to solve, and requiring students to complete a large number of them before receiving reinforcement may result in students becoming frustrated and giving up. Interval schedules of reinforcement can be used for behaviors that occur infrequently but that continue for longer periods.

The key to understanding interval schedules is recognizing that they focus on the availability of reinforcement after a certain time has passed. One way to view interval schedules is as "gatekeepers" to reinforcement. Imagine that the gate to a roomful of treasure opens only once every 15 minutes and only after a person says "Great balls of fire." Until the 15 minutes are up, it doesn't matter how many times "great balls of fire" is said. Only after the time has elapsed will the behavior of saying "Great balls of fire" result in access to the treasure room—that is, in reinforcement. The geyser Old Faithful, in Yellowstone National Park, is another example of an interval schedule. Tourists can engage in the behavior of looking at the geyser off and on for 59 minutes without ever being reinforced. However, if they look at the geyser 59 minutes and 59 seconds after the previous eruption, their behavior will be reinforced with a spectacular sight.

With a **fixed-interval (FI) schedule,** the first instance of a particular behavior being performed after a fixed period (usually measured from the time of the previous reinforcement or beginning of a lesson) is reinforced. All that is required for reinforcement to occur is that students engage in the behavior after the reinforcement becomes available because of the passage of time. For example, a teacher may designate that a 5-minute interval must pass before a student working a word problem receives reinforcement. After 5 minutes, the next time the teacher observes the student working on a word problem, he is reinforced. This is an FI-5 schedule. Provided that the length of the interval has been increased fairly gradually, the characteristic effect of an FI schedule is relatively steady responding just prior to reinforcement, followed by a pause immediately after reinforcement. The length of this pause depends on the length of the fixed interval—the longer the interval, the longer the pause. Viewing Old Faithful is an example of an FI schedule.

A disadvantage of FI schedules is that students readily figure out how much time must pass before they have the opportunity to receive reinforcement. In the previous example, the student could figure out that 5 minutes had to pass before he could receive reinforcement. Therefore, he could sit and do nothing for 5 minutes but then, at the end of this interval, begin working on a story problem and receive reinforcement. With a variable-interval schedule, this problem is less likely to occur.

Variable-Interval Schedule of Reinforcement

A **variable-interval(VI) schedule** is similar to an FI schedule except that the time that must elapse before reinforcement becomes available, rather than being constant, changes unpredictably from one reinforcement to the next. The interval varies around some average similar to the VR schedule. The average amount of time required before a response will produce reinforcement is designated in the abbreviation of the schedule. Returning to the example of getting the student to complete math word problems, with a VI-5 schedule, he might have the opportunity to receive reinforcement by performing the behavior after 3 minutes, then 8 minutes, then 2 minutes, and so on. Because the student is unsure how much time must elapse before reinforcement might occur, he is more likely to engage in the behavior continuously so as not to miss the opportunity to receive reinforcement.

An example of a VI schedule in the natural world is whale watching. A tourist does not know when a whale will surface, which means that the reinforcer (seeing a whale) is on a VI schedule. The tourist can increase her chances of seeing a whale by looking continuously at the water. Looking away, of course, decreases her likelihood of spotting a whale.

The good behavior game, described in Chapter 9, is based on a variable-interval schedule of reinforcement.

Interval Schedules with Limited Hold

An interval schedule with a **limited hold** is the same as an FI or VI schedule with a slight modification, but one that has a powerful effect on behavior. Students must perform the behavior within a set amount of time after reinforcement becomes available. That is, once the initial interval has elapsed and students have the opportunity to earn reinforcement, its availability is "held" for only a limited period (hence the term *limited hold*). In the case of the student doing math word problems, the teachers may want to hold the availability of reinforcement for only 1 minute. This means that after the initial 5-minute interval has elapsed the student has only 1 minute to engage in the behavior (working on the problems) to earn the reinforcement. If he fails to engage in the behavior after 1 minute, then another 5-minute interval begins and the sequence is repeated.

In the natural environment, waiting for a bus is an example of an FI/limited-hold schedule. Buses usually run on a regular schedule—for example, one every 20 minutes. We may arrive at the bus stop just before the bus is due or just after it arrives—it makes no difference because we will still catch the bus. So far, this resembles a simple FI schedule. However, the bus will wait only a limited time, perhaps 1 minute. If we are not at the bus stop within this limited period, we will miss the bus and have to wait for the next one.

A real-world example of behavior on a VI/limited-hold schedule is telephoning a friend whose line is busy. As long as the line is busy, we will not get through to our friend no matter how many times we dial, and we have no way of predicting how long the line will be busy. However, after finishing the call, our friend may leave or may receive another call. In each case, if we do not call during one of the limited periods in which the line is free and our friend is at home, we miss the reinforcement of talking to our friend and must wait another unpredictable period before we again have an opportunity to gain this reinforcer.

Limited-hold interval schedules can easily be employed in educational settings. For example, a teacher faced with a classful of rambunctious young students might use an FI 30-minutes/limited-hold-2-seconds schedule to reinforce in-seat behavior. That is, if the students are quiet sometime during a 2-second period after a 30-minute interval, they will receive reinforcement such as points that can be accumulated toward early dismissal or extra free time. However, with this schedule, the students are likely to learn that they can be out of their seats for much of the 30-minute interval. A better schedule is a VI-30-minutes/limited-hold-2-seconds schedule. This is less predictable because students cannot know when reinforcement is available and must perform the behavior fairly continuously in order not to miss it.

Fixed-Duration Schedule of Reinforcement

On a **fixed-duration** (FD) schedule, reinforcement occurs after the behavior has been engaged in for a certain continuous period. For example, if 10 continuous seconds of the behavior are required per reinforcement, this is an FD-10-second schedule. Provided that the amount of time students must engage in the behavior increases gradually, the characteristic effect of an FD schedule is that the behavior occurs continuously for long periods. As with FR schedules, however, a pause occurs immediately after reinforcement and before students begin working toward the next reinforcement. The length of this pause depends on the time requirement of the FD schedule: The longer the time students are required to perform a behavior, the longer the pause after receiving reinforcement.

The natural environment provides a number of examples of FD schedules. For instance, the behavior of a worker who is paid by the hour might be considered to be on an FD schedule. Melting solder might also be an example of behavior on an FD schedule. To melt the solder, the worker must hold the tip of the soldering iron on the solder for a continuous fixed period. If the tip is removed, the solder cools quickly, and the worker has to start over again and apply heat for the same continuous period. A common example of an FD schedule involves students who play a musical instrument. Many of them are required by their parents to practice their instrument for a half hour after school. Parents often tell them that they cannot go out and play until they have practiced for a solid half hour.

This schedule represents a natural progression once behavior is being reinforced on an interval schedule. Think about the student who has the opportunity to receive reinforcement for doing math word problems after a specific interval has elapsed. Even with a VI/limited-hold schedule, he does not have to work on the problems continuously to receive reinforcement. Therefore, we may want to move to a duration schedule. In this case, the student must work on the problems continuously for a set time—say, 15 minutes—to receive reinforcement.

Variable-Duration Schedule of Reinforcement

A **variable-duration** (VD) schedule resembles an FD schedule except that the amount of continuous time the behavior must be engaged in to produce reinforcement changes unpredictably from one reinforcement to the next. Like all variable schedules, the amount of time required differs around some average. For example, if the average is 25 seconds, then 15 continuous seconds of engaging in the behavior may be required to produce the first reinforcement, 50 to produce the second, 30 to produce the third, 5 to produce the fourth, and so on. Provided that the average amount of time required for the behavior to be reinforced increases gradually, the characteristic effect of a VD schedule is that the behavior occurs continuously for long periods.

There are many real-life examples of VD schedules. For example, rubbing two sticks together to start a fire involves a VD schedule because the amount of time it takes varies as a function of factors such as the size, shape, and dryness of the sticks. A childhood example might involve burning a hole in a leaf using a magnifying glass. The magnifying glass must focus the sun's rays and be held continuously on the leaf in order to burn a hole. But the amount of time it takes to burn the hole will vary depending on what time of day it is, how big the magnifying glass is, and whether clouds pass in front of the sun.

PRINCIPLES RELATED TO DECREASING BEHAVIOR

Various principles have the opposite effect of reinforcement—to decrease or eliminate behaviors. Punishment is the most common principle associated with decreasing behaviors. Like reinforcement, punishment is defined in terms of

The typical response for dealing with students who display extremely challenging behaviors is to punish them more severely. This approach results in linear interventions that represent "more of the same" and seldom work. If punishment were effective for students with challenging behaviors, then their behaviors would no longer be challenging.

its effect on behavior. Any stimulus, when presented after the occurrence of a behavior, that *decreases* the future occurrence of that behavior is a punisher. Also like reinforcement, punishment has two parts: (1) If, in a given situation, somebody does something that is followed immediately by a certain consequence, (2) then that person is less likely to do the same thing again when he or she next encounters a similar situation. Two types of punishment are described in this section, as well as two additional principles that reduce or eliminate behavior.

Application of Contingent Stimulation Punishment (Type I)

The first type of punishment (sometimes called type I punishment or positive punishment) is produced by the **application of contingent stimulation.** This involves following a specific behavior with some stimulus. We cannot automatically call the stimulus that is applied aversive because what one student finds aversive another may not. Therefore, we still define this type of punishment by its effect on behavior. For example, if a student is talking to a peer and we administer the verbal reprimand "Stop talking, now!" and the behavior decreases, then we can say that the reprimand was an example of contingent stimulation punishment. However, if the student continues talking, then the verbal reprimand was not a punisher. And if the student talks more frequently, then the verbal reprimand was a reinforcer because it had the effect of increasing behavior—a common occurrence with some students who would rather receive negative attention (not negative reinforcement) than no attention at all. Another example of contingent application of stimulation punishment is spanking.

Contingent Withdrawal of a Positive Reinforcer Punishment (Type II)

The second type of punishment (sometimes called type II punishment or negative punishment) is produced by **contingent withdrawal of a positive reinforcer.** In a sense, any positive reinforcer can become a punisher if it is removed after a problem behavior. For example, if a student is throwing paper wads around the room the teacher tells her that she must stay in from recess, and, as a result of withdrawing this positive reinforcer, her subsequent paper wad throwing decreases, then punishment has occurred. But as we know, some students don't find recess reinforcing. For these students, we would not expect paper throwing to decrease simply because recess is withdrawn. In some cases, paper wad throwing may even increase because the student finds it more reinforcing to be around the teacher than to be out on the playground. Other examples of this type of punishment occur when parents ground their child or take away phone, television, and stereo privileges for misbehavior.

This type of punishment often is called a **response cost** because some behavior (or response) costs the individuals something they like. Applications of response costs appear in many aspects of our society as a method of controlling inappropriate behaviors. A common example is when a police officer issues a speeding ticket. That ticket "costs" something the speeder values as a positive reinforcer—money! Any type of fine imposed for engaging in inappropriate behavior is a response cost or Type II punisher. Fines are also conditioned punishers.

Chapter 11 describes the appropriate uses of response costs with students.

Conditioned Punishment

Just as a stimulus that signals reinforcement becomes reinforcing itself, so, too, can a stimulus that signals punishment become punishing itself. The exclamations "No!" and "Stop that!" are examples of stimuli that become **conditioned punishers** because they often are followed by type I or type II punishment if the person continues to engage in the inappropriate behavior. Moreover, punishing tokens in addition to reinforcing ones, are sometimes used. The demerit system used in the military is an example of a punishing-token system. The demerits are not punishing in and of themselves but become punishing when paired with some other punisher such as latrine or KP duty.

Extinction

Withholding reinforcement for a conditioned response leads to **extinction**. Extinction has two parts: (1) If, in a given situation, somebody emits a previously reinforced response and it is not followed by the usual reinforcing consequence, (2) then that person is less likely to perform the same behavior again when she next encounters a similar situation. If a response has been increased in frequency through positive reinforcement, then completely ceasing to reinforce the response will cause it to decrease in frequency. For example, imagine a student who constantly makes grunting noises when raising his hand to answer a question. His teacher may respond to these noises by telling him to be quiet. If the grunting noises continue, then we can assume that the teacher's verbal reprimand is reinforcing. Therefore, to decrease the student's grunting behavior, the teacher must completely *ignore* it. If grunting decreases as a result of withholding reinforcement (i.e., ignoring it), then we can say that this behavior has been extinguished.

Like punishment, extinction results in a decrease in a behavior. Sometimes type II punishment (contingent withdrawal from a positive reinforcer) and extinction are incorrectly seen as identical. However, extinction is different because reinforcement that previously followed the response is withheld. Therefore, the response no longer produces reinforcement. The precise time at which extinction is introduced is controlled by the teacher. The removal or reintroduction of reinforcement is not controlled by the student. Conversely, with type II punishment, the response emitted by the student has the immediate and direct effect of removing a reinforcer that was already available. The removal of the reinforcer is directly controlled by the student—as her inappropriate behavior decreases, the reinforcer is no longer withheld. With extinction, the student's behavior has no effect on the availability of reinforcement. For example, extinction could be said to have occurred if a student's grunting decreases as a result of the teacher ignoring him. However, once grunting has decreased, the teacher will not then reintroduce reinforcement (i.e., her attention) for grunting in the future. But a student who loses recess privileges for grunting can earn them back once grunting has decreased.

Extinction Curve   Extinction of behavior takes place gradually until the behavior occurs no more often than it did prior to being reinforced. During extinction, the behavior may increase before it begins to decrease. For example, once the teacher begins ignoring the student's grunting noises, that behavior may increase for a while. The reason for the increase should be obvious: The student is no longer getting the attention he finds reinforcing from his teacher. Therefore, he tries grunting even more in an attempt to win back her attention.

Extinction usually doesn't eliminate behavior, but merely reduces it to preconditioned levels. Therefore, it is important, when using extinction, to provide reinforcement to students for exhibiting appropriate behaviors. Otherwise, they will simply begin displaying different inappropriate behaviors to obtain teacher attention.

Spontaneous Recovery   Behavior that is completely suppressed through the use of extinction or punishment may subsequently reappear. The reappearance of an extinguished behavior following a break is called **spontaneous recovery.** The amount of behavior that spontaneously resurfaces is sometimes less than the amount occurring prior to extinction. However, sometimes the spontaneous recovery of the behavior may be at a level higher than that originally displayed. Therefore, once we decide to use extinction, it is important that we "gut it out." Returning again to the previous example, the teacher may notice that the student's grunting behavior spontaneously reemerges after a period of nonoccurrence. If it spontaneously reoccurs at a high level at 2:30 on a Friday afternoon and the teacher impulsively tells the student to be quiet, she has just reinforced grunting at a level higher than the one originally conditioned. Spontaneous recovery is less of a problem after providing several additional extinction sessions and after reinforcing the student for engaging in an appropriate behavior. We should anticipate that spontaneous recovery will occur occasionally. It does not indicate, in and of itself, that a behavioral intervention was ineffective but rather that additional reinforcement should be administered for a student displaying appropriate behavior.

Forgetting

A decrease in a behavior as a result of not being able to perform it over time is called **forgetting.** Forgetting involves preventing a response from occurring for a period after it has been conditioned. For example, at the beginning of every school year, most elementary school teachers spend several weeks reviewing content that students learned at the end of the previous year. The reason is that students usually do not study academics during summer vacation. Because the behavior (i.e., knowledge of content) did not occur over some period (about 3 months), students forget it.

Forgetting is different from extinction. In forgetting, the behavior does not occur for a while because of the lack of opportunity to respond. With extinction, the behavior occurs but reinforcement is withheld. Both are similar in that they consist of a decrease in the rate of responding. They are different in that forgetting is caused by the lack of an opportunity to respond whereas extinction is caused by a response without reinforcement.

STIMULUS CONTROL AND RELATED TERMS

In Chapter 1, antecedents were described as stimuli that cue or prompt the occurrence of behaviors. Antecedents are very important because, once they are identified, we can manipulate them to cue appropriate behaviors. In addition, the A-B-C analysis technique was presented as a way to help us organize antecedents, behaviors, and consequences in a logical sequence. We will be revisiting the A-B-C analysis in Chapter 7 as a means to determine the purpose a behavior serves. But for now, the nature and impact of antecedents are elaborated on by conceptualizing them as stimulus control. Several related terms that have implications for behavior management are discussed as well.

Stimulus Control

Antecedent stimuli have the capability to cue and alter a response. Recall that a stimulus is any physical event or object in the environment. Teachers, peers, materials, and written directions are all relevant stimuli. Certain behaviors occur in the presence of some stimuli and not others—a phenomenon known as **stimulus control.** Two everyday examples of stimulus control are the phone ringing and a traffic light changing color. The ring represents a stimulus that controls picking up the phone, and a traffic light that turns red controls stopping the car. These stimuli exert a powerful control over behavior whereas others have no appreciable effect. For example, receiving a piece of junk mail rarely elicits the behavior of reading it. The reason is that, although stimuli cue or prompt behavior, it is the consequences that ultimately control whether the behavior will be performed in the future. For example, if the phone rings once every 5 minutes for an hour and no one is at other end, then the behavior of picking up the receiver will extinguish because most of us view talking to someone on the other end (except for salespersons) to be reinforcing.

The term *stimulus control* is somewhat misleading. Stimuli do not control a behavior but rather "set the stage" for a behavior to occur. The consequences are actually what controls behavior.

Stimulus Discrimination

The procedure by which students learn to express appropriate behavior in the presence of the "right" stimuli and not the "wrong" stimuli is called **stimulus discrimination.** This procedure involves reinforcing a behavior in the presence of one stimulus and not reinforcing it (i.e., extinguishing it) in the presence of other stimuli. Students' figuring out which teachers are lenient and which are strict is an example of stimulus discrimination. Consequently, students may talk to their classmates more in Mr. Wilson's room and be quieter in Ms. Smith's room. The teachers become a stimulus for receiving either reinforcement (the fun of talking to a classmate) or punishment (a verbal reprimand from the teacher).

Stimulus Generalization

The opposite of stimulus discrimination is **stimulus generalization,** which occurs when individuals respond in a similar manner to different stimuli. A behavior conditioned in the presence of one discriminative stimulus tends to occur in the presence of other stimuli.

Stimulus generalization can have either positive or negative effects on behavior. A positive example is when a student learns to say "Excuse me" when he burps. The burp is a stimulus to engage in the behavior of saying "Excuse me." However, if the student also says "Excuse me" when trying to enter a conversation with peers or after accidentally bumping into someone, stimulus generalization has occurred. Entering a conversation and accidentally bumping someone are different stimuli that elicit the same behavior of saying "Excuse me." A negative example is when a student learns how to add a pair of two-digit numbers without regrouping and then applies this strategy for the addition

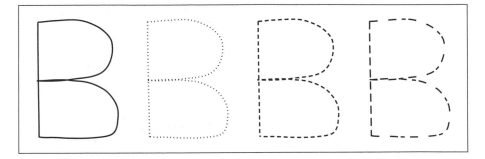

FIGURE **4.2**

Example of Fading

of a pair of two-digit numbers with regrouping (e.g., 48 + 67 = 1015 rather than 115).

Fading

The gradual change of the stimulus controlling a behavior, such that the behavior eventually occurs as the result of a partially changed or completely new antecedent stimulus, is called **fading.** For example, fading can be used to teach students how to write letters of the alphabet. The teacher might begin by printing the letter *B* on the chalkboard and asking students to trace it. Next, the teacher writes the letter *B* in dots and has students trace it. Then, the teacher writes the letter *B* using only several dashes as a cue for students to trace. Finally, the teacher fades the cue completely by requiring students to write the letter *B* without any visual cue. This basic process is depicted in Figure 4.2.

Fading can be a useful technique for changing the stimulus control in a situation in which a stimulus is a powerful cue to perform a behavior. Fading should not be confused with shaping. Although both are procedures of gradual change, the similarity ends there. Recall that shaping involves reinforcing slight changes in a behavior so that it gradually comes to resemble the desired target behavior. The stimulus situation generally stays about the same, and the behavior changes from an initial behavior (not necessarily resembling the target) to the final target behavior. In contrast, fading involves reinforcing the final behavior while slightly changing the stimulus so that it gradually comes to resemble the stimulus that we wish to eventually control the desired response. Thus, shaping involves the gradual change of a behavior while the stimulus stays the same, and fading involves the gradual change of a stimulus while the behavior stays the same.

RESPONSE CLASS AND RELATED TERMS

The use of the principles described in this chapter can help us increase the occurrence of desired student behaviors while decreasing undesired behaviors. This process can be accomplished by using positive reinforcement, shaping, fading, extinction, and stimulus control, and by understanding the nature of a response class and related terms.

Response Class

A **response class** refers to a group of responses (behaviors) that have at least one characteristic in common. One obvious characteristic of responses is the movement they involve; another is the effect they have on the environment—that is, the purpose they serve. Behaviors may encompass different movements, but they are all similar in that they lead to a common result. For example, the following student behaviors make up a response class: raising a hand, grunting, making animal noises, walking up to the teacher's desk, calling the teacher's name, and tugging on the teacher's sleeve. The common characteristic they all share is getting teacher attention even though some of the behaviors are appropriate (e.g., raising a hand, calling out the teacher's name) and others are inappropriate (e.g., grunting, making animal noises). Here is another response class: knocking, ringing the bell, using the door knocker, and yelling. The common purpose these behaviors serve, of course, is getting someone to answer the door.

Differential Reinforcement

Differential reinforcement involves reinforcing a certain behavior (or behaviors) from a response class and extinguishing all other members of that class. We can illustrate this process using the first response class described previously. Specifically, in the case of the response class for getting teacher attention, we want to reinforce two or three of the members—raising a hand, calling the teachers' name, and walking up to the teacher's desk—while ignoring the others. By doing this, we say that raising a hand, walking up to the teacher's desk, and calling the teacher's name have been differentially reinforced. Differential reinforcement leads to response differentiation.

Response Differentiation

After certain members of a response class are repeatedly reinforced while the others are extinguished, students begin to differentiate which behaviors will result in reinforcement and which ones will not. Once students are able to make this distinction, **response differentiation** is said to have occurred. The example of the response class for getting someone to answer the door illustrates this point. The most desirable behavior of that response class to reinforce is knocking because not all houses or apartments have doorbells or door knockers. Knocking is differentially reinforced by having the person answer only to a knock but stay inside if someone uses the doorbell or knocker or yells. Once the individual learns to approach the door and immediately knock rather than performing any of the other behaviors in the response class, response differentiation has occurred.

SUMMARY

This chapter described basic principles and terms of behavior modification. Positive reinforcement is the most important principle because it has the effect of increasing students' appropriate behaviors. Positive reinforcement can be used to shape the occurrence of new student behaviors that enhance learning and social skills. However, several guidelines should be followed for positive reinforcement to be maximally effective. Intermittent schedules of reinforcement ensure that new behaviors are performed at a high rate without requiring continual reinforcement. When positive reinforcement is used in conjunction with extinction and the establishment of stimulus control, response differentiation is more likely to occur. Students are then more likely to perform appropriate behaviors when cued by the teacher or some other aspect of the environment.

Principles of punishment are also important. However, the need to use punishment is dramatically reduced when the other principles are applied in conjunction. In addition, there are many negative side effects of punishment that may work against students performing desirable behaviors. The concerns over the uses of punishment are discussed in Chapter 11.

Response class refers to a group of behaviors that share some common characteristic, typically the purpose they serve or the topography (appearance) displayed. The goal is to reinforce appropriate members of a response class while ignoring others. This process makes use of differential reinforcement and extinction. When students understand what behaviors will be reinforced and what ones will be extinguished, response differentiation is said to have occurred.

ACTIVITIES

1. Observe children on a playground. Note whether they give each other more reinforcing or punishing comments. Do teachers use this same ratio, and is that good or bad?

2. Here's a fun experiment to try with your friends or family. In a group of people, have someone volunteer to leave the room. Then pick a behavior you want to see that person perform when she or he reenters the room. But you are not going to tell the person what behavior you've selected. Rather, you are going to "shape" that behavior by using the old game of "getting hotter or colder." For example, suppose you want the volunteer to pick up a certain book on a shelf. When that person reenters the room, have everyone else begin clapping their hands as he or she gets closer to picking up the particular book. In no time at all, the volunteer will have picked up the book through the use of shaping.

3. Think back to when you were in grade school. Remember how in some teachers' classrooms you did exactly what they said on the first request whereas in other teachers' classrooms you blew off their request? Make a list of the differences between these teachers, and examine the list. What do you observe and how is it related to stimulus control?

REVIEW QUESTIONS

1. What effect does reinforcement have on behavior?
2. What guidelines should be followed to increase the effectiveness of positive reinforcement?
3. What effect do punishment and extinction have on behavior?
4. What is the difference between negative reinforcement and punishment?
5. What role do satiation and deprivation play in the effectiveness of reinforcement?
6. How do shaping and fading differ from each other?
7. Provide an example for each schedule of reinforcement. Describe situations in which each schedule would be desirable.
8. Describe the two types of punishment and provide an example for each.
9. How do contingent withdrawal of a reinforcer and extinction differ?
10. How might it be demonstrated to someone that, although stimulus control elicits behavior, it is the consequence that actually controls the behavior?
11. Give an example of how the concepts of response class, differential reinforcement, and response differentiation work together.

REFERENCES

Cautela, J. R. (1981). *Behavioral analysis forms for clinical intervention: Volume 2*. Champaign, IL: Research Press.

Cooper, J. O., Heron, T. E., & Heward, W. L. (1987). *Applied behavior analysis*. Columbus, OH: Merrill.

Levitt, L. K., & Rutherford, R. B., Jr. (1978). *Strategies for handling the disruptive student*. Tempe: College of Education, Arizona State University.

Malott, R. H., Malott, M. E., & Trojan, E. A. (2000). *Elementary principles of behavior* (4th ed.). Englewood Cliffs, NJ: Prentice-Hall.

Martin, G., & Pear, J. (1999). *Behavior modification: What it is and how to do it* (6th ed.). Upper Saddle River, NJ: Prentice-Hall.

Patterson, G. R. (1975). *Families: Applications of social learning to family life*. Champaign, IL: Research Press.

Premack, D. (1959). Toward empirical behavioral laws: I. Positive reinforcement. *Psychological Review, 66,* 219–233.

Walker, J. E., & Shea, T. M. (1995). *Behavior management: A practical approach for educators* (6th ed.). New York: Macmillan.

Wielkiewicz, R. M. (1995). *Behavior management in the schools: Principles and procedures* (2nd ed.). Boston: Allyn & Bacon.

COUNTING AND RECORDING BEHAVIOR

CHAPTER OVERVIEW

- Reasons Counting Behavior Is Important
- Considerations Prior to Recording Behavior
- Factors to Consider When Pinpointing a Target Behavior
- Techniques for Recording Behavior
- Methods for Calculating Interobserver Reliability

CHAPTER OBJECTIVES

After completing this chapter, you will be able to do the following:

1. Discuss the reasons it is important to count behavior.
2. Recognize what factors should be considered before recording behavior.
3. Identify factors to consider when pinpointing target behaviors.
4. Explain how to implement the different techniques for recording behavior.
5. Explain the uses for permanent product recording.
6. Describe the advantages and disadvantages of frequency (event) recording.
7. Describe the advantages and disadvantages of duration recording.
8. Describe the advantages and disadvantages of interval recording.
9. Describe the advantages and disadvantages of time sample recording.
10. Identify methods for calculating interobserver reliability.

In the previous chapter, we learned about principles of behavior that form the basis for many of the interventions described later in this book. Before we can intervene, however, we need to know exactly what behavior is of concern to us, how often it occurs, and what purpose it serves. These processes require that we target and define a behavior, select a technique for recording our counts, and then place the results on a graph so that we have a visual representation of the behavior. This chapter is concerned with the first procedures—targeting and defining a behavior, and counting and recording its occurrences. Chapter 6 focuses on how to graph the results of our counts. A solid working knowledge of the information in these two chapters is necessary for understanding functional assessment—one of the most important aspects of behavior management, as discussed in Chapter 7. Specifically, this chapter focuses on the various ways in which behavior can be counted and recorded reliably. The reasons it is important to count behavior, the factors to consider before recording behavior, issues to address when pinpointing a target behavior, and methods for recording behavior and for determining interobserver reliability.

REASONS COUNTING BEHAVIOR IS IMPORTANT

Recall the definition of applied behavior analysis (ABA) from Chapter 1: a systematic, performance-based, self-evaluative method for changing students' behaviors. Therefore, ABA is based on direct measurement of behavior because we are counting and recording students' behaviors before, during, and after implementing interventions in classroom situations. Note that it is insufficient to count and record behavior only once before and after implementing an intervention. This procedure is similar to pretesting students at the beginning of the year and posttesting them at the end of the year. Instead, the process of counting and recording behavior should be frequent and continuous.

Frequent and continuous counting and recording of students' behavior can be time consuming, and so generally is reserved for students with the most challenging behaviors.

Cooper, Heron, and Heward (1987) suggested two reasons counting should be direct and continuous. First, it reduces the likelihood of our introducing error into the behavior management process. Unlike with standardized tests, direct recording of students' behaviors help us avoid the problem of inferring the meaning of students' behavior. Any time we must make an inference, we introduce error into the evaluation process. Second, direct and continuous counting reduces the likelihood of our either prematurely terminating an effective intervention or unduly continuing an ineffective one. Figures 5.1 and 5.2 illustrate these two important reasons.

Figure 5.1 depicts the performances of four students before and after they received the same intervention using only two observations—a pretest and a posttest. Let us assume that the target behavior was "number of times student

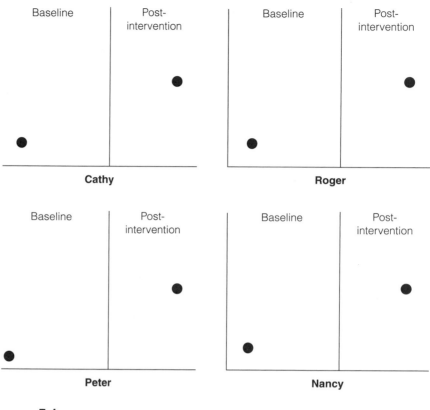

FIGURE 5.1

Pretest and Posttest Performance of Two Students

raises hands before answering a question." Let us also assume that the intervention was to give the students a piece of candy every time they raised their hands before answering a question. The vertical line indicates when the **baseline**—that is, the data collected on the target behavior prior to intervention—stopped and intervention began. The pretest observation was conducted early on during the baseline, and the posttest observation was conducted after the intervention had been in effect for a while. An examination of the graphs in Figure 5.1 seems to indicate that the intervention was equally effective for all four students. Based on these results, we may feel confident continuing the intervention for all four students and even consider implementing it with other students in the class.

However, a different picture emerges when we examine the students' behaviors as depicted in Figure 5.2. These graphs show the effects of intervention after collecting continuous data on their hand raising prior to answering a

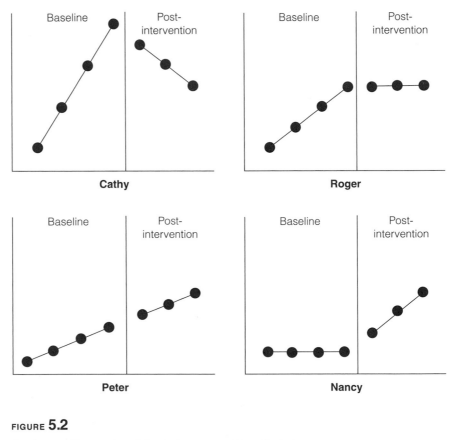

FIGURE 5.2

Continuous Observation of the Performance of Four Students

question. For example, for Cathy, the effect of intervention was to decrease her hand raising. In Roger's case, his hand raising hit a plateau when intervention was implemented. Although the intervention did not have as negative an effect on hand raising for Roger as it did for Cathy, it nevertheless terminated any progress he was making on his own. The intervention had no effect on Peter's hand raising. An examination of his graph shows that the behavior was gradually increasing during the baseline and that this trend continued when intervention was implemented. The intervention was only effective for Nancy, whose hand raising was not improving at all until intervention was implemented.

This example graphically illustrates the importance of collecting frequent and continuous data. Unfortunately, some teachers view collecting data to be, at best, unnecessary and, at worst, as irrelevant. This belief is unfortunate because researchers have consistently found that teachers who collect frequent and continuous data make better decisions than do teachers who say they keep data "in their heads" (e.g., Fuchs & Fuchs, 1986; Fuchs, Fuchs, & Stecker, 1989). In addition, students make better progress when teachers collect frequent and continuous data (Fuchs, Deno, & Mirkin, 1984).

Given this information, it may be tempting to think that frequent and continuous data should be collected for *all* students. However, there are few students in the general education classroom whose behavior is so inappropriate as to warrant using the type of counting and recording procedures described in this chapter. We typically only record students' scores on assignments, quizzes, and tests, and perhaps document misconduct for the purposes of disciplinary action or information if a student is referred for special education evaluation. Yet, for students with challenging behaviors, counting and recording is essential for several reasons.

Precounting to Help Evaluate the Effectiveness of Intervention

We need a precount of behavior to accurately evaluate the effectiveness of an intervention. Evaluation involves comparing performance to some standard and noting any discrepancies (Howell & Nolett, 2000). Figure 5.3 provides a simple illustration of the process of evaluation.

Precount data are the baseline—a term previously introduced. The baseline can be thought of as our standard: It is what we use to determine whether a discrepancy exists between performance (or behavior) and our standard. If we consider our standard to be the ongoing behavior of a student prior to intervention, then our intervention is effective if a large discrepancy exists in the desired direction after the intervention. Figure 5.4 shows two graphs of a student's behavior. The horizontal lines indicate the average performance of the student during baseline and intervention. As these lines show, a small discrepancy exists between baseline and intervention. Accordingly, the intervention was ineffective. However, in Figure 5.5, there is a large discrepancy between the student's behavior recorded during baseline and intervention. The precount gives us a standard indicating that this intervention was effective.

The importance of counting and recording behavior can be seen in many aspects of our society—from the graph that appears on the front page of the *Wall Street Journal* to information appearing on billboards.

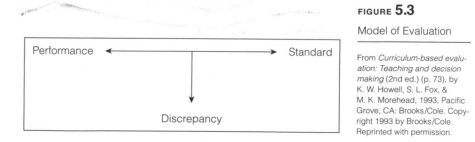

FIGURE 5.3

Model of Evaluation

From *Curriculum-based evaluation: Teaching and decision making* (2nd ed.) (p. 73), by K. W. Howell, S. L. Fox, & M. K. Morehead, 1993, Pacific Grove, CA: Brooks/Cole. Copyright 1993 by Brooks/Cole. Reprinted with permission.

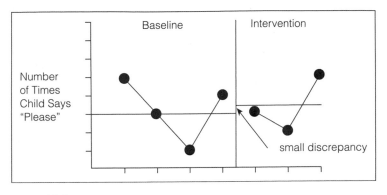

FIGURE 5.4

Hypothetical Data of an Ineffective Intervention

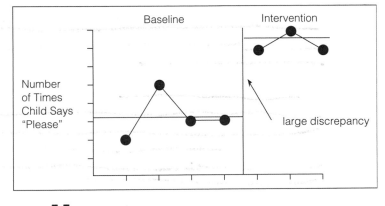

FIGURE 5.5

Hypothetical Data of an Effective Intervention

Counting to Identify the Correct Behavior

Counting helps us determine whether the targeted behavior is actually the one causing the problem (Levitt & Rutherford, 1978). For example, we might complain about a student who is continually out of his seat. Consequently, "out of seat" becomes the behavior we want to change. However, when the student is out of his seat, he also hits peers, knocks books off desks, and tosses paper on the floor. In this instance, the behaviors the student engages in when he is out of his seat are more relevant targets for intervention. But we will not acquire this information without first counting and recording out-of-seat behavior.

Here is another example, using the opposite behavior: "in seat." We might complain that a student is never in her seat. However, the instructionally relevant issue is what behaviors we want her to perform when sitting in her seat. Counting the frequency or duration of the student sitting in her seat makes it apparent that her work completion is a more important behavior than being out of seat. The reason is that, the more work the student completes, the longer she remains in her seat. When we count one behavior, we are also collecting information on other behaviors that may be more important targets for interventions.

Identifying Behavior Deserving of Intervention

Obtaining a count of the target behavior helps to determine whether the problem is actually severe enough to warrant intervention. Because teachers are human, their perceptions of students' behavior may be biased. For example, knowing that a student has been labeled "behaviorally disordered" may automatically indicate that he will talk excessively in class. However, if we count the actual number of "talk outs" of this student and compare them to our counts of the number of "talk outs" of other students, we may realize that the behavior of the student with the behavior disorder is no more severe than that of his peers. Unfortunately, when some teachers find out that students have a behavior disorder, they tend to *expect* those students to behave better than their peers. Therefore, we should count not only the behavior of target students but also that of other students.

This practice helps us determine whether an intervention is effective (Maag, Rutherford, & DiGangi, 1992). Take, for example, a student who was attending to task 30 percent of the time prior to intervention. Intervention produced a 25 percent increase, so that she now attends to task 55 percent of the time. This figure may seem low. However, if we identify the percentage of time other students attended to task to be 60 percent, then the intervention is, in fact, successful. Therefore, evaluating the effectiveness of an intervention requires counting the occurrences of target behaviors in other students.

Evaluating Our Successes

Counting and recording behavior is a way to validate our own success because it demonstrates to us that we can be effective in changing students' behavior by doing something different (Levitt & Rutherford, 1978). This point is important because students with behavior problems present us with constant challenges. We may feel helpless to affect changes in their behavior. Yet selecting one behavior, counting and recording it, and implementing an intervention provide us with proof of the effect we can have on students. And nothing impresses parents, administrators, and other teachers as much as a visual representation of the improvement we made in a student's behavior.

CONSIDERATIONS PRIOR TO RECORDING BEHAVIOR

The crucial elements in counting and recording behavior are consistency and accuracy. Levitt and Rutherford (1978) identified several questions to consider before counting behavior. These questions and their corresponding answers are summarized in Table 5.1. Counting and recording behavior is generally an easy process. All of the recording systems described in this chapter are appro-

TABLE 5.1   QUESTIONS TO CONSIDER BEFORE COUNTING

Question	Answer
Who can make the observations?	Depending on the behavior targeted for a count, it can be done by a number of people. Many behaviors can be counted on the edge of a lesson plan page using a digit counter. Or they can be counted by a student in the room, a paraprofessional, a parent, a student teacher, another teacher, or the principal—anyone who is responsible enough to be accurate and who knows the precise behavior to count.
What will be observed?	The targeted behavior must have a movement cycle—a beginning and an end—so we know when the behavior ends and another cycle begins. If the targeted behavior is "talks out loud without raising his hand," then we may define a cycle as "each talk without hand raised out consists of words spoken and heard by an observer, and a new cycle will begin when a pause of 5 seconds elapses between each group of words." This, or any other description of a cycle, gives the counter an accurate description of when the behavior starts and stops, and enables a more accurate count of the frequency or duration.
Where will the observation take place?	A teacher decide this, again depending on the pinpointed behavior. If it is a classroom behavior, lunch time and recess will not be part of the observation. If it is a playground-related behavior, it may be counted there exclusively, or in conjunction with counting in the classroom. Count it where it is a problem.
When will it be counted?	If the behavior is infrequent, the whole day might be the set time span to count the behavior, and it can probably be done by the teacher. If it is a frequent behavior, counting during just one set time each day may be appropriate. "Biting other students" might be counted all day if it occurs periodically during the school day. But "whispering to the child behind him" might be counted only during reading time if that is the one time the behavior seems to occur most often. Set the time depending on the behavior.
How will it be recorded?	There are several different techniques to record counts. Each is appropriate for different types of behaviors.

priate for everyday classroom use, depending on the situation and the type of behavior being targeted. First, however, there are several factors to consider when targeting a behavior to record—factors that are important to address in order to obtain useful information from counts of behavior.

FACTORS TO CONSIDER WHEN PINPOINTING A TARGET BEHAVIOR

These factors not only have practical implications for counting behavior but also highlight, in a user-friendly manner, how behavior management is more than a series of cut-and-dried strategies.

To accurately count behavior, we first must decide precisely what it is we are going to observe. However, not all behaviors represent appropriate targets for assessment. In this section, four factors Kaplan (1995) identified as being critical for pinpointing appropriate target behaviors are described. Ignoring these factors makes it difficult to accurately count behaviors for which we want to intervene.

Stranger Test

As pointed out in Chapter 2, we all have our own reality from which we view phenomena. Consequently, our standards and tolerance levels for disruptive behavior will vary (Walker, 1986). This variance has been shown to exist between general and special educators—with the latter group tending to judge behavior as less deviant and to be more tolerant of misbehavior (Fabre & Walker, 1987; Safran & Safran, 1987; Walker, 1986). Therefore, depending on personal standards, one teacher may consider a student's behavior inappropriate whereas another will not. Because interpretations necessarily vary from teacher to teacher, it is important to describe students' behaviors in terms that will pass what is called the **stranger test** (Kaplan, 1995).

According to this test, a behavior should be defined precisely enough that a stranger could walk into the classroom and observe the student's behavior equally accurately. If a behavior passes the stranger test, then we can say that it has been operationally defined. An **operational definition** involves breaking down a broad concept, such as "hostility," into its observable and measurable components (Sulzer-Azaroff & Mayer, 1977). Otherwise, a stranger may interpret "hostility" as "hits," "bites," "shoves," and "kicks," whereas we may have meant "provocative language" (e.g., verbal threats or profanity directed at peers). If we take the time to define "hostility" for the stranger as meaning "each instance of an unprovoked hit," where "unprovoked" means that it was not in retaliation for a physical or verbal attack from a peer, we and the stranger will be more likely to obtain the same results because we will be looking for the same thing.

Another factor to consider when operationally defining a behavior is whether it has a **movement cycle.** A movement cycle exists if a behavior has a specific beginning and ending point. For example, we may be tempted to believe that "hand raising" is easy to observe and that it will pass the stranger test. But what exactly constitutes a "hand raise"? What if a student puts her hand above her head and waves it three times? Does that action constitute three episodes of hand raising or one? What if the student raises her left hand and also raises her right hand? Does that action constitute one or two episodes of hand raising? To answer these questions, we must define "hand raising" with a movement cycle: "Hand raising begins when a student raises one hand over the head and ends when the hand is lowered below the shoulder." Now the behavior has a movement cycle and, consequently, is more likely to pass the stranger test.

The term *movement cycle* was first used in the context of precision teaching—an evaluative system that summarizes changes in performance over time through direct and daily measurement of behaviors.

The So-What Test

Once we have targeted a behavior that passes the stranger test, we want to ask, "So what?" In other words, do we really want to take the time to count the behavior? To answer this question, we can apply the **so-what test** (Kaplan, 1995). This test consists of asking ourselves if there is evidence that some behavior is presently or potentially harmful to students' own or their peers' social, physical, emotional, or academic well-being. If the answer is "yes," then it passes the so-what test and will be an appropriate target for intervention. For example, hitting other students obviously passes the so-what test because it's dangerous to peers. If a student is hitting others, we are probably spending too much time trying to manage the student and keep the classroom safe for peers. In this situation, the academic progress of all students will suffer.

Other behaviors do not meet the so-what test. For example, a student teacher whom the author supervised was conducting an interesting interactive reading lesson. However, during the lesson, a boy in the back of the room lost interest. It was winter, and he was wearing a heavy coat with a furry hood. While students took turns reading, he put the hood over his head and pulled the drawstrings so tight that he looked like a walrus. At this point, the student teacher could have stopped what was a smooth-flowing lesson and reprimanded the boy. But doing so probably would have prompted peers to turn around to see what their classmate was doing. They might have started laughing at his walrus-like appearance, thereby providing him with attention for his behavior and disrupting the lesson. Instead, believing that this behavior did not pass the so-what test, the student teacher ignored the boy and carried on with the lesson. After about 2 minutes, the boy removed the hood, probably because it was getting hot under there, and proceeded to reengage himself in the lesson.

Fair Pair

A common, but unfounded, criticism of behavior modification is that it creates docile, orderly students willing to dutifully follow any teacher (e.g., Kohn, 1993). Although it may not be beneficial to create "docile" students, instructional activities nevertheless run more smoothly when students are compliant (Maag, 2001). The criticism was valid many years ago. For example, in a review of research studies using behavior modification techniques, Winett and Winkler (1972) determined that the most prevalent behaviors targeted for intervention were "being out of seat" and "talking to peers." They concluded that teachers wanted the model student to stay in her or his seat all day, maintain continuous eye contact, avoid talking with peers and laughing or singing at inappropriate times, and pass silently in the halls.

Although much progress has been made in targeting appropriate behaviors for intervention, some teachers still spend an inordinate amount of time focusing on the negative. They tend to catch kids being "bad" and to ignore them when they're being "good." Students with challenging behaviors quickly learn that the only way to get attention from teachers is to misbehave. Teachers who punish these students severely enough to suppress the annoying behavior will quickly realize that the students simply begin performing another inappropriate behavior that serves the same purpose. Sigmund Freud called this phenomenon symptom substitution; behaviorists call it response covariation; teachers call it a pain in the neck.

The **fair pair** can help us avoid this problem (Kaplan, 1995). The meaning of the term *pair* is obvious; we are talking about two things—in this case, two behaviors. The term *fair* refers to the idea that it is acceptable to weaken students' maladaptive behavior only if an appropriate behavior is strengthened in its place. Therefore, the term *fair pair* refers to our targeting an appropriate behavior to increase when we target an inappropriate behavior to decrease. When we target a behavior with a similar topography to the inappropriate behavior that is incompatible, the inappropriate behavior often decreases automatically. A topographically similar behavior is one that shares movement or appearance with the inappropriate behavior. An incompatible behavior is one that, when students perform it, makes it impossible for them to simultaneously engage in the inappropriate behavior. For example, we might target a student's nose picking to decrease. We then want to target an appropriate behavior that shares the same movement as nose picking but makes it impossible for the student to pick her nose if she is performing the appropriate behavior. A fair-pair behavior might be using a Kleenex. It has a similar movement to nose-picking (hands and nose), but the student cannot pick her nose while using a Kleenex appropriately. Therefore, by increasing the use of a Kleenex, nose-picking automatically decreases.

The problems caused by decreasing behavior through the use of punishment are elaborated on in Chapter 11.

The Dead Man's Test

Kaplan (1995) suggested that we can apply the **dead man's test** to determine whether we have a fair pair. Here is the key question posed by the dead man's test: Can a dead man perform the target behavior? If the answer is "yes," the behavior does not pass the dead man's test, and it isn't a fair pair; if the answer is "no," it is a fair pair. For example, suppose a teacher wants a fair-pair target behavior for "swears at peers." The teacher comes up with the target behavior "does not swear at peers." Does this behavior pass the dead man's test? No, because a dead man certainly could refrain from swearing at peers. What would be better? How about "speaks to peers courteously"? This behavior passes the dead man's test because a dead man does not have the power to speak. Similarly, the target behavior of "sits quietly in seat" does not pass the dead man's test because a dead man is perfectly capable of sitting quietly. But do most teachers want a student to sit quietly as an end unto itself? No. They most likely want the student to be actively engaged in the task—for example, completing a worksheet with 25 addition problems. Therefore, a fair pair for sitting quietly would be writing the answers to addition problems, because this behavior is one that a dead man cannot perform.

> The term *dead man's test* has been used since the early 1970s, which accounts for its gender-specific designation.

TECHNIQUES FOR RECORDING BEHAVIOR

There are many different techniques for recording counts of behavior, but not all of them are appropriate for everyday classroom use. In addition, some recording systems are fairly complicated and may never be used by teachers. A summary of the most applicable recording techniques is presented in Table 5.2 and described in greater detail here.

Direct Measurement of Permanent Products

Many behaviors, particularly academic ones, leave a permanent product after a student performs them. These products can be observed, counted, and recorded in what are called **permanent products recordings.** All teachers assign grades to students' work (e.g., the percentage of math problems a student gets correct on a quiz or test) as part of the permanent product. Parents use permanent products to evaluate whether their children clean their room appropriately (e.g., the arrangement of a child's clothes, toys, and books).

Permanent products are the end results of students' behavior. The behavior occurs, and later on we count the results of that behavior. The behavior does not necessarily have to be observed while it is occurring to be counted. For example, we don't have to observe a student completing a math assignment to

	TABLE 5.2	**COMMON RECORDING TECHNIQUES**

Recording Method	Description	Indications
Permanent product	Counting the by-products of a student's behavior (e.g., number of pencils snapped, problems completed)	Appropriate for behaviors that leave a by-product that can later be counted
Frequency recording	Counting the number of times a target behavior occurs	Appropriate for behaviors with a short movement cycle; inappropriate for high-rate behaviors or those occurring over an extended time
Duration recording	Measuring how long a behavior lasts	Appropriate for behaviors that occur infrequently but continue for long periods
Latency recording	Measuring how long it takes for a behavior to be performed	Appropriate for assessing how long it takes a student to begin a behavior once given a direction
Interval recording	Measuring the occurrence or non-occurrence of a behavior within specified intervals; a mark is made if the behavior occurred during any part of the interval (partial) or entire interval (whole); the percentage of intervals marked is computed	Provides an estimate of both frequency and duration; easy to use but requires the observer's undivided attention
Time sampling	Same as interval recording except that the observer looks at the child at the end of the interval and records if the behavior is or is not occurring at that instant	Does not require the observer's undivided attention; allows for longer interval lengths than interval recording

evaluate her performance; we can simply count the number of correct answers. Here are some additional examples of permanent products including both desirable academic behaviors and disruptive misbehaviors:

- A list of words spelled correctly
- The number of multiplication facts answered on a quiz
- The number of paper airplanes thrown
- The number of pencils snapped in pieces
- The number of notes written to friends
- The number of marks on a student's desk
- The number of spit wads on the floor

Cooper, Heron, and Heward (1987) described several advantages of using permanent products as a recording technique. First, permanent products represent the outcomes of academic instruction. For example, a teacher may believe that a student getting out of his seat is a serious behavior requiring intervention. However, a more important fair-pair behavior is the number of multiplication problems he answers correctly. The more problems a student completes, the longer he is staying in his seat. This behavior also helps us determine how effectively the student is learning multiplication. Second, behavior that does not leave a permanent product can be recorded as a permanent product by using audiovisual equipment. For example, the number of inappropriate verbalizations is a major factor in students' failing to complete seatwork (Mastropieri & Scruggs, 1994). During a seat-work activity, we can simply turn on a tape recorder to obtain a permanent product of the number of a student's inappropriate verbalizations. Third, using permanent products allows us to spend our time teaching rather than observing students. After a lesson is over, we can go back and count the product left by the behavior, such as the number of words spelled correctly. Fourth, permanent products can be translated into numbers and placed on graphs. Alberto and Troutman (1999) recommended that teachers keep an up-to-date count of the permanent products of students whose behavior is troublesome so that the problems can easily be corroborated at a later date when intervention or verification for special education services may be warranted.

Cooper, Heron, and Heward (1987) also described two situations in which permanent products should be avoided. First, they should not be used for behaviors that do not naturally produce permanent products. For example, it would be unwise to determine the number of times a student interacts with peers during recess by counting the number of rocks used to play hopscotch because she may play hopscotch many times using the same rock. Or she may be interacting with other peers playing hopscotch but infrequently participate in the game. Consequently, playing hopscotch may not be a good indicator of how many times she interacts with peers. Second, permanent products should not be used when there are multiple behaviors that could result in the product. For example, it would be inappropriate to count the number of cigarettes in an adolescent's cigarette pack as an indicator of how many times he left school grounds to have a smoke because the product could be produced by any number of behaviors: He may have given peers cigarettes to smoke, or he could have borrowed cigarettes from a friend, thereby not depleting his own pack.

Frequency (Event) Recording

Frequency or **event recording** involves a tally or count of the number of times a targeted behavior occurs. It is the most commonly used technique, as well as the most advantageous, because it is fairly easy to do, produces a number that can be graphed, and applies to many disruptive behaviors in the class-

Making a videotape of a student's behavior is another form of permanent product recording because the teacher can go back later to watch and count the target behavior.

Student:	Clyde
Observer:	Ms. Harrison
Behavior:	Raises hand over head

Date	Time		Notations of Occurrences	Total Occurrences
	Start	Stop		
10-7-97	11:10	11:25	//// //	7
10-8-97	11:10	11:25	//// //// //	12

FIGURE 5.6

Frequency Recording Sheet

room, such as "hits peers," "runs out of room," "raises hand," and "asks for help." A count of the number of times a student engages in the target behavior can be tallied on a data sheet such as the one in Figure 5.6. Or it can be tallied on any easy-to-carry device such as a wrist counter, hand-tally digital counter, wrist tally board, or masking tape wrapped around the wrist. Or pennies, buttons, or paper clips can be moved from one pocket to another each time the target behavior occurs (Cooper, Heron, & Heward, 1987).

For frequency recording to yield useful information, the target behavior must have a movement cycle. Without a movement cycle, it is difficult to determine when one episode of a behavior ends and another begins, rendering any count of the behavior uninterpretable. For example, Maag, Wolchik, Rutherford, and Parks (1986) investigated ways to decrease two self-stimulatory behaviors—hand clapping and hand gazing—in a student with autism. The researchers thought that they would simply have to count the frequency of their occurrence. However, they failed to take into account two important features of the two behaviors. First, the student engaged in the behaviors interchangeably and often simultaneously. Second, the student would pause for random lengths of time between clapping his hands. Consequently, it was difficult to determine when an episode of one behavior ended and another behavior started. The researchers solved the problem by operationally defining the behaviors to include a movement cycle. Hand clapping was defined as the student bringing the palms of his hands together at least twice, with a 3-second interval between claps constituting the beginning of a new episode. Hand gazing occurred when the student's hands were above his shoulders while his face was oriented toward his extended fingers. A new episode of gazing was marked if a 3-second interval of nongazing occurred or if the child began clapping and then turned to gazing.

The results of the Maag et al. (1986) study point out that sometimes determining the best recording technique is based on trial and error.

There are several desirable aspects of using a frequency count (Alberto & Troutman, 1999; Cooper, Heron, & Heward, 1987). First, it is an easy recording system to implement. All we have to do is note whether the target behavior is occurring. Second, because of its simplicity, it rarely interferes with ongoing classroom activities. For example, we can conduct a lesson with a group of students while making tally marks on a strip of masking tape or moving paper clips from one pocket to another. Third, frequency recording regularly produces numbers that can be easily graphed and interpreted.

There are two situations in which it is inappropriate to use frequency recording. First, frequency recording should not be used for behaviors that occur at such a high rate that it becomes difficult to keep track of them, such as pencil tapping, chair rocking, or steps taken while running. In the case of hand clapping and hand gazing, Maag and colleagues (1986) ultimately determined that, even after using a movement cycle, a different type of recording technique would be preferable for clapping because it occurred at such a high rate. Second, frequency recording is inappropriate for behaviors that occur over an extended time. For example, a frequency count may reveal that a student has only two tantrums during the day—certainly a manageable number for most teachers. However, if the two episodes each lasts for 45 minutes, then a frequency count will be misleading. A total of 90 minutes of tantrum indeed represents a problem worthy of intervention.

Duration Recording

Duration recording is useful when we want to measure how long behavior lasts. It is most appropriate for behaviors that occur infrequently but continue for some length of time or for behaviors that occur at a high rate of speed so that one episode blends into the next, such as pencil tapping. Here is a partial list of behaviors for which duration recording is appropriate:

- Crying
- Writing a paper
- Drumming on the desktop
- Returning to class after the recess bell
- Finishing a math assignment

Duration recording provides a better record of these behaviors than does frequency recording. It is more important to know that "Jason cried for 12 minutes without stopping" than simply that "Jason cried one time today," or that "Paula was out of her seat for 17 minutes, then 10 minutes, then 23 minutes" than simply that "Paula was out of her seat three times today." These behaviors are more aptly described in terms of how long they last rather than how many times they occur (Levitt & Rutherford, 1978).

Date	Time		Duration
	Behavior Begins	Behavior Ends	
4-23-96	9:45	10:02	17 minutes
4-24-96	9:53	10:00	7 minutes
4-25-96	9:51	10:04	13 minutes

Student: Saul
Observer: Mr. Case
Behavior: Time spent conversing with peers at recesses

FIGURE **5.7**

Duration Recording Sheet

Like frequency recording, duration recording is most appropriate for behaviors that can be defined in terms of a movement cycle. Even though how long a behavior lasts is being recorded, it is still important to know precisely when the behavior began and ended. For example, "crying" may begin when a tear appears on the face and end when the student's face is dry. Some people may not like this definition because a student can wipe the tears away and begin a fresh bout, or cry without shedding tears. Therefore, an alternative movement cycle for this behavior might involve voice intonation, volume, or pitch.

Duration recording can be performed in a variety of ways. The easiest is to use a stopwatch or digital wristwatch that has a stopwatch feature. An alternative method is to use a tape recorder to record the duration of verbal behavior. Remember, an audiotape or videotape of students' behavior leaves a permanent product. Therefore, a tape recorder can simply be turned on whenever a student begins to cry; later, the teacher can note how long the episode lasted simply by replaying the tape. Or a videotape can be replayed when there is more time to determine how long a student was out of his seat. In the latter case, it is a simple matter to have a video recorder pointed at a student's desk to record when he is in and out of his seat. Figure 5.7 gives an example of a duration recording data sheet.

There are several ways to determine how long a behavior lasts, including total duration, duration per occurrence, and average duration (Alberto & Troutman, 1999; Cooper, Heron, & Heward, 1987). **Total duration** refers to the entire time students engage in the target behavior during a specified observation period. For example, a teacher may be interested in the total time a student was out of her seat during a 45-minute independent-seatwork assignment. Let us assume that the student was out of her seat for 5 minutes,

3 minutes, and 7 minutes during this time. Therefore, the total duration recorded and graphed is 15 minutes (5 + 3 + 7 = 15). **Duration per occurrence** involves recording the length of time per episode that students engage in the target behavior. Therefore, the duration per occurrence that the student was out of her seat is recorded as 5, 3, and 7 (i.e., three numbers rather than one). Unlike duration per occurrence, **average duration** produces only one number to graph. Using the data from the out-of-seat example, the average duration is 5. Here, we are adding together the duration for each episode the student was out of her seat and dividing that number by the total number of times she was out of her seat ([5 + 3 + 7]/3 = 5). Each of these three measures is easy to compute. Total duration and average duration yield one number to record, whereas duration per occurrence results in as many numbers to graph as there were occurrences of the target behavior.

A variation of duration recording is **latency recording,** which involves recording how long it takes students to begin engaging in a behavior after instructing them to perform it. According to Alberto and Troutman (1999), this technique "measures the length of time between the presentation of an antecedent stimulus and the initiation of the behavior" (p. 133). For example, a teacher will be concerned with the latency of a student's response if he is told to put in the wastebasket a piece of paper (antecedent stimulus) that he threw on the floor, and it takes him 7 minutes to perform the behavior. The duration recording sheet shown in Figure 5.7 can be used to measure latency. Instead of recording how long the behavior lasted, we record how long it took for a student to begin a target behavior once its performance had been requested.

Although duration and latency measures are similar, they do provide somewhat different "snapshots" of students' behavior. Whether duration or latency recording is desired depends on whether the problem involves an inappropriate behavior that persists or an appropriate behavior that is not displayed when requested.

Interval Recording

Interval recording measures the occurrence or nonoccurrence of behavior within specified time intervals. We divide the total observation time into equal intervals and record whether the behavior occurs during those intervals. The length of the intervals typically ranges from 5 to 30 seconds. Figure 5.8 shows an interval recording sheet with 10-second intervals.

To construct an interval recording sheet, we first determine how long the observation period will last. In Figure 5.8, the total observation period is quite brief—5 minutes. We then divide this observation period into equal intervals. In Figure 5.8, the 5-minute observation period is divided into 10-second intervals. Next, we construct boxes for each 10-second interval. To determine the number of boxes required, we divide the total number of seconds of the observation period into the interval length. The total observation period should be converted into seconds because that typically is the standard used for the individual intervals. In Figure 5.8, we have 300 seconds (5 × 60) divided into 10-second intervals, so we need 30 boxes. For the sake of convenience, these are

Student: Chris

Observer: Ms. Satchell

Behavior: Percentage of time Chris talks to child directly across aisle

Total Observation Time Equals Five Minutes

	10 seconds	10 seconds	10 seconds	10 seconds	10 seconds	10 seconds
1 minute	o	o	x	x	o	o
2 minutes	x	o	x	o	x	x
3 minutes	o	o	o	x	x	o
4 minutes	x	o	o	o	o	o
5 minutes	o	x	o	x	o	x

Percentage of Time Talking   40%

x = Talking
o = Not talking

FIGURE **5.8**

Interval Recording Sheet

arranged in five rows of six boxes apiece. Each row represents the passage of 1 minute of the 5-minute observation period.

To use the observation form in Figure 5.8, we make only one mark in each box depending on whether the target behavior occurred. If the target behavior occurred during any part of a 10-second interval, then we place an "X" in that box. If the target behavior did not occur during the 10-second interval, then we place an "O" in that box. It is important to remember that only one mark is made per interval. Therefore, it does not matter whether the target behavior occurred one time or five during a given 10-second interval. For example, a student could speak to his neighbor three times during a 10-second interval—once each at the beginning, middle, and end of the interval; however, only one mark is made for the occurrence of the behavior during that interval. Consequently, this recording technique is sometimes called **partial interval recording,** because we are only interested in whether the target behavior occurred at any time during the interval (Cooper, Heron, & Heward, 1987).

Because we are dividing an observation period into intervals, the results are given in percentages. We do not record the total number of "X's" appearing on the observation form. Remember, one "X" represents any number of times the behavior occurred during a given 10-second interval. Instead, we are interested in the percentage of intervals in which the student engaged in the target behavior. In Figure 5.8, there are a total of 30 intervals. The student engaged in the target behavior during 12 of those intervals, which means he engaged in the target behavior during 40 percent of the intervals during the 5-minute observation period. This calculation appears below:

$$\frac{\text{(intervals talking)}}{\text{(total intervals)}} \quad \frac{12}{30} \times 100 = 40\%$$

Interval recording is usually conducted by placing the recording sheet on a clipboard and attaching a stopwatch or wristwatch to the clip with a rubber band. Then we try to look at both the student and stopwatch simultaneously to determine whether the target behavior occurred during the intervals. Interval recording requires our undivided attention. Consequently, a disadvantage of the clipboard- and-stopwatch method is that we must occasionally look away from the student to the stopwatch to determine when an old interval ends and a new interval begins.

An alternative method for conducting interval recording is to use a small cassette tape recorder with an earphone to signal the beginning and end of intervals (Cooper, Heron, & Heward, 1987). With this method, we do not have to split our attention between observing the student and looking at the stopwatch. Sometimes students can be taught to count behavior using interval recording for short periods (Levitt & Rutherford, 1978).

A variation of this technique is **whole interval recording,** in which the target behavior must be displayed for the entire duration of an interval (Cooper, Heron, & Heward, 1987). For example, with this variation, we mark the target behavior of "talks" with an "X" only in the interval boxes for which it occurred for the entire 10 seconds. As a general rule, whole interval recording is the method of choice when we want to increase an appropriate behavior, such as having the student academically engaged for the entire work period. As with the previous interval procedure, whole interval recording requires our undivided attention.

There are two major advantages of interval recording (Alberto & Troutman, 1999; Cooper, Heron, & Heward, 1987). First, it provides an estimate of both the frequency and the duration of behavior. If the target behavior occurs often or for a long time, a mark will appear in many of the interval squares. If the observation sessions are conducted over several periods of the day and for several days, it is possible to identify activities or times that may prompt the student to perform the behavior. Second, interval recording helps us determine whether the target behavior is more likely to occur at the beginning, middle, or end of an observation session. This information can help us to develop interventions. For example, interval recording during a 20-minute math lesson may reveal that a student was talking to peers excessively only during the latter part

A variety of cueing devices can be used to implement interval recording. Prerecording tones on a tape recorder or setting the timer on regular watches are two ways to use interval recording while still maintaining attention on the primary task at hand.

of the period. The math period was structured so that at the beginning of class the teacher provided direct instruction in the skill, in the middle had students work in cooperative learning groups as a guided practice activity, and at the end had students complete math sheets independently. We now can generate some hypotheses as to why the student talked excessively during the latter part of the period. Perhaps he did not learn the skill sufficiently to complete the worksheet independently. Therefore, he may either be asking peers for assistance or be frustrated and occupying his time by talking.

There are also several disadvantages of interval recording. First, as previously mentioned, we have to give our undivided attention to both the student and the stopwatch. Consequently, we may miss an occurrence of the behavior while looking at the stopwatch, which, in turn, will distort the obtained information. Second, because only one mark is made for a given interval if the behavior occurs at all, we do not have information on exactly how many times a behavior occurs. In perusing Figure 5.8, all we can say is that the student talked during the third 10-second interval of the first minute of observation, although the student may have talked three, four, or five times. Similarly, the student may have begun talking at the end of one interval and continued for a second or two into the next. If we are using a frequency count, we record only one instance of talking. However, with interval recording, we mark an "X" in both interval boxes because talking occurred in each interval. In the latter case, this number may overestimate the severity of the problem. Third, because intervals are usually no longer than 30 seconds (Cooper, 1981), it is difficult to observe a student for more than 15–20 minutes at a time. Teachers rarely have time to give their undivided attention to observing a student every 10 seconds for periods that exceed 15 or 20 minutes.

Time Sampling

A method of interval recording that is easier for teachers to use is **time sampling.** With this approach, we record the target behavior only if it occurs at the end of an interval. The process of creating a time sampling recording sheet is similar to that employed with interval recording. The only difference is that we can use longer intervals in time sampling because we are observing students only at the end of intervals. Therefore, we are free to concentrate on teaching during the intervals. Recording behavior using time sampling give us a broader picture of that behavior. Figure 5.9 provides an example of a time sampling recording sheet. Note that this sheet is similar to the interval recording sheet in Figure 5.8, with two notable exceptions: (1) The intervals in Figure 5.9 are 5 minutes long, and (2) the total observation period lasts for 2 hours instead of 5 minutes.

	Student:	Martha

Student: __Martha_____

Observer: __Mr. Clutch_____

Behavior: __Percentage of time Martha makes animal noises_____

Total Observation Time Equals Two Hours

	5 minutes	5 minutes	5 minutes	5 minutes	5 minutes	5 minutes
30 minutes	x	o	x	x	o	o
1 hour	x	o	x	o	x	x
1½ hours	o	x	o	x	x	o
2 hours	x	x	x	x	o	x

Percentage of Time Making Animal Noises __63%__

x = Animal noise
o = No animal noise

FIGURE 5.9

Time Sampling Recording Sheet

Time sampling is a fairly straightforward procedure. First, we set a kitchen timer to ring at the end of the specified interval. Alternatively, we can use an audiocassette tape recorder, recording a tone every 5 minutes. Then we simply record whether the target behavior is occurring at the end of each interval, when we hear the recorded tone. As with other forms of interval recording, we mark each interval box only once and report the final number as a percentage. Figure 5.9 shows that the student made animal noises at the end of the first, third, and fourth 5-minute intervals during the first 30 minutes of observation.

The key advantage of time sampling is that we do not have to give our undivided attention to observing students' behavior. Instead, we are free to engage in other activities and observe students only when cued by the taped tone that signals the end of an interval. If we are concerned that students may hear the recorded tones and figure out when they occur, we can record them randomly. However, we want the tones to sound within some specified interval length; in Figure 5.9, it is 5 minutes. The reason for not wanting students to figure out when the tones occur is because otherwise they might refrain from engaging in the inappropriate behavior at the end of the interval, and so the behavior will not appear to be a problem requiring intervention.

There are also several disadvantages associated with time sampling (Alberto & Troutman, 1999). First, as with other forms of interval recording, we obtain only limited information on how often the behavior occurs. For example, a student may have made animal noises 12 times during the first 4 minutes of the second interval. However, if she refrains from making animal noises at the end of this interval, there will be no mark in this interval box, which will give the erroneous impression that no animal noises occurred during that interval. In this example, time sampling underestimates the occurrence of the target behavior. Second, one of the major advantages of time sampling—the use of longer intervals than with interval recording—can also be a disadvantage. The correspondence between the information collected on the time sampling recording sheet and the actual occurrence of the target behavior may be reduced (Saudargas & Zanolli, 1990). Therefore, Alberto and Troutman (1999) recommended using time sampling only for behaviors that occur often or last for long periods. Third, it can be tempting to use time sampling as a schedule of reinforcement because the intervals are set—as with the fixed-interval reinforcement schedule described in Chapter 4. The problem with this arrangement is that students can easily figure out the reinforcement schedule and perform the appropriate behavior only at the end of an interval to get reinforcement. This problem can be minimized by using a variable interval schedule with limited hold.

METHODS FOR CALCULATING INTEROBSERVER RELIABILITY

We are a fallible species. It may be helpful to think back to the discussion of paradigms in Chapter 2 and the differences that exist in the eyewitness accounts of crimes. The point was that we interpret situations and fill in missing information based on our belief systems. It is not uncommon for two people to observe the same phenomenon and get two distinctly different impressions. We have a tendency to see what we are looking for. The placebo and Hawthorne effects—two interrelated phenomena—provide good examples of this tendency.

The **placebo effect** refers to the process by which individuals' behavior changes as a result of believing that they received a treatment when, in reality, they received something that lacked any intrinsic treatment value. For example, a student may think he was given Ritalin—a stimulant medication used to treat attention-deficit/hyperactivity disorder—when, in fact, he got a sugar pill. Nevertheless, both the student and his teachers view his behavior as improved. The **Hawthorne effect** refers to the phenomenon of working harder and producing more because of a feeling of participating in something new and special even when the innovations have no corrective merit.

It is easy for us to lose our objectivity when observing students' behavior. A loss of objectivity can occur for a variety of reasons—some may be asso-

The placebo and Hawthorne effects illustrate how humans can see only what they are looking for.

ciated with the placebo and Hawthorne effects—and can result in different behaviors being observed and recorded than those originally targeted. This phenomenon, called **observer drift,** and can occur even when a target behavior is operationally defined and passes the stranger test. Cooper, Heron, and Heward (1987) suggested that observer drift can be minimized by ensuring that the teacher observing students' behavior receive ongoing training and feedback. Another approach to ensure that we accurately and reliably observe behavior is to have a second person observe as well. The two observers then compare findings to see how consistently and accurately they recorded the target behavior.

This latter approach to determining the reliability of recording depends on establishing **interobserver agreement**—the extent to which two observers record the same behavior accurately. The method used depends on the type of recording technique employed; options include counting permanent products and using frequency, duration, interval, or time sample recording techniques. Regardless of the method, it is desirable to have at least 80 percent agreement between observers in order to have confidence that the observations accurately and consistently reflect the original operational definition of the target behavior.

The type of calculation used to compute reliability will largely depend on the type of recording technique used.

Achieving interobserver agreement can be time intensive in terms of people and resources because two persons must observe and record the target behavior. However, the second person usually has to observe only a quarter to a third of the session. This approach saves some person resources while ensuring that the primary observer continues to record the target behavior accurately. In addition, most methods for obtaining interobserver agreement are easy and quick to calculate.

One caution is warranted before proceeding: Observer drift can still occur even when two observers are recording the same behavior. Therefore interobserver agreement can be high (e.g., 80 percent conformity) even as both recordings deviate from the original definition of the target behavior. Multiple observer drift can occur when primary and secondary observers work in close physical proximity, such that they can visually examine each other's recordings or communicate when they are marking the target behavior. The easiest way to avoid multiple observer drift is to physically separate the two observers so that they are still able to observe students but are not close enough to see each other's recording sheets or overhear each other's conversations.

Permanent Product and Interobserver Reliability

Recording permanent products requires counting the remnants from behavior, such as the number of pencils snapped, words spelled correctly, or pieces of paper thrown on the floor. Interobserver reliability for permanent products is obtained by dividing the number of agreements by the number of agreements plus disagreements, and multiplying by 100. The following formula is used to calculate the percentage of interobserver agreement:

$$\frac{\text{agreements}}{\text{agreements} + \text{disagreements}} \times 100 = \% \text{ of agreement}$$

For example, suppose a teacher counts that a student spelled 13 out of 15 words correctly words correctly while the paraeducator counts that the student spelled 14 words correctly. Therefore, they agree on 13 words spelled correctly and disagree on 1 word. The percentage of agreement is computed by taking the number of agreements (13), dividing it by the number of agreements and disagreements (13 + 1 = 14), and multiplying by 100; the result is 93 percent. Not suprisingly, this percentage is high. After all, we would not expect there to be much disagreement when two people are counting a permanent product such as number of words spelled correctly. However, interobserver agreement is trickier when actual behavior is involved.

Frequency Recording and Interobserver Reliability

Computing interobserver reliability for frequency recording involves having two observers independently but concurrently record the number of times a target behavior occurs (Cooper, Heron, & Heward, 1987). Reliability is determined by dividing the smaller number by the larger number and multiplying by 100, as in the following formula:

$$\frac{\text{smaller number}}{\text{larger number}} \times 100 = \% \text{ of agreement}$$

For example, a teacher may count that a student raised her hand and waited to be called on to answer questions five times during a 15-minute question-and-answer session. A paraeducator records that the student raised her hand four times. Using the formula, interobserver agreement would be 80 percent ([4 / 5] × 100).

A potential problem in computing interobserver agreement for frequency recordings is that the two observers may have high levels of agreement without having observed the same behavior at the same time. Figure 5.10 displays hypothetical frequency recording data for two people observing the number of times a student raises her hand. These observations can be used to obtain an interobserver agreement of 80 percent using the formula just stated. However, this figure is misleading because the teacher and paraeducator only twice

Observer	Number of Times Student Raises Hand							
Teacher	x		x		x	x	x	Total = 5
Paraeducator		x	x	x			x	Total = 4

Hypothetical Frequency Recording Data for Two Observers

saw the hand raising at the same time (as indicated by the shaded boxes in Figure 5.10). Therefore, they have only two agreements (for seeing the behavior at the same time) and five disagreements, which results in a reliability level of 40 percent ($[2 / 5] \times 100$).

Duration and Latency Recording and Interobserver Reliability

The process of calculating interobserver agreement for duration and latency recording is similar to that used for frequency recording. However, instead of dividing the small number by the larger, as with frequency recording, the shorter duration is divided by the longer duration:

$$\frac{\text{shorter duration}}{\text{longer duration}} \times 100 = \% \text{ of agreement}$$

For example, a teacher may observe that a student has a tantrum for 55 seconds whereas the paraeducator records the tantrum as lasting for 38 seconds. Therefore, the interobserver agreement is 69 percent ($[38 / 55] \times 100$).

There are two problems associated with using this approach for determining interobserver agreement. The first is similar to that described for frequency recording. In this instance, the problem is that observers may not begin their observations at the same time. Therefore, one observer might start his observations at 9:15 A.M. and end at 9:16 A.M. while the other might begins at 9:14 A.M. and end at 9:15 A.M. In this case, reliability will be even lower than the 69 percent just calculated. Observervations that differ by even a few seconds can substantially affect interobserver agreement. The second problem is that observers may not be able to accurately determine when a behavior starts and stops. For example, a student may be throwing a tantrum and pause briefly to take a breath for a fresh scream. Does this pause signal the beginning of a new tantrum, or is it simply a continuation of the previous tantrum? This prob-

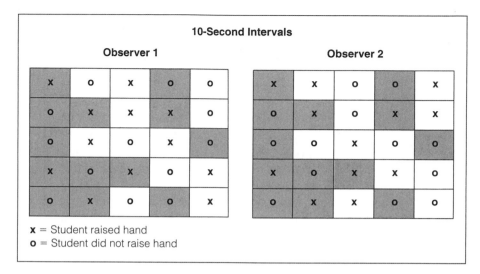

FIGURE 5.11

Two Observers' Interval Recording Sheets for the Target Behavior of "Raises Hand"

lem can be reduced by ensuring that the target behavior definition has a movement cycle.

Interval and Time Sampling and Interobserver Reliability

The most commonly used method for calculating interobserver reliability for interval and time-sampling recordings is the interval-by-interval agreement method. With this method, every interval is used to calculate interobserver reliability. Interobserver reliability is based on the number of intervals observers agree that the target behavior occurred or did not occur. This approach avoids the problem for computing interobserver reliability for frequency data in which observers count the same number of the target behavior but witness it at different times. The formula is similar to that used for permanent products except that intervals instead of products are inserted into the calculation:

$$\frac{\text{agreements intervals}}{\text{agreements + disagreements intervals}} \times 100 = \% \text{ of agreement}$$

Figure 5.11 provides an example of the interval-by-interval method in which two observers record intervals of the target behavior "raises hand." A comparison of these two recording sheets might lead us to incorrectly assume that the interobserver reliability is 100 percent because both observers marked 12 intervals in which the behavior occurred and 13 intervals in which it did not occur. However, they agreed that the behavior occurred at the same interval only 6 times and agreed that the behavior did not occur at the same interval 7 times, for a total agreement on 13 of the intervals. In Figure 5.11, the shaded boxes indicate the agreements for occurrences and nonoccurrences between observers. Using the formula just stated, the interval-by-interval interobserver agreement is 52 percent ($[13 / 25]$) $\times$ 100).

SUMMARY

This chapter focused on methods of collecting continuous information on the occurrence of students' behaviors. Collecting continuous data helps teachers become better decision makers. There are several factors to consider when pinpointing behaviors. A behavior passes the stranger test when it is operationally defined. The so-what test helps teachers determine whether a behavior interferes with students' or peers' academic and social well-being. The fair pair requires that, before teachers try to eliminate an inappropriate behavior, they target an appropriate behavior to increase. The dead man's test helps teachers determine whether a behavior is a fair pair.

The various recording techniques for counting students' behaviors all have both advantages and disadvantages. The recording technique selected depends on the type of target behavior, availability of teachers to make observations, and length of observations desired. Interobserver reliability is calculated to make sure that the teacher is observing a behavior based on its original definition. It requires that a second person occasionally observe the target behavior. The method selected for calculating interobserver reliability should correspond to the type of recording technique used.

ACTIVITIES

1. Identify a time when you told your roommate, spouse, or significant other that he or she *always* or *never* does something. Here are some examples: "You always forget to lock the door," "You never vacuum the carpet," "You always forget to give me messages," or "You never wash the dishes." Then, for one week, keep a frequency count of the actual number of times he or she engages in the behavior. Finally, based on your observations, ask yourself whether the person really "never" or "always" performs the behavior. Reflect on how this experience compares to what some teachers do when they are informed that a student has a behavioral or academic problem.

2. Develop an interval recording sheet similar to the one in Figure 5.8. However, instead of having five rows with six 10-second intervals, make it with five rows of six 30-second intervals. Your recording sheet should give you a total observation time of 15 minutes. Make two copies of this sheet. At the top write "Running." Then invite a friend over to watch some sporting event on television that involves some running. Take off your watch, set it to beep at 30-second intervals, and place it on a table close to you and your friend. Tell him or her that you're playing a game to see who can most accurately note when some athlete on television is running, and that when running occurs that he or she should mark the corresponding box with an "X." At the end of the 15-minute session, you and your friend should figure out the percentage of intervals running occurred. Finally, you and your friend should use the formula for interval recording to calculate the interobserver reliability. Did the reliability between you and your friend reach 80 percent? If not, to what factors do you attribute the low reliability ?

REVIEW QUESTIONS

1. Why it is important to count behavior?
2. Give an example of an incorrect conclusion that can be reached by observing behavior only once during the baseline and intervention.
3. What factors should be considered before counting and recording behavior?
4. What are the advantages and disadvantages of permanent product recording?
5. Give an example of two types of behaviors for which frequency (event) recording is inappropriate.
6. Give an example of how duration recording may be conducted.
7. What are the advantages and disadvantages of interval and time-sampling recording techniques?
8. What is the purpose of calculating interobserver reliability?
9. In what ways can interobserver reliability be calculated?

REFERENCES

Alberto, P. A., & Troutman, A. C. (1999). *Applied behavior analysis for teachers* (5th ed.), Columbus, OH: Merrill.

Cooper, J. O. (1981). *Measuring behavior* (2nd ed.). Columbus, OH: Merrill.

Cooper, J. O., Heron, T. E., & Heward, W. L. (1987). *Applied behavior analysis.* Columbus, OH: Merrill.

Fabre, T. R., & Walker, H. M. (1987). Teacher perceptions of the behavioral adjustment of primary grade level handicapped pupils within regular and special education settings. *Remedial and Special Education, 8*(5), 34–39.

Fuchs, L. S., Deno, S. L., & Mirkin, P. K. (1984). The effects of frequent curriculum-based measurement and evaluation on pedagogy, student achievement, and student awareness of learning. *American Educational Research Journal, 21*, 449–460.

Fuchs, L. S., & Fuchs, D. (1986). Effects of systematic formative evaluation: A meta-analysis. *Exceptional Children, 53*, 199–208.

Fuchs, L. S., Fuchs, D., & Stecker, P. M. (1989). The effects of curriculum-based measurement on teachers' instructional planning. *Journal of Learning Disabilities, 22*, 51–59.

Howell, K. W., & Nolet, V. (2000). *Curriculum-based evaluation* (3rd ed.). Belmont, CA: Wadsworth.

Kaplan, J. S. (1995). *Beyond behavior modification: A cognitive-behavioral approach to behavior management in the school* (3rd ed.). Austin, TX: Pro-Ed.

Kohn, A. (1993). *Punished by rewards: The trouble with gold stars, incentive plans, A's, praise, and other bribes.* Boston: Houghton Mifflin.

Levitt, L. K., & Rutherford, R. B., Jr. (1978). *Strategies for handling the disruptive student.* Tempe: College of Education, Arizona State University.

Maag, J. W. (2001). Rewarded by punishment: Reflections on the disuse of positive reinforcement in schools. *Exceptional Children, 67*, 173–186.

Maag, J. W., Rutherford, R. B., Jr., & DiGangi, S. A. (1992). Effects of self-monitoring and contingent reinforcement on on-task behavior and academic productivity of learning-disabled students: A social validation study. *Psychology in the Schools, 29*, 157–172.

Maag, J. W., Wolchik, S. A., Rutherford, R. B., Jr., & Parks, B. T. (1986). Response covariation on self-stimulatory behaviors during sensory extinction procedures. *Journal of Autism and Developmental Disorders, 16*, 119–132.

Mastropieri, M. A., & Scruggs, T. E. (1994). *Effective instruction for special education* (2nd ed.). Austin, TX: Pro-Ed.

Safran, J. S., & Safran, S. P. (1987). Teachers' judgments of problem behaviors. *Exceptional Children, 54*, 240–244.

Saudargas, R., & Zanolli, K. (1990). Momentary time sampling as an estimate of percentage time: A field validation. *Journal of Applied Behavior Analysis, 23*, 533–537.

Sulzer-Azaroff, B., & Mayer, G. R. (1977). *Applying behavior-analysis procedures with children and youth.* New York: Holt, Rinehart & Winston.

Walker, H. M. (1986). The Assessment for Integration into Mainstream Settings (AIMS) assessment system: Rationale, instruments, procedures, and outcomes. *Journal of Clinical Child Psychology, 15,* 55–63.

Winett, R. A., & Winkler, R. C. (1972). Current behavior modification in the classroom: Be still, be quiet, be docile. *Journal of Applied Behavior Analysis, 5,* 499–504.

GRAPHING BEHAVIOR

CHAPTER OVERVIEW

- Benefits of Graphing Behavioral Observations
- Elements of a Graph
- Collecting Baseline Data
- Designs for Graphing Behavioral Observations

CHAPTER OBJECTIVES

After completing this chapter, you will be able to do the following:

1. Explain the benefits of graphing behavioral observations.

2. Identify the parts of a graph.

3. Recognize the four types of baseline data patterns.

4. Describe an AB design including its advantages and disadvantages.

5. Describe an ABAB (reversal) design including its advantages and disadvantages.

6. Describe a multiple baseline design including its advantages and disadvantages.

7. Describe other types of designs including their advantages and disadvantages.

The numbers that appear below represent the products of observing and recording the target behavior of "writes answers." The numbers, which could have been obtained through the use of various recording techniques, are called data. The word *data* designates the numerical results of intentional, programmed, and controlled observations (Cooper, Heron, & Heward, 1987). Although the definition of data is straightforward, interpreting their meaning can be more difficult. For example, we could assume that an intervention was implemented after, say, the ninth data point was collected. Given the following list of numbers, was the intervention effective in increasing the target behavior of "writes answers"?

12, 16, 7, 13, 8, 10, 15, 13,
11, 22, 24, 19, 26, 20, 25

It is difficult to determine whether the intervention was effective by looking at these numbers. Instead, making an informed and accurate assessment of its effectiveness requires plotting the numbers on a graph so that we can visually inspect their relation to one another. Figure 6.1 shows what these data look like on a graph. From the graph, we can see that the student's performance steadily improved after the intervention was implemented. Now we can say, with some certainty, that the intervention was effective.

In this chapter, the benefits of graphing behavioral observations are elaborated on, and the various parts of a graph are described. Knowledge of the parts of a graph helps us quickly plot and interpret data for the purpose of making decisions regarding the effectiveness of interventions. Next, the importance of collecting baseline data is discussed. Several baseline trends are described that can serve as a guide for determining appropriate conditions under which to implement an intervention. Finally, six different designs for graphing data are described.

BENEFITS OF GRAPHING BEHAVIORAL OBSERVATIONS

As with counting and recording behavior, there are several benefits of graphing data acquired through behavioral observations. The importance of how graphing provides a visual representation of the target behavior has already been noted. Furthermore, the benefits of counting and recording behavior, discussed in Chapter 5, also pertain to graphing behavior. Cooper, Heron, and Heward (1987) described several additional benefits for graphing data.

The benefits of graphing data are similar to those described in the previous chapter for counting and recording behavior.

First, graphing data provides us with immediate feedback on students' behavior when the numbers obtained are plotted immediately after the observation. Teachers do not typically create visual records of students' behavior immediately after it occurs. As a result, decisions regarding that behavior tend to

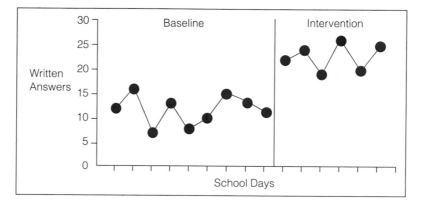

FIGURE 6.1

Numerical Data Plotted on a Graph

be made infrequently and may be biased due to the passage of time since the behavior occurred.

Second, plotting data points on a graph and connecting them with a line allows us to visually examine trends in students' behavior. These trends are important for making decisions as to whether an intervention should be continued, discontinued, or modified. Recall the data trends in Figure 5.2, in which data were plotted for four students: Cathy, Roger, Peter, and Nancy. Based on the trends in the data, we determined that the intervention was effective only for Nancy. Teachers can make such determinations only by plotting and connecting data points.

Third, graphing data provides a vehicle for others to independently judge the effectiveness of an intervention. There are few more powerful ways of making a statement to colleagues, administrators, parents, and students as to the effectiveness of an intervention than showing them a graph. Graphing makes use of the saying "Don't tell me, show me." People respond positively to visual representations of behavior because graphs provide a permanent record that reflects students' progress. In addition, graphs document teachers' intervention efforts and demonstrate their accountability.

Fourth, graphs represent an important source of feedback for students regarding their behavior. When students either see graphs of their behavior or actually graph their own performance, they are more likely to evaluate their own performance. And as students meet certain standards, they tend to adjust them upward and to engage in reinforcing self-statements (Mace, Brown, & West, 1987). Consequently, having students graph their own behavior tends to promote self-management (DiGangi, Maag, & Rutherford, 1991).

Media-savvy politicians recognize the positive impact of graphs, using them when interviewed on TV or when giving speeches in Congress while the C-SPAN cameras are rolling.

TABLE 6.1	DESCRIPTION OF PARTS OF A GRAPH
Part	**Description**
1. Horizontal axis	The horizontal (X) axis is a straight line representing the passage of time and the numerical value of the target behavior. The horizontal axis is marked in equal intervals representing equal increments of time. In Figure 6.2, each interval on the horizontal axis represents successive days that the number of compliments was measured.
2. Vertical axis	The vertical (Y) axis, which is a line drawn upward from the left-hand end of the horizontal axis, represents the numerical property of the behavior being measured. The vertical axis is usually divided into equal intervals. In Figure 6.2, the vertical axis depicts the number of compliments.
3. Phase change lines	Vertical lines are drawn upward from the horizontal axis at those points in time when changes in the intervention are made (e.g., going from baseline to intervention). In Figure 6.2, phase change lines are drawn to coincide with the introduction or withdrawal of reinforcement.
4. Phase/condition labels	Single words or brief descriptive phrases are written at the top of the graph, parallel to the horizontal axis. These labels identify the different conditions in effect during each phase of the intervention.
5. Data points	Each data point on a graph represents (1) the numerical amount of the target behavior recorded during an observation period and (2) the time when and intervention conditions under which a particular observation was conducted. For example, on day 11, the last day of the first baseline condition, 3 compliments were observed, and on day 12, the first day of organized games, 7 compliments were recorded.
6. Data path	When successive data points within a given phase (condition) are connected with straight lines, a data path is created. The data path represents the relation between the behavior being observed and the intervention used to effect change on the behavior.
7. Legend	The figure legend is a short description that provides the reader with sufficient information to identify the target behavior and intervention.

Source: Cooper, Heron, and Heward (1987).

ELEMENTS OF A GRAPH

Cooper, Heron, and Heward (1987) described seven parts to a graph, which are summarized in Table 6.1. Line graphs, which are frequently used in behavior management, contain certain elements. All graphs have horizontal and vertical axes on which are marked the number of sessions and the target behavior, respectively. They also have vertical lines indicating when the baseline ended and intervention was implemented. The number of these lines will vary depending on whether we plan to implement several variations of an intervention or to withdraw the intervention to see its long-term effect on students'

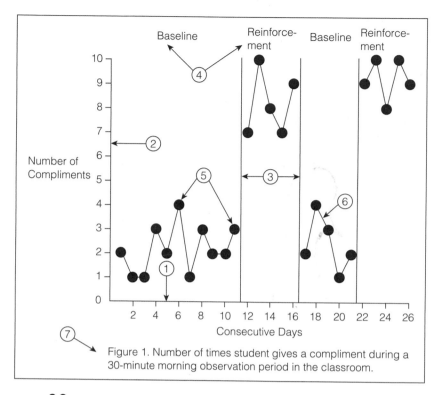

Figure 1. Number of times student gives a compliment during a 30-minute morning observation period in the classroom.

behavior. Line graphs have both data points and a data path. The data points are a numerical summary of the target behavior recorded during a particular observation session. A data path is created by connecting the data points with straight lines. The data path allows us to determine whether a behavior is increasing or decreasing during both baseline and intervention. Finally, all graphs have a figure legend or title indicating the information contained.

Figure 6.2 shows a graph, similar to one depicted by Cooper, Heron, and Heward (1987), in which the seven parts described in Table 6.1 are labeled. Each number corresponds to the numbered part described in Table 6.1. For example, in Figure 6.2, the number "1" has an arrow pointing down to the horizontal axis, the first part described in Table 6.1. Similarly, the number "2" in Figure 6.2 points to the vertical axis, which was the second part described in Table 6.1, and so on.

Collecting Baseline Data

The four reasons for collecting baseline data are similar to those given in Chapter 5 on the importance of recording behavior.

Recall that the data collected on the target behavior before intervention serve as the baseline. Baseline data give us a picture of the extent to which a behavior is performed before we implement intervention. There are several reasons for establishing a baseline (Alberto & Troutman, 1999; Cooper, Heron, and Heward, 1987; Kazdin, 1982):

- The baseline provides an objective method for evaluating the effectiveness of an intervention.
- The baseline helps us identify any environmental conditions that exist right before (antecedents) or after (consequences) the behavior occurs.
- Baseline data can help us set an initial standard of acceptable behavior for a student to receive reinforcement.
- Baseline data make it possible to determine whether the target behavior is actually a problem that requires intervention.

The baseline is most useful when the data pattern reflects a stable baseline, as depicted in Figure 6.3. In Figure 6.3, note that all of the data points are bunched together to form a fairly limited range. Therefore, we can reasonably assume that there are few antecedent events affecting the performance of the target behavior, and so any subsequent changes may be attributed to the intervention rather than to some idiosyncratic variables.

Figures 6.4 and 6.5 provide a graphic representation of an ascending baseline and a descending baseline, respectively. The data path in Figure 6.4 reflects an increasing trend in the behavior over time; the data path in Figure 6.5 shows a decreasing trend. If at all possible, an intervention should be avoided when these trends are present. Ascending and descending baselines indicate that the target behavior is already in the process of changing. Therefore, it makes little sense to introduce an intervention under these conditions, because the baseline will not provide an accurate standard by which to judge the intervention's effectiveness. The baseline should be continued until the trend has stabilized before implementing an intervention. Sometimes the trend will not stabilize, or it may not be feasible to establish a baseline over an extended time because of the intensity, severity, or frequency of the problem behavior. For example, it is unwise to extend baseline for a student who is displaying self-injurious behavior, such as biting his arm.

The fourth type of baseline pattern, depicted in Figure 6.6, is an unstable or variable trend. As with either an ascending or a descending trend, it is unwise to introduce an intervention in the presence of such variability. In all likelihood, the variability is due to a host of environmental factors that are not accounted for. The effectiveness of an intervention cannot be determined until

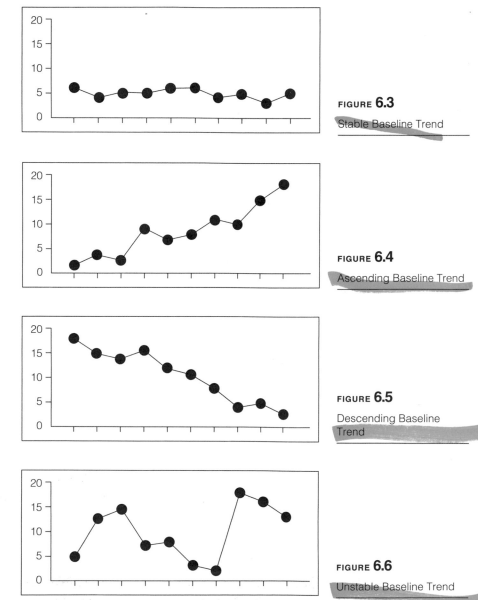

FIGURE **6.3**
Stable Baseline Trend

FIGURE **6.4**
Ascending Baseline Trend

FIGURE **6.5**
Descending Baseline
Trend

FIGURE **6.6**
Unstable Baseline Trend

Fitness trainers typically collect baseline data on their clients' initial performance levels in order to assess their physical condition and to set attainable goals. This process routinely occurs in any profession between an employer and employee.

the source of such variability is identified and eliminated. For example, let's assume that the target behavior in Figure 6.6 is swearing at peers. The data seem to suggest that on some days the student swore at peers frequently (e.g., data point 8) while on other days she swore infrequently (e.g., data points 6 and 7). Based on an A-B-C analysis, we might determine that the student was involved in cooperative learning activities on days when swearing occurred infrequently

In real-life situations such as the classroom, it is not always possible to establish a stable baseline trend. Sometimes a student's behavior is too variable, and other times it is impractical to continue the baseline long enough to establish a stable trend. In these cases, we collect the best data we can and proceed within the constraints imposed by the classroom.

Functional assessment techniques, described in the next chapter—of which an A-B-C analysis is one—represent the best way to determine the reasons for variability in data.

and in independent seat-work activities on days when swearing occurred frequently. Perhaps she doesn't know how to complete the independent assignment successfully or found it boring and was swearing to escape the task. The unstable baseline may prompt us to investigate the behavior in more detail.

DESIGNS FOR GRAPHING BEHAVIOR

There are a variety of techniques, or designs, for graphing behavior. Alberto and Troutman (1999) identified six types of designs, which are summarized in Table 6.2 and described in detail in this section. All of the designs help us determine the effectiveness of an intervention. Consequently, selecting a design to graph behavior is important for monitoring students' performance while an intervention is in effect. Another purpose of designs is to help us determine whether changes in the target behavior resulted from the intervention or were due to chance or to variables that were not accounted for. The more precisely we can control extraneous variables, the more confidently we can predict the impact an intervention will have on a target behavior (Shores, 1988).

TABLE 6.2   COMMON DESIGNS FOR GRAPHING BEHAVIOR

Design	Description	Advantages	Disadvantages
AB design	Baseline data collected during the A phase, and intervention implemented in the B phase	Provides the teacher with a quick, uncomplicated means of comparing behavior before and after intervention	Cannot be used to make a confident assumption of a functional relation
ABAB (reversal) design	Sequential application and withdrawal of intervention following initial baseline	Provides a simple means to analyze effects of intervention	Requires withdrawal of effective intervention to determine a functional relation
Multiple baseline design	Simultaneous analysis of behaviors, students, or settings	Can establish a functional relation without withdrawing intervention	Is not always practical to apply intervention to several behaviors, students, or settings
Changing criterion design	Successive increase or decrease in criteria for reinforcement in a stepwise fashion	Can establish a functional relation while always changing the behavior in a positive direction	Relies on gradual behavior change, which may not be appropriate for behaviors requiring rapid modification
Changing conditions design	Successive change in conditions for performance of behavior to evaluate comparative effects of intervention	Allows the teacher to compare the effects of several interventions on student behavior	Cannot determine a functional relation and may reflect cumulative rather than differential effects of interventions
Alternating treatments design	Random alteration of two or more to compare their effectiveness	Is an efficient way for the teacher to determine the most effective intervention	Requires replication to establish a functional relation

Source: Alberto and Troutman (1999).

AB Design

The **AB design** is the most basic design. The AB designation refers to the two phases of the design: (1) the A, or baseline phase, and (2) the B, or intervention, phase. During the A phase, baseline data are collected and recorded. Once a stable baseline trend has been established, a vertical phase change line is drawn, and an intervention is introduced that signifies the beginning of the B phase. In this phase, intervention data are collected and recorded. We can evaluate the effectiveness of the intervention by comparing the data trend during the B phase to the behavioral observations collected during the A phase. We can use this information, in turn, to help us decide to either continue, modify, or discontinue an intervention. The AB design is depicted in Figure 6.7.

The major advantage of an AB design is that it is simple to use. As can be seen in Figure 6.7, baseline and intervention data points are plotted and connected, with the phases separated by a vertical phase change line. We now have a swift, easy method for comparing students' behavior before and after intervention.

The major disadvantage of the AB design is that it is impossible to rule out alternative explanations for any behavior change that takes place during intervention. For example, suppose that the intervention plotted in Figure 6.7 consisted of our verbally praising a student every time he spelled a word correctly. Based on a visual inspection of the results, we might conclude that the intervention was effective. However, what if a desirable peer was coincidentally seated next to the student while the intervention was implemented? We may erroneously conclude that the intervention was responsible for the increase in

Collecting baseline data will not appear to be such an onerous chore once teachers understand that this process will make them better decision makers.

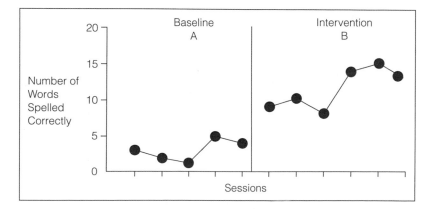

FIGURE 6.7

AB Design

Some teachers tend to ignore the problems with the AB design because it is so easy to implement. A common response to the problems the design poses is that, as long as the behavior improves, the problems can be overlooked.

spelling words written correctly when, in fact, the student was completing more work simply to impress his peer. Without knowing this information, we may continue using verbal praise with the student even though it was not responsible for the change in behavior. If the desirable peer is moved to another desk, the number of spelling words written correctly may decrease, and we will be at a loss to explain it.

ABAB (Reversal or Withdrawal) Design

The **ABAB design,** commonly referred to as the reversal or withdrawal design, involves temporarily removing the intervention in order to evaluate its effects on students' behavior. In other words, we are evaluating whether the effectiveness of an intervention can be replicated. If it can be replicated, then we have established a functional relation between the behavior and the intervention. If it cannot be replicated, then the change in behavior was due to some extraneous variables.

The ABAB design has four distinct phases, as shown in Figure 6.8. In the initial baseline (A_1) phase, we collect behavioral observations on the target behavior under circumstances that existed prior to the intervention. After a stable baseline trend has been established, the intervention (B_1) is implemented. This intervention continues until a stable trend is established in the direction of the desired behavior change. At this point, the first two phases, in isolation, mirror the AB design described previously. However, unlike with the AB design, two additional phases are added. The third phase is a return to the original baseline (A_2) conditions by withdrawing the intervention. The final phase involves rein-

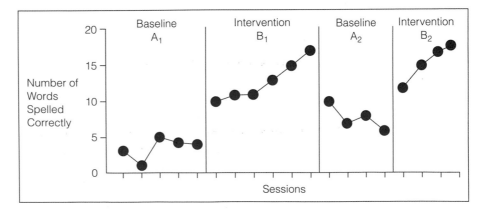

FIGURE 6.8

ABAB or Reversal Design

troducing the intervention (B_2) to see if the original change in behavior that occurred during the second phase of the design (B_1) can be replicated.

There are two classic variations on the reversal (ABAB) design (Zucker, Rutherford, & Prieto, 1979). In the first variation, the intervention is implemented when the student is not performing the target behavior during the return to the baseline condition. That is, the intervention is present in all phases after the initial baseline. To conceptualize this variation, look at the data in Figure 6.8. During the return to the baseline (A_2) phase, the teacher still provided the student with verbal praise but did so randomly, and not while the student was writing spelling words. If verbal praise were responsible for the increase in correct spelling words during the intervention (B_1), then the number of correct spelling words would decrease when it was applied randomly.

The second variation involves applying the intervention during the return to the baseline (A_2) phase to a behavior other than the one targeted. If the target behavior decreases during the second baseline, we have demonstrated that the intervention produced the desired behavior change. If the target behavior remains high, then some other extraneous factor may be responsible for the behavior change. If the target behavior remains high and the nontarget behavior improves, then the intervention may have been very powerful.

There are several advantages to the reversal (ABAB) design. First, it allows us to determine a functional relation between the intervention and any changes in the target behavior. If the behavior change can be replicated, then we can say that the intervention, and not some extraneous factor, was responsible. Second, it is a method of providing accountability. If a functional relation does not exist, then we implement a different intervention. If a functional relation does exist, then we have documentation proving our ability to modify students' behavior. Third, it can be used as a teaching tool. We can demonstrate to a student, administrator, or parent that, for example, verbal praise results in positive changes in behavior. Fourth, it may help us move students away from continuous schedules of reinforcement and toward more intermittent schedules because it involves alternating phases of baseline and intervention.

There are two circumstances in which it is inappropriate to use a reversal (ABAB) design (Alberto & Troutman, 1999):

1. When the target behavior is dangerous, for example, aggressive behavior directed toward other students (hitting) or self-injurious behavior. Because the reversal design calls for a second baseline condition to be implemented after a change in the target behavior rate, ethical considerations would prohibit withdrawing a successful technique.

2. When the target behavior is not reversible. Many academic behaviors, for example, are not reversible because the behavior change is associated

with a learning process. Under such conditions, a return to baseline performance is not feasible: information cannot be "unlearned." (p. 164)

There are two other related concerns (Zucker, Rutherford, & Pricto, 1979). First, some behaviors, once they are acquired, are no longer dependent on the intervention because they are maintained by naturally occurring reinforcers in the environment. For example, we may develop an intervention to teach a student to interact appropriately with peers during recess. Once she learns to interact appropriately, her peer group may reinforce her behavior with positive comments even after a return to the baseline. Although this may make it difficult to evaluate the effectiveness of intervention, it nevertheless is a desirable effect. Second, we may not be able to accurately replicate the baseline conditions that existed prior to the intervention. For example, it may be difficult for us to reproduce the exact rate of attention provided for appropriate behavior and denied for inappropriate behavior during the initial baseline phase.

Multiple Baseline Design

The **multiple baseline design** provides a way to evaluate the effectiveness of an intervention when a reversal (ABAB) design is not desirable because of the limitations noted previously. As the title implies, a multiple baseline design allows us to analyze the effects of intervention on three variables (Alberto & Troutman, 1999):

1. Two or more behaviors associated with one student in a single setting; for example, John's out-of-seat and talking-out behaviors in social studies class (multiple baseline across behaviors).
2. Two or more students exhibiting the same behavior in a single setting: for example, the spelling accuracy of Sara and Janet in English class (multiple baseline across individuals).
3. Two or more settings in which one student is exhibiting the same behavior: for example, Kurt's cursing during recess and also in the school cafeteria (multiple baseline across settings). (pp. 173–174)

Some teachers frown on the use of reversal and multiple baseline designs because of the time involved in implementing them. This thinking can be dangerous because using the simpler and more time-efficient AB design may lead to an ineffective intervention in which other variables have not been accounted for.

Consequently, the multiple baseline design is most appropriate when we want to use an intervention with two or more students, behaviors, or settings. In addition, because the multiple baseline design does not include a reversal phase, it may be used for a target behavior that involves aggression (or another behavior we don't want to reverse) or for academic learning (that can't be reversed).

Figure 6.9 provides an example of a multiple baseline design across three academic behaviors for one student: (1) math problems completed correctly, (2) words spelled correctly, and (3) reading questions answered correctly.

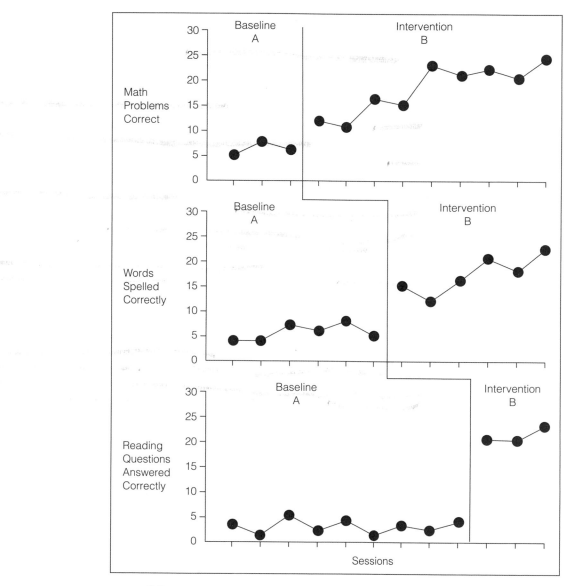

FIGURE 6.9

Multiple Baseline Design Across Behaviors

Although Figure 6.9 may look complicated, we can easily conceptualize it as a series of three AB designs. Take a piece of paper and cover the portion of the graph in Figure 6.9 for "words spelled correctly" and "reading questions answered correctly," so that only the graph for "math problems correct" is showing. Notice how there is an initial baseline (A) phase consisting of three data points. This phase is followed by nine data points during intervention. Repeating this process with the other two behaviors reveals three AB designs in which the application of interventions is staggered—they are not implemented at the same time.

The first step in using the multiple baseline design is the same as that for an AB design or reversal design: Collect baseline data until a stable trend is established. The crucial difference in a multiple baseline design, as shown in Figure 6.9, is that the baselines are successively longer for the second and third behaviors. Thus, once a stable trend was established for "math problems correct," an intervention was implemented while baseline data were still being collected for spelling words and reading questions. After intervention produced a stable trend for "math problems correct" (three data points into the intervention), an intervention was implemented for the second behavior, "words spelled correctly." Baseline data collection continued for the third behavior, "reading questions answered correctly," until a stable trend was established during intervention for "words spelled correctly." Finally, intervention was implemented for "reading questions answered correctly."

The idea behind the multiple baseline design is actually quite simple. Continuing the baseline on the second behavior after intervention has been started for the first behavior allows us to determine if a functional relation exists between the target behavior and the intervention. It is a way to determine whether the intervention or some other extraneous factor is responsible for the behavior change. Here's an example of how it works: In Figure 6.9, notice that for the first three data points of intervention for "math problems correct," the corresponding data points for the last part of the baseline for "words spelled correctly" remained stable and low. This pattern tells us that the intervention probably was responsible for the behavior change observed in "math problems correct." Conversely, if the baseline trend for "words spelled correctly" began to increase at the same time the intervention was implemented for "math problems correct," then we may suspect that some unaccounted-for variable was responsible for the change in behavior. This same process is in effect for the second and third behaviors in Figure 6.9 as well.

There are two major advantages to the multiple baseline design. First, unlike with the reversal design, the intervention does not have to be withdrawn to establish a functional relation between the target behavior and the intervention. Therefore, a multiple baseline design can be used for situations in which the target behavior is irreversible (e.g., academic learning) or in which reversals are undesirable because the behavior is dangerous to the student or others (e.g., aggression). Second, a multiple baseline design can be used in situations in which multiple behavior changes are desired. Unlike with the reversal design, which is usually limited to interventions on a single behavior, the multiple baseline design provides an opportunity to systematically intervene on several behaviors over the course of an intervention program. These advantages make the multiple baseline design particularly desirable for classroom use (Alberto & Troutman, 1999).

Like every other design for graphing behavior, the multiple baseline design has some limitations. Alberto and Troutman (1999) described two situations in which the multiple baseline design is inappropriate:

1. When the target behavior calls for immediate action. The multiple baseline design calls for a considerable delay in delivery of the intervention procedure for the second and subsequent dependent variables.
2. When the behaviors selected for intervention are not independent. In such a case, intervention with one behavior will bring about a change in the related behavior; therefore, the teacher will be unable to evaluate clearly the effects of the procedure. For example, if two behaviors targeted for a student are cursing and fighting, the teacher might find that after the student's cursing decreases, there are fewer fights. In this case, the two behaviors are clearly not independent. (pp. 183–184)

The second point in particular deserves some elaboration. Recall that the idea of a multiple baseline design is to establish a functional relation without reversing the intervention. That is, we do not want to see the second behavior change after an intervention is implemented for the first one. If the second behavior changes during baseline at the same time that an intervention is applied to the first behavior, then we may assume that some extraneous factor, and not the intervention, is responsible for improvements in the target behavior. However, there are two other possible explanations. First, the second behavior may be part of the same response class as the first behavior. Recall from Chapter 4 that a response class is a group of behaviors that have at least one characteristic in common. In Figure 6.9, "words spelled correctly" and "reading questions answered correctly" may be members of the same response class (if the same story was used to generate both spelling words and questions). Therefore, an intervention applied to one member of the response class may bring about a change in another member. Second, the intervention may have been so powerful that it transferred to the second behavior. Both explanations represent positive aspects of an intervention. However, the multiple baseline design does not allow us to determine which of these factors are responsible for the behavior change.

Changing Criterion Design

The **changing criterion design** is used to evaluate a slow and orderly increase or decrease in performance levels by changing the criterion for students to receive interventions in a stepwise fashion (Alberto & Troutman, 1999). An

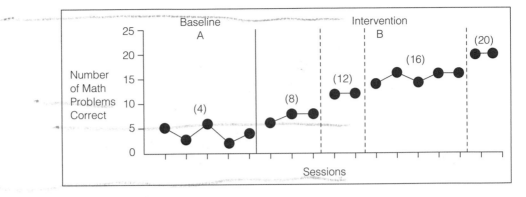

FIGURE 6.10

Changing Criterion Design

example of this design appears in Figure 6.10. Although this figure seems to present a lot of data, it is merely an extension of the AB design. The main difference is that the intervention (B) phase is divided into subphases indicated by the three vertical dashed lines. Each subphase of intervention requires a closer approximation of the target behavior than the previous phase. In this respect, this design takes advantage of the behavioral principle of shaping. This design is particularly appropriate when achieving the terminal goal of the intervention requires a considerable length of time or when measuring the effectiveness of a shaping program (Alberto & Troutman, 1995).

The first step in implementing the changing criterion design is to collect baseline data, just as with the designs previously described. Three tasks must be accomplished after a stable baseline rate has been established. First, the average performance of the student during baseline must be determined. In Figure 6.10, that number is 4 ([5 + 3 + 6 + 2 + 4]/5 = 4), as indicated in parentheses above the baseline data. The second task is to determine the target criterion for acceptable performance. The easiest way is to identify the average performance of other students who have mastered the target behavior; this number represents the terminal goal. The third task is to determine interim levels of performance. These standards ensure that students are making sufficient progress toward the target criterion for acceptable performance.

Alberto and Troutman (1999) described four ways to determine interim levels of performance:

1. The interim criterion for performance can be set at, and then increased by, an amount equal to the mean of the stable portion of the baseline data. This technique is appropriate when the goal of the behavior-change program is to increase a level of performance and when the student's

present level is quite low. For example, if a teacher wanted to increase the number of questions a student answered and the student's mean baseline level of correct responses was two, that teacher might set two correct answers as a first interim criterion. Each subsequent subphase would then require two additional correct answers.

2. Interim levels of performance can be determined by taking 50% of the computed mean of baseline data (or the stable portion of the baseline data). For example, suppose that a student's number of problems correct was noted for one week and that the following data were recorded:

   Monday   9
   Tuesday   10
   Wednesday   7
   Thursday   6
   Friday   8

3. Interim criteria can be based on selecting the highest (or lowest, depending on the terminal objective) level of baseline performance. This is probably most appropriate for use with social behavior, for example, out-of-seat, positive peer interactions, rather than for an academic behavior. The assumption is that if the student were able to perform at that high (or low) level once, the behavior can be strengthened (or weakened) and maintained at that level.

4. Interim criteria can be based on a professional estimate of the student's ability. This procedure is particularly appropriate when the student's present level of performance is zero. (pp. 168–169)

In Figure 6.10, the interim criterion was set by first determining the mean number of math problems completed correctly during the baseline phase, which was 4. Then the four subsequent interim criteria were each increased by 4 problems correct. These interim criteria appear in parentheses in Figure 6.10. The last subphase of intervention has an interim criterion of 20, which becomes the final task standard.

Thus far, we have collected baseline data and determined the interim and terminal criteria for acceptable performance. We should avoid the pitfall of making the changing criterion design more difficult than it really is. The only data that have been graphed so far are baseline data. The next step is the same as in an AB design: implementing intervention. However, unlike with the AB design, students receive an intervention only when they reach the criterion for the first subphase. In Figure 6.10, students received the intervention only when a stable trend was established and they averaged 8 math problems correct. It is important to analyze the appropriateness of the first interim level of performance. If students do not meet the criterion after a reasonable number of trials, the standard was probably set too high; conversely, if they reach it too quickly, it was set too low. In either case, the first interim criterion level should be adjusted accordingly.

Intervention is implemented after students' performance reaches the first interim criterion either for a predetermined number of consecutive sessions (usually two) or for average performance. Then, the intervention is not administered until students reach the second interim level. This process continues until the terminal goal is reached or the behavior either increases 100 percent or ceases, depending on the purpose of the intervention (Alberto & Troutman, 1999).

There are several advantages to the changing criterion design (Alberto & Troutman, 1999; Cooper, Heron, & Heward, 1987). First, it can establish a functional relation between behavior and intervention while the target behavior continues to change in a positive direction. Second, unlike the reversal design, it does not require withdrawing the intervention to establish a functional relation. Third, unlike the multiple baseline design, one behavior at a time can be targeted for intervention, thereby saving time while focusing on the most important problems students present.

There are also some disadvantages to the changing criterion design (Alberto & Troutman, 1999; Cooper, Heron, & Heward, 1987). First, it requires changing the target behavior gradually. Consequently, it may be unsuitable for behaviors that a teacher wants to either increase (e.g., acquiring study skills for a test) or decrease (e.g., acting aggressively) quickly. Second, the changing criterion design can be used only for behaviors that students already possess. For example, this design will be inappropriate for increasing the number of division problems a student completes correctly if he does not know how to divide. Third, the changing criterion design will not work with behaviors that do not lend themselves to a stepwise modification. For example, it will be counterproductive to systematically increase the number of times a student asks a question because the goal is to have her work independently. There probably is an optimal number of times for students to ask questions during a set period. Asking questions below an optimal level may lead to incorrect answers; asking too many questions may inhibit independence. Fourth, the changing criterion design may reduce the amount of reinforcement students receive because they are systematically required to perform more behaviors. Finally, Tawney and Gast (1984) noted that the major problem in using the changing criterion design is setting interim criterion levels that allow us to determine whether a functional relation exists between the target behavior and the intervention without interfering with students' optimal learning rates. If students are not reaching an interim criterion level, then we may have to withdraw the intervention by returning to a lower criterion and then reinstating a higher criterion.

A changing criterion design has much in common with the continuous assessment technique called curriculum-based measurement (CBM). With CBM, trend lines are established as a way to monitor students' progress through various content areas.

Changing Conditions Design

A **changing conditions design** is used to determine the effectiveness of two or more interventions on a target behavior (Alberto & Troutman, 1999). Sometimes this technique is called an ABC design (not to be confused with A-B-C analysis). As in an AB design, A refers to the baseline while B designates the intervention. In a changing conditions design, the C designates the application of a second intervention. In fact, with any design, letters other than A (which always refers to the baseline) designate different interventions. Therefore, in a changing conditions design, we are implementing different interventions consecutively without ever returning to the baseline. This design reflects how most teachers implement interventions: They keep trying different interventions consecutively until they find an effective one. As is the case with an AB design, a functional relation between a target behavior and intervention cannot be determined. The only conclusion we can reach is whether a target behavior changed in the desired direction at the time intervention was implemented (DiGangi & Maag, 1992). Figure 6.11 shows an example of a changing conditions design.

Notice that in Figure 6.11 the first two phases mirror an AB design: baseline (A) and intervention (B). In this case, the intervention (B) was self-monitoring—a technique described in more detail in Chapter 12. However, what makes Figure 6.11 a changing conditions design is that five data points of self-

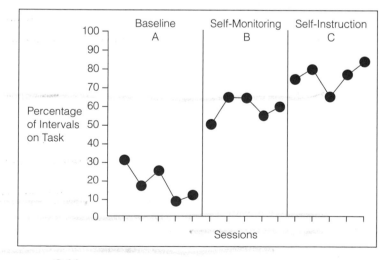

FIGURE 6.11

Changing Conditions Design

monitoring (B) were immediately followed by a second intervention, self-instruction (C)—a technique discussed in Chapter 13.

As with all designs, the first step in using a changing conditions design is to collect behavioral observations during the baseline phase. Once a stable trend is established, the first intervention is implemented. In Figure 6.11, five sessions of self-monitoring resulted in an increase in the percentage of intervals the student was on task. "On task" was defined as the student's writing answers, looking at a book, or asking the teacher a question. The student's on-task behavior improved to 60 percent of the intervals when self-monitoring was implemented. But the teacher thought that this increase was insufficient, so self-instruction (C) was implemented after a stable trend was established for self-monitoring. Alberto and Troutman (1999) stated that the second intervention can be either a complete change from the previous one or a slight modification.

The main advantage of the changing conditions design is that it allows us to determine which intervention will be most effective. On the basis of the data graphed in Figure 6.11, we may conclude that self-instruction was a more effective intervention than self-monitoring for increasing the percentage of time the student was on task.

The main disadvantage of the changing conditions design is that, in the case of the data appearing in Figure 6.11, we may incorrectly conclude that self-instruction was more effective than self-monitoring. The reason is that the increase in on-task behaviors during self-instruction may be due to carryover effects rather than the superiority of this intervention (Barlow & Hersen, 1984). In other words, the apparent superiority of self-instruction may be caused by the cumulative effects of both interventions. For example, in Figure 6.11, even though self-monitoring was discontinued before self-instruction was implemented, the student may have retained some of the knowledge of the first intervention that positively influenced his performance following the second intervention. The other disadvantage of this design is that it is impossible to determine a functional relation between the target behavior and the intervention. These disadvantages can be remedied by inserting a return to the baseline condition in between the two interventions.

Alternating Treatments Design

Like the changing conditions design, the **alternating treatments design** allows us to determine the differential effectiveness of more than one intervention for a target behavior. However, unlike the changing conditions or reversal designs, different interventions are randomly alternated from session to session regardless of the stability and level of behavior of previous data points. The data points of the same intervention are connected with a line. The trend that the

> Some teachers like the changing conditions design because it involves using two interventions back-to-back, which is often viewed as a more powerful option than one employing only a single intervention.

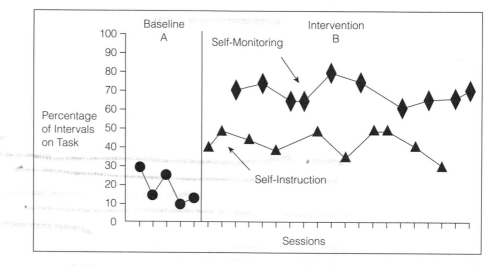

FIGURE **6.12**

Alternating Treatments Design

line creates is then visually compared with the lines for the other interventions. In this way, we can answer the question of which intervention will be most effective for a given student. This arrangement is presented in Figure 6.12 using the same two interventions as in the example of the changing conditions design.

A visual inspection of Figure 6.12 helps us evaluate which intervention was most effective. Self-monitoring is depicted by the diamond data points, and self-instruction by the triangular data points. The trend line for self-monitoring is much higher than that for self-instruction. Clearly, self-monitoring was more effective than self-instruction for increasing the percentage of time the student was on task. Figure 6.12 also shows that self-monitoring and self-instruction were randomly implemented. For example, self-instruction was implemented for the first 2 sessions of the intervention phase, followed by 1 session of self-monitoring, 1 session of self-instruction, 1 session of self-monitoring, 1 session of self-instruction, 2 sessions of self-monitoring, and so forth, until a total of 10 sessions for each intervention was implemented.

As with all designs, once a stable baseline trend is established, the intervention phase is begun by alternating the treatments. An important consideration is determining the order the treatments are implemented. Alberto and Troutman (1999) suggested that the interventions should be counterbalanced, with the intervention that was implemented first used second in the second session. This counterbalancing ensures that students do not receive one intervention more frequently than the other. An alternative approach is to imple-

ment the interventions randomly, with the condition that no intervention occur in more than three consecutive sessions (Maag, Reid, & DiGangi, 1993).
Figure 6.12 depicts this latter approach.

Several authors have discussed the advantages of the alternating treatments design (Alberto & Troutman, 1999; Barlow & Hersen, 1984; Kazdin &
Hartmann, 1978; Ulman & Sulzer-Azaroff, 1975). Cooper, Heron, and Heward
(1987) synthesized these authors' comments into six advantages. First, the major benefit of the alternating treatments design is that it minimizes sequence
effects. Sequence effects refer to the possibility that the order in which two or
more interventions are implemented affect their outcome. Second, the alternating treatments design does not require withdrawing possibly effective interventions simply to demonstrate a functional relation. Third, because the
interventions are alternated quickly, their differential effectiveness can be determined within several sessions rather than waiting for a stable trend to be established for the first intervention or returning to baseline before implementing the second intervention. Fourth, this design can reveal differences between
interventions even if the target behavior cannot be reversed, as is the case with
academic learning. For example, we can determine whether drill and practice
or a mnemonic strategy will be most effective for students learning math facts.
Fifth, it is possible to assess whether a behavior generalizes from one intervention to another. Finally, an alternating treatments design can be implemented without collecting any baseline data. Although baseline data are important for a variety of reasons, they are not necessary if we are only interested
in determining which intervention is most effective for a given situation.

As with all designs, this one is not without its disadvantages, which Cooper,
Heron, and Heward (1987) summarized. First, the rapid back-and-forth
switching of interventions represents an artificial arrangement. It is more common in education to implement one intervention over time in order to assess
its effectiveness. Second, multiple treatment interference is likely to occur
when two or more treatments are alternated rapidly. That is, carryover effects
are occurring from one intervention to the next. Consequently, we may be
evaluating the combined effectiveness of two interventions rather than their
differential impact on the target behavior. Carryover effects can be minimized
by providing distinctive discriminative stimuli that signal the onset of a new intervention. For example, Lloyd, Bateman, Landrum, and Hallahan (1989) implemented two discriminative stimuli procedures to minimize carryover effects when evaluating the effectiveness of two self-monitoring techniques on
students' math performance: (1) All math practice worksheets and self-monitoring cards were color coded, and (2) the signal tones used to prompt students
to self-monitor differed in pitch for each self-monitoring procedure. Third, the
alternating treatments design is limited in the number of possible interventions
that can be evaluated at one time. In practice, three interventions are probably

Although the alternating treatments design is somewhat complicated, it offers teachers the option of not having to first collect baseline data. If teachers are interested in which interventions are effective, it is less important what level the target behavior was at prior to alternating the treatments.

the maximum capacity of this design if proper precautions are taken to minimize carryover effects and to carefully counterbalance the interventions. Fourth, if the interventions are too similar, it will be almost impossible to minimize carryover effects. Therefore, the interventions that are being evaluated should be substantively different from each other.

SUMMARY

This chapter focused on graphing behavior. Graphing data provides us with immediate feedback on students' behavior, allows us to visually examine trends in students' behavior, provides a vehicle by which others can independently judge the effectiveness of interventions, and offers an important source of feedback to students regarding their behavior. Baseline data provides important information about behavior and helps us develop appropriate interventions.

Six types of designs can be used to graph behavioral observations. The AB design is easy to apply but does not enable us to rule out alternative explanations. The ABAB, or reversal, design permits us to determine a functional relation between a behavior and an intervention but should not be used for behaviors that are dangerous to the student or others or for academic learning that cannot be reversed. The multiple baseline design allows us to determine a functional relation between a behavior and an intervention without returning to the baseline, but it is time consuming. The changing criterion design is good for evaluating the effectiveness of an intervention for improving academic performance although it may be difficult to set intermediate criterion levels. The changing conditions design permits us to evaluate the effectiveness of two or more interventions, but without returning to baseline between interventions, we cannot rule out carryover effects. The alternating treatments design does not require a baseline to evaluate the effectiveness of two or more treatments, but it is not always desirable to interchange two or more treatments quickly. All six designs have advantages and disadvantages. The goal is to select the design that meets the needs of the student, target behavior, intervention, and setting in which it is implemented.

ACTIVITIES

1. Watch 10 minutes of the nightly news (either local or national) for 5 days. Jot down how many times graphs appear as a way to illustrate a point or story. If very few graphs are used, ask yourself how many stories could have been better reported with graphs.

2. List all the situations and professions in which collecting baseline data is important. For example, doctors measure patients' glucose levels before prescribing insulin, and pediatricians want parents to take their child's temperature every hour for at least a day before prescribing an antibiotic. In what situations and professions do others collect some type of baseline data?

3. Think of two situations in which you might use a reversal design to determine the effectiveness of an intervention. Did you select behaviors that are desirable or possible to reverse?

REVIEW QUESTIONS

1. How can graphing data, rather than simply looking at a series of numbers, help teachers make better decisions regarding the effectiveness of an intervention?

2. Describe, and provide an example, of the benefits of graphing behavioral observations.

3. Describe and draw the different elements of a graph.

4. Why is it important to establish a baseline before implementing an intervention?

5. Describe the four types of baseline patterns and their implications for implementing and evaluating the effectiveness of an intervention.

6. Describe the six designs for graphing behavior including their advantages and disadvantages.

REFERENCES

Alberto, P. A., & Troutman, A. C. (1999). *Applied behavior analysis for teachers* (5th ed.). Columbus, OH: Merrill.

Barlow, D. H., & Hersen, M. (1984). *Single case experimental designs: Strategies for studying behavior change* (2nd ed.). New York: Pergamon.

Cooper, J. O., Heron, T. E., & Heward, W. L. (1987). *Applied behavior analysis*. Columbus, OH: Merrill.

DiGangi, S. A., & Maag, J. W. (1992). A component analysis of self-management training with behaviorally disordered youth. *Behavioral Disorders, 17,* 281–290.

DiGangi, S. A., Maag, J. W., & Rutherford, R. B., Jr. (1991). Self-graphing of on-task behavior: Enhancing the reactive effects of self-monitoring on on-task behavior and academic performance. *Learning Disability Quarterly, 14,* 221–230.

Kazdin, A. E. (1982). *Single-case research designs.* New York: Oxford University Press.

Kazdin, A. E., & Hartmann, D. P. (1978). The simultaneous-treatment design. *Behavior Therapy, 9,* 912–922,

Lloyd, J. W., Bateman, D. F., Landrum, T. J., & Hallahan, D. P. (1989). Self-recording attention versus productivity. *Journal of Applied Behavior Analysis, 22,* 315–323.

Maag, J. W., Reid, R., & DiGangi, S. A. (1993). Differential effects of self-monitoring attention, accuracy, and productivity. *Journal of Applied Behavior Analysis, 26,* 329–344.

Mace, F. C., Brown, D. K., & West, B. J. (1987). Behavioral self-management in education. In C. A. Maher & J. E. Zins (Eds.), *Psychoeducational interventions in the schools* (pp. 160–176). New York: Pergamon.

Shores, R. E. (1988). Highlighting analysis in applied behavior analysis: Designing and analyzing single subject research. In R. B. Rutherford, Jr., & J. W. Maag (Eds.), *Severe behavior disorders of children and youth* (Vol. 11, pp. 144–155). Reston, VA: Council for Children with Behavioral Disorders.

Tawney, J., & Gast, D. (1984). *Single subject research in special education.* Columbus, OH: Merrill.

Ulman, J. D., & Sulzer-Azaroff, B. (1975). Multi-element baseline design in educational research. In E. Ramp & G. Semb (Eds.), *Behavior analysis: Areas of research and application* (pp. 371–391). Englewood Cliffs, NJ: Prentice-Hall.

Zucker, S. H., Rutherford, R. B., Jr., & Prieto, A. G. (1979). Teacher directed interventions with behaviorally disordered children. In R. B. Rutherford, Jr., & A. G. Prieto (Eds.), *Severe behavior disorders of children and youth* (Vol. 2, pp. 49–61). Reston, VA: Council for Children with Behavioral Disorders.

FUNCTIONAL ASSESSMENT OF BEHAVIOR PROBLEMS

CHAPTER OVERVIEW

- An Overview of Functional Assessment
- Stages of Functional Assessment
- Writing Behavioral Support Plans
- Issues in Functional Assessment

CHAPTER OBJECTIVES

After completing this chapter, you will be able to do the following:

1. Describe the advantages of functional assessment.

2. Understand the three foundational aspects of functional assessment.

3. Identify the types of hypotheses that can be generated for functional assessment.

4. Describe procedures for generating and testing hypotheses regarding the functions problematic behaviors serve.

5. Describe the process and components for writing behavioral support plans from functional assessment information.

6. Explain how behavioral, cognitive, and self-control deficiencies contribute to teaching replacement behaviors.

7. Identify the advantages and limitations of naturalistic versus contrived assessment, and the situations in which each should be used.

8. Describe multiply controlled behaviors and transfer of functions, and ways to solve the problems they present.

9. Understand implications for an expanded repertoire of behavioral functions.

From information presented in the two previous chapters, we now know how to target and define a behavior of concern, count and record its occurrence, and plot the ensuing data on a graph in order to visually inspect trends. We are now ready to conduct functional assessment—arguably the most important component of effective behavior management.

The assessment of students' challenging behaviors is more complex than simply punishing students when they misbehave. If behavior management were that easy, you would be neither reading this book nor taking the class for which this book is required. The reality is that students' behavioral repertoires are—for better or for worse—wonderfully diverse and versatile. Most students, at certain times in their lives, display behaviors usually considered inappropriate. Hops, Bieckel, and Walker (1976) identified behaviors that are characteristic of students who act out in the classroom; Table 7.1 lists these behaviors. What should become apparent from this list is that many students display these behaviors in classrooms. For example, what student, at some point, does *not* run around the room, complain, disturb peers, argue, ignore the teacher, distort the truth, decline to follow directions, or fail to complete an assignment?

What separates students whose behavior requires intervention from those whose behavior does not are not the behaviors themselves but rather the frequency, duration, and intensity with which they are displayed. Let's take one of the behaviors appearing in Table 7.1—complains—for illustrative purposes. Almost every student complains at one time or another. But what if a student complains 10 times during a 50-minute period? Or what if she complains only once—but the episode of complaining lasts for 25 minutes? Or what if a student complains at the top of his voice rather than mumbling his objections? In these instances, the frequency, duration, and intensity of the behavior, respectively, probably exceed the social norm of the class environment.

The goal here is not to suggest that no behaviors are bizarre and atypical in and of themselves. Certainly, students who refuse to leave the house, or hurt animals require swift and rigorous interventions regardless of the frequency, duration, and intensity. The point is that giving attention to the types of behavior students exhibit provides little information about the nature of their problems or appropriate interventions. Instead, collecting information on the function (purpose) students' behavior serves provides the key to selecting and implementing effective interventions. Once the functions maladaptive behaviors serve have been identified, we can alter the antecedents and consequences to make the behaviors less likely to occur while also teaching students replacement behaviors (and reinforcing their use) that will help them appropriately obtain the same outcomes. This process involves conducting functional assessment.

This chapter focuses on several aspects of functional assessment including the foundational assumptions of functional assessment and the types of hy-

TABLE 7.1	BEHAVIORS CHARACTERISTIC OF ACTING-OUT STUDENTS
Is out of seat	Destroys property
Yells	Does not comply with adult commands or directions
Runs around the room	Argues (talks back)
Disturbs peers	Ignores other teachers
Hits or fights	Distorts the truth
Ignores the teacher	Has temper tantrums
Complains	Is excluded from activities by peers
Fights excessively	Does not follow directions
Steals	Does not complete assignments

Functional assessment is sometimes considered to be traditional assessment in reverse because the teacher manipulates variables to assess the function the behavior serves rather than conducting assessment before intervening.

potheses that can be generated for functional analyses, the two primary stages of functional assessment, and ways to develop behavioral support plans from functional assessment results. The last section of this chapter presents issues related to conducting functional assessment. The key to understanding functional assessment is to view it as traditional assessment *in reverse*. That is, we usually think of assessing prior to intervening. However, with functional assessment, we are intervening first—manipulating the environment (antecedents and consequences) in order to determine what purpose the challenging behavior serves. Successful environmental manipulations and performance of replacement behaviors form the basis for the behavioral support plan.

AN OVERVIEW OF FUNCTIONAL ASSESSMENT

Traditional approaches in assessing students' behavior problems typically follow the medical-disease model described in Chapter 2. Assessment approaches based on this model focus on deficits inherent to children and provide only a limited range of information.

Assessment typically is conducted for one of two reasons: (1) to determine whether students are eligible for special education services under the Individuals with Disabilities Education Act (IDEA), or (2) to pave the way for an intervention. It might seem that assessment for special education services would yield information applicable for developing interventions. However, traditional assessment techniques—such as standardized tests of intelligence and achievement, behavior ratings, assessments of peer relations, and physical and psychophysiological measures—have few implications for intervention. Several authors have provided information on the appropriateness and usefulness of these and other techniques (Epanchin, 1991; Kauffman, 2001; Morgan & Jenson, 1988). However, what is often missing from some authors' discussions of assessment is any exploration of the functions inappropriate behaviors serve.

The term *functional assessment* can be misleading. For instance, it can imply that traditional approaches for assessing behavior problems are nonfunc-

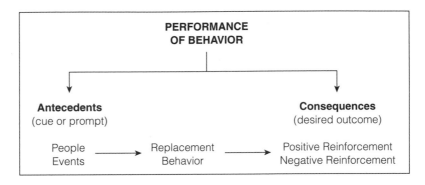

FIGURE 7.1

Process and Goal of Functional Assessment

tional (Maag & Reid, 1994, 1996). To say that one approach is more, or less, functional than another is a difficult distinction to make. The degree to which obtained information helps us determine the purpose a behavior serves is what makes one approach more functional than another. Interestingly, the dictionary definition of the word *function* is "involving functions rather than a physiological or structural causes." This definition ignores the role of physiological factors in favor of purposeful relations between environmental variables and students' behavior. Simply stated, **functional assessment** involves engaging in activities to identify (1) environmental factors that affect the performance of a behavior and the desired outcome that behavior serves, and (2) a replacement behavior that is an appropriate way for students to obtain a desired goal. Figure 7.1 depicts the process and goal of functional assessment.

In Figure 7-1, the performance of behavior depends on the antecedents (people and events) that cue or prompt it and the consequences that maintain it. The behavior is maintained if it accomplishes a desired goal. Desired goals (i.e., functions) can usually be categorized as positive reinforcement (gaining attention or access to objects or activities) or negative reinforcement (escaping or avoiding something aversive). Manipulating antecedents and consequences changes the conditions under which the behavior is performed. These manipulations may result in intervention suggestions for a behavioral support plan. However, no behavioral support plan is complete unless it includes teaching students a replacement behavior and reinforcing them when it is performed. In this way, the students will have in their repertoire an appropriate way to obtain a desired goal.

In this section, the basic assumptions of functional assessment and the types of hypotheses that can be generated for functional analyses are described. This knowledge is important for effectively implementing functional assessment.

Basic Assumptions of Functional Assessment

Three basic and interrelated assumptions about behavior are essential to understanding functional assessment: (1) Context affects how a behavior is displayed and interpreted, (2) all behavior is purposeful and serves some function, and (3) replacement behaviors allow students to appropriately obtain desired outcomes. All three assumptions deserve elaboration because they are the key to understanding and using functional assessment.

Behavior Is Affected by Context   Recall from Chapter 1 that behavior does not occur in a random or unorganized fashion. Students' behaviors attain meaning from the context—situation or circumstances—that exists in a particular environment. Therefore, a major aspect of functional assessment involves analyzing antecedents and consequences. To review briefly, antecedents refer to the circumstances that exist in the environment before a behavior is exhibited and that prompt its performance. Consequences refer to a change in the environment shortly after a behavior is displayed. Consequences function to either maintain, increase, decrease, or eliminate a behavior. It may be helpful to reexamine Table 1.2 and Figure 1.1, which portray aspects of the A-B-C model of analysis, because functional assessment makes extensive use of this model.

Antecedents are similar to stimulus controls, discussed in Chapter 4. Recall that a stimulus is anything in the environment that prompts, but does not cause, the occurrence of certain behavior.

Behavior Is Purposeful   All behavior is purposeful and serves some function for students. Neel and Cessna (1993) used the term **behavioral intent** to describe the relation between the behavior exhibited and the outcome desired. When students act, even with behaviors considered to be inappropriate, they do so to achieve some result. The desired result, or outcome, can be viewed as the intent or function of the behavior. In turn, the intent of the behavior will affect the form (i.e., appearance) the behavior takes to achieve a desired outcome. The function a behavior serves may be appropriate, but the form it takes may be inappropriate. For example, a student who makes animal noises may be doing so to obtain attention from his peers or to escape a task he perceives to be aversive. There is nothing inherently wrong with a student wanting attention from peers or escaping something perceived to be aversive. However, there are appropriate behaviors, through which, and times and situations in which, to obtain these outcomes.

It is not always easy to identify the function a behavior serves. For example, early researchers conducting functional assessment with children and adults with developmental disabilities identified more than 30 functions of inappropriate behaviors (e.g., Donnellan, Mirenda, Mesaros, & Fassbender, 1984; Evans & Meyer, 1985). Researchers subsequently demonstrated that it is more theoretically parsimonious and practical to condense multiple functions into positive or negative reinforcement (O'Neill et al., 1997; Repp & Horner, 1999). Positive reinforcement includes obtaining attention from others, access to tan-

TABLE 7.2   CLASSIFICATION OF BEHAVIORAL INTENT

Outcome	Description
Power/control	When a student's outcome is the control of an event and/or situation; characterized by a student acting to stay in a situation and keep control.
Protection/escape avoidance	When a student's outcome is to avoid a task or activity, escape a consequence, or terminate or leave a situation.
Attention	When a student becomes the focus of a situation or draws attention to him- or herself, puts him- or herself in the foreground of a situation, discriminates him- or herself from the group for a time; a distinguishing feature is "becoming the focus" as the end product of the behavior.
Acceptance/ affiliation	When a student connects to or relates with others; mutuality of benefit is present.
Expression of self	When a student develops a forum of expression; this could be a statement of needs or perceptions, or a demonstration of skills and talents.
Gratification	When a student is self-rewarded or pleased; a distinguishing characteristic is that the reward is self-determined; others may play agent role.
Justice/revenge	When a student settles a difference, provides restitution, or demonstrates contrition; settling the score.

Source: From "Behavioral intent: Instructional content for students with behavior disorders" by R. S. Neel & K. K. Cessna, 1993, in K. K. Cessna (Ed.), *Instructionally Differentiated Programming: A Needs-Based Approach for Students with Behavior Disorders* (p. 35), Denver, CO: Colorado Department of Education. Copyright 1993 by Kay K. Cessna, Jefferson County Public Schools, Golden, Colorado. Adapted with permission.

gible items or preferred activities, and sensory stimulation. Sensory reinforcement is primarily identified among students with developmental disabilities (e.g., autism and stereotypy), although it has been argued that some students with attention-deficit hyperactivity disorder (ADHD) may engage in certain maladaptive behaviors to gain sensory stimulation (Barkley, 1998). Negative reinforcement includes performing behaviors to either escape something aversive (e.g., a difficult or boring task) or to avoid it altogether.

Not all conceptualizations of behavioral intent focus on positive and negative reinforcement (Maag, 1999, 2001). For example, Neel and Cessna (1993) developed a comprehensive classification system, which is presented in Table 7.2. They believed that human behavior is too complex simply to function in terms of positive and negative reinforcement. Constructs such as power, control, and affiliation may also be valid functions of behavior. Research has yet to corroborate their assumptions although their taxonomy has commonsense appeal. Issues related to the number and types of functions are presented in the last section of this chapter. But suffice it to say here that determining the functions that behaviors serve for students is necessary to subsequent performance of replacement behaviors.

Replacement Behaviors Need to Be Taught   As mentioned previously, replacement behaviors are appropriate behaviors that allow students to obtain the same outcomes as an inappropriate behavior. Behavioral support plans (the by-product of functional assessment) are incomplete if they do not include replacement behaviors that students can be taught and reinforced for displaying. Simply manipulating antecedents and consequences is insufficient and will not help students perform appropriate behaviors in different settings and situations. For example, a student may make animal noises to get the attention of peers sitting around him. We can modify the environment by moving him away from those peers—a manipulation that may effectively reduce or eliminate the animal noises. But what happens when he wants to get the attention of peers in the cafeteria or on the playground? Making animal noises in these situations may alienate him from, rather than involve him with, peers. However, teaching an appropriate way to gain peer attention (e.g., tell a funny story or talk about sports) may be useful for a variety of situations in which we do not have direct control.

Teaching students replacement behaviors will help them use the behaviors in other settings and situations.

Inappropriate behavior does not always need to be decreased if we can identify replacement behaviors. For example, a student may get out of her seat as a way to get the teacher's attention and help. However, simply teaching and reinforcing the student for raising her hand may accomplish the same outcome as her leaving her seat. Consequently, the inappropriate behavior may no longer be performed.

Types of Hypotheses

Functional assessment provides a way of examining relations and generating hypotheses regarding the functions of behaviors and environmental factors contributing to the performance of inappropriate behaviors (Dunlap & Kern, 1993). Generating hypotheses is essential for conducting functional assessment. Hypotheses represent the vehicle for selecting appropriate replacement behaviors, implementing appropriate interventions to reinforce their occurrence, and modifying antecedents and consequences. Three types of hypotheses may be generated for functional assessment: functional, contextual, and curricular.

Functional Hypotheses   A major emphasis of functional assessment is on generating hypotheses related to the function, or intent, a behavior serves. For example, the hypothesis "Juan throws tantrums in order to get the teacher's attention" focuses on the desired outcome or purpose of behavior. Functional hypotheses tend to lead to interventions that address replacement strategy training—teaching an appropriate behavior that serves the same purpose. Therefore, the teacher will want to teach Juan an appropriate way to get her attention (e.g., raise his hand, ask for help, and approach the teacher).

Functional hypotheses are most likely to address the issue of **social validity**—the extent to which the outcomes of intervention enhance the quality of students' lives (Wolf, 1978). Neel and Cessna (1993) cautioned educators that, if the function of a behavior is not addressed by teaching replacement strategies that serve the same function as the problematic behavior but have greater social acceptability, students are unlikely to experience growth in environments outside the controlled classroom setting. Cessna and Borock (1993) believed that outcomes or intents are legitimate social goals. Therefore, programs should be designed to give students immediate access to increased levels of the desired outcome and then to teach replacement behaviors within a context of decreased frustration. In sum, teaching and reinforcing students for using functionally equivalent replacement behaviors enhances the social validity of interventions and, consequently, the likelihood of obtaining maintenance and generalization beyond the walls of the classroom.

Contextual Hypotheses Although the previously described benefits of generating functional hypotheses are substantial, contextual hypotheses appear quite frequently in the functional assessment literature. There may be two reasons for this. First, contextual manipulations (e.g., antecedents and consequences) usually result in rapid changes in behavior. For example, Cooper, Peck, Wacker, and Millard (1993) demonstrated the effectiveness of manipulating task preference and teacher attention to decrease the disruptive behavior of a student with mild disabilities. Second, contextual manipulations are typically within the control of teachers and can usually be designed so that they are implemented with little disruption to classroom routines and activities. For example, Dadson and Horner (1993) reduced the disruptive and nonattentive behaviors of a high school student simply by manipulating certain classroom routines that cued the occurrence of the inappropriate behaviors.

Contextual hypotheses are frequently generated by examining the antecedents and consequences surrounding the performance of inappropriate behavior. One of the most basic, and still one of the best, ways to generate contextual hypotheses is through the use of an A-B-C analysis, first described in Chapter 1. To review briefly, a piece of paper is turned sideways, and three columns are formed and labeled with the words "antecedents," "behavior," and "consequences." Observations are then numbered and recorded according to whether they were antecedents, behavior, or consequences such as those appearing in Figure 1.2.

Contextual hypotheses typically result in interventions aimed at modifying some aspect of the environment. This approach was used by Umbreit (1995) with Corey, an 8-year-old boy with ADHD who displayed disruptive behavior in a general education classroom. Based on data collected from an A-B-C analysis, Umbreit generated two hypotheses: (1) Corey's behavior during independent work would improve if he was seated away from others, and (2) Corey's behavior in group work would improve if the group did not contain his friends. After confirming these hypotheses by manipulating the environment and noting the occurrence of misbehavior, four interventions were implemented: (1) Corey was assigned to a special work area away from his peers, (2) he worked in groups that did not contain his friends, (3) he was taught to request a break when needed, and (4) instructional staff ignored his disruptive behaviors. The results of this intervention were striking: Disruptive behavior was eliminated.

Curricular Hypotheses   Several authors have investigated the use of curricular hypotheses (Dunlap, Kern-Dunlap, Clarke, & Robbins, 1991; Kern, Childs, Dunlap, Clarke, & Falk, 1994). Curricular hypotheses focus on identifying the types of curricular, task, and instructional demands that may prompt the occurrence of inappropriate behavior. These factors are then modified to increase the occurrence of appropriate behavior. The idea of the curriculum being an antecedent to behavior is further elaborated on in Chapter 8. Suffice it to say here that curricular variables such as student preference, choice making, length of task, type of task, and task difficulty can substantially influence the occurrence of undesirable behavior (Dunlap et al., 1991). For example, DePaepe, Shores, Jack, and Denny (1996) found that, when two students with behavioral disorders were presented with difficult math tasks, they engaged in higher rates of disruptive behavior and spent less time on task than when presented with an easy assignment.

The word *curricular* is used loosely to describe hypotheses and manipulations that focus on various aspects of academic tasks: shuffling the curriculum, breaking the task into smaller components, changing the instructional format or strategy, and modifying the materials, to name but a few.

A common hypothesis that has been generated from the research on curricular variables is that difficult academic activities are aversive to some students and that disruptive behavior may function as a means by which they escape or avoid these activities. For example, DePaepe and colleagues (1996) found that the two boys in their study each displayed a similar pattern of skipping problems that were more complex during difficult conditions even though they both had been directed to complete each problem. In addition, one of the boys engaged in the alternative activity of drawing pictures on the back of the difficult math materials. This self-initiated drawing activity may have allowed him to escape the difficult task. When the boys were presented with easy tasks, their disruptive behaviors decreased and their academic performance improved. These findings resulted in such curricular modifications as shortening task periods, assigning relevant tasks, and allowing student choice of activity or materials.

STAGES OF FUNCTIONAL ASSESSMENT

Conducting a functional assessment entails following a certain procedure to arrive at socially valid interventions (i.e., behavioral support plans). This procedure involves (1) defining a behavior, (2) interviewing knowledgeable adults (and, when appropriate, students) about occurrences and nonoccurrences of the behavior, (3) observing occurrences and nonoccurrences of the behavior, (4) developing hypotheses about the potential function of, and effect of context on, the behavior, and (5) verifying or testing hypotheses by manipulating controlling variables (Foster-Johnson & Dunlap, 1993; Fowler & Schnacker, 1994; Mayer, 1996; Tobin, 1994).

There are a variety of models for implementing functional assessment. However, one approach that has empirical support for classroom use is the framework developed by Dunlap and Kern (1993). Their functional assessment process consists of two stages: (1) hypothesis development and (2) hypothesis testing. Note that the process of functional assessment is not performed in a one-shot, 30-minute session, but is continuous and ongoing. Students who display challenging behaviors quickly adapt to interventions and find ways to defeat our efforts. Students' behaviors do not become challenging overnight, and they are not fixed overnight. Therefore, we should view functional assessment the same way we do curriculum and instruction—as always present and evolving to meet the needs of students. This means that behavioral support plans (the culmination of functional assessment) must also be flexible and address areas of concern.

Before exploring the steps involved in each stage, let us take a brief look at an "advance organizer" for subsequent information. Functional assessment begins when we identify a student whose behavior is interfering with her or his own and/or peers' academic and social progress. However, we may have only a vague idea of the behavior of concern. For example, we may say that the student is "disruptive," "off task," "uncooperative," "hyperactive," or "under achieving." Sometimes we may initially use more objective terms to describe the behavior. In either case, the first step is to interview knowledgeable adults, peers, and the student (if possible) about the circumstances under which the behavior occurs. We then collect behavioral observations of the student in the settings and situations identified in the interviews as areas of concern. The purpose of these behavioral observations is to confirm our interview findings, to identify any discrepancies, and to begin to refine the definition of the behavior of concern. Next, we collect additional behavioral observations using a scatter

Unlike traditional assessment, functional assessment is ongoing. Because the information from functional assessment leads to socially valid interventions, its application is continuous. Teachers should have the mindset that functional assessment (in one shape or another) is conducted for every challenging behavior students display.

plot technique. This technique helps us pinpoint specific days, times, and activities during which the challenging behavior is most likely to occur. Then we conduct an A-B-C analysis to isolate the immediate antecedents and consequences surrounding the behavior. Using the functional assessment hypothesis generation protocol developed by Larson and Maag (1998), we define the behavior precisely in objective terms and generate hypotheses to test. Hypotheses testing (also called functional analysis) is accomplished by observing, recording, and graphing the target behavior before and after making curricular or contextual modifications or teaching a replacement behavior. This information is used to write a behavioral support plan, as described in the next main section of this chapter.

Stage 1: Hypothesis Development

The entire process of functional assessment can be conceptualized as a series of hypothesis testing sequences (Elliott, Gresham, & Heffer, 1987). Hypotheses, or our best guesses, are generated based on available information collected from interviews and observations in order to determine probable relations between students' behavior and environmental variables. Elliott and colleagues described this process as proceeding from global behavioral information to more specific information. For example, we might observe that a student continually interrupts peers' conversations or games during recess (one of the diagnostic criteria for ADHD). A traditional hypothesis would be that this inappropriate behavior is caused by the underlying ADHD. However, another hypothesis may be that she interrupts conversations because that is the only way she can get attention from her peers. And although her peers may respond to the intrusion negatively, negative attention often is better than no attention at all. From this general information, more specific hypotheses can be generated and tested. For example, we might manipulate the composition of the peer group or reinforce peers for ignoring the target student's inappropriate behavior and providing positive feedback if she engages in more appropriate behavior. If the appropriate behavior results from these manipulations, then we have determined the functional relations among the behavior of interrupting, the outcome desired by the student, and the impact of her peers' responses to the behavior.

To begin the process of developing hypotheses, it is necessary to engage in four activities: (1) Pinpoint a behavior of concern, (2) interview adults, peers, and the student of concern (when applicable) to determine environmental factors that affect behavior, (3) directly observe the target behavior in a natural setting, and (4) refine the definition of the behavior and generate hypotheses. While engaging in these activities, it is important to remember that hypothesis testing simply represents a best guess. As such, we may want to generate several hypotheses. Furthermore, we should not become discouraged if our first hypothesis does not pan out. The very nature of functional assessment lends itself to disproving hypotheses as much as proving them. In addition, disproving a hypothesis provides information useful in developing the next hypothesis to test.

Defining a Target Behavior   Teachers involved in functional assessment need to precisely define a behavior so that its occurrences and nonoccurrences can be reliably noted. O'Neill and colleagues (1997) suggested that an operational definition of a behavior should include its topography (appearance), frequency (number), duration (length), and intensity (severity). For example, defining a behavior as "strikes peers on back with open hand for 2 seconds five times a day" is preferable to "hits peers a lot." Classroom teachers, who usually work most closely with students, may be able to provide the greatest specificity in behavioral definitions. When multiple persons are involved in a functional assessment, properly defining a behavior provides all involved parties with criteria by which to judge the importance of the behavior and ensures that everyone is observing the same thing. It may be necessary to modify the definition of the target behavior after collecting information from interviews and behavioral observations.

Interviewing   Interviewing adults and students (where applicable) is an initial step to understanding the conditions under which students' behavior occurs. The use of interviews presupposes that the functional assessment will be a collaborative process between two or more school personnel. The more people who are interviewed, the greater the likelihood that no important information will be omitted.

Dunlap and Kern (1993) recommended that at least two school personnel involved with the student and his or her parents be interviewed. The purpose of interviewing multiple people is to determine whether certain behaviors occur in some, but not other, contexts and conditions. In addition, it is helpful if both male and female teachers are interviewed, because students' behaviors sometimes vary depending on the gender of the adult.

Dunlap and Kern (1993) also recommended that the interviews focus on two core questions: (1) Under what conditions or circumstances is the behavior most likely to occur? and (2) Under what conditions or circumstances does the behavior rarely or never occur? Figure 7.2 shows a sample interview form. The information acquired through interviews is still fairly global and often appears in nonbehavioral terms. For example, one teacher may say that a student is off task during independent seat-work whereas another may say that the student is inattentive during lectures. "Off task" and "inattentive" are not specific behaviors. Nevertheless, this information gives a contextual starting point from

How long has respondent known the student? _____

Approximate time spent with the student per week _____

1. What do you see as the major problems? Prioritize problems from most to least severe.

2. In what situations do these behaviors occur?

3. In what situations is behavior most appropriate?

4. What are the student's greatest strengths?

5. What are the student's greatest weaknesses?

6. Why do you think the student acts in the way s/he does?

7. What do you think needs to be done to help the student? How?

8. What does the student like the most?

9. What does the student like the least?

10. What events or actions seem to trigger inappropriate behavior during:

    teaching   lunch

    recess   unstructured time

11. What can be done to increase the likelihood of appropriate behavior during:

    teaching   lunch

    recess   unstructured time

FIGURE 7.2

Sample Interview Form

From "Assessment and intervention for children within the instructional curriculum" by G. Dunlap & L. Kern, 1993, in J. Reichle & D. Wacker (Eds.), *Communicative Alternatives to Challenging Behavior: Integrating Functional Assessment and Intervention Strategies* (p. 190). Baltimore, MD: Brookes. Copyright 1993 by Paul H. Brookes Publishing, P.O. Box 10624, Baltimore, MD 21285-0624. Adapted with permission.

which to refine the definition of the behavior and formulate a hypothesis that can be tested using direct observation methods.

The interview form in Figure 7.2 is fairly short and easy to use. These characteristics are important because most interviewing techniques originally were developed for use by teachers working with students with severe disabilities whose cognitive and interpersonal skills were limited. Consequently, the forms or protocols relied heavily on adults' interpretations of students' behaviors, tended to be quite lengthy, and required substantial collaboration among persons involved in the functional assessment. In contrast, the form in Figure 7.2 can be used by teachers conducting functional assessment in general education classrooms with minimal consultative services. An alternative approach is to have classroom teachers engage in a process of self-interview/reflection that replaces the need for outside interviewers. Although there are certainly ratio-

Materials / Tasks (What is the student being asked to do?)	Appropriate Student Behaviors		Inappropriate Student Behaviors	
	Ask Question	Finish Work	Talk Out	Out of Seat
Paper-Pencil			///	//
Listening Activity			//	//// /
Class Discussion	//	//		
Workbook			////	///
Individual Lesson			////	////
Group Lesson	///	///		
Transition			////	
Lecture	//	////		
Free Time				

Student: Lisa Lightly   Date: 3/21
Observer: Ms. Bishop   Time Began: 9:00   Time Ended: 9:20

FIGURE **7.3**

Sample Behavior Observation Chart

nale for the inclusion of multiple perspectives in the observation/identification process (Cessna & Borock, 1993), the classroom teacher still remains the most significant source of information on the occurrence of students' behavior over time.

Observing Behavior   Although important information may be obtained from interviewing others, it is important to corroborate these results, identify discrepancies, and determine specific controlling environmental variables through the use of direct observations of behavior. Useful behavioral observation tools and techniques include the behavior observation chart, the scatter plot, and A-B-C analysis. These three techniques are used in the order presented as a way to obtain increasingly detailed information about the conditions under which the behavior of concern is performed.

Behavior observation charts and scatter plots can be easily modified for use in a variety of settings and under many conditions.

Behavior observation charts like the one shown in Figure 7.3 are used to confirm information acquired through interviews and also to identify any discrepancies. In this chart, we list the various materials, tasks, and activities that students are involved in during the day along the vertical axis. We then record, in each column, the types of appropriate and inappropriate behaviors observed for each activity/task listed on the vertical axis. We can now compare this information to that obtained through interviews. In Figure 7.3, two appropriate behaviors ("ask question" and "finish work") and two inappropriate behaviors ("talks out" and "out of seat") were targeted. From the data appearing in this figure, the student engaged in inappropriate behaviors during individual-type lessons/assignments and transition, and behaved appropriately during group-type lessons and activities. This suggests that the student may not possess the skills to work independently and so may misbehave as a way to escape the task or lesson. But this hypothesis requires further observation before testing it in stage 2 of functional assessment. An alternative use of the behavior observation chart is to list two or three specific appropriate and inappropriate behaviors obtained from interviews. We then make tally marks every time one of those behaviors occurs during the task/activity appearing on the vertical axis.

We should now have an emerging picture of the behavior of concern and the situations in which it occurs. The original behavior of concern may now be more precisely defined and observed using the **scatter plot** method appearing in Figure 7.4. The scatter plot, which was developed by Foster-Johnson and Dunlap (1993), helps us further determine not only the settings and situations

---

Student: Lisa Lightly   Date Began: 3/21

Observer: Ms. Bishop   Date Ended: 4/2

Target Behavior: Talking without permission

Directions: Make a tally mark each time the student exhibits the target behavior.

Activity	Time	Days									
		M	T	W	TH	F	M	T	W	TH	F
Warm up	8:30–9:00	### //	/		/		///		/		//
Reading Groups	9:00–9:30	//		/		///	### //	//		/	
Spelling	9:30–10:00	////	/	//	/		///		//		
Recess	10:00–10:30										
Math	10:30–11:00	///		//	///	//	### //	//	///	///	////
Lunch	11:00–11:30										
Social Studies	11:30–12:00	###	///	/		/	### //	/		/	
Science	12:00–12:30	///	//		///	//	////	/	/		/
Catch-up	12:30–1:00										

FIGURE **7.4**

Sample Scatter Plot Observation Form

From "Using functional assessment to develop effective, individualized interventions for challenging behaviors" by L. Foster-Johnson & G. Dunlap, 1993, *Teaching Exceptional Children, 25*(3), p. 48. Copyright 1993 by the Council for Exceptional Children. Adapted with permission.

in which the behavior occurs, but also the number of times the behavior occurs in a given situation and day.

In a scatter plot, the days for several weeks are listed on the horizontal axis. This results in a grid in which instances (or noninstances) of a behavior can be charted over a period of weeks, thereby making it possible to identify certain patterns. For example, suppose an examination of the scatter plot in Figure 7.4 reveals that math period seemed to be an important antecedent for the occurrence of problem behavior. This determination is made by making tally marks for the number of times the behavior occurs in the appropriate box. The behavior of concern also appeared to occur more often on Mondays. Conversely, recess, lunch, and catch-up had no episodes of inappropriate behavior. This suggests that these activities may be used as reinforcers to maintain appropriate behavior at other times.

The final behavioral observations we make during the hypothesis generation phase of functional assessment involve A-B-C analysis. This enables us to pinpoint specific antecedents and consequences affecting the performance of the behavior of concern. For example, again suppose that information obtained from a scatter plot indicates that math period is an important antecedent for the behavior. Therefore, we conduct a fine-grained A-B-C analysis during math period—not only on Mondays but also on another day of the week, because the behavior of concern occurs more on Mondays than any other day of the week. We may discover that task demands on Mondays differ from those on other days. Once we have done several A-B-C analyses, we can generate hypotheses to be tested.

Generating Hypotheses   Once data are collected from interviews and direct observation, testable hypotheses may be generated. In many instances, this requires collaborative efforts between consultants and classroom teachers. Dunlap and colleagues (1993) reported that hypotheses resulting in effective interventions for five elementary students with emotional disturbances were generated when consultants and classroom teachers shared information. Other researchers, however, have reported that classroom teachers can generate hypotheses and effective interventions by themselves (Cooper et al., 1993).

To improve the ability of teachers to generate hypotheses, Larson and Maag (1998) developed the protocol that appears in Figure 7.5. This protocol is designed to address all the steps in the hypothesis development stage of functional assessment, enabling teachers to formulate plans for contextual and curricular manipulations and replacement behavior training with little or no consultation from professionals. Combining elements of other checklists and interview and observation forms, the protocol guides teachers through the process of (1) operationally defining a behavior, (2) identifying setting events and functions (intent) associated with the occurrence of the behavior, and (3) conducting a

I. BEHAVIOR DEFINITION

A. Definition Components: Operationally defining the problem behavior is the first step in conducting an effective functional assessment. In order to arrive at a reliable definition that can be observed and measured, answer the following questions:

1. What does the problem behavior look like? (check one that is of greatest concern)

___ talks out/disrupts class   ___ tardy/late to class
___ insubordination   ___ out of seat/place
___ not completing work   ___ excessive movement/fidgeting
___ inappropriate language   ___ threatening
___ destruction of property   ___ theft
___ aggression   ___ other (specify) _____

2. How is the behavior performed (topography)? *Consider the following categories: type of physical movement; use of objects*

_____

_____

_____

3. How long does it last when it occurs (duration)? *Check box that corresponds to the approximate length of action and circle the appropriate time measurement*

___ 1 – 2 seconds/minutes   ___ 15 – 20 seconds/minutes
___ 3 – 5 seconds/minutes   ___ 20 – 25 seconds/minutes
___ 5 – 10 seconds/minutes   ___ 25 – 30 seconds/minutes
___ 10 – 15 seconds/minutes   ___ other _____

4. How often does it occur (frequency)? *Indicate the rate of occurrence using formula:*

_____ times per _____. *Ex: three or four times an hour.*

5. How damaging or destructive is the behavior (intensity)? *Ex: with no physical injury.*

_____

_____

_____

6. Where does the behavior occur and who is typically involved (setting)?

_____

_____

_____

continues

B. Definition Summary: Using the answers to the questions above, write an operational definition of the target behavior. *Ex: During transition periods when new students are present, Jane uses aggression by striking peers with an open hand on the back for one to two seconds three or four times a period with no physical injury.*

_____

_____

_____

II. FACTOR IDENTIFICATION

A. Setting Events: Using the checklists below, identify factors that usually occur prior to or as a result of the problem behavior.

1. Factors that appear to set off and/or precede the problem behavior:

Teacher behaviors:
___ Task explanation/demand
___ Performance feedback/evaluation
___ Lesson presentation/lecture
___ Teacher reprimand
___ Teacher encouragement/praise
___ Individual attention to student
___ Independent work/lack of attention

Student behaviors:
___ Drowsy/sleepy appearance
___ Physical complaints (hunger, pain, etc.)
___ Disturbed affect (sad, angry appearance)
___ Excessive motor activity (fidgety, restless)
___ Peer attention (negative)
___ Peer attention (positive)

Environmental factors:
___ Elevated/excessive noise levels
___ Presence of unusual/extra adult(s)
___ Presence of unusual/extra peer(s)
___ Transition task/activity (expected/routine)
___ Transition task/activity (unexpected/irregular)
___ Access/availability of preferred activity/task
___ Termination of preferred activity/task
___ Access/availability of food

2. Factors that appear to maintain/follow the occurrence of problem behavior:

Teacher behaviors:
___ Teacher reprimand
___ Teacher encouragement/praise
___ Task removal
___ Withdrawal of teacher attention/ignoring

continues

Student behaviors:
___ Peer attention (negative)
___ Peer attention/affirmation (positive)
___ Withdrawal of peer attention/isolation

Environmental factors:
___ Access/availability of preferred activity/task
___ Removal of student to alternative setting

B. Behavioral Intent Identification: Using the checklist below, identify the possible functions or outcomes that the behavior may serve for the student. If more than one function appears to be a reasonable explanation, rank order your responses from 1 to 3 with 1 being the most likely function of the behavior.

___ Attention   ___ Acceptance/affiliation/approval
___ Tangible reward   ___ Sensory stimulation
___ Gain access to objects/activities   ___ Expression of self
___ Gratification   ___ Justice/revenge
___ Escape/avoid task/event   ___ Escape/avoid attention
___ Power/control   ___ Other_____

III. OBSERVATION

Observer: _____   Date Began: _____

Target Behavior: _____

_____

ACTIVITY	TIME	DAYS									
		M	T	W	TH	F	M	T	W	TH	F

continues

IV. FUNCTIONAL HYPOTHESIS

  A. Hypothesis Statement: Using the information from sections I, II, and III, construct an hypothesis statement according to the form.

When _____
                                        (identify setting events)

_____ will _____
            student   behavior

in order to _____
                                    (intended outcome/function)

  B. Functional Analysis Plan: In order to test the hypothesis, the following functional analysis will be attempted:

  1. Contextual Modification: (What changes in environment and/or teacher behaviors will be attempted?)

_____

_____

_____

  2. Curricular Accommodation: (What changes in instructional materials/techniques will be attempted?)

_____

_____

_____

  3. Replacement Strategy: (What new behaviors/strategies will be taught?)

_____

_____

_____

FIGURE 7.5

Functional Assessment Hypotheses Formulation Protocol

From "Applying functional assessment in general education classrooms: Issues and recommendations" by P. J. Larson & J. W. Maag, 1998, *Remedial and Special Education*, 19(6), 338–349. Copyright 1998 by Pro-Ed. Reprinted with permission.

systematic observation of the behavior. The use of the protocol culminates in the development of a hypotheses statement and the formulation of a functional analysis plan.

Stage 2: Hypothesis Testing

The second stage of functional assessment, often referred to as functional analysis, consists of testing hypotheses by systematically manipulating contextual and curricular variables and teaching a replacement behavior while observing these effects on the target behavior (Mace, Lalli, & Lalli, 1991). An example using two manipulations—curricular and replacement behavior training—in response to the problem behavior of "tantruming" illustrates the functional analysis (hypothesis testing) phase of functional assessment.

Suppose we hypothesize that the function (intent) of a student's tantruming is to escape from a difficult task. We observe the occurrences of tantruming for several sessions and then institute a curricular manipulation while continuing to observe the occurrences of tantruming. The curricular manipulation may be to replace the difficult task with an easy, high-interest task while holding other behavioral and environmental variables constant. If tantruming decreases, then the hypothesis that the behavior serves an escape function has been confirmed. The logic is simple: If a student tantrums to escape a difficult task (e.g., sent to time-out, the hallway, or the principal's office) then she has no reason to tantrum to escape an easy, high-interest task. The difficult task can be reintroduced to further corroborate this hypothesis: If tantruming increases, then the difficult task most likely is a relevant and controlling variable.

We can also test whether tantruming serves the function of escape by teaching the student a replacement behavior. Suppose we present her with three possible replacement behaviors to use when the task becomes too difficult: (1) Raise her hand to ask for help, (2) raise her hand to ask for a break, or (3) raise her hand to ask for an easier task. She might initially select the replacement behavior she wants to try, and we reinforce her for using it. If tantruming decreases, then the hypothesis that it serves an escape function is validated. The logic is straightforward: The student should have no reason to continuing tantruming to escape the difficult task because she has been given, and reinforced for using, a more appropriate behavior that serves the function of escape.

The two manipulations described previously demonstrate the general approach for testing a hypothesis. However, four specific steps should be followed:

1. Operationally define the target behavior.
2. Select a recording technique for observing and counting the target behavior.
3. Observe the target behavior before and after manipulating variables (e.g., curricular, contextual, or functional).
4. Graph the results of behavioral observations to provide a visual representation of the effects of the manipulations.

Let as examine these steps in detail, again using the example of tantruming.

Throughout the hypothesis generation phase of functional assessment, the definition of the target behavior is refined as more information is obtained. However, by the time the protocol appearing in Figure 7.5 is completed, the

The importance of operational definitions was discussed in Chapter 5 in the section "The Stranger Test." That information is equally applicable here.

target behavior should be precisely defined using objective (rather than subjective) terms. It is the first step in testing our hypothesis. You may want to review the information on objective versus subjective descriptors of behavior in Chapter 1, as well as the stranger test in Chapter 5. In our example, tantruming is defined as "stomping foot on ground while slamming book on desk or tabletop."

The second step in testing our hypothesis is to observe the behavior over several days or sessions before we implement the manipulation. We must also select a recording technique with which to document the target behavior. Recall that with these techniques (described in detail in Chapter 5) we can record how many times the behavior occurs (frequency), how long the behavior lasts (duration), or both. In this case, we record the number of times tantruming occurs (frequency) because it is fairly easy to tally the number of times the student stomps her foot and slams books. We want to collect at least five separate observations of the target behavior before we implement the manipulation. The reason is that we will plot the number for each observation on a graph and connect them with lines. Plotting five or more numbers enables us to visually inspect trends in the graphed behavioral observations.

The third step is to implement the manipulation while continuing to observe and record occurrences of the target behavior—in our example, the number of times the student tantrums when completing a task. We want to observe the behavior at least five times while the manipulation is in effect for the same reason as stated previously: to visually inspect the plotted frequency trend in the graphed numbers.

The fourth step is to graph the numbers from our behavioral observations before and during manipulation. It is preferable to plot the numbers of the behavioral observations on the graph after each observation, rather than waiting until the end of the manipulation period, so that we can determine how well the manipulation is working. Our graph will have a vertical and a horizontal axis. We can label the vertical axis "Number of Tantrums" and the horizontal axis either "Days" (if we observe the behavior only once a day) or "Sessions" (if we observe the behavior more than one time a day). Next, we write the letter "A" and the word "Baseline" at the top of the graph corresponding to our plotted numbers prior to instituting a manipulation. Then we draw a vertical line after the last baseline observation number to indicate that we are now changing the conditions under which the target behavior is observed. Finally, we label the second phase (to the right of the vertical phase change line) with the letter "B" and the word "Manipulation."

Contextual, curricular, and replacement behavior training manipulations form the basis for developing effective behavioral support plans.

Figures 7.6, 7.7, and 7.8 depict line graphs of behavioral observations before and after making contextual, curricular, and functional manipulations, respectively, for the target behavior "number of tantrums." From these graphs, we can determine how effective each manipulation is at reducing the number

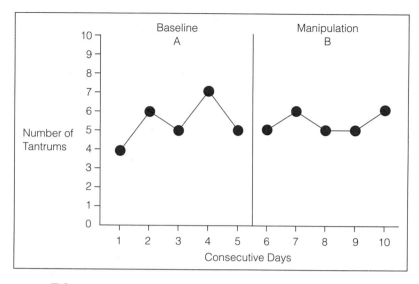

FIGURE **7.6**

Contextual Manipulation (moving student)

A simple AB design, as described in Chapter 6, is used to evaluate the effectiveness of our manipulations.

of tantrums in response to difficult work. These graphs, and their corresponding manipulations, help us determine whether tantruming is maintained by escape and which manipulation is most effective.

Figure 7.6 presents a graph of the tantrums the student displayed before and after the contextual manipulation of moving her to the opposite side of the room. This manipulation may be undertaken if we believe that the student tantrums to escape sitting next to several peers whom she fears may make fun of her inability to complete the work. What should become apparent from this graph is that the frequency of the student's tantruming remained relatively stable. Therefore, she did not seem to be trying to escape any particular peers.

Given the data in Figure 7.6, a different type of manipulation may be warranted to test the escape function of tantruming. Figure 7.7 presents a graph of the results of the curricular manipulation of giving the student an easy, high-interest task. As a result of this curricular manipulation, the frequency of tantruming decreased substantially during the B (manipulation) phase. Therefore, the curricular hypothesis that she tantrumed to escape difficult work appears to be confirmed.

Based on the data appearing in Figure 7.7, a functional manipulation, teaching a replacement behavior, was undertaken. Specifically, in Figure 7.8, the number of tantrums was recorded before and after teaching the student the replacement behavior "asking for help." As Figure 7.8 shows, this replacement behavior also resulted in a decrease in tantruming. More importantly, replace-

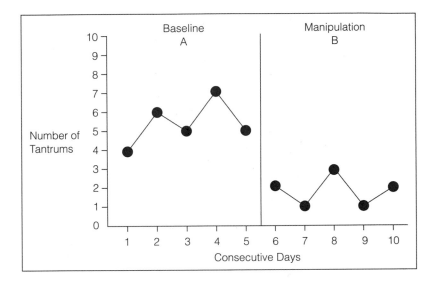

FIGURE 7.7

Curricular Manipulation (providing easy, high-interest work)

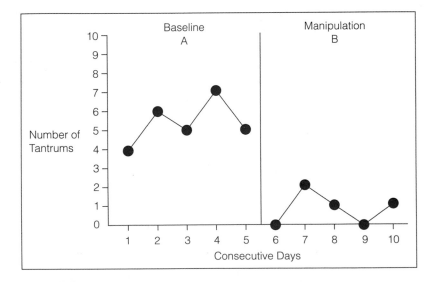

FIGURE 7.8

Functional Manipulation (asking for help)

ment behaviors have a greater likelihood of resulting in generalized and durable change in the target behavior because the student can use them in a number of situations when presented with a difficult task.

WRITING BEHAVIORAL SUPPORT PLANS

Behavioral support plans are formulated based on information collected from functional assessment (O'Neill et al., 1997). They represent our best strategy for keeping inappropriate behavior from resurfacing. They also provide recommendations that other teachers and school personnel who interact with students can follow. O'Neill and colleagues (1997) described several components of a good behavioral support plan, including the following:

Behavioral support plans should be written so that any school personnel can read them and implement their recommendations.

- *They describe behavior.* That is, they define in detail the changes expected in the behavior of relevant teachers, paraeducators, and other school personnel (as well as family members, when applicable).
- *They are built from functional assessment results.* This information enables teachers and others to identify specific changes in the classroom that will influence patterns of behavior.
- *They are technically sound.* They achieve this by applying the principles of behavior discussed in Chapter 4.
- *They make problem behaviors irrelevant.* This involves identifying those situations (antecedents) that give rise to problem behaviors and organizing the environment to reduce the likelihood that these conditions are encountered. For example, the behavior of a student who screams as a way of getting attention in an otherwise boring environment may become irrelevant if a more active and interesting schedule of daily events is developed.
- *They make problem behaviors ineffective.* This involves providing alternative ways of obtaining reinforcers. For example, moving a student who screams to get peer attention away from peers or teaching the student how to get peer attention appropriately (e.g., by sharing a favorite story or movie with them) makes the behavior ineffective.
- *They include a replacement behavior.* The key element in behavioral support plans is identifying replacement behaviors, describing how they will be taught, and developing a intervention to reinforce students who perform them.

With these considerations in mind, we are ready to write a behavioral support plan. These plans typically contain four sections: (1) a summary of the findings, (2) the general approach, (3) areas of concern, and (4) monitoring and evaluation procedures.

Summary of the Findings

Behavioral support plans typically begin with a summary of the findings from both the hypothesis generation and hypothesis testing phases of the functional assessment. It is important to restate the final operational definition of the target behavior that was the subject of the manipulation(s) so that anyone unfamiliar with the initial functional assessment has a clear understanding of the nature of the problem.

The initial section of the behavioral support plan also contains a summary of the manipulations conducted. This information lets readers know what manipulations were most effective. In many cases, behavioral support plans are a logical extension of manipulations conducted during functional analysis. Consequently, this information is often translated into accommodations and/or interventions for students (Dunlap & Kern, 1993).

The General Approach

This section of the behavioral support plan describes the intervention procedures. The goal is to identify the set of procedures that make problem behaviors irrelevant, inefficient, and ineffective. In most cases, this section includes at least four subsections: (1) setting event strategies, (2) instructional interventions, (3) consequent interventions, and (4) future replacement behaviors. The section should clearly define what school personnel will do to reduce the problem behaviors.

Setting events refer to those antecedents that cue or prompt the occurrence of the target behavior. This section focuses on the types of antecedent modifications that are recommended to decrease future occurrences of the target behavior. Examples of possible setting event manipulations include (but are not limited to) shuffling the student's schedule, changing class size and seating arrangements, using more or fewer desks or study carrels, and using partitions. Whatever the instructional antecedents, a rationale should be provided.

Instructional interventions focus on changing some aspect of the instruction students receive. Many behavior problems arise because students either lack the prerequisite skills to perform the task or find the task boring or irrelevant. Therefore, potential interventions include embedding the task in a relevant context. For example, instead of teaching the multiplication of decimals in isolation, this skill could be presented within the context of a student computing his favorite baseball players' batting averages. In addition, criterion-referenced testing (described in Chapter 8) can be used to assess students' instructional levels. This assessment is important when assigning students independent paper-and-pencil seat-work. To work independently, students should be at least 85 to 95 percent proficient at a task with teacher guidance.

Instructional interventions may also focus on how instruction is presented. For example, the student who tantrums to escape a difficult lesson may perform better while working in a cooperative learning group or receiving peer tutoring because others can give her ongoing feedback.

Consequent interventions—as the term suggests—focus on the consequences of misbehavior. Good behavioral support plans include positive reinforcement interventions such as those described in Chapter 9. Positive reinforcement serves three functions: (1) promotes the use of replacement behaviors, (2) reinforces the absence of the target behavior (see Chapter 10), and (3) reinforces peers who ignore the student displaying the inappropriate behavior. Recall from Chapter 4 that we can reinforce peers for ignoring students' inappropriate behavior as a way to extinguish it.

Identifying replacement behaviors is the final task in the "general approach" section of the behavioral support plan. Describing potential replacement behaviors is important because doing so helps students generalize the results of the functional assessment to other settings. The basic idea is that, by teaching students appropriate behaviors that serve the same function as the inappropriate behavior, and reinforcing them for performing the appropriate behaviors, the inappropriate behavior is less likely to occur. For example, teaching a student to ask his teacher for a break may allow him to escape an aversive task just as effectively as did making animal noises. And the student sees that asking for a break actually works better (i.e., he is reinforced rather than punished) than making animal noises, he is more likely to perform the behavior in other situations and settings.

It is relatively simple to identify replacement behaviors when we think in terms of response classes. Recall from Chapter 4 that a response class is a group of behaviors that share some common characteristic—most notably, the same function. In this case, we generate lists of appropriate behaviors (e.g., asking for help, requesting a break, or asking for an easier task) that allow students to escape aversive tasks. We then ask the students to list any additional behaviors that might serve this same function and to rank order the behaviors. Finally, we teach and reinforce students for performing the replacement behavior. And we try to continually identify possible replacement behaviors so that students' repertoires eventually expand, thus further promoting generalization.

Areas of Concern

No behavioral support plan is foolproof. Like functional assessments, behavioral support plans should be flexible and evolve along with the needs of students. Here, a simple yet profound axiom applies: Take what students give you. As this axiom points out, the very nature of students with problematic behaviors represents a challenge. No one intervention will work forever. This suggests that functional assessment is ongoing—we are always trying to find new and more effective manipulations that lead to improved behavioral support plans. This process is enhanced when we plan for unexpected events that become areas of concern. There are two main areas of concern in a behavioral support plan: (1) key routines and (2) difficult situations.

Key routines are crucial components in responding to the most dangerous and difficult behaviors. Although we want to develop proactive procedures that decrease the likelihood of problem behaviors occurring (through antecedent and instructional modification), we should nevertheless assume that any problem behaviors displayed by students in the past will recur in the future. A behavioral support plan that does not have clearly defined procedures for responding to these difficult situations is incomplete. Therefore, our key routines should describe difficult behaviors and present strategies for preventing their occurrence. For example, in a previous example, three manipulations were described for a student who tantrumed to escape a difficult task. Key routines address other possible inappropriate behaviors the student may display to escape the task, such as poking other students or making animal noises. We also want to reiterate strategies to reduce the likelihood of peers inadvertently reinforcing the student for performing these behaviors.

Describing difficult situations goes hand in hand with outlining key routines. Here, we want to elaborate on one or two specific situations that past experience indicates may trigger other problematic behaviors. For example, if we identify "animal noises" as a second way that the student escapes a difficult task, specific interventions should be emphasized to remedy this problem.

Monitoring and Evaluation Procedures

Behavioral support plans should be monitored and evaluated on an ongoing basis. The two key questions for any plan are (1) Is the plan having any impact on the behavior of the personnel in the target setting? and (2) Is the plan having any impact on the behavior of the target student (O'Neill et al., 1997)? The section of the plan that defines monitoring and evaluation procedures should indicate the system that will be used for collecting data and the process for data review (how often and by whom). In most cases, the behavioral recording technique used during functional analysis can be used to monitor progress. In a previous example, the frequency of tantruming before and during manipulations was recorded and graphed by counting its occurrence. This observation, recording, and graphing process should continue throughout the school year. The only modification is that, instead of collecting and graphing behavioral observations daily, we can collect them once or twice a week. This provides us with information more sporadically but over a longer period, enabling us to assess the long-term effects of the behavioral support plan.

ISSUES IN FUNCTIONAL ASSESSMENT

Several issues have an impact on the way functional assessment is conducted and the results we obtained. These include (1) the role of individual-specific deficiencies in selecting replacement behaviors, (2) the collection of information using naturalistic versus contrived methods, (3) problems related to identifying behavioral intent, and (4) an expanded repertoire of potential functions to assess.

Individual-Specific Deficiencies and Replacement Behaviors

The importance of selecting replacement behaviors was previously covered. However, there is an important issue related to this selection process: Can the student perform it? Just because we have selected a replacement behavior does not automatically mean that the student knows how to perform it. Replacement behaviors are similar to academic behaviors in that students do not automatically come to school knowing them—they must be taught. For students to perform a replacement behavior, they must possess the requisite skills, assemble and sequence subtasks into a task strategy, select a task strategy, and monitor their performance (Maag, 1992). Deficiencies in any of these individual-specific areas may prevent students from learning and performing replacement behaviors.

Deficiency areas can be condensed into behavioral, cognitive, and self-control. The most important area, and the easiest to assess, is behavioral deficiency. Functional assessment cannot proceed unless students possess the requisite skills for performing replacement behaviors. Cognitive and self-control deficiencies are more difficult to assess, and doing so requires that students have the requisite skills for performing replacement behaviors. Consequently, this section presents a specific plan for determining a behavioral skill deficiency but only an overview of self-control and cognitive deficiencies (Chapters 12 and 13, respectively, cover these two deficiencies in detail).

Figure 7.9 presents a model of behavior developed by Howell and Nolet (2000) and modified here to address the role of deficiencies in the performance of a replacement behavior. In Figure 7.9, inappropriate behavior is the focus of functional assessment. Conducting functional assessment helps us identify the function (purpose) the inappropriate behavior serves, and in addition to po-

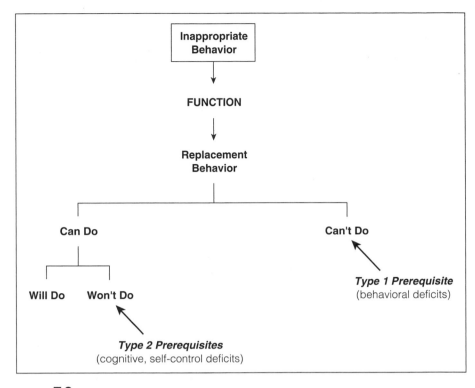

FIGURE 7.9

Model for Understanding Deficiencies Related to Performing a Replacement Behavior

From *Curriculum-based evaluation: Teaching and decision making* (3rd ed.) (p. 390) by K. W. Howell & V. Nolet, 2000, Belmont, CA: Wadsworth/Thomson Learning. Copyright 2000 by Wadsworth/Thomson Learning. Adapted with permission.

tentially offering contextual and curricular modifications, we want to teach students a replacement behavior. The key issue at this point is whether students can perform the replacement behavior. If students can and will perform the behavior, then no further training is necessary. Instead, we develop a reinforcement program—like those described in Chapter 9—to reinforce its occurrence. Eventually, we can phase out the reinforcement program because students will discover that performing the replacement behavior is reinforcing in and of itself, in that it results in the same outcome as the inappropriate behaviors.

However, some students can't perform the replacement behavior because they lack the requisite behavioral skills. For example, a student can't join in a peer group conversation as a way to appropriately obtain attention if he does not know how to identify a peer group, stand an appropriate distance away, maintain eye contact with the person talking, and so forth; Table 7.3 summarizes the requisite skills for joining such a conversation. Sometimes students can perform the replacement behavior but nevertheless won't. In this case,

TABLE 7.3	**REQUISITE SKILLS FOR JOINING IN A PEER GROUP CONVERSATION**

1. Locates a peer group
2. Stands at an appropriate distance
3. Looks at the person talking
4. Waits for a pause in the conversation
5. Asks to join in the conversation
6. Waits for a response
7. Says something relevant to the topic
8. Waits for a response

they may have some cognitive deficiency (e.g., lack the problem-solving strategies or interpret the situation incorrectly) or be unable to monitor and evaluate their own and others' behaviors (self-control deficit).

It is important to understand that when students won't perform a replacement behavior, something has interfered with their selecting it. They may not have consciously, and with intent to irritate us, selected to do so. Moreover, selecting an inappropriate behavior is not the same thing as deciding to behave inappropriately. We select behaviors automatically; that is, automatic responses become habitual through repeated use and so are unconscious. Thus, the student may not be purposely irritating us, but rather may be automatically selecting an inappropriate behavior without giving conscious thought to the consequences.

Behavioral Skill Deficiency   This category of deficiency is based on Bandura's (1977) social learning theory, discussed in Chapter 3. To review briefly, students learn behaviors by observing the consequences they see others receive for offering various responses to certain situations; obtaining verbal instructions from teachers, parents, and peers; and receiving direct reinforcers and punishers from these individuals. And as noted previously, students may behave inappropriately simply because they lack the requisite skills for behaving appropriately.

Determining whether a behavioral deficiency exists is a fairly straightforward process. First, a powerful reinforcer must be selected to motivate students to perform a behavior if they indeed possess it in their repertoire. There are several important things to recognize in selecting a reinforcer:

- *Reinforcement is individual.* Not every student likes the same things. We might erroneously believe that our choice of reinforcement has universal appeal to all the students in our class. Do not assume that all students will perform a target behavior simply because we think we've found the best reinforcer.

- *The best way to determine a powerful reinforcer is to observe individual students.* Observing what students do when they have free time will help us identify powerful reinforcers. In essence, by identifying what students like to do when given free access, we can use these behaviors as reinforcers for students engaging in the target behavior.

- *Students must not have access to a reinforcer other than when they perform the target behavior.* We must strictly adhere to this recommendation to avoid satiation. A powerful reinforcer is not only something students like but also something over which we have control.

After selecting a powerful reinforcer, we want to precisely define the replacement behavior and its subcomponents, and observe them using an observation form similar to the one in Figure 7.10. Again, it is important that the replacement behavior and its subcomponents be as precisely defined as the original inappropriate behavior that was the target of functional assessment.

With a task analysis observation form like the one in Figure 7.10 in hand, suppose we observe a student attempting to join in a peer group conversation (the replacement behavior). If a given subcomponent is displayed, then we place an "X" in the "present" column; if a subcomponent is not being displayed,

Detailed guidelines for providing positive reinforcement appeared in Chapter 4.

	Subcomponents	Child's Performance		Comments
		Present	Absent	
1.	Locates a peer group	X		
2	Stands at an appropriate distance	X		
3.	Looks at the person talking		X	Child looked at one person in group but not one who was talking
4.	Waits for a pause in the conversation		X	
5.	Asks to join in the conversation	X		
6.	Waits for a response		X	
7.	Says something relevant to the topic	X		Topic was baseball and child talked about football
8.	Waits for a response		X	

FIGURE 7.10

Task Analysis Observation Form for Determining the Presence or Absence of Subcomponents for "Joining in Peer Group Conversation."

then we place an "X" in the "absent" column. The right-hand column is for recording comments. As Figure 7.10 shows, the student was able to perform four out of the eight subcomponents correctly. However, the teacher made comments regarding the student's performance on subcomponents 3 and 7. Based on these comments, the teacher might observe the student again, specifically noting his performance on those two subskills to determine whether they existed in his repertoire.

Observations can take place in the naturalistic environment or after setting up a role-play scenario. It is preferable to observe students' performance on the subskills of the target behavior in the natural environment. However, two problems may arise when trying to do so. First, there often are too many extraneous variables to control. For example, it is difficult to observe a student attempting to join in a peer group conversation if the peer group runs away as she approaches. Second, students do not always perform the behaviors they possess on demand for us to observe in the real world. Therefore, it may be necessary to observe students and assess their ability to perform the replacement behavior during staged situations. This approach provides students with a structured opportunity to perform the replacement skill by interacting with peers selected to participate in a role-play. As with naturalistic observation, students should have the opportunity to earn a powerful reinforcer contingent on performing the target behavior.

There are four basic steps in setting up a role-play (Feindler & Ecton, 1986; Goldstein & McGinnis, 1997):

1. *Develop a semistructured script.* A script includes a description of the scene, a lead-in narration, and co-actors who interact with the target student. Scenes should be developed that are most relevant to students. Role-playing past events that have little relevance for future situations is of limited value to students. An example of a role-play script appears in Figure 7.11.
2. *Select peers to participate with the student in the role-play.* The behaviors that peers are to engage in should be specified; these behaviors include the initiations and responses to the target student. Peers should be reinforced for engaging in the specified behaviors.
3. *Provide participants with both a rationale for the role-play and general instructions to guide them.* Role-playing should be defined for students as acting the way they might if this ever actually happened to them. It's also important to specify the conditions under which the role-play will occur, as well as the participants' roles.
4. *Assess whether the student performed the skill and its subcomponents successfully.* This decision is based on the completion of a task analysis observation form like the one in Figure 7.10.

Instructions to Target Child	You (target child) see a group of kids talking over by the jungle gym during recess. You want to go over and join in their conversation.
Target Child	Walks over to peer group to initiate conversation
Instructions to Peers	You three are talking about scary movies. You all take turns telling each other about one scary movie you've seen. When (target child) comes over, he will want to join your conversation. Let him join in your conversation but continue to act as naturally as if you were talking on your own. When (target child) comes over, each of you can earn points for saying "Hi," asking what scary movie he likes, and looking at him while he's talking.
Peer 1	"I saw Nightmare on Elm Street Part Six and it was really scary. Freddy Krueger was awesome."
Peer 2	"That sounds great. I saw Tales from the Crypt. Two of the stories were really cool but the other two were kind of corny."
Peer 3	"Hi (target child). We're talking about scary movies. Have you seen any lately?"

FIGURE **7.11**

Script for Role-Playing "Joining in Peer Group Conversation"

Once missing requisite skills are identified, they can be taught through the use of instructions, modeling, rehearsal, role-playing, and reinforcement— approaches that have been used to teach students a variety of interpersonal skills (Ager & Cole, 1991; Schloss, Schloss, Wood, & Kiehl, 1986; Singh, Deitz, Epstein, & Singh, 1991; Zaragoza, Vaughn, & McIntosh, 1991). In sum, identifying behavioral skill deficiencies helps us determine if we need to teach students any aspects of the replacement behavior before expecting them to perform it.

Cognitive Deficiencies   The basic assumption here is that cognitive activity mediates behavior. That is, the way students interpret situations leads to the particular behaviors they exhibit. For example, suppose an 11-year-old girl is confronted with this situation: A boy comes up to her at recess and tells her he thinks her shirt is unusual. If the girl interprets his comment as meaning "he thinks I'm a dork," then she may react by either saying something nasty to him or running away. But if she interprets his comment as meaning "he must like me if he's paying this much attention to me," then her behavior may be to smile back at him and carry on a conversation.

There are two types of cognitive problems students may experience: deficit or distortion. A **cognitive deficit** refers to the absence of reflective thinking that governs behavior. For example, a student may fail to maintain a conversation with his peers because he has not learned the specific strategies for selecting appropriate behaviors from his repertoire. A **cognitive distortion** refers to an interpretation that does not match the facts of a situation. For example, a student may fail to perform the behaviors for initiating and maintaining a conversation in the belief that his peers are making fun of him because they are laughing. There are many innocent reasons peers may be laughing, yet this interpretation interferes with his motivation for performing the replacement behaviors.

Self-Control Deficiencies   **Self-control** refers to the range of activities, both obvious and subtle, in which students may engage that increase or decrease the likelihood of some behavior being performed (Mace, Brown, & West, 1987). Self-control is initiated when students focus attention on the particular task or situation (Kanfer & Gaelick-Buys, 1991). Achieving self-control, then, requires students to engage in three activities: (1) self-monitoring, (2) self-evaluation, and (3) self-reinforcement.

More specific information pertaining to self-control and cognitive factors appears in Chapters 12 and 13, respectively.

To illustrate this process, imagine a student who is unaware of the negative comments he makes to teammates during basketball games until his coach tells him that unless he stops he will be removed from the team. The first activity, self-monitoring, occurs when students are aware of their own behavior and self-record when it is and is not performed. In our example, the student must first be aware of what constitutes negative comments during a basketball game and then keep track of them. The second activity is self-evaluation, in which students compare their behavior to some self-selected standard. The boy in our example may hold the standard that it's okay to make no more than three negative comments to teammates per game. By self-monitoring his behavior, he decides whether his performance is acceptable. If he determines that it is acceptable, he might give himself a pat on the back—self-reinforcement—a process that has both feedback and feed-forward effects (Kanfer & Gaelick-Buys, 1991). The feed-forward effect may be that he alters his standard of acceptable negative comments to fewer than his teammates make.

Naturalistic Versus Contrived Assessment

The issue of whether to use naturalistic or contrived assessment takes us back to the phases of conducting functional assessment. To generate and test hypotheses, we have to observe the target behavior. There are two approaches to observing behavior: (1) in vivo (naturalistic) assessment and (2) analogue (role-play) assessment.

In vivo (naturalistic) assessment is the most desirable because we are observing students' behavior in real-life situations. For example, in our example of a student trying to join a conversation, we can observe in a context in which conversation naturally takes place, such as an art project, cooperative learning group, or free time. We note changes in the student's behavior (or his

In vivo assessment makes use of the direct observation techniques elaborated on in Chapter 5.

performance on the prerequisite skills) to such factors as peers involved in the conversation, the topic of conversation, and the location in which the conversation took place. These observations could be recorded on a chart similar to the one shown in Figure 7.10.

It is preferable to observe students' behavior naturalistically. However, there are three potential problems with this approach. First, real-world conditions have extraneous variables we cannot always control (e.g., peer composition and reactions). Second, just because a situation exists for students to perform the target behavior does not automatically mean they will. Few students will display a behavior simply because we request it (Maag, 1989). Third, not all naturalistic situations are conducive to students' performing a behavior. For example, some teachers have classroom structures that minimize peer interaction (e.g., study carrels and work placed in folders). These problems have led to the use of analogue assessment.

Analogue (role-play) assessment involves observing students' behavior during staged situations. The advantage of this approach is that we can elicit and observe the target behavior while controlling or manipulating situational and contextual events (Feindler & Ecton, 1986). In addition, we may be better able to control and manipulate certain variables. For example, different peers can participate in the role-play, enabling us to determine whether any of them serve as a prompt or cue (i.e., antecedent) for the student performing the target behavior. A variation is to instruct peers to provide several different types of feedback to the student: ignoring inappropriate behavior, reinforcing appropriate behavior, and punishing inappropriate behavior. Another variation is to alter the topic of conversation while observing its effect on the student's behavior. These variables also can be placed on an observation chart similar to the one in Figure 7.10.

The major advantage of the analogue approach is that it allows us to control and manipulate variables of interest. In addition, it can help students who participate in the role-play to learn appropriate behaviors from peers with whom they interact. Students who receive reinforcement from peers are more likely to use appropriate behaviors in the future. There is, however, a major limitation to this approach. Because of the artificial nature of the method, the information obtained may not correspond to that obtained through naturalistic observations (Gresham, 1985). Consequently, we should use analogue assessment only when our best efforts to observe students naturalistically have failed.

Multiple Control and Transfer of Function

It is difficult to get clear-cut answers from functional assessment. Rather, it is a process in which we observe students' behavior and then make our best guesses as to the functions it serves. Sometimes our hypotheses will be confirmed; other times they will be refuted. When they are refuted, we continue observing behavior, generating new hypotheses, and testing them. The process may be tedious (most things worth having are), but it certainly is not tricky—or is it? There are two thorny issues that impact our ability to obtain useful information from a functional analysis: (1) multiply controlled behaviors and (2) transfer of function.

We may confidently assign a single function to a behavior and so be surprised when, after making subsequent observations to test our hypothesis, it is refuted. On the one hand, this is to be expected because functional assessment involves disconfirming as much as confirming hypotheses. Disconfirming hypotheses may be more helpful in formulating future behavior support plans than having them initially confirmed because we have, in essence, ruled out certain variables. On the other hand, our best, and repeated, efforts to generate and test hypotheses may leave us with no more information than when we started.

One explanation for the failure to identify a single function may be that behaviors are multiply controlled or serve multiple functions for students. For example, a student may make animal noises to get the attention of peers or to avoid a difficult or boring task. Researchers have suggested that, given this phenomenon, we need to implement more complex functional assessments (Day, Horner, & O'Neill, 1994; Lalli & Casey, 1996; Smith, Iwata, Vollmer, & Zarcone, 1993). Unfortunately, this involves establishing rigorous experimental control over long periods—an approach that is, at best, impractical and, at worst, undoable for most teachers juggling various classroom tasks and demands. Therefore, multiply controlled behaviors can cause substantial logistical problems unless a consultant is employed.

Another explanation for the failure to identify a single behavioral function is that it may change depending on the situation. We may successfully decrease or eliminate an inappropriate behavior only to have it reoccur to serve a different function (Lerman, Iwata, Smith, Zarcone, & Vollmer, 1994). For example, a transfer of function may occur if a student initially makes animal noises to escape a difficult task but later does so to get attention from peers. When transfer of function occurs, we want to generate and test additional hypotheses rather than simply "throw the baby out with the bath water." This problem should be addressed in the behavioral support plan in the "areas of concern" section.

An Expanded Repertoire of Behavioral Intent

Earlier in the chapter, functions of behavior were characterized in terms of either positive reinforcement (obtaining attention, an object, or activity) or negative reinforcement (escaping or avoiding something aversive). These two

Multiply controlled behaviors and transfer of function seem to be difficult problems. In reality, however, they can be addressed by conducting functional assessment on an ongoing basis. In this way, teachers are always getting up-to-date information on the purposes students' inappropriate behaviors serve.

functions have been consistently reported in over 97 studies of children or adults with severe developmental disorders (Nelson, Roberts, Mathur, & Rutherford, 1999). However, only seven studies have examined students with mild disabilities in general education classrooms for which attention or escape were the controlling functions (Reid & Nelson, 2002).

It seems logical, however, to think that humans are too complex to condense the functions of their behaviors in terms of either attention (positive reinforcement) or escape (negative reinforcement). For example, is a parent who stops engaging in a tedious activity to comfort her injured child (e.g., hug her, wipe away her tears, and tell her she will be okay) doing so to obtain attention from the child or to escape the previously-engaged-in task? Or is a more sophisticated function, such as compassion, involved? Functions of behaviors may become more varied and complex as we mature and move through various developmental stages (Kohlberg, 1969; Maslow, 1962; Piaget, 1954). In this section, two additional functions of behavior—power/control and affiliation— are presented, and methods for testing for their presence described.

Power/Control   Few interactions advance very far before elements of power and control come into play. In fact, the mathematician and philosopher Bertrand Russell (1938) stated that power is the most fundamental concept in the social sciences, just as energy is the most fundamental concept in physics. **Power/control** can be defined in terms of social influence. It basically involves one person causing another person to perform a behavior that is contrary to the latter's desire (French & Raven, 1959). Although there are various dimensions of power, its influence can be seen in such areas as African-American women's professional achievements, emerging delinquency, and parental discipline styles (Cain, 1994; Hagan, Simpson, & Gillis, 1987; Leiber & Wacker, 1997). Perhaps nowhere is the impact (or lack thereof) of power so apparent as in individuals with anorexia nervosa. Bruch (1973) suggested that by losing weight the anorexic gains control of her own body and, ultimately, control of the dynamics of the entire family.

We can easily test whether a behavior serves the function of power, because power is based on the effect context has on behavior. When the context surrounding a behavior changes, the meaning attached to that behavior also changes, and inferences can then be drawn about the purpose the behavior serves (Maag, 1999). Note that these approaches rely on *permitting* students to engage in the unwanted behavior. Therefore, we do not want to test for power with behaviors that are dangerous to students or others (i.e., aggressive and self-injurious behaviors). Keeping this caution in mind, there are four ways that the context can be changed: time, location, amount, and topography. Each of these is described using an example of a student telling jokes in class.

It is no more difficult to assess for power/control and affiliation than to assess for attention getting and escape. Testing for these two additional functions helps teachers develop a more varied repertoire of interventions for addressing students' challenging behaviors.

Recall from Chapter 2 that behavior derives its meaning from context. When teachers change the context surrounding the behavior, the stimulus–response chain (see Chapter 4) is disrupted.

Changing the time involves asking the student to begin telling jokes at a time when joke telling is not occurring. For example, we might say, "Billy, you've gotten pretty good at telling jokes. Why don't you take a few minutes before I begin the lesson and tell the class jokes." Changing the location involves directing the student to tell jokes in a special place, such as a designated "joke chair." For example, we might say, "Billy, I have a special chair that you can sit in whenever you want to tell jokes." Changing the amount usually involves instructing the student to perform more of the behavior. For example, we might say, "Billy, that was a pretty good joke. Last year I had a student who told seven jokes during a math lesson. Let's see if you can break that record by telling even more jokes." Changing the topography involves having the student perform the behavior with a different physical action than is normally displayed. For example, we might say, "Billy, those jokes are so good, next time, why don't you wave your arms for greater effect."

The logic underlying these manipulations is straightforward: If joke telling functions as an attention getter, then the student will have no problem following our directions because in all four instances they will result in his obtaining more attention. Conversely, if the student refuses to follow our directions, then the hypothesis that the behavior functions as an expression of power has been confirmed. This hypothesis can be further verified by teaching the student a replacement behavior. The simplest replacement behavior for power is to give the student choices. Most individuals believe that their personal power is enhanced when they have a choice or say-so in a situation (Hagan, Simpson, & Gillis, 1987).

Affiliation   Humans enjoy joining together with others of their species to form groups (Aronson, 1988). This process is called **affiliation.** Schachter (1959), the noted social psychologist, conducted pioneering research on people's need to affiliate. He placed individuals in anxiety-producing situations, manipulated the amount of information they received, and then assessed their desire to affiliate with other people. Schachter and others (Gerard, 1963; Gerard & Rabbie, 1961; Wills, 1981) demonstrated that individuals under stress affiliate both to gain information and to reduce anxiety levels. Another reason students affiliate is to obtain the perceived rewards of membership (Fagan & Wilkinson, 1998; Klein, 1995). Students who feel disconnected from their own family units may participate in a variety of behaviors that we find inappropriate as a way to be accepted by some group (e.g., a gang).

Determining whether a behavior functions to help students affiliate is almost as straightforward as using manipulations for power, attention, and escape. However, the process is somewhat more complicated because affiliation involves associations with others. This means that more variables need to be considered. There are three conditions that can be manipulated to test for affiliation: (1) students from the same versus different ethnic/cultural groups, (2) familiar versus unfamiliar activities, and (3) high- versus low-stress activities.

First, a student's maladaptive behavior may be observed during a lesson or activity with students from the same ethnic/cultural group and one with students from a different ethnic/cultural group. If the target student misbehaves when in the group with members from the same ethnic/cultural group—and that group values others who perform the behavior—then the function of affiliation may be the controlling factor (Dunphy, 1972; Fagan & Wilkinson, 1998; Klein, 1995). Conversely, if the target student displays the inappropriate behavior during an activity or lesson with students from a different ethnic/cultural group, then the functions of attention getting or escape may be maintaining the behavior and so require further analysis.

Second, a student's behavior can be observed during a familiar activity in which the norms and rules are known and during an unfamiliar activity in which the norms and rules are unknown. The rationale for this manipulation is that people tend to affiliate when seeking information (Gerard, 1963; Gerard & Rabbie, 1961; Wills, 1981). If the target student misbehaves during an activity in which the norms and rules are unfamiliar, then the function of affiliation may be assumed to be the controlling variable. However, if the student misbehaves during an activity in which the norms and rules are familiar, then the functions of attention getting and escape may be maintaining the behavior and so require further analysis.

Third, a student's behavior can be observed during a lesson that is stressful and one that entails little or no stress. The rationale for this manipulation is that people tend to affiliate when in high-stress situations that engender anxiety (Gerard, 1963; Gerard & Rabbie, 1961; Wills, 1981). Affiliation may be the controlling function if the student misbehaves during the high-, but not low-, stress condition. Otherwise, the functions of attention getting and escape may be maintaining the behavior and so require further analysis.

As stated previously, testing for affiliation is somewhat complex because of the number of variables to be manipulated. However, interventions based on affiliation are fairly easy to implement. Specifically, for these students, lessons and activities should be conducted (1) with mixed (or nondominant) ethnic/cultural groups, (2) under conditions in which all students are familiar with the norms and rules, and (3) with reduced levels of stress and anxiety. These conditions are easy to implement when classroom rules are clearly stated, students possess the requisite skills to perform requested tasks, and we convey a warm, caring, and inclusive attitude.

SUMMARY

Functional assessment is used to determine the purpose an inappropriate behavior serves so that socially valid interventions can be developed and implemented. Unlike traditional assessment, functional assessment involves manipulations of contextual, curricular, and replacement behavior strategies. There are two basic assumptions of functional assessment: (1) Behavior is contextually defined, and (2) behavior is purposeful. Three types of hypotheses can be generated for functional assessment: (1) contextual (manipulating the environment), (2) curricular (modifying the curriculum, instructional methods, and materials), and (3) replacement behavior training (teaching a student an appropriate way to achieve the same outcome as with the inappropriate behavior).

Functional assessment typically has two stages. The first stage, hypothesis generation, involves interviewing others and collecting behavioral observations in order to make an informed guess about the purpose a behavior serves. The second stage, hypothesis testing (also called functional analysis), is designed to confirm or deny hypotheses. During this phase, the target behavior is observed prior to the baseline and during the implementation of a manipulation.

Information obtained during these two stages of functional assessment is used to develop behavioral support plans. These plans include various components that help teachers maintain students' appropriate behaviors and provide suggestions for dealing with the reoccurrence of inappropriate ones. Like functional assessment, behavioral supports plans are always changing to meet the behavioral challenges students present.

In functional assessment, the point of assessing students' individual-specific skill deficiencies is to determine whether they have the requisite skills for performing a replacement behavior. It is preferable to observe students' behaviors naturalistically. However, sometimes students will not display their behavior for us to observe, or the environment is not conducive for students to perform behaviors. In these cases, contrived assessment may help us determine if students possess the skills for performing replacement behaviors. Two thorny issues—multiply controlled behaviors and transfer of function—are factors that can interfere with the development of effective behavioral support plans. Power/control and affiliation are potential functions of students' inappropriate behaviors and so are valid targets for functional analysis.

ACTIVITIES

1. At a party, try to identify the purposes your friends' behaviors serve. Do some people behave in a way to escape or avoid interactions with others? Do some people behave in a way to get attention from others? Do the attention-seeking behaviors differ if the object of the attention is male to male, male to female, or female to female? How do you account for any differences?

2. Briefly interview both a high school mathematics and science teacher. Ask them which students in their classes possess the requisite skills for doing the assigned work. Then ask them to identify the students who pose the greatest behavioral challenges in their classrooms. The two lists should be similar because students who do not know how to do the work are also those who misbehave the most. Or these students may be the ones who participate and interact with others the least. Do these statements seen to apply?

3. Watch a television show and try to determine if one of the characters acts the same way as another but for different reasons. Is that person's conduct an example of multiply controlled behavior, and if so, how?

REVIEW QUESTIONS

1. Why have traditional assessment approaches failed to provide pertinent information for intervention?

2. What is the definition of functional assessment?

3. What are the two basic assumptions of functional assessment?

4. List three types of hypotheses that can be generated for functional assessment.

5. Describe the steps involved in collecting information during the hypothesis generation stage of functional assessment.

6. Why is the second stage of functional assessment often called "functional analysis"?

7. How are hypotheses tested, and why is this stage important?

8. Provide examples of contextual, curricular, and functional (replacement behavior) hypotheses.

9. What are the components of a behavioral support plan, and what types of information should be included for each component?

10. Why is it important to assess individual-specific deficiencies when identifying replacement behaviors?

11. How can teachers determine whether students have behavioral skill deficiencies?
12. What are the circumstances under which naturalistic and contrived assessment should be used?
13. What are multiply controlled behaviors and transfer of function, and how can these problems be addressed?
14. Why should teachers look beyond positive and negative reinforcement as functions of behavior?
15. How can teachers test for the presence of power/control and affiliation in controlling students' inappropriate behaviors?

REFERENCES

Ager, C. L., & Cole, C. L. (1991). A review of cognitive-behavioral interventions for children and adolescents with behavioral disorders. *Behavioral Disorders, 16,* 276–287.

Aronson, E. (1988). *The social animal* (5th ed.). New York: Freeman.

Bandura, A. (1977). *Social learning theory.* Englewood Cliffs, NJ: Prentice-Hall.

Barkley, R. A. (1998). *Attention-deficit hyperactivity disorder: A handbook for diagnosis and treatment* (2nd ed.). New York: Guilford.

Bruch, H. (1973). *Eating disorders, obesity, anorexia nervosa and the person within.* New York: Basic Books.

Cain, R. A. (1994). Perception of power/control among African Americans: A developmental approach. *Western Journal of Black Studies, 18,* 164–174.

Cessna, K. K., & Borock, J. (1993). Instructionally differentiated programming: Suggestions for implementation. In K. K. Cessna (Ed.), *Instructionally differentiated programming: A needs-based approach for students with behavior disorders* (pp. 53–65). Denver: Colorado Department of Education.

Cooper, L. J., Peck, S., Wacker, D. P., & Millard, T. (1993). Functional assessment for a student with a mild mental disability and persistent behavior problems. *Teaching Exceptional Children, 25*(3), 56–57.

Dadson, S., & Horner, R. H. (1993). Manipulating setting events to decrease problem behaviors: A case study. *Teaching Exceptional Children, 25*(3), 53–55.

Day, H. M., Horner, R. H., & O'Neill R. E. (1994). Multiple functions of problem behaviors: Assessment and intervention. *Journal of Applied Behavior Analysis, 27,* 279–289.

DePaepe, P. A., Shores, R. E., Jack, S. L., & Denny, R. K. (1996). Effects of task difficulty on the disruptive and on-task behavior of students with severe behavior disorders. *Behavioral Disorders, 21,* 216–225.

Donnellan, A. M., Mirenda, P. L., Mesaros, R. A., & Fassender, L. L. (1984). Analyzing the communicative functions of aberrant behavior. *Journal of the Association of the Severely Handicapped, 9,* 201–212.

Dunlap, G., & Kern, L. (1993). Assessment and intervention for children within the instructional curriculum. In J. Reichle & D. Wacker (Eds.), *Communication alternatives to challenging behavior: Integrating functional assessment and intervention strategies* (pp. 177–203). Baltimore: Brookes.

Dunlap, G., Kern-Dunlap, L., Clarke, S., & Robbins, F. (1991). Functional assessment, curricular revision, and severe behavior problems. *Journal of Applied Behavior Analysis, 24,* 387–397.

Dunlap, G., Kern, L., dePerczel, M., Clarke, S., Wilson, D., Childs, K. E., White, R., & Falk, G. D. (1993). Functional analysis of classroom variables for students with emotional and behavioral disorders. *Behavioral Disorders, 18,* 275–291.

Dunphy, D. C. (1972). Peer group socialization. In F. J. Hunt (Ed.), *Socialization in Australia* (pp. 200–217). Sydney: Angus & Robertson.

Elliott, S. N., Gresham, F. M., & Heffer, R. W. (1987). Social-skills interventions: Research findings and training techniques. In C. A. Maher & J. E. Zins (Eds.), *Psychoeducational interventions in the schools* (pp. 141–159). New York: Pergamon.

Epanchin, B. C. (1991). Assessment of social and emotional problems. In J. L. Paul & B. C. Epanchin (Eds.), *Educating emotionally disturbed children and youth* (2nd ed., pp. 307–349). New York: Macmillan.

Evans, I. M., & Meyer, L. H. (1985). *An educative approach to behavior problems: A practical decision model for interventions with severely handicapped learners.* Baltimore: Brookes.

Fagan, J., & Wilkinson, D. L. (1998). Social contexts and functions of adolescent violence. In D. S. Elliott, B. A. Hamburg, & K. R. Williams (Eds.), *Violence in American schools* (pp. 31–54). New York: Cambridge University Press.

Feindler, E. L., & Ecton, R. B. (1986). *Adolescent anger control: Cognitive-behavioral techniques.* New York: Pergamon.

Foster-Johnson, L., & Dunlap, G. (1993). Using functional assessment to develop effective, individualized interventions for challenging behaviors. *Teaching Exceptional Children, 25*(3), 44–50.

Fowler, R. C., & Schnacker, L. E. (1994). The changing character of behavioral assessment and treatment: An historical introduction and review of functional analysis research. *Diagnostique, 19,* 79–102.

French, J. R. P., Jr., & Raven, B. (1959). The bases of social power. In D. Cartwright (Ed.), *Studies in social power* (pp. 118–149). Ann Arbor, MI: Institute for Social Research.

Gerard, H. B. (1963). Emotional uncertainty and social comparison. *Journal of Abnormal and Social Psychology, 66,* 568–573.

Gerard, H. B., & Rabbie, J. M. (1961). Fear and social comparison. *Journal of Abnormal and Social Psychology, 62,* 586–592.

Goldstein, A. P., & McGinnis, E. (1997). *Skillstreaming the adolescent: New strategies and perspectives for teaching prosocial skills.* Champaign, IL: Research Press.

Gresham, F. M. (1985). Utility of cognitive-behavioral procedures for social skills training with children: A critical review. *Journal of Abnormal Child Psychology, 13,* 411–423.

Hagan, J., Simpson, J., & Gillis, A. R. (1987). Class in the household: A power-control theory of gender and delinquency. *American Journal of Sociology, 92,* 788–816.

Hops, H., Bieckel, S., & Walker, H. M. (1976). *CLASS (Contingencies for Learning Academic and Social Skills): Manual for consultants.* Eugene: University of Oregon, Center for Research in Behavioral Education of the Handicapped.

Howell, K. W., & Nolet, V. (2000). *Curriculum-based evaluation* (3rd ed.). Belmont, CA: Wadsworth.

Kanfer, F. H., & Gaelick-Buys, L. (1991). Self-management methods. In F. H. Kanfer & A. P. Goldstein (Eds.), *Helping people change: A textbook of methods* (4th ed., pp. 305–360). New York: Pergamon.

Kauffman, J. M. (2001). *Characteristics of emotional and behavioral disorders of children and youth* (7th ed.). Columbus, OH: Merrill.

Kern, L., Childs, K. E., Dunlap, G., Clarke, S., & Falk, G. D. (1994). Using assessment-based curricular intervention to improve the classroom behavior of a student with emotional and behavioral challenges. *Journal of Applied Behavior Analysis, 27,* 7–9.

Klein, M. W. (1995). *The American street gang: Its nature, prevalence, and control.* New York: Oxford University Press.

Kohlberg, L. (1969). Stage and sequence: The cognitive-developmental approach to socialization. In D. Goslin (Ed.), *Handbook of specialization theory* (pp. 347–480). New York: Rand McNally.

Lalli, J. S., & Casey, S. D. (1996). Treatment of multiply controlled problem behavior. *Journal of Applied Behavior Analysis, 29,* 391–395.

Larson, P. J., & Maag, J. W. (1998). Applying functional assessment in general education classrooms: Issues and recommendations. *Remedial and Special Education, 19,* 338–349.

Leiber, M. J., & Wacker, M. E. (1997). A theoretical and empirical assessment of power-control theory and single-mother families. *Youth and Society, 28,* 317–350.

Lerman, D. C., Iwata, B. A., Smith, R. G., Zarcone, J. R., & Vollmer, T. R. (1994). Transfer of behavioral function as a contributing factor in treatment relapse. *Journal of Applied Behavior Analysis, 27,* 357–370.

Maag, J. W. (1989). Assessment in social skills training: Methodological and conceptual issues for research and practice. *Remedial and Special Education, 10*(4), 6–17.

Maag, J. W. (1992). Integrating consultation into social skills training: Implications for practice. *Journal of Educational and Psychological Consultation, 3,* 233–258.

Maag, J. W. (1999). Why they say no: Foundational precises and techniques for managing resistance. *Focus on Exceptional Children, 32*(1), 1–16.

Maag, J. W. (2001). *Powerful struggles: Managing resistance, developing rapport.* Longmont, CO: Sopris West.

Maag, J. W., & Reid, R. (1994). Attention deficit-hyperactivity disorder: A functional approach to assessment and treatment. *Behavioral Disorders, 20,* 5–23.

Maag, J. W., & Reid, R. (1996). Treatment of attention deficit-hyperactivity disorder: A multi-modal model for schools. *Seminars in Speech and Language, 17,* 37–58.

Mace, F. C., Brown, D. K., & West, B. J. (1987). Behavioral self-management in education. In C. A. Maher & J. E. Zins (Eds.), *Psychoeducational interventions in the schools* (pp. 160–176). New York: Pergamon.

Mace, F. C., Lalli, J. S., & Lalli, E. P. (1991). Functional analysis and treatment of aberrant behavior. *Research in Developmental Disabilities, 12,* 155–180.

Maslow, A. H. (1962). *Toward a psychology of being.* Princeton, NJ: Van Nostrand.

Mayer, G. R. (1996). Why must behavior intervention plans be based on functional assessments? *California School Psychologist, 1,* 29–34.

Morgan, D. P., & Jenson, W. R. (1988). *Teaching behaviorally disordered students: Preferred practices.* Columbus, OH: Merrill.

Neel, R. S., & Cessna, K. K. (1993). Behavioral intent: Instructional content for students with behavior disorders. In K. K. Cessna (Ed.), *Instructionally differentiated programming: A needs-based approach for students with behavior disorders* (pp. 31–39). Denver: Colorado Department of Education.

Nelson, J. R., Roberts, M. L., Mathur, S. R., & Rutherford, R. B. (1999). Has public policy exceeded our knowledge base? A review of the functional behavioral assessment literature. *Behavioral Disorders, 24,* 169–179.

O'Neill, R. E., Horner, R. H., Albin, R. W., Sprague, J. R., Storey, K., & Newton, J. S. (1997). *Functional assessment and program development for problem behavior: A practical handbook* (2nd ed.). Pacific Grove, CA: Brooks/Cole.

Piaget, J. (1954). *The construction of reality in the child.* New York: Basic Books.

Reid, R., & Nelson, J. R. (2002). The utility, acceptability, and practicality of functional behavioral assessment for students with high-incidence problem behaviors. *Remedial and Special Education, 23,* 15–23.

Repp, A. C., & Horner, R. H. (1999). *Functional analysis of problem behavior: From effective assessment to effective support.* Belmont, CA: Wadsworth.

Russell, B. (1938). *Power: A new social analysis.* London: Allen & Unwyn.

Schachter, S. (1959). *The psychology of affiliation.* Palo Alto, CA: Stanford University Press.

Schloss, P. J., Schloss, C. N., Wood, C. E., & Kiehl, W. S. (1986). A critical review of social skills research with behaviorally disordered students. *Behavioral Disorders, 12,* 1–14.

Singh, N. N., Dietz, D. E. D., Epstein, M. H., & Singh, J. (1991). Social behavior of students who are seriously emotionally disturbed: A quantitative analysis of intervention studies. *Behavior Modification, 15,* 74–94.

Smith, R. G., Iwata, B. A., Vollmer, T. R., & Zarcone, J. R. (1993). Experimental analysis and treatment of multiply controlled self-injury. *Journal of Applied Behavior Analysis, 26,* 183–196.

Tobin, T. (1994). Recent developments in functional assessment: Implications for school counselors and psychologists. *Diagnostique, 19,* 5–28.

Umbreit, J. (1995). Functional assessment and intervention in a regular classroom setting for the disruptive behavior of a student with attention deficit hyperactivity disorder. *Behavioral Disorders, 20,* 267–278.

Wills, T. A. (1981). Downward comparison principles in social psychology. *Psychological Bulletin, 90,* 245–271.

Wolf, M. M. (1978). Social validity: The case for subjective measurement or how applied behavior analysis is finding its heart. *Journal of Applied Behavior Analysis, 11,* 203–214.

Zaragoza, N., Vaughn, S., & McIntosh, R. (1991). Social skills interventions and children with behavior problems: A review. *Behavioral Disorders, 16,* 260–275.

PREVENTATIVE APPROACHES

CHAPTER OVERVIEW

- Curricular Considerations
- Direct Instruction
- Environmental Accommodations

CHAPTER OBJECTIVES

After completing this chapter, you will be able to do the following:

1. Describe the focus of prevention.

2. Explain the impact of curricular considerations on students' behavior problems.

3. List the components of direct instruction.

4. Describe the types of environmental accommodations that can be made to prevent behavior problems from occurring.

The best behavior management techniques are those that anticipate and prevent behavior problems from occurring. Several decades ago, Levitt and Rutherford (1978) coined the term **positive teaching** to describe not so much a set of techniques as an attitude toward teaching that focuses on manipulating antecedents. More recently, Wielkiewicz (1995) described prevention from a schoolwide perspective and provided techniques for preventing behavior problems in both general and special education classroom settings.

Preventative approaches are those that focus on antecedents rather than consequences of behavior. The idea is that, if we can alter the antecedent conditions under which a behavior occurs, we can prevent it from occurring again. With this proactive approach, the idea is not to react to misbehavior by administering punitive consequences. Rather, the goal is to replace the pervasive "reactive punishment mentality" with positive proactive strategies to prevent behavior problems from occurring by manipulating antecedents.

The possible types and combinations of antecedent manipulations are endless, but most can be categorized as either curricular, instructional, or environmental. We may be tempted to conclude that these manipulations are peripheral to the topic of behavior management because it is typically conceptualized in terms of methods for applying consequences—either positive or negative. Yet the main reason for schooling is to help students acquire knowledge of the curriculum. This knowledge is transmitted through various instructional strategies or techniques. In turn, the effectiveness of these strategies depends, to a great extent, on the way we structure the classroom environment. Therefore, what students learn, how they learn it, and where they learn it will all have an impact on their behavior.

Unfortunately, as Figure 8.1 indicates, very little of students' time in school is spent on academic responding. This is relevant because students are less

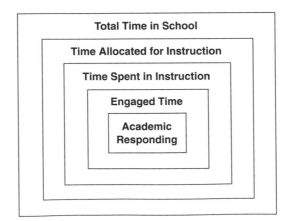

FIGURE **8.1**

Proportion of Time Students Spend on Certain Activities During a School Day

Recall from Chapter 5 that the fair pair refers to the process of increasing an appropriate behavior that is incompatible with the inappropriate behavior. If students are academically engaged in writing answers to problems, they will not be running around the classroom knocking peers' materials off their desks.

likely to be disruptive when they are academically engaged in meaningful tasks. Obviously, some common school activities (e.g., lunch, recess, parties, movies, field trips, and assemblies) conflict with maximizing academic engaged time. However, many things are within our control. When we provide a relevant curriculum with effective and interesting instructional strategies in classrooms with friendly and structured environments, students' academic engaged time increases and their inappropriate behaviors decrease. Therefore, this chapter is devoted to describing the impact of and techniques for curricular, instructional, and environmental modifications.

CURRICULAR CONSIDERATIONS

The main responsibility of teachers is to ensure that students acquire the knowledge and skills articulated in the curriculum. The **curriculum** is a structured set of learning outcomes or objectives (Howell & Nolet, 2000). The curriculum reflects the content school districts decide students should know and the sequence in which it will be learned. A complete curriculum includes numerous objectives covering different content areas such as reading, science, mathematics, and history, to name but a few. Because of the large number of objectives and types of content to be covered, the curriculum is subdivided according to various objectives, with different content taught at different grades, in different classes, and at different times of the year.

Choosing what to teach means targeting long-term outcomes for students, delineating the skills necessary to achieve those outcomes, and assessing students on an ongoing basis. To accommodate students, the sequence of the curriculum may be shuffled, its tasks may be broken into small pieces or combined into larger ones, its organizational structure may be altered, and it may be reassigned to different teachers (Howell & Nolet, 2000). The key factor in making curricular decisions is encouraging students to view the content as meaningful (Glasser, 1992). Teachers do not always have the authority to develop novel curricular areas, but they can embed the curriculum in contexts students find personally meaningful. The more meaningful the curriculum is to students, the longer they will stay academically engaged, and the fewer behavior problems will occur.

There are several critical aspects of the curriculum that affect students' classroom behaviors: (1) the curriculum as an antecedent for behavior problems, (2) the use of task analysis to evaluate students' knowledge of the curriculum, and (3) curriculum modification to promote appropriate classroom behavior. The curriculum is an important antecedent to managing students' behaviors. What we choose to teach students is what they are likely to learn. And when we have a clear vision of what we want to teach students, we are likely to use effective instructional strategies and to create stimulating class-room environments that meet the objectives outlined in the curriculum.

The Curriculum as an Antecedent for Behavior Problems

Students are expected to master one year's worth of curriculum for every year they are in school. The curriculum at any grade level often is conceptualized in terms of "scope and sequence"—that is, the total amount of content to be covered and the order in which it is presented (Mastropieri & Scruggs, 1994). Special education services may be provided to students who fail to progress at an adequate rate through the curriculum. Figure 8.2 illustrates this point. The vertical axis represents the years in the curriculum and the horizontal axis represents the years in school. The diagonal line indicates the progress schools want to see students make—mastering one year's worth of curriculum for every year in school. The dots represent clusters of specific content mastered. The dots in Figure 8.2 show a substantial deviation from the expected progress around the third year (grade). Thus, a decision was made to provide the student with special education services as indicated by the box surrounding the three dots.

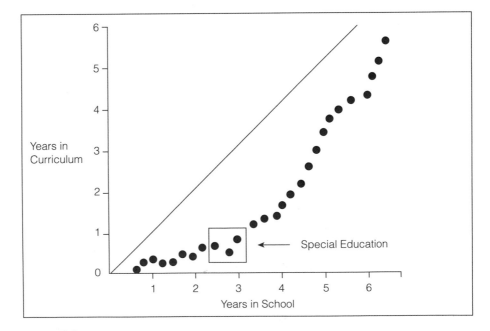

FIGURE 8.2

Hypothetical Lack of Progress in the Curriculum

From *Curriculum-based evaluation: Teaching and decision making* (2nd Ed.) (p. 8), by K. W. Howell & V. Nolet, 2000, Belmont, CA: Wadsworth. Copyright 2000 by Wadsworth. Adapted with permission.

An important issue involves what to do to remedy the discrepancy between years in school and the amount of curriculum mastered. For many years, the answer was **remediation**—the process of providing students with special instruction with the goal of eventually "catching them up" in the curriculum. These students typically received their education in either a resource room or a self-contained classroom. The main problem with this approach was that it was unrealistic to expect these slow learners to learn at a *faster* pace than their nondisabled peers. For example, a student may be expected to master 30 math objectives by the time he enters the third grade. However, suppose that by the fourth week into the third grade he has mastered only 10 math objectives. The task of catching him up will be daunting because he must learn not only the 20 previous objectives but also the 10 new ones his peers will have learned by the end of third grade. In other words, he must master 30 math objectives during third grade while his nondisabled peers need to master only 10.

The compensatory curriculum has become so much a part of secondary special education that many teachers frown on teaching adolescents basic skills such as reading decoding (i.e., phonics). Ironically, most adult literacy programs focus on having their clients learn phonics skills.

The problem just described is especially acute for students in middle and high school. It is unrealistic to expect a 15-year-old sophomore who is having difficulty with multiplication and division to master geometry by the end of the year after receiving remedial special education. Instead, the curriculum of many high school special education programs is altered to meet the reality of time constraints. In what is sometimes called a **compensatory curriculum,** high school students in special education classes may be taught a variety of nontraditional skills including vocational skills, school survival skills, self-management skills, life skills, and self-help skills, to name but a few.

Now we are in the age of inclusion, in which students with learning and behavioral problems are reintegrated into the general education classroom and curriculum in which they experienced failure. Students who do not possess the requisite skills to master the curriculum are likely to misbehave in order to escape and avoid difficult tasks. The typical response of many teachers is to punish these students. This unfortunate situation can be avoided by ensuring that students are placed in the appropriate curriculum and possess the skills necessary to achieve.

Effective curriculum modifications require teachers to have a clear vision of what they want students to learn. Evans, Evans, Gable, and Schmid (1991) described several guidelines for developing a relevant, multifaceted curriculum:

1. Focus on an agreed-on series of goals and objectives.
2. Offer a common core of courses.
3. Include a diversity of educational experiences and activities.
4. Organize the presentation of the instructional program.

The key thing to remember is that schools serve a broad range of students who vary widely in their interests and skill levels. For example, the narrow goal of college preparation often results in a curriculum that is boring and irrelevant for some students. For these students, a college preparation curriculum is an antecedent for behavior problems.

The curriculum typically is determined by a small group of administrators or consultants and so may not always reflect the needs of the community and its consumers. Therefore, curriculum modifications should be undertaken by having parents, teachers, and students assist in identifying the goals of the curriculum. A common core of courses will emerge when goals are identified. Sometimes these courses reflect traditional content areas such as reading, mathematics, history, and science; other times they focus on self-help, social, vocational, and survival skills. Regardless of the core content, it should be delivered using diverse educational experiences and activities. Once the curriculum is identified, a hierarchy of skills is developed for each content area. However, an overreliance on curriculum hierarchies leads to student boredom and subsequent behavior problems.

> Curricular modifications are probably grossly underused in schools. One reason may be that "what to teach" become highly politicized and overshadows the creative ways in which content can be delivered to students.

Types and Sequencing of Curricula

The first step in curriculum modification entails determining which types of curricula are most appropriate for a given student. In most instances, general education curricula cause few problems, and approximately 80 percent of students progress through the curriculum at an adequate rate. However, students with learning and behavioral problems have often failed in traditional curricula and require a substantively different curriculum. Meier (1992) described five types of curricula that seem to be more appropriate for students with disabilities; Table 8.1 summarizes these curricula.

In many cases, teachers have no choice but to follow the curriculum prescribed by the school district. General educators must follow the curriculum whereas special educators have more latitude to develop their own curricula for students with disabilities. However, all teachers have the ability to sequence the curriculum in a way that best meets the needs of their students.

Content in a grade-level curriculum typically is sequenced from easy to difficult, based on the assumption that content is hierarchical. However, not all content progresses in such a fashion. In many instances, we can sequence content of equal difficulty in ways that students find interesting, relevant, and, consequently, motivational. Howell and Morehead (1987) stated that "sequencing content allows us to recognize a coordinated series of objectives and the lessons used to teach them" (p. 32). They also provided several ways to sequence content of equal difficulty:

- *Logically.* Grouping content logically means finding some similarity. For example, vegetables and fruits might be studied based on the geographic

TABLE 8.1	CURRICULA APPROPRIATE FOR STUDENTS WITH DISABILITIES
Type of Curriculum	**Description**
Parallel curriculum	Is identical to that for students without disabilities but with fewer, and less complex, content area skills. The problem is ensuring that students with disabilities do not get a watered-down curriculum.
Functional curriculum	Focuses on teaching students skills for satisfactorily functioning in real-world situations. For example, mathematical computation is taught within the context of balancing a checkbook, completing an income tax form, or making a household budget.
Community-based curriculum	Represents an adaptation and extension of the functional curriculum. Students are taught functional skills for successfully negotiating various demands of community living, such as ordering a meal from a restaurant, getting on a bus, washing clothes at a laundromat, and purchasing food from a grocery store.
Life management curriculum	Resembles the previous two approaches except that it consists exclusively of skills necessary for independent living, including such skills as grooming, traveling, and using a telephone.
Specialized curriculum	Includes skills not found in the general education curriculum, such as social skills and self-management skills.

Source: Meier (1992).

region in which they are grown. Studying vegetables grown in the Midwest is not more difficult than studying vegetables grown in the Southeast.

- *Chronologically.* That is, content is delivered as it evolves or is discovered by students. For example, students initially may be studying what dinosaurs ate, which may lead them to ask which dinosaurs ate meat and which ate plants. The teacher then moves to this second area of content.
- *Student interest.* Sometimes the most effective way to sequence content is to ask students what they want to study. Students become equal participants in their education. They are more likely to view content as relevant and exciting when they have a voice in selecting what to study.
- *Utility.* This refers to how students will use the content. For example, some teachers may view cooperative learning skills as essential for students to learn other parts of the curriculum. The content generated from this approach will vary considerably depending on the adults and children in a given community.

Analysis of Content Knowledge

Once an appropriate curriculum has been selected and sequenced, students' knowledge of prerequisite skills should be analyzed so that we present content that they can successfully learn. Content that is too difficult for students to learn is an antecedent for their engaging in inappropriate out-of-seat behaviors. This problem frequently occurs when students are assigned worksheets for which they do not possess the requisite skills to complete independently. Many teachers respond to the inappropriate behaviors by punishing the student, thereby exacerbating the problem.

The best way to determine whether students possess the requisite skills to learn new content or to practice content independently is to assess their skill level using criterion-reference testing. **Criterion-referenced testing** compares students' performance on a specific curricular objective to some standard (Howell, Kaplan, & O'Connell, 1979). If students cannot perform the desired **task,** then we have created an antecedent for behavior problems. The question becomes, Is it our goal to have students sit quietly holding pencils, with their eyes on the paper, pretending to do work they cannot complete independently?

Criterion-referenced tests are created by breaking a skill down into its subcomponents (i.e., task analysis). Task analysis is "the process of isolating, sequencing, and describing the essential components of a task" (Howell & Nolet, 2000, p. 487). All tasks are composed of subtasks and strategies.

Subtasks are the simpler requisite skills students must possess in order to competently perform the main task. For example, in order for a student to learn division, she must first possess the requisite skills of multiplication, subtraction, and addition. The number of subtasks a task has depends on how finely it is broken down. For example, we can take the subtask of addition (a prerequisite for subtraction, division, and multiplication) and break it down into several subtasks: (1) three or more single digits in a column, (2) two digits to one digit without regrouping, (3) two digits to one digit with regrouping, (4) two digits to two digits without regrouping, (5) two digits to two digits with regrouping, and (6) three or more digits to three or more digits with or without regrouping. These statements become the subtasks for the task of addition, which, in turn, can be a subtask for subtraction, multiplication, and so on.

Task strategy refers to the procedure, strategy, or algorithm that links subtasks together so that students can perform some task competently. Students may be skilled at all the subtasks but still not be able to perform the task if they lack the task strategy. For example, a student may know how to add, subtract, and multiply but still not be able to perform the task of division if he lacks the necessary task strategy. The division task strategy consists of the steps involved in executing the subtasks. Howell and Nolet (2000) provided an example of a task analysis of fractions; Figure 8.3 shows the example. Task strategies represent our explanations to students of how to perform a task. They are not products in and of themselves.

Criterion-referenced testing is primarily used to determine how well students have mastered skills. This information is important for developing appropriate instructional objectives.

In essence, one task's subtasks can become another subtask's task. Although this may sound confusing, it simply points out that any task can become a subtask for a higher-level task.

Task

Add or subtract fractions without common denominators that do not have common factors between denominators. Convert to simplest form.

Task Strategy

(a) Decide if denominators are the same.
(b) Find the least common denominator.
(c) Produce the equivalent fractions.
(d) Decide what operation (add or subtract) is called for.
(e) Carry out the operation.
(f) Decide if the answer is in simplest form. If it isn't,
(g) Convert it.

Essential Subtasks

5. Converting fractions to simplest form
4. Adding and subtracting fractions that do have common factors
3. Multiplication and division facts
2. Finding least common denominators
1. Addition facts

FIGURE **8.3**

Task Analysis of Functions

For example, given the task strategy and subtasks in Figure 8.3, what should we make of a student who writes the following answer?

$$\frac{6}{8} \times \frac{6}{3} = \frac{36}{24}$$

The answer is wrong because it was not converted to its simplest form. It may be that the student knows how to convert (subtask 5) but forgot the final step in the task strategy (step g). A good instructional strategy might be to have the student memorize the strategy rather than repeatedly drilling him on multiplication facts. In the latter case, multiplication worksheets would be an antecedent for misbehavior.

Once content has been task analyzed, we can formulate behavioral objectives. It is from behavioral objectives that criterion-referenced tests are generated. Behavioral objectives represent a way to operationally define the tasks that make up the curriculum. They typically contain a description of the content, the necessary behavior, the conditions under which the behavior is to occur, and the criterion for acceptable performance (CAP). Here is an example of a math objective:

Given 1-digit to 2-digit addends with regrouping, the student will write the answers on a worksheet at a rate of 70 digits correct per minute.

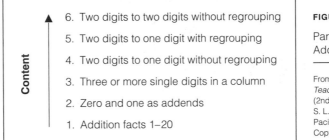

FIGURE **8.4**

Partial Task Analysis of Addition Content

From *Curriculum-based evaluation: Teaching and decision making* (2nd Ed.) (p. 48), by K. W. Howell, S. L. Fox, & M. K. Morehead, 1993, Pacific Grove, CA: Brooks/Cole. Copyright 1993 by Brooks/Cole. Adapted with permission.

This objective contains the content (1-digit to 2-digit addends with regrouping), behavior (write), conditions (worksheet), and criterion (70 digits correct with no errors).

The first component of objectives, **content,** refers to the specific subject matter from the curriculum we want students to learn. We derive specific content statements from our task analysis. Figure 8.4 presents a partial task analysis for addition. Notice that we can select any particular subtask to be the content statement in a behavioral objective. Howell and Morehead (1987) recommended that teachers ask themselves the following questions when selecting content for a behavioral objective:

1. *Is it relevant?* Is the main task of value to the student?
2. *Is it complete?* Has any essential content been omitted?
3. *Is it trivial?* Is content included which is too easy for the target student?
4. *Is it necessary?* Is all content necessary to master the main task?
5. *Is it redundant?* Do any of the content statements overlap with other content statements? (p. 32)

The **behavior** component represents the actions students undertake to indicate that they have knowledge of the content. We cannot measure learning directly because it involves covert cognitive activity. Therefore, we infer that it has taken place by observing behavior. Two classes of behavior appear in behavioral objectives: identifying and producing. Identifying behaviors such as pointing, circling, or crossing out indicate that students can recognize content. Producing behaviors such as writing answers or saying answers aloud typically indicate a higher level of knowledge. Identification behaviors usually appear in an objective only if we are interested in whether students can accurately perform a task. Production behaviors help us determine whether students have internalized and can apply content in a larger context.

Conditions reflect the situation or circumstances under which a behavior is performed; they represent how we add context and relevance to a task. For example, learning compound words (e.g., *airport, firehouse, sunshine, barn-*

Identification behaviors (e.g., multiple choice, true/false, or matching items) indicate a lower level of proficiency at a task than do production behaviors (e.g., fill-in-the-blanks, short-answer, or essay items).

yard) in the context of an interesting story probably has more relevance for students than repeating them when shown flash cards. Altering the conditions also indicates different levels of students' mastery of the content. For example, let's assume that the specific content being taught is subtracting three or more digits from three or more digits, and the behavior is "writes answers." One condition may be that students write the answers on a piece of paper with the problems supplied. A second condition may be that students write the answers while balancing a checkbook. The second condition makes the objective more difficult because the students have to not only subtract but also enter check numbers, purchases, and check amounts.

The **criterion** is simply the standard for judging whether students successfully learned the content in the behavioral objective. Howell and Nolet (2000) stressed the importance of not setting arbitrary criteria. A typical criterion level in many objectives is 80 percent. However, there are some tasks in which 100 percent accuracy is not only desirable but necessary. For example, would we want to fly in a jet airliner with a pilot who was only 80 percent accurate at landing? Or would we be satisfied to balance our checkbook with 80 percent accuracy? The consequences of an 80 percent criterion for these content areas can be devastating. Conversely, there are some situations in which an 80 percent criteria is too high. The example that comes to mind is the "cloze" technique for evaluating reading comprehension. With this technique, students are provided with a reading passage in which every fifth word is omitted (the first and last sentences are left intact). Students must supply the omitted words. This task has a criterion level of 40 percent (Howell & Morehead, 1987).

Howell and Nolet (2000) provided the following example of how a behavioral objective can be modified in terms of its content, behavior, conditions, and criterion:

Howell and Nolet (2000) published "tables of specification" that contain criteria for the accuracy, fluency, and automaticity levels for reading decoding and mathematics. It is more difficult to find published criteria for other content areas, such as science and history.

Original objective
Pam will write the answers to addition facts on a worksheet at a rate of 40 correct per minute.

Content modification
Pam will write the answers to subtraction facts on a worksheet at a rate of 40 correct per minute.

Modification of behavior
Pam will say the answers to addition facts on a worksheet at a rate of 40 correct per minute.

Condition modification
Pam will write the answers to addition facts in a checkbook at a rate of 40 correct per minute.

Criterion modification
Pam will write the answers to addition facts on a worksheet with 100% accuracy. (p. 44)

Objective: Given 1-digit to 2-digit addends with regrouping, the student will write the answers on a worksheet at a rate of 70 digits correct per minute.				Practice Items		27 +7	43 +9	38 +5	77 +4
29 +5	54 +8	17 +9	83 +9	86 +6	64 +8	58 +5	35 +7	46 +4	29 +3
35 +9	24 +8	83 +7	24 +6	48 +9	69 +5	56 +6	26 +8	32 +8	25 +6
37 +7	64 +7	25 +7	89 +4	55 +8	49 +6	29 +7	44 +9	66 +6	28 +8
39 +1	27 +8	63 +9	46 +7	86 +4	57 +3	29 +9	48 +3	37 +4	75 +6
63 +8	26 +5	35 +5	74 +9	52 +8	88 +3	49 +4	29 +1	67 +8	75 +4
51 +9	34 +7	28 +8	95 +5	62 +8	16 +8	47 +9	75 +6	38 +5	86 +4

FIGURE **8.5**

Sample Probe for One-Digit to Two-Digit Addends with Regrouping

Once we have task analyzed content and created specific behavioral objectives, criterion-referenced tests can be created. These tests, often called probes, are keyed to specific objectives. Criterion-referenced tests can help us determine whether students possess the subskills necessary to perform a task. Figure 8.5 provides an example of a probe sheet. Two aspects of the objective's criterion appearing in Figure 8.5 deserve elaboration. First, the rate is 70 digits, not 70 problems, per minute. "Digits correct" more accurately reflects students' knowledge of this task (or subtask, depending on where it appears in a task sequence). The reason is that each problem in Figure 8.5 requires adding twice. Therefore, if students add the first column correctly but make an error in the second column, they still get credit for getting one digit correct. The second aspect of the objective's criterion is that students must complete 70 digits correct in one minute. The reason for a timed test is to determine what levels of proficiency students have achieved on a given task.

Three proficiency levels reflect the extent to which students have learned a skill: accuracy, fluency, and automaticity. The **accuracy** level focuses solely on whether students can do a task correctly. **Fluency** refers to the ability to do a task correctly and quickly. The objective and accompanying probe in Fig-

Changing the proficiency level (accuracy, fluency, automaticity) creates an entirely new behavioral objective because it requires different behaviors to be performed.

ure 8.5 reflect the fluency level of proficiency. Fluency is a prerequisite for the last, and most important, level of proficiency—automaticity. **Automaticity** refers to the ability to perform some task quickly and accurately within a relevant context. For example, a relevant context for multiplication is figuring out how much of a tip a restaurant server deserves. If we are fluent at multiplication, we can allocate our conscious awareness to variables related to the task at hand, such as evaluating the quality of service we received. Similarly, students who are fluent at multiplication will learn division much more quickly because they can allocate their conscious awareness to learning the division strategy.

DIRECT INSTRUCTION

Once the curriculum, or content (what to teach), has been established, appropriate instructional strategies (how to teach) are implemented. Instructional strategies represent the vehicle for students to learn the skills delineated in the curriculum. Literally hundreds of instructional strategies have been described by various authors (e.g., Lovitt, 1984; Mastropieri & Scruggs, 1991; Meyen, Vergason, & Whelan, 1988; Pressley, 1990). The intent in this section is not to provide a laundry list of instructional strategies. Although many teachers might find that approach desirable, it is beyond the scope and purpose of this book. Instead, the focus is on a model for delivering instruction known as direct instruction—the best methodology we currently possess for teaching students with disabilities and minimizing their behavior problems.

Direct instruction emerged from the teacher effectiveness research conducted over the past 20 years that has helped us identify behaviors and activities linked to student achievement gains (Mastropieri & Scruggs, 1994). For our purposes, **direct instruction** refers to a series of behavioral techniques, including scripts, prompts, cues, correction procedures, and teacher responses, to help students acquire content skills (Howell & Nolet, 2000). Although the sequence sometimes varies and the steps may be combined or isolated, the basic elements of direct instruction are the same:

1. Explain the goals and objectives of the lesson.
2. Sequence content.
3. Review requisite skills.
4. Deliver information.
5. Give clear instructions and explanations and relevant examples.
6. Provide guided practice.
7. Check for comprehension.
8. Provide quick and specific feedback.
9. Provide independent practice.
10. Conduct formative evaluation.

Direct instruction is sometimes viewed as a series of empirically tested steps as are presented here. Direct instruction also refers to specific programs of reading and math (e.g., DISTAR) that have been empirically tested.

The elements of direct instruction can be used to teach students in both small- and large-group arrangements.

Explain Goals and Objectives

The first step in delivering a lesson is to state its purpose to students so that they can focus their attention on the new information to be presented. As with behavior, the more precisely a goal is described, the easier it is for students to attain it. Academic achievement increases when students understand the specific goals, the importance of the content, and its relation to previously learned material.

We can communicate the goals and objectives of lessons to students using anticipatory sets. An **anticipatory set** refers to statements of activities that introduce students to the content of the lesson, help them recognize important points, and offer them motivation for learning the material (Hunter, 1981). We can write the objectives and goals of the lesson on the chalkboard along with important pieces of information to which students should pay particular attention as the lesson progresses. It is also helpful to have a brief activity relating the to-be-learned information to students' previous knowledge of the topic. For example, if we teach a lesson on dinosaurs, it helps to initially ask students if they have ever been to a museum that contained dinosaur bones or fossils. This question serves two purposes: (1) It helps us determine students' current knowledge of dinosaurs, and (2) it may increase students' interest by making the to-be-learned information more contextually relevant.

Sequence Content

In direct instruction, content is introduced to students in small, incremental, and sequential steps (Hunter, 1981; Rosenshine, 1986). Task analysis, as described previously, is a method for identifying the sequence of discrete steps that lead to mastery of a skill.

In general, the more content covered, the more students will be actively engaged, and, the fewer inappropriate behaviors they will display. The term **pacing** is sometimes used to describe the speed at which material is presented. A quickly paced lesson consisting of concrete and relevant materials and examples maximizes the number of objectives students reach while minimizing classroom disruptions (Mastropieri & Scruggs, 1994). Most school districts specify the quantity of content to be covered (scope) and the order in which it will be introduced (sequence). It is important to remember that these predetermined factors only represent *opportunities* to cover content. Effective teachers make the most of the time constraints in which they have to work. Mastropieri and Scruggs (1994) recommended the following strategies for increasing the amount of content covered:

1. Identify the district's scope and sequence.
2. Match instructional material to the district's scope and sequence.

3. Estimate the amount of time necessary to maintain the year's content.
4. Estimate the monthly pace necessary to obtain yearly goals.
5. Monitor progress and adjust instruction accordingly.
6. Prioritize objectives.
7. Incorporate regular reviews to ensure retention and maintenance of previously mastered objectives.
8. Use the teacher-effectiveness variables.
9. Maximize engaged time-on-task.
10. Ensure that all activities are relevant to instructional objectives. (p. 5)

Review Requisite Skills

The next step of direct instruction is to review the skills students need to master the new material. This can be accomplished with 5- to 10-minute daily reviews. Daily reviews also provide us with an opportunity to monitor student learning, provide corrective feedback, and make last-minute adjustments in the material to be presented. Mastropieri and Scruggs (1994) described several ways to conduct a daily review:

- Teachers can engage students in brief question-and-answer sessions focusing on the requisite skills.
- Teachers can review students' homework from the previous lesson by quizzing students orally, having students check each others' assignments, or having students review homework in small groups.
- Students can work either alone or in small groups to generate summaries of the requisite skills and either share their summaries with the class or generate questions over previously learned material for classmates to answer.

Deliver Information

Mastropieri and Scruggs (1994) described a process to help us remember the important teacher behaviors for effectively delivering information; the acronym SCREAM summarizes the method:

S = structure
C = clarity
R = redundancy
E = enthusiasm
A = appropriate rate
M = maximum engagement

First, a structured lesson ensures that strategies have been implemented for obtaining students' attention prior to presenting the information. Here, we should provide an overview of the lesson, including a description of what the objectives are, when to expect critical information, and when transitional points will occur. A structured lesson also includes ongoing summaries and reviews of material. Second, lessons are clear when we focus on only one objective at a time, refrain from using ambiguous language, and provide relevant, concrete examples. Third, presentations should provide redundancy, particularly when important concepts and rules necessary for more complex knowledge are involved. Fourth, students are more likely to pay attention when we are enthusiastic about the information being presented. Fifth, students are more likely to pay attention and master objectives when we cover material at a quick rate. Sixth, students master the material when we provide opportunities for maximum engagement. To achieve this, Mastropieri and Scruggs (1994) suggest using the following strategies:

1. Verbally praise students who are actively engaged in the instructional task.
2. Reinforce students for completing assignments quickly and accurately.
3. Question students frequently and provide opportunities for them to respond aloud or on paper.
4. Schedule more difficult material earlier in the day when student interest and energy are at their highest.
5. Use a kitchen timer to ring at random intervals. If all students are engaging in prespecified appropriate behaviors, they earn a reward.
6. Select instructional strategies and materials to make learning concrete and contextually relevant.

Give Clear Instructions and Explanations and Relevant Examples

The teacher effectiveness literature has reported that teachers who give extensive and elaborate descriptions and examples of content are the most successful at promoting learning in their students (Evertson, Emmer, & Brophy, 1980). Three specific techniques contribute to explanations and examples being relevant and useful: instructions, modeling, and prompts.

Instructions   Essentially, **instructions** refer to rules or guidelines indicating that specific behaviors will pay off in particular situations (Martin & Pear, 1992). Instructions become meaningful to us when they state explicitly that compliance will be followed either by reinforcement ("If you vacuum the carpet, you can watch an hour of television") or the avoidance of punishment ("If you don't stop teasing Susie, I'll bring you in the house"). In other words, instructions are verbal antecedent stimuli that gradually came to modify our behavior (Martin & Pear, 1992).

A good lesson always contains instructions that can be easily followed. Using instructions appropriately can produce behavior change much more rapidly than shaping or trial-and-error experiences with reinforcement and extinction. Martin and Pear (1992) provided the following guidelines for using instructions effectively:

1. Instruction should be within the understanding of the individual to whom it is applied.
2. Instruction should specify the behavior in which the individual is to engage.
3. Instruction should specify contingencies involved in complying (or not complying) with it, and these contingencies should be applied consistently.
4. Complex instruction should be broken down into easy-to-follow steps.
5. Instruction should be sequenced so that it proceeds gradually from very easy to more difficult behavior for the individual being treated.
6. Instruction should be delivered in a pleasant, courteous manner.
7. Fading should be used as necessary to phase out instruction if you want other stimuli that are present to take control of the behavior. (p. 215)

Modeling   Modeling is one of the most powerful techniques for helping students acquire new information. **Modeling** refers to learning by imitation. Cooper, Heron, and Heward (1987) stated that **imitation** consists of three environmental manipulations: (1) A model is presented that prompts the same behavior from students, (2) students imitate the modeled behavior within a specified time, and (3) students are reinforced for performing the modeled behavior. Students do not have to imitate the behavior exactly as the teacher demonstrated it in order for modeling to take place. However, modeling is said to occur when the teacher's behavior serves as an antecedent for students to engage in a reasonably similar behavior.

Modeling is a term associated with social learning theory, which was described in Chapter 3.

Goldstein and McGinnis (1997) described several modeling enhancer characteristics that fall into three categories: (1) model characteristics, (2) modeling display characteristics, and (3) observer characteristics. Model characteristics are the traits and qualities possessed by the person who is modeling the behavior. Modeling display characteristics involve procedures for effectively presenting the behavior to be imitated. Observer characteristics refer to personal traits of the individual doing the modeling. These characteristics, summarized in Table 8.2, increase the speed and accuracy with which students imitate appropriate behavior. In addition, Stowitschek, Stowitschek, Hendrickson, and Day (1984) described three highly effective modeling procedures: (1) antecedent modeling, (2) error-dependent modeling, and (3) partial modeling.

Antecedent modeling occurs when we perform each subskill needed to complete a lesson immediately before requesting that students imitate it. We do not want to wait for students to make an error before modeling the correct response. Combining the following four steps with reinforcement may result in errorless learning:

TABLE 8.2	MODELING ENHANCERS
Characteristic	**Modeling Enhancers**
Model characteristics	More effective modeling will occur when the model:
	(1) seems to be highly skilled or expert
	(2) is of high status
	(3) controls rewards desired by a child
	(4) is of the same sex, approximate age, and social status as a child
	(5) is friendly and helpful
	(6) is rewarded for the given behaviors
Modeling display characteristics	More effective modeling will occur when the modeling display shows the behaviors to be imitated:
	(1) in a clear and detailed manner
	(2) in order from least to most difficult behaviors
	(3) with enough repetition to make overlearning likely
	(4) with as little irrelevant detail as possible
	(5) when several different models, rather than a single model, are used
Observer characteristics	More effective modeling will occur when the person observing the model is:
	(1) told to imitate the model
	(2) similar to the model in background or in attitude toward the skill
	(3) friendly toward or likes the model
	(4) rewarded for performing the modeled behaviors

1. Model (teacher).
2. Request (teacher).
3. Respond correctly (student).
4. Praise (teacher).

With error-dependent modeling, we use the following nine steps, modeling a skill only when a student makes a mistake:

1. Request (teacher).
2. Respond correctly (student).
3. Praise (teacher).
4. Request (teacher).
5. Respond incorrectly (student).
6. Model (teacher).

7. Request (teacher).
8. Respond correctly (student).
9. Praise (teacher).

In the third approach, partial modeling, we model only the part of a response that is incorrect. This approach is most effective for students who can learn much information on their own.

Modeling can be so effective that some students hesitate to give correct answers without first having them modeled. In these instances, a fading technique can be used to reduce the amount of help we are providing. Stowitschek and colleagues (1984) described several ways in which fading can be implemented:

- The number of steps modeled can be reduced.
- The type of assistance provided can be reduced (e.g., from physical assistance to partial physical assistance to modeling to verbal assistance).
- The amount of assistance in a given period can be reduced (e.g., one prompt per 5-minute session).

Prompts   In situations in which students fail to imitate a model behavior in spite of our best efforts, we can provide them with prompts. **Prompts** refer to contrived antecedent stimuli that supplement natural stimuli to help students perform a desired behavior (Zirpoli & Melloy, 1997). For example, a natural prompt for getting students' attention is to ring the bell; an additional, and contrived, prompt is to flick the lights in the classroom on and off. Zirpoli and Melloy (1997) described five types of prompts, which are summarized in Table 8.3. Alberto and Troutman (1999) suggested that prompts should be related to the original antecedent, be as weak as possible so students do not overrely on them, and be faded out as quickly as possible.

Some people try to make a distinction between prompts and cues. To their way of thinking, prompts involve physical guidance whereas cues involve verbal guidance. The word *prompts* is used because it is more descriptive, but the two terms are synonymous.

Provide Guided Practice

Students need opportunities to practice what they have learned. Guided practice is a way to accomplish this by providing students with structured time to use newly acquired skills under our supervision (Mastropieri & Scruggs, 1994). Examples of guided practice activities include teacher-led question-and-answer sessions, peer tutoring, and cooperative learning.

Two particularly useful approaches are the model-lead-test and time-delay strategies (Rosenshine, 1986). With the **model-lead-test strategy,** we model and orally present the task, guide students in understanding the process through prompts and practice, and then test for mastery. The **time-delay strategy** consists of five steps: (1) Present the task to students and ask them to respond, (2) prompt students immediately (zero-second delay) by providing

TABLE 8.3	TYPES OF PROMPTS
Type of Prompt	**Description**
Natural prompts	Represent environmental stimuli that originate in our interactions in various contexts and situations. For example, the morning sun shining in a bedroom window is a natural prompt for getting up. It is important to maximize students' reliance on natural prompts because they promote maintenance and generalization.
Verbal stimuli	Represent the most prevalent kind of prompt. Many verbal prompts can be considered natural. For example, having a teacher ask a question is a verbal prompt for students to raise their hands. Verbal prompts can supplement naturally occurring prompts. For example, a parent telling a child to pick up a ringing phone is a verbal prompt to supplement the natural prompt of the ring.
Gestural prompts	Involve some body movements or signals that direct students to perform a desired behavior. For example, a teacher may augment the verbal prompt of asking a question by looking at a particular student and slightly nodding her head as a sign for the student to raise his hand.
Physical prompts	Involve physically guiding students in the performance of a target behavior. They are the most intrusive and should be used only when other types of prompts have failed to elicit the target behavior. There are two dangers in using physical prompts: (1) The physical contact students receive when they initially fail to perform the desired behavior may reinforce noncompliance, and (2) students may become embarrassed or angry when an adult physically aids them in performing a behavior.

Source: Zirpoli and Melloy (1997).

the correct answer during several trials, (3) have students respond and give them feedback based on their responses, (4) have them repeat prior steps while incrementally increasing the amount of time between the presentation of the content and the provision of the correct response, and (5) fade out assistance so that students can respond quickly and independently.

Check for Comprehension

We can check for comprehension by questioning students after they complete guided practice activities. The purpose is to see if students acquired the information or if reteaching some, or all, of the lesson is warranted. Mastropieri and Scruggs (1994) recommended that to maximize student learning we should ensure that students are at least 80 percent correct in answering questions. We want to provide students with rapid and frequent questioning and encourage them to display high rates of correct responding. Students should be questioned equally. If they are hesitant to answer questions, we can have them respond chorally—saying the answer aloud together. Or we can provide them with slates and chalk to use in writing down correct answers; they can then hold their slates in front of them for us to see. With either technique, the class should be monitored to ensure that students are not simply copying answers from each other.

There is a common teacher questioning technique that should be avoided: Do not question students who do not seem to be paying attention during a lesson. There are two problems with this approach. First, if the student says "I don't know," nothing has been proved because the probability of giving correct answers decreases when students are off task. Second, some students may actually give the right answer, which only sends the message to other students that they do not have to pay attention in order to answer questions correctly. A better technique for students who are off task is to "catch them" being good and reinforce them with verbal praise.

Teachers are good at catching students being bad. This attention, in the form of a question or reprimand, may be reinforcing to students. Remember, negative attention is better than no attention at all.

Provide Feedback

We want to provide students with overt feedback after they have answered our questions. Overt feedback may take the form of a teacher repeating the correct answer, providing elaboration to the answer, saying "good job," or nodding her head. We should provide feedback on an intermittent basis, following the guidelines for giving reinforcement described in Chapter 4, for several reasons. First, if students are getting answers correct, they are probably reinforcing themselves internally, and we do not want to distract them during this process. Second, some students may be embarrassed to receive elaborate feedback, in which case feedback is punishing rather than reinforcing. Third, excessive feedback takes up time that otherwise could be devoted to presenting content.

Mastropieri and Scruggs (1994) provided several suggestions for giving students feedback depending on the correctness of their answers. Specifically, the type of feedback we give students will vary depending on whether they provide answers that are correct, partially correct, or incorrect. In addition, there are specific ways to respond to students who fail to provide overt responses to our questions. Table 8.4 summarizes their suggestions.

Provide Independent Practice

Most lessons conclude with independent seat-work activities, the purpose of which is to provide students with practice to demonstrate mastery of the skills. In order to promote automaticity, seat-work activities should be directly related to the content presented in the lesson. Students should be highly proficient at the skill (at least 85 to 95 percent accurate) during guided practice before independent practice activities are implemented. Any lesser degree of accuracy will become an antecedent for behavior problems.

	TABLE 8.4 FEEDBACK TO STUDENT RESPONSES
Response	**Feedback**
Correct	Overt acknowledgment ("That is correct."). Not overly elaborate; appropriate to response. Should be more limited during rapid-paced drill activities.
Partially correct	Acknowledge correct aspect of response. Provide prompt or rephrase question. Provide answer or call on another student if necessary. Repeat question later in the lesson.
Incorrect	State simply that the response is incorrect. Do not prod or probe students who obviously do not know the answer. State correct response or call on another student. Do not criticize the student unless incorrect response is due to inattention, lack of effort, or refusal to follow directions; be judicious with criticism.
Lack of overt response	Question further to determine source of nonresponding. Elicit an overt response, even if "don't know" is most appropriate. When response is overt—correct or incorrect—respond as described above.

Source: From *Effective Instruction for Special Education* (2nd ed.) (p. 16) by M. A. Mastropieri & T. E. Scruggs, 1994, Austin, TX: Pro-Ed. Copyright 1994 by Pro-Ed Publishing Company. Reprinted with permission.

Mastropieri and Scruggs (1994) described three considerations in providing beneficial seat-work activities. First, seat-work activities should reflect the instructional objective. We are trying to build either fluency or automaticity during independent practice activities, and not simply engage students in busy-work. Second, students should possess the requisite skills for doing seat-work independently. This determination can be made through the use of task analysis and criterion-referenced tests. Third, we should provide assistance to students in the initial stages of independent practice so that they gain confidence in their ability to complete the assignment on their own. For example, we can have the entire class work the first two problems of a math worksheet while providing guidance and corrective feedback. However, our direct involvement should be quickly faded out so that students are working independently.

One way to reduce our involvement during independent practice activities while also ensuring that students succeed is to create **sure-fire work folders** (Paine, Radicchi, Rosellini, Deutchman, & Darch, 1983). These folders contain work that students can complete without our assistance or instruction. They are helpful for students who can perform a task but need to build fluency and automaticity. Paine and colleagues (1983) provided the following instructions for developing sure-fire work folders:

1. Obtain construction paper (one large piece for each student in the class), a marking pen, and tape or a stapler.

2. Fold the paper in half lengthwise and cut a 4-inch slit on the fold at one end. This will give you two 4- by 10-inch tabs.
3. Fold over each of the tabs and fasten them with tape or staples to form pockets on the inside of the folder.
4. Write each student's name on a different folder along with the label "Sure-Fire Work."
5. Place a 1 day's to 1 week's supply of sure-fire work in each student's folder, adjusting the level of work to each student's ability. (pp. 112–113)

By design, our direct involvement with students during independent practice is reduced. However, this lack of involvement may also increase the likelihood of student disruptions. Mastropieri and Scruggs (1994) suggested that we instruct students on what they are expected to do, how they can obtain extra help, and what to do when they complete an assignment. In addition, students' seats should be organized so that we can observe the entire classroom at a glance. Finally, if we do not provide small-group instruction while the rest of the class completes seat-work, we should circulate among students to provide feedback, answer questions, and monitor student engagement. A major antecedent for behavior problems is a stationary teacher.

Paine and colleagues (1983) devised a nondisruptive way for students to obtain assistance during independent seat-work activities. We create **assistance cards** for each student that are placed on students' desks and used to signal us for help with assigned work. To construct assistance cards, obtain a piece of paper or tagboard about the size of notebook or photocopy paper, and fold it four times, as shown in Figure 8.6. On the first fold, write "Please Keep Working," and on the second fold, write "Please Help Me." Then fold the paper into a triangular shape and tape or staple it together. During seat-work

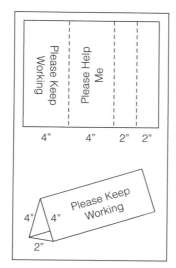

FIGURE 8.6

Constructing an Assistance Card

From *Structuring your classroom for academic success* (p. 111) by S. C. Paine, J. Radicchi, L. C. Rosellini, L. Deutchman, & C. B. Darch, 1983, Champaign, IL: Research Press. Copyright 1983 by the authors. Reprinted with permission.

activities, we acknowledge requests for help from students who use the card. If we are busy with another student or task, we momentarily stop, walk over to the student's desk, and flip the card up so that the statement "Please Keep Working" faces the student. Students who continue to work and patiently wait for assistance are reinforced. Obviously, we do not want to wait too long to provide assistance, or students will become frustrated.

Assistance cards can be placed on the tops of students' desks when they are given their sure-fire work folders. Paine and colleagues (1983) described the following procedures for using these two techniques together:

1. Provide students with instructions on how to use the assistance cards.
2. Model the use of the cards for students.
3. Make sure students' cards are visible from all parts of the classroom.
4. Scan the classroom to determine which students request assistance.
5. Reinforce students who use the card.
6. Reinforce students who are working while they wait and those who are working without asking for assistance.
7. Ignore students who do not use the cards.
8. Initially review procedures for students using the cards.
9. Ensure that students have enough daily work in their sure-fire work folders.

Conduct Formative Evaluation

The last component of direct instruction is the formative evaluation. This involves collecting information on a regular basis throughout the school year and graphing the data to help us make more informed instructional decisions. Table 8.5 provides some examples of formative evaluation techniques for six content

TABLE 8.5   CONTENT-AREA EXAMPLES OF FORMATIVE EVALUATION PROCEDURES

Content Area	Formative Evaluation Procedure
Math facts	Daily rate of correct digits
Grammar	Number of times noun–verb agreement correctly used
Decoding	Daily rate of CVC words (*hat, met, bit*) said aloud correctly
Spelling	Daily number of words spelled correctly
Science	Number of elements correctly identified from the periodical chart of elements
Social studies	Number of state capitals written correctly

areas. Formative evaluation techniques help us assess not only students' performance but, more importantly, their progress through the curriculum.

Graphing formative evaluation data can help us determine whether students are making adequate progress toward mastering instructional objectives. If the data reveal insufficient rates of progress, we should determine what instructional modifications are required to improve their learning. The first step should be to increase the amount of engaged time. By maximizing the time on task, more material can be covered. A second step might be to increase the pace at which information is covered, perhaps by modifying the way the curriculum is sequenced. A third step might be to alter the structure and clarity with which information is delivered. A fourth step might be to modify the types of questioning and feedback or guided and independent practice activities.

ENVIRONMENTAL ACCOMMODATIONS

The classroom is the environment in which most teachers and students interact. Making the classroom a pleasant place is beneficial for both students and teachers. A disorganized classroom environment is a major antecedent for student disruptions. Conversely, a well-organized classroom environment can exert a powerful influence on students' behavior and lead to high levels of academic engagement. Academic engagement, in turn, is an antecedent for appropriate student behavior. Smith and Rivera (1993) described several factors to consider when making environmental accommodations to prevent behavior problems from occurring.

First, most classrooms contain high-traffic zones such as group work areas, pencil sharpeners, trash cans, doorways, bathrooms, bookshelves, and supply areas. These areas provide students with opportunities to engage in disruptive behavior such as talking to or getting physical with one another. The contribution of high-traffic zones to student disruptions can be lessened by keeping the areas separated, providing plenty of space, and ensuring easy access to the areas (Evertson et al., 1994). We can identify potential high-traffic areas by observing students' movements during independent seat-work activities.

Second, the arrangement of students' seating may contribute to disruptive behavior. In addition, the presence of independent workers, students who are easily distracted, attention seekers, and daydreamers may dictate different seating arrangements. For example, some teachers prefer to arrange seating in rows to minimize interaction. The advantage of this arrangement is that students are less likely to disrupt others; the disadvantage is that their positive interactions are also reduced, making it difficult to use techniques such as cooperative learning effectively. Regardless of how carefully teachers initially

---

Formative evaluation involves techniques similar to those presented in Chapters 5 and 6 for counting, recording, and graphing behavior. However, with formative evaluation, permanent products of students' behavior in content-area subjects are collected.

The environment includes concrete and tangible events such as the students and adults in a room and the tables, chairs, chalkboards, materials, and tasks. Some events can be less visible and abstruse. For example, social norms and cultural mores have a profound effect on how behavior is expressed and interpreted.

consider students' seating, it will most likely change as the year progresses. Therefore, teachers must remain flexible as environmental demands change.

Third, students should have easy access to any materials required for instructional activities. A considerable amount of time is lost when both teachers and students are searching for materials. When teachers search for materials, students have less supervision. And when students search for materials, they have an ideal opportunity to engage in various off-task behaviors such as talking to peers and getting out of their seats. Once materials have been located, it takes additional time to get students' attention so the lesson can begin. These problems can be minimized by having designated areas for materials and a schedule for students to obtain them.

The three factors described by Smith and Rivera (1993) provide a good preview for the subsequent discussion on techniques for making environmental accommodations. This information is based primarily on the work of Paine and colleagues (1983), who field-tested and evaluated their procedures for structuring classrooms for success over several years. Several of their procedures are discussed here, including techniques for arranging the classroom area, developing classroom rules, managing transition time, handling materials, and managing students' paperwork.

Arranging the Classroom Area

There are a variety of factors to consider before deciding how the classroom area should be arranged. Most classrooms have student and teacher desks, chalkboards, countertops, bookshelves, and various materials. Additional items in some elementary classrooms may include a sink, partitions, work and activity centers, bulletin boards, a coatroom, and perhaps a bathroom. And all classrooms have wall space to be arranged.

Paine and colleagues (1983) identified several advantages of well-arranged classrooms. First, they minimize student noise and disruption. For example, seating students at separate desks instead of tables reduces the likelihood that they will talk to each other and increases attending behaviors. Second, they facilitate positive peer interactions through the use of cooperative learning techniques and activity centers. Third, they result in higher levels of student engaged time. Fourth, they prompt teachers to praise students, provide them with corrective feedback, and circulate around the classroom.

There are eight components for arranging classrooms to maximize students' learning and minimize distractions (Paine et al., 1983). First, desks should be placed in rows facing toward the chalkboard and away from windows. Students with behavior problems should be placed in the front and in between well-behaved students who can serve as models for appropriate behavior. Second, the teacher's desk should be in a front corner of the room, facing students' desks. A paraeducator's desk can be placed in the back, on the opposite side of the room. Third, portable partitions, such as chalkboards, can be used to change the structure of the room to meet the demands of a particular lesson. For example, a partition might be placed between cooperative learning groups to minimize distractions. Fourth, teaching stations can be placed in the corners not occupied by the teacher's and paraeducator's desks. Students' chairs should face toward the wall to minimize distractions, but the teacher's chair should face the classroom so she can monitor students. Fifth, a table and several chairs can be placed near a wall to serve as a self-correction station. Sixth, a materials station consisting of a large table can be located in the front of the room to allow easy access for both teacher and students. Seventh, activity centers can be arranged in various parts of the room that do not inhibit the flow of traffic or interfere with students working at desks. Activity stations can be used to provide reinforcement or to give extra practice to build fluency and automaticity. Finally, bulletin boards can be used for posting rules, announcements, student artwork, and seasonal displays.

Developing Classroom Rules

A classroom is a microcosm of society, and like any society, it needs rules to function in an orderly fashion. The rules that are selected, and the way they are introduced, can have a substantial effect on students' classroom behaviors. Rules serve two important functions (Paine et al., 1983; Smith & Rivera, 1993). First, they communicate our expectations for students. This means that when students misbehave they do not have the convenient excuse of pleading ignorance, but instead can be held accountable. Second, rules help us catch students being good. Teachers who occasionally reinforce students for following the rules, rather than focusing exclusively on students who break them, generally run more efficient classrooms.

Good rules share certain characteristics (Paine et al., 1983; Smith & Rivera, 1993). First, students should participate in developing rules. They acquire ownership of the rules by participating in this process and so are more likely to follow them. We can encourage their participation by asking them questions such as "What do you consider to be appropriate and inappropriate classroom behavior?" and "Why do you think (the behavior they generate) is inappropriate?" Second, only three to four rules should be written for any particular activity or lesson so that students can remember them. Third, the wording of the rules should be kept simple so that students understand them. Fourth, rules should be stated positively—for example, not "No talking," but "Raise your hand if you have something to say." Fifth, different rules should be used for different situations. Generating a list of rules for every classroom situation is too burdensome for students. Sixth, rules should be posted in a con-

First-year and novice teachers should place their desk away from the rest of the class. This forces them to move around the room rather than standing by the desk, which limits their vision.

The acronym KISS is sometimes used to describe rules: Keep It Simple, Stupid. Although the last word in the acronym is pejorative, it nevertheless points out how teachers often create elaborate rules that are too complicated for some students to follow.

TABLE 8.6	STEPS FOR ESTABLISHING RULES
Steps	**Description**
Tell students the importance of having rules in the classroom.	Inform students that rules are required so that they will know what is expected of them and that discipline will be fair and clearly understood. The appearance of a repressive environment should be avoided.
Tell students that they will help write the rules for the classroom.	Remind students that it is their classroom and education that are being structured and that they will be part of it. Make sure students realize that the teacher is the classroom manager and that she will teach and enforce the rules after they are written. Let students know as well that the teacher will impose her own rules if they cannot follow the ones generated together.
Tell students which classroom activities will need to be covered by rules.	Have students discuss what types of behavior will be appropriate for each classroom activity. Moderate the discussion so that it stays on topic and all students participate equally in generaing rules. Guide the discussion toward rules believed to be best for a classroom activity. Write the rules on the board. Condense the rules into three or four for each activity.
Once the rules lists have been refined, write each list down on a large piece of tagboard.	Use a wide felt-tipped marker to write the rules so that they will be visible from all parts of the classroom. Groups of students can be assigned to write the various lists and make the charts as a group art project. Students can also help choose a spot for each chart and hang up the charts.

Source: Paine, Radicchi, Roselline, Deutchman, and Darch (1983).

spicuous spot that provides students with a visual reminder of the expectations for a given activity.

Rules should be established early in the morning on the first day of school so that students recognize their importance (Paine et al., 1983). Furthermore, structuring a group discussion to solicit student input provides them with ownership for the development and enforcement of rules. Paine and colleagues described four steps for establishing rules, which are summarized in Table 8.6.

After rules are established for each classroom activity, they need to be implemented. Paine and colleagues (1983) suggested providing students with 3- to 5-minute minilessons in which the rules for a given activity are taught. These lessons should take place just prior to the first time students engage in the activity. The goal is to have students follow the rules and not simply regurgitate them. Therefore, at the end of each minilesson, time should be set aside for students to practice rule-following behaviors. Smith and Rivera (1993) provided the following tips for implementing rules:

1. Decide what code of conduct and expectations must be in place in the classroom.
2. Discuss ideas for rules with students.

3. Determine no more than seven rules that can be followed and understood by all.
4. Phrase rules in the positive as much as possible.
5. Identify positive consequences for rule observance.
6. Identify logical negative consequences for infractions.
7. Enforce the rules and apply the consequences consistently.
8. Inform parents and administrators about classroom rules and consequences.
9. Teach the rules.
10. Remind students about the rules.
11. Praise students for following the rules.
12. As circumstances change, revise rules accordingly.
13. Be sure the rules are age appropriate. (p. 63)

Managing Transition Time

Classroom transitions constitute a major source of off-task activities (Mastropieri & Scruggs, 1994). Transitions occur when students move from one activity to the next. During these times, student behaviors such as sharpening pencils, using the bathroom, obtaining drinks from the water fountain, and socializing can reduce the amount of engaged time. Obviously, some of these transitions are necessary and appropriate. However, activities such as using the bathroom, getting drinks, and sharpening pencils should be arranged so that they do not interfere with lessons. In addition, students can be taught to engage in appropriate transition behaviors.

Several steps can ensure that students learn appropriate behavior during transition time (Mastropieri & Scruggs, 1994; Paine et al., 1983; Smith & Rivera, 1993). First, we should prepare all materials for each lesson in advance and place them in the room where they are to be used. This frees us to monitor students during transition time. Second, we should provide a signal letting students know they have a specified (e.g., 10 minutes) amount of time to finish their work. This signal prepares students for the upcoming transition to another activity. Third, we want to gain students' attention before the transition occurs. For example, in elementary school classes, music can be played to signal the impending transition and then stopped to indicate that we now want students' attention. Fourth, after obtaining students' attention, we can give them instructions on how to make the transition (e.g., lining up according the color of their shirts) and what the expected behavior is (e.g., walking quietly and quickly while keeping their hands to themselves). Fifth, we can use positive reinforcement techniques such as verbal praise, tokens, and stickers for prompt transitions. Sixth, we should provide a negative consequence for students who do not follow the transition plan. For example, students can be informed that time lost during transitions will be made up either during free time or recess or after school.

Handling Classroom Materials

In many instances, students need materials to participate in an activity or complete an assignment that are not typically kept at their desks or work areas. Materials such as workbooks, papers, worksheets, special writing utensils, and content-area specialty items (e.g., chemicals and containers for science) typically are distributed and then collected each time they are used. The distribution of these materials represents a specific type of transition time that can detract from academic engagement.

Paine and colleagues (1983) described several inefficient methods for distributing and collecting materials. First, we should avoid handing out materials to each student, a practice that consumes large amounts of time and is distracting to students. And assigning this task to students does not save much time and may result in their engaging in inappropriate socialization. Second, we want to avoid having students distribute and collect their own materials. This practice is extremely disruptive and is a definite antecedent for inappropriate behavior. Third, we should avoid having the last, or first, student in a row hand out or collect materials. This practice often leads to talking, poking, waving, paper dropping, and other such disruptions.

Indeed, using any one of these three techniques can easily lead to students spending 5 to 10 minutes simply handling papers for an activity. If this figure is multiplied by six instances per day, students can spend 30 to 60 minutes a day distributing and collecting papers. Paine and colleagues (1983) made four recommendations for managing materials efficiently: (1) Develop supplementary materials, (2) have needed materials ready, (3) store materials conveniently, and (4) develop distribution and collection procedures.

Develop Supplementary Materials It is important for teachers to develop supplementary materials before the school year begins, although they may need to generate additional supplementary materials as time passes. Supplementary materials provide students with additional practice to develop fluency and automaticity while also keeping them appropriately engaged in tasks for which they possess the requisite skills. In addition, supplementary materials often are useful for modifying traditional curricular and textbook materials that students with disabilities initially may find too difficult.

Paine and colleagues (1983) described two methods for modifying and supplementing traditional textbooks. First, extra worksheets can be developed to provide certain students with additional drill and practice in skills for which they need to build fluency and automaticity. Although some textbooks offer extra worksheets, they usually are neither specific nor extensive enough to provide the intensive practice low-achieving students require. Second, instructional games can be developed that are directly related to instructional objectives.

Have Needed Materials Ready   The most efficient way to handle materials is to have them readily accessible. Distributing and collecting materials should not interfere with the time allocated for instruction. In addition, a large supply of needed materials such as pencils, paper, erasers, rulers, and markers should be on hand. Some students may purposely forget these supplies in an attempt to avoid participating in the lesson or completing an assignment (or they may simply find it reinforcing to disrupt the lesson). These problems can be avoided by providing students with the needed materials immediately.

Some teachers do not like to give out extra materials because they believe it is students' responsibility to be prepared. Although the logic may be sound, this approach can result in some students not learning the content. An alternative approach to this dilemma is to institute a point system whereby students must "pay" for supplies with points earned for displaying good behavior. They can use extra points to purchase privileges.

Store Materials Conveniently   All materials and extra supplies should be stored near the instructional area. For example, materials for cooperative learning activities can be kept by the tables designated for this purpose. Or books can be kept on a shelf close to the area where small-group reading instruction takes place. An area should be designated for collecting work materials and assignments to be graded. In addition, boxes or "cubbyholes" can be provided for each student containing folders for each academic subject. Each box can have a partition in the middle, with the front designated as the place where students hand in assignments to be graded and the back as the place where teachers place graded assignments.

Develop Distribution and Collection Procedures   The most effective procedures for handing out and collecting papers involve several students at a time acting as paper monitors. These students should be selected carefully, taught how to distribute and collect papers, and reinforced. Paine and colleagues (1983) described five basic rules for handing out and collecting papers:

1. Pass or collect materials quietly.
2. The paper monitors pick up the materials quickly.
3. Paper monitors pass or collect in their zone only.
4. Pass or collect without touching other people.
5. Monitors return material to the correct storage area. (p. 103)

For these rules to work, about 20 minutes should be spent practicing the procedures. In addition, all needed materials should be readily available. Generally, the classroom can be divided into two or three zones, or areas, with one student responsible for each zone. Materials monitors can be rotated so that all students get a chance to participate in this activity. Many students find this job highly reinforcing in and of itself; other students may require external reinforcement to perform the task appropriately. If these latter students still are unable to follow the rules correctly, warn them that they risk forfeiting the privilege of being a monitor.

Managing Students' Paperwork

The management of students' paperwork is an important aspect of preventing behavior problems. The less time teachers spend correcting papers, the more time they have for monitoring students' behaviors, reinforcing them for staying on task, and providing certain students with more individual attention. Paine and colleagues (1983) described three techniques for correcting students' papers efficiently: (1) correction while circulating, (2) student self-correction, and (3) group self-correction.

Teacher Correction While Circulating It is easy to handle the time-consuming task of correcting papers by doing it while providing students with assistance during seat-work activities. We can use different-colored pens or pencils so that our marks can be distinguished from marks students make on their own papers. Sometimes it is helpful to carry the answer key, especially for tasks that may involve multistep computations, such as math problems. We should correct lower-achieving students or those with their "help me" cards raised first so that they get immediate feedback. Gradually circulate around to all students, marking at least two items for each. Mark correct items with a "C" or star; these marks serve as reinforcers. Mark incorrect items with a small dot, which is less conspicuous and may minimize student embarrassment. We want to circulate several times, replacing the dots with a "C" or star when the student corrects the item. It is important to provide students with verbal praise and encouragement while circulating.

Student Self-Correction There are many types of assignments for which students can correct their own work. For example, we can prepare answer keys for many math and reading assignments. Having students self-correct their papers serves two important purposes. First, it frees up time that can be used for helping students and managing their behavior. Second, it teaches students self-management skills because they are active participants in their own education. Students tend to be more motivated and thorough when they participate in the correcting and grading aspects of assignments (Glasser, 1992).

A prerequisite for establishing self-correction procedures is a checking station consisting of a table and several chairs visible to the teacher. The station should have correcting markers, teacher-prepared answer keys, and a box in which students can place their checked work. Paine and colleagues (1983) described four rules for using a checking station:

1. Only one person at each answer key.
2. Leave your pens or pencils at your desk (only correcting pens are allowed at the station).
3. Check your work without talking.
4. Put all corrected work in the box. (pp. 123–124)

It is important that we monitor the checking station to ensure that students are using it properly. Paine and colleagues (1983) described the following procedures for using a checking station:

HOW STUDENTS SELF-CORRECT

1. Students complete the assignment and "double-check" it at their desks to make sure that all items have been completed.
2. Students go to the checking station and circle any errors with the colored pen.
3. Students return to their seats to correct the errors.
4. They go to the checking station to recheck their corrections.
5. When their assignments are 100% correct, the students place them in the box for completed assignments.
6. If all the answer keys are being used, students work on another assignment while waiting to use the checking station.

HOW TO PREPARE FOR STUDENT SELF-CORRECTION

1. Prepare the checking station for only one subject at first. Math is an easy subject for students to correct. Language or other subjects can be added later.
2. Post the rules at the station.
3. Introduce self-checking to students by using the script and by modeling it.
4. Set expectations for proper use of the checking station by reviewing the rules frequently with students.
   a. For the first week, review rules every day.
   b. The second week, review them every other day (M, W, F).
   c. In succeeding weeks, review the rules the first day of each week and when it appears that students are not following them. Also, review rules the first day after a break in the school schedule.
5. Reinforce correct checking. It is important to focus on encouraging students to find all their errors. Praise careful checking: "Good, you found that mistake."
6. Spot check at least some of the student's papers each day to determine their accuracy at self-correction.

REWARDS AND CONSEQUENCES FOR SELF-CORRECTION

1. Rewards should be given for correct work and correct checking. The teacher or aide should select one paper at random from among those each student has corrected to check for accurate self-correction. It is important that students have no idea which paper will be checked.
2. If a student checks a paper incorrectly, there should be a consequence. Cheating in any way could cost points, time from recess, staying after school, and the like.
3. The teacher should stress both the importance of doing a good job on assignments and checking them correctly for errors.

4. The student can earn a plus, or some other positive mark, for final accuracy on the paper if all items are properly corrected.
5. When students are checking their papers, the teacher and/or aide should always praise them for correct checking behaviors (following the rules) and for finding errors. The praise should be given frequently at first and then generally phased out when the students consistently follow the rules while checking. (pp. 124–125)

Group Self-Correction   The benefits of group self-correction are similar to those for a checking station: efficiency, immediate feedback and practice, and detection of error patterns. An additional advantage is that we immediately know which students have mastered a skill. Group self-correction can be used at the end of a daily review session, for the following lesson, or as an independent practice activity. As with guided practice, we want to lead the self-correction activity as students check their work with a colored pen or pencil. Paine and colleagues (1983) described six steps for using group self-correction:

1. Have the answers ready to display on an overhead projector or chalkboard.
2. When all students have completed the assignment, ask them to pick up their correcting pens. Check to see that everyone has done so.
3. Uncover the first answer on the overhead or chalkboard.
4. Point to the first answer and say (for example): "Give yourself a plus if you spelled (word) correctly. Circle any incorrect answers and correct them with the correcting pen."
5. Continue until all answers are checked, one at a time.
6. As with individual self-correcting, stress finding all mistakes. (p. 127)

As with the procedures for using the checking station, it is important to spot-check students' answers after they are collected. Students should be reinforced for accurate self-correction.

SUMMARY

Preventing behavior problems from occurring requires that we examine the curriculum, instruction methods, and classroom management techniques. The curriculum can serve as an antecedent for behavior problems if students do not possess the skills for completing assignments correctly. Sequencing curricular content of similar difficulty levels can increase student interest. Writing behavioral objectives, conducting task analysis, and using criterion-referenced tests help teachers determine at what instructional level the curriculum should be presented to students. Direct instruction is an effective, data-based approach for teaching students the curriculum. Finally, behavior problems can be minimized when teachers make environmental accommodations. These accommodations are often referred to as classroom management.

ACTIVITIES

1. Interview a principal, teacher, and parent, and ask them if the curriculum meets the needs of most students. Questions to ask include "Do all students benefit from the curriculum?" "Does the curriculum reflect what students will need to know in real life as adults?" and "What accommodations can be made for students who are not adequately learning the curriculum?" You should identify differences between the answers given by the principal, teacher, and parent.
2. Ask a teacher and a principal if the popular practice of requiring teachers to spend time teaching students how to take standardized tests enhances or inhibits their learning the curriculum.
3. Get on the Internet and search for "direct instruction." Write down four important characteristics of direct instruction, and note how these characteristics differ from traditional ways in which teachers deliver instruction.
4. Observe two teachers' classrooms. Identify what aspects of the room arrangement both prevent and aggravate the occurrence of behavior problems. Then list the classroom arrangements you would use to minimize behavior problems.

REVIEW QUESTIONS

1. How can the curriculum actually cause behavior problems?
2. What are the components of tasks, and how is a task analysis conducted?
3. What are the five types of curricula that are appropriate for students with disabilities?
4. Describe the components of behavioral objectives.
5. Discuss techniques for sequencing content of equal difficulty.
6. Describe the steps of direct instruction.
7. What factors should be considered when arranging the classroom to minimize behavior problems?
8. What are the characteristics of good rules, and how can they minimize classroom disruptions?
9. Discuss the importance of transition time and ways in which teachers can teach students appropriate transition behaviors.
10. Describe the four procedures for handling classroom materials efficiently.
11. What are the three procedures for managing students' paperwork?

REFERENCES

Alberto, P. A., & Troutman, A. C. (1999). *Applied behavior analysis for teachers* (5th ed.). Columbus, OH: Merrill.

Cooper, J. O., Heron, T. E., & Heward, W. L. (1987). *Applied behavior analysis.* Columbus, OH: Merrill.

Evans, W. H., Evans, S. S., Gable, R. A., & Schmid, R. E. (1991). *Instructional management for detecting and correcting special problems.* Boston: Allyn & Bacon.

Evertson, C. M., Emmer, E. T., & Brophy, J. E. (1980). Predictors of effective teaching in junior high mathematics classrooms. *Journal of Research in Mathematics Education, 11,* 167–178.

Evertson, C. M., Emmer, E. T., Clements, B. S., Sanford, J. P., & Worsham, M. E. (1994). *Classroom management for elementary teachers* (3rd ed.). Englewood Cliffs, NJ: Prentice-Hall.

Glasser, W. (1992). *The quality school* (2nd ed.). New York: HarperCollins.

Goldstein, A. P., & McGinnis, E. (1997). *Skillstreaming the adolescent: A structured learning approach to teaching prosocial skills* (2nd ed.). Champaign, IL: Research Press.

Howell, K. W., Kaplan, J. S., & O'Connell, C. Y. (1979). *Evaluating exceptional children: A task analysis approach.* Columbus, OH: Merrill.

Howell, K. W., & Morehead, M. K. (1987). *Curriculum-based evaluation for special and remedial education.* Columbus, OH: Merrill.

Howell, K. W., & Nolet, V. (2000). *Curriculum-based evaluation* (3rd ed.). Belmont, CA: Wadsworth.

Hunter, M. (1981). *Increasing your teaching effectiveness.* Palo Alto, CA: Learning Institute.

Levitt, L. K., & Rutherford, R. B., Jr. (1978). *Strategies for handling the disruptive student.* Tempe: College of Education, Arizona State University.

Lovitt, T. C. (1984). *Tactics for teaching.* Columbus, OH: Merrill.

Martin, G., & Pear, J. (1992). *Behavior modification: What it is and how to do it* (4th ed.). Englewood Cliffs, NJ: Prentice-Hall.

Mastropieri, M. A., & Scruggs, T. E. (1991). *Teaching students ways to remember: Strategies for learning mnemonically.* Cambridge, MA: Brookline Books.

Mastropieri, M. A., & Scruggs, T. E. (1994). *Effective instruction for special education* (2nd ed.). Austin, TX: Pro-Ed.

Meier, F. E. (1992). *Competency-based instruction for teachers of students with special learning needs.* Boston: Allyn & Bacon.

Meyen, E. L., Vergason, G. A., & Whelan, R. J. (Eds.). (1988). *Effective instructional strategies for exceptional children.* Denver, CO: Love.

Paine, S. C., Radicchi, J., Rosellini, L. C., Deutchman, L., & Darch, C. B. (1983). *Structuring your classroom for academic success.* Champaign, IL: Research Press.

Pressley, M. (1990). *Cognitive strategy instruction that really improves children's academic performance.* Cambridge, MA: Brookline Books.

Rosenshine, B. V. (1986). Synthesis of research on explicit teaching. *Educational Leadership 43*(7), 60–69.

Smith, D. D., & Rivera, D. M. (1993). *Effective discipline* (2nd ed.). Austin, TX: Pro-Ed.

Stowitschek, J. J., Stowitschek, C. E., Hendrickson, J. M., & Day, R. M. (1984). *Direct teaching tactics for exceptional children: A practice and supervision guide.* Rockville, MD: Aspen.

Wielkiewicz, R. M. (1995). *Behavior management in the schools: Principles and procedures* (2nd ed.). Boston: Allyn & Bacon.

Zirpoli, T. J., & Melloy, K. J. (1997). *Behavior management: Applications for teachers and parents* (2nd ed.). New York: Macmillan.

REINFORCEMENT TECHNIQUES FOR INCREASING BEHAVIOR

CHAPTER OVERVIEW

- Token Economies
- Behavioral Contracting
- Group-Oriented Contingencies
- Novel Applications of Positive Reinforcement

CHAPTER OBJECTIVES

After completing this chapter, you will be able to do the following:

1. Describe the purpose and advantages of a token economy and the steps for implementing one.

2. Explain the mechanisms underlying a behavioral contract and the components for implementing one.

3. Describe the types of group-oriented contingencies and the rationale for and ethical considerations in using them.

4. Identify various novel ways for using reinforcement.

Positive reinforcement is the most powerful and effective method for increasing or maintaining appropriate behavior. Positive reinforcement always works. If a behavior does not increase when it is followed by some stimulus, then, by definition, that stimulus is not a positive reinforcer. Conversely, if the behavior subsequently increases, then the consequence is a positive reinforcer.

As indicated in Chapter 1, criticisms of positive reinforcement are pervasive, grounded in cultural mores, and not likely to disappear despite empirical evidence for its effectiveness provided in many journal articles. Only when teachers have the will and foresight to use positive reinforcement proactively, however, will its effectiveness be acknowledged by others. Once teachers experience its effectiveness first-hand, they are more likely to use it. With positive reinforcement, everyone comes out a winner. It is responsive to students' natural need for attention and approval, and it decreases the likelihood that students will exhibit inappropriate behavior to obtain attention.

Positive reinforcement can be administered in many ways. It may be incorporated into and implemented through a token economy or a behavioral contract with individuals. It can also be applied to groups or an entire class of students. Methods for implementing reinforcement can involve dependent, independent, and interdependent group-oriented contingencies. There are literally countless ways in which positive reinforcement can be administered; we are restricted only by our lack of creativity and unwillingness. This chapter discusses the use of token economies, behavioral contracts, group-oriented contingencies, and six easy-to-implement methods.

Before describing these procedures, a summary for determining reinforcers may help. (This information was presented in detail in Chapter 4.) Regardless of the approach, we should obtain reinforcers using the follow procedure:

1. Ask students what they find reinforcing. Write down everything they say even though some comments may be inappropriate. The purpose here is to encourage students to "brainstorm" as many reinforcers as possible. We can always eliminate inappropriate reinforcers from the list later on.

2. Ask other adults who interact with the students (i.e., teachers, administrators, parents) what they believe the students might like as reinforcers. Add these items, privileges, and activities to the initial list.

3. Observe students to see what they like to do when they are free to do whatever they want. This approach makes use of the Premack principle, described in Chapter 4. We add our observations to the list.

4. Present the compiled list to the students and have them rank order them from most to least desirable.

We now have reinforcers that can be incorporated into a token economy, behavioral contract, group-oriented contingency, or some other novel approach for delivering reinforcement.

TOKEN ECONOMIES

Why is money so highly valued in our society? Because we can use it to purchase a variety of highly reinforcing items and activities. Money is a special type of reinforcer—a conditioned reinforcer. There is nothing inherently reinforcing about money; after all, it is just paper. Imagine being stranded on a deserted island with nothing with which to start a fire except a suitcase full of money. If our prospects for rescue are slim, how long will we wait before burning the money to cook our food? In this situation, money loses its reinforcing properties, other than as a flammable substance, because it cannot be exchanged for anything desirable. The reinforcing power of a conditioned reinforcer depends, to a large degree, on the number of backup reinforcers available (Martin & Pear, 1996). **Backup reinforcers** are the items and activities that can be purchased using the conditioned reinforcer—in this case, money. Money is a generalized conditioned reinforcer because it can be exchanged for a virtually limitless number of items and activities. Imagine what would happen to the reinforcing power of money if it could only be used to purchase socks and lamps!

There are many real-life examples of conditioned reinforcers. Grocery stores used to give customers "green stamps" that they could redeem for merchandise from an accompanying catalogue. More recently, American Express offers gift certificates that have become popular Christmas and birthday presents for the "hard-to-shop-for" relative or friend. The person receiving the gift certificate also receives a catalogue of items from which to choose.

The tangible objects, such as money, trading stamps, or gift certificates, that are exchanged for items or activities are called **tokens.** Any token that is a generalized conditioned reinforcer can be used to increase students' appropriate behaviors. A token economy is a way to administer reinforcement. Students earn tokens that can be exchanged for a variety of backup reinforcers. Cooper, Heron, and Heward (1987) described key aspects of a **token economy:**

- Behaviors to be reinforced are identified and defined.
- A medium of exchange is selected. A medium of exchange refers to some symbol or token that individuals receive after successfully completing the target behavior.
- Backup reinforcers are provided that can be purchased with the tokens.

There are several advantages of token economies (Alberto & Troutman, 1999; Kazdin, 1985; Martin & Pear, 1996):

- Tokens can be administered immediately after a target behavior occurs and subsequently exchanged for backup reinforcers. Therefore, they "bridge the gap" between the time when students perform the desired behavior and the time when they have access to the backup reinforcers.

- It is easier for teachers to dispense tokens than verbal reinforcement when dealing with students as a group.
- Unlike edible or activity reinforcers, tokens can be used to reinforce students' behavior any time without interrupting the lesson or leading to satiation.
- Tokens will maintain students' behavior over time.
- Tokens can be given to students who have different preferences in backup reinforcers.

Token economies are most often used with students who have not responded to teacher approval and praise alone. Token economies involve presenting tokens after students perform certain behaviors—usually no more than three. After some specified time has elapsed, students exchange the tokens for backup reinforcers. Tokens quickly become conditioned reinforcers because they are exchanged for backup reinforcers. Teacher praise and approval should be paired with tokens in order to increase their effectiveness.

Reasons for the Effectiveness of Token Economies

Cooper, Heron, and Heward (1987) provided several reasons token economies are an effective method of dispensing reinforcement.

The Time Gap Is Bridged Between Behavior and Backup Reinforcer

It is not always possible for us to stop in the middle of a lesson to reinforce students. The problems with a procedure in which students get 5 minutes of free time for every 10 math problems completed correctly on a sheet of paper containing 30 problems should be obvious: The students will be going back and forth between task and reinforcement, which is disruptive to other students and wastes time. However, we can circulate around the room while teaching a lesson and unobtrusively dispense tokens that students can later exchange for backup reinforcers.

The Amount of Reinforcement Is Immediately Obvious to Students

Tokens provide students with visible and tangible proof that they are working toward obtaining backup reinforcers. Students also can see the progress they are making as they accumulate tokens. For example, a student may place stickers on a bar graph, as in Figure 9.1, in order to keep track of how many tokens he has earned. Or we can place marbles in a jar every time a student engages in a target behavior.

Tokens Are Unaffected by the Mood of the Praiser

Teachers are human, and like anyone else, they have both good and bad days. Verbal praise,

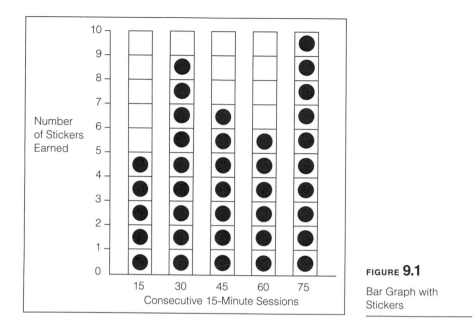

FIGURE 9.1

Bar Graph with Stickers

a form of positive reinforcement, is more effective when we deliver it in a pleasant, courteous manner. Students are not likely to find our verbal praise very reinforcing if we deliver it while clearly in a bad mood. The use of a token economy may circumvent this problem because the value of a token does not decrease if it is delivered when we are in a bad mood. Tokens can still be exchanged for backup reinforcers regardless of our mood when we delivered them.

Tokens Make Use of Generalized Conditioned Reinforcers   Students are less likely to experience satiation because tokens can be exchanged for a variety of backup reinforcers. Furthermore, given this variety of backup reinforcers, our inability to restrict access to one of them is not likely to affect students' motivation to obtain others. Finally, all students respond equally well to tokens because they can exchange them for backup items that they individually find reinforcing.

Tokens Provide Stimuli That Control Teacher Behavior   One of the most important reasons token economies work is because tokens serve as a cue to remind us to reinforce students. For example, we can fill up our pockets with marbles to dispense as tokens. The weight of the marbles in our pocket serves as a reminder to catch students being good as a way to reduce the weight. Therefore, the tokens function as a discriminative stimulus—leading to a marble-dispensing response in the presence of certain stimuli. In addition, we are negatively reinforced because the weight and bulk of the tokens is aversive.

TABLE 9.1	RULES FOR ESTABLISHING A TOKEN ECONOMY
1. Select a target behavior.	7. Designate a time when students can exchange tokens for rewards.
2. Develop rules.	8. Implement the token economy.
3. Select an appropriate token.	9. Provide immediate token reinforcement for acceptable behavior.
4. Establish reinforcers for which tokens can be exchanged.	10. Gradually change from a continuous to a variable schedule of reinforcement.
5. Establish a ratio of exchange.	11. Revise the menu frequently.
6. Develop a reward menu and post it in the classroom.	

Tokens also control teacher behavior (i.e., dispensing tokens) through the principle of negative reinforcement. The weight of the marbles represents an aversive stimulus that can be terminated by dispensing marbles for appropriate behavior.

We can eliminate (escape) this aversive stimulus by catching students being good and dispensing tokens. The more tokens we dispense, the less weight we have to bear.

Procedures for Establishing a Token Economy

Setting up a token economy at the beginning of the year takes considerable time and effort. However, the time spent doing so is well worth the return of having students' behaviors under control for the rest of the year. Table 9.1 summarizes rules for establishing a token economy.

There are two main concerns in establishing a token economy. First, we should introduce the token economy gradually because it can be difficult for students to understand and complicated for us to administer. It is best to introduce it in steps, explain it clearly and precisely to students, and answer all their questions. At first, we may want to implement the token economy for only a brief period during the day—perhaps initially for a 30-minute lesson. Second, we should field-test the token economy before actually implementing it (Cooper, Heron, & Heward, 1987). For 3 to 5 days, we should tally the number of tokens each student might earn without actually dispensing tokens. Field-testing the system provides us with information that can be used to answer the following questions:

1. Are students actually deficient in the targeted skills?
2. Are some students demonstrating mastery of behaviors targeted for the system?
3. Are some students not receiving tokens?

Select a Target Behavior Cooper, Heron, and Heward (1987) made several recommendations regarding the selection of target behaviors for a token economy. First, target behaviors should be operationally defined so that they pass the stranger test. An operational definition ensures that both teachers and students are fully aware of the behaviors that will earn tokens, which makes misunderstandings less likely to occur. Second, the criteria for acceptable performance (CAP), or task standards, should be clearly specified. This helps us determine whether the task or behavior was performed at a satisfactory level. Third, it is important to begin with a small number of behaviors—no more than three to five—so that both students and teachers are less likely to become confused. Fourth, one or two easy behaviors should be included to set up students for success and make them more likely to "buy into" the token economy. We can gradually add more difficult behaviors and administer tokens on a more intermittent basis after everyone has bought into the system. Fifth, students must have the requisite skills for performing the targeted behaviors. This determination can be made by conducting a thorough task analysis before implementing the token economy.

Post the Rules and Review Them Frequently For elementary school students, rules should be posted on either the chalkboard or a bulletin board. For secondary school students, rules can be stapled to the inside of a folder each receives. These folders might also contain a tally card for keeping track of the number of tokens earned and a menu of backup reinforcers. Just as with classroom rules, which were discussed in the previous chapter, rules for a token economy should be frequently reviewed with students. Cooper, Heron, and Heward (1987) suggested rules for operating a token economy, which are summarized in Table 9.2.

The effectiveness of a token economy can be enhanced by giving students copies of the rules and reviewing them on a regular basis, using the guidelines in Chapter 8 for teaching rules.

Select Tokens Items frequently used as tokens include washers, checkers, coupons, poker chips, tally marks, teacher initials, and cards with holes punched in them. Almost any object can serve as a token as long as it cannot be easily counterfeited. Younger students often prefer physical objects such as stickers or poker chips because their accumulation provides them with a visual representation of their progress. Older students may find physical objects "babyish" and prefer a form similar to a check register on which token earnings can be recorded. Cooper, Heron, and Heward (1987) described several criteria for selecting tokens, which are summarized in Table 9.3.

Establish Backup Reinforcers Recall that backup reinforcers are items, activities, and privileges that students can purchase with the tokens they acquired for engaging in target behaviors. Tokens can be used to buy time to play a popular game, listen to music, have lunch with a favorite teacher or peer, or write and deliver a note to a friend. It is also helpful to have some candy, gum, and trinkets as backup reinforcers. These items typically do not cost much money. And teachers can ask parents or parent–teacher organizations to con-

TABLE 9.2	RULES FOR OPERATING A TOKEN ECONOMY
Rule	**Description**
Specify procedures for dispensing tokens.	Teachers state that they, or a paraprofessional, will circulate around the room and dispense tokens or points to students who remain quiet and don't continuously ask for them.
Describe how tokens are to be exchanged.	For elementary school students, a "store" with backup reinforcers can be displayed at certain times. For secondary school students, a menu can be developed similar to ones used in restaurants.
Describe consequences for "bootlegging" tokens.	Tokens can be confiscated for bootlegging. Students shouldn't lose more tokens than they earn. A ratio of one token lost for every five earned prevents students from losing all their tokens.
Establish a policy for playing with tokens.	Students may play with tokens for a specified length of time in order to establish them as reinforcers. After several days, a storage system can be introduced.
Establish a policy for purchasing backup reinforcers.	Students may not purchase backup reinforcers because they don't have enough tokens or enjoy "hoarding" tokens. Students can purchase items on "layaway" by presenting tokens until they are able to purchase the backup reinforcer. Hoarding can be dealt with by having students start with zero tokens after the store is closed. This prevents students who have earned enough tokens early in the day from purchasing a backup reinforcer and then misbehaving.

Source: Cooper, Heron, and Heward (1987).

tribute a small amount of money to a token economy fund to finance the purchase of backup reinforcers.

Backup reinforcers can be identified by asking students what they might like to purchase with their tokens, interviewing adults as to what students might like, and observing students. Students then rank order the combined list to help us determine the cost of backup reinforcers. Students should not be permitted to debate the cost (number of tokens) of the various backup reinforcers after we have established prices. However, they can participate in frequently revising the backup reinforcers on the menu to avoid boredom and satiation. We should have as many activities and privileges that are naturally available in schools as possible. This prevents students from sticking out from their peers and also helps us eventually fade out the token economy. The types of backup reinforcers vary depending on whether the token economy is used for elementary or secondary school students.

Elementary school students often like trinkets that secondary school students view as childish. Many stores supply trinkets at a very low cost. The little trinkets that fast food restaurants put in their "kids meals" also make excellent backup reinforcers for younger students. It is perfectly appropriate for most elementary school students to purchase backup reinforcers at a class "store." This store may consist of a table containing the backup reinforcers, with their prices displayed. Some teachers use a locked cabinet as a store; the cabinet is unlocked when the store is open. A price sheet can be taped to the back of the cabinet door specifying the amount of tokens required to purchase various items and activities.

Table 9.4 lists naturally occurring activities and privileges that can be used as backup reinforcers for elementary school students. As this table shows, a token economy can be implemented without relying exclusively on trinkets, toys, candy, magazines, and other objects. For students who have difficulty reading, a picture of the activity or a snapshot of a student engaging in the activity, with the number of tokens the activity costs, can be included on the menu. It may be more difficult to come up with reinforcers for teenagers because they often find certain items gimmicky or childish. Creative descriptions of various activities might enhance their desirability for this group. For example, a one-sentence blurb about taking a note to a friend might read, "Here's your only legitimate chance to get that special person a note during the day." And items that are not being purchased can be removed or used as a "daily special" that students can obtain at a reduced rate. Table 9.5. shows a possible reinforcer menu for teenagers.

TABLE 9.3 CRITERIA FOR SELECTING TOKENS

Criteria	Description
Tokens should be safe.	Tokens should not be potentially harmful to students. For young students, tokens should not be an item that can be swallowed. For older students with behavior problems, they should not be items that can be used as weapons.
Token presentation is controlled by the teacher.	Students should not be able to bootleg tokens. If tally marks are used, they should be made on a special card or with a special marking pen that is available only to the teacher. Likewise, if holes are punched in a card, the paper punch should be available only to the teacher.
Tokens should be durable.	Tokens probably will be used for an extended period of time. Therefore, they should last and be easy to carry, handle, bank, store, and accumulate.
Tokens should be readily accessible to the teacher.	Tokens should be readily available at the moment they are to be dispensed. It is important that they be provided immediately after the target behavior occurs.
Tokens should not be a desirable object.	One teacher used baseball cards as tokens, but the students spent so much time interacting with the token (e.g., reading about players' stats and trading cards) that the token itself distracted them from the purpose of the system.

Source: Cooper, Heron, and Heward (1987).

TABLE 9.4 BACKUP REINFORCERS FOR ELEMENTARY SCHOOL STUDENTS		
Reinforcer	**Time**	**Cost**
Listening to music	10 minutes	20 tokens
Cutting and pasting	5 minutes	10 tokens
Finger painting	12 minutes	25 tokens
Playing marbles	10 minutes	15 tokens
Showing a hobby to classmates	5 minutes	10 tokens
Reading a story out loud to classmates	10 minutes	30 tokens
Visiting another class	15 minutes	20 tokens
Running an errand	————	15 tokens
Helping the librarian	15 minutes	30 tokens
Getting first selection of recess toys	————	35 tokens
Decorating the bulletin board	————	30 tokens
Borrowing a book	————	5 tokens
Leading student groups	15 minutes	20 tokens
Choosing a game for the class	————	25 tokens
Moving a desk	————	30 tokens
Eating lunch with the teacher	————	15 tokens
Getting extra free time	10 minutes	10 tokens
Visiting the nurse	10 minutes	20 tokens
Reading morning announcements	————	15 tokens
Having a project displayed	————	25 tokens
Erasing the chalkboard	————	5 tokens
Bringing a positive note home to parents	————	15 tokens
Using a learning center	15 minutes	30 tokens
Calling home	5 minutes	25 tokens
Visiting the principal	10 minutes	30 tokens

After developing a backup reinforcement menu, we need to decide how frequently students may exchange tokens for activities and privileges. Too long a delay may cause some students, especially younger ones, to lose interest in earning tokens. Some students may need to purchase backup reinforcers as often as every hour. Other students may need to have the store open twice a day (once before lunch and once before going home). Still others can maintain appropriate behavior if they have access to backup reinforcers only once a day or even once a week. The goal is to gradually increase the amount of time that

TABLE 9.5   **REINFORCEMENT MENU FOR ADOLESCENTS**

Reinforcer	Time	Cost
Listening to music	10 minutes	20 tokens
Playing a game	10 minutes	20 tokens
Writing a note to a friend	————	25 tokens
Borrowing a book	48 hours	35 tokens
Watching a music video	15 minutes	30 tokens
Talking to a friend	10 minutes	15 tokens
Showing a hobby to classmates	5 minutes	10 tokens
Eating lunch with a friend	————	25 tokens
Delivering a note to a friend	————	30 tokens
Using gym equipment after school	30 minutes	30 tokens
Choosing an activity for the class	————	10 tokens
Running the film projector	————	5 tokens
Visiting another class	————	20 tokens
Running an errand	————	15 tokens
Helping a teacher	15 minute	30 tokens
Sitting out an activity	————	35 tokens
Moving a desk	————	20 tokens
Telling a secret to a friend	————	30 tokens
Making a phone call	5 minutes	20 tokens
Eating a snack or drinking a soda	————	15 tokens
Getting free time	10 minutes	10 tokens
Playing a game	15 minutes	20 tokens
Being excused from a quiz	————	30 tokens
Visiting another class	30 minutes	30 tokens
Running an errand	————	15 tokens
Rearranging the room	————	20 tokens
Playing a computer game	20 minutes	25 tokens
Working on a hobby	15 minutes	20 tokens
Being excused from a homework assignment	————	30 tokens

elapses between students' earning tokens and their purchasing backup reinforcers. Managing and supervising exchanges of tokens takes time away from instruction. Nevertheless, the time and effort devoted to managing a token economy is paid back in the form of better-run classrooms and more academically engaged students.

Establish a Ratio of Exchange   The initial ratio between the number of tokens earned and the price of backup items should be small so as to ensure that students enjoy immediate success. The quickest way to sabotage a token economy is to have students who are unable to purchase backup reinforcers the first time the store is open. We also want to dispense tokens immediately after students perform the target behaviors. This practice reduces their concern that the system may be unfair or may require too much effort. Students are more likely to perform the target behaviors when they are sure they will receive tokens at the proper time. As in dispensing any type of positive reinforcement, the ratio of exchange can be changed in the direction of a more intermittent schedule after target behaviors are being performed with some regularity. Cooper, Heron, and Heward (1987) described several considerations when adjusting a ratio of exchange:

- Students are allowed to spend only the number of tokens they have earned; they may not borrow tokens.
- Students shouldn't be able to purchase backup reinforcers and have tokens left over because they can misbehave and still have enough tokens for a purchase the next time the store is open.
- The number of highly preferred backup reinforcers should increase as students earn more tokens so that the behaviors are being performed at a high level. In order for students to see some "payoff" for their efforts, some highly preferred backup items and activities that do not initially appear on the reinforcement menu can be made available.

There are many purposes for token economies and many ways in which they can be implemented. Token economies require time and effort, but they represent a powerful application of positive reinforcement.

The Multipurpose Point Sheet

An additional component that can combined with a token economy is a multipurpose point sheet (Walker & Shea, 1995). This feature can help students perform appropriate classroom behaviors consistently throughout the school day regardless of the subject or teacher.

A multipurpose point sheet like the one appearing in Figure 9.2 is stapled to the inside left portion of a manila file folder. (We want to make multiple copies of this sheet because a new one is attached every day.) Operational definitions of the behavioral categories, like those appearing in Table 9.6, as well as the number of points students can earn, are stapled to the right inside portion of the folder. A reinforcement menu, including a schedule for exchanging

Student's Name _____				Date _____	
Class Periods	**On Time to Class**	**Bring Materials**	**Complete Homework**	**Social Behavior**	**Work Success**
8:15–8:50					
9:00–9:50					
10:00–10:50					
11:00–11:50					
Lunch					
12:30–1:20					
1:30–2:20					
2:30–3:20					

FIGURE 9.2

Daily Point Sheet

From *Behavior management: A practical approach for educators* (6th ed.) (p. 379) by J. E. Walker & T. M. Shea, 1995, New York: Macmillan. Copyright 1995 by Macmillan. Adapted with permission.

TABLE 9.6   OPERATIONAL DEFINITION SHEET

Behavioral Category	Description of Behavior
Attendance	Students can earn three tokens if they are in their seats when the bell rings. Walking in the room or standing by a desk talking to a classmate is unacceptable.
Materials	Students can earn one token each for (1) bringing a writing instrument, (2) bringing notebook paper, and (3) bringing the appropriate textbook.
Homework	Students can earn five tokens for bringing the completed home-work assignment to class. Students who bring an assignment that is at least 80 percent accurate can earn five additional tokens.
Social behavior	Students can earn one token each for the following behaviors: (1) ignoring a verbal taunt from classmates, (2) raising a hand and waiting to be called on before talking, and (3) saying "hello" to a classmate or teacher upon entering the room.
Work success	Students can earn one token for every 2 minutes of class time that they are looking at the teacher, asking a question related to the material, or working on an assignment.

Child's Name _____   Date _____

Teachers: *Please rate this child's behavior today in the areas listed below. Use a separate column for each subject or class period. Use the following ratings: 5 = excellent, 4 = good, 3 = fair, 2 = poor, and 1 = very poor. Then initial the box at the bottom of your column. Add any comments about the child's behavior today on the back of this card.*

Behaviors to Be Rated	**Class Periods/Subjects**						
	1	**2**	**3**	**4**	**5**	**6**	**7**
Teacher's Initials							

FIGURE 9.3

Daily School Behavior Report Card

From *Attention-deficit hyperactivity disorder* (2nd ed.) (p. 476) by R. A. Barkley, 1998, New York: Guilford. Copyright 1998 by Guilford. Adapted with permission.

points for backup reinforcers, is then stapled to the back of the folder. Students lose the points entered on sheets if they destroy them. However, they can purchase, for a token fee, replacement sheets.

Initially, students should be able to purchase backup reinforcers at the end of every day. A paraeducator or volunteer might run the "store," or we might take on this job ourselves. In the short term, some instructional time is lost while we administer the store. However, in the long run, we end up with far more engaged time because students are better behaved.

The daily school behavior report card appearing in Figure 9.3 has been effectively used for students with attention-deficit/hyperactivity disorder (Barkley, 1998; DuPaul & Stoner, 1994). It is a good example of a multipurpose point sheet that teachers and parents can use cooperatively to keep each other abreast of students' behavior. The target behaviors are listed along the left-hand side of the card. Numbered columns across the top of the card correspond to each class period at school. Teachers give a number rating that reflects how well a student did for each of the behaviors listed during each class period. These marks can be added to the student's token earnings.

The success of this system depends upon the cooperation between teachers. Each teacher must mark down how many points the student earned for that particular class. Some teachers are hesitant to perform this task because they either view it as too time consuming or dislike having to reinforce students whom they expect to be good. These problems are minimized when there is strong administrative leadership and a team of teachers committed to working together to improve students' behaviors.

BEHAVIORAL CONTRACTS

Behavioral contracting is another way to deliver reinforcement. A **behavioral contract** is a written document specifying who is involved, what behaviors are targeted, when and where the behaviors are to be performed, and how much reinforcement students will receive. In behavioral contracts, each individual's behaviors and the accompanying reinforcers to be administered for successfully completing the behaviors are specified more precisely than in a verbal agreement. One person's behavior (e.g., a student coming to class on time) is dependent upon the other person's behavior (e.g., a teacher allowing the student to write a note during the last 10 minutes of class). Table 9.7 lists essential features that should be considered when developing a behavioral contract.

Unlike the contracts used in many business contexts, behavioral contracts focus on ensuring that all involved parties are treated fairly.

TABLE 9.7   ESSENTIAL FEATURES OF A BEHAVIORAL CONTRACT

1. The contract must be negotiated and agreed on by all parties.
2. The contract payoff (reinforcer) should be immediate.
3. Contracts should initially call for and reinforce approximations of target behavior.
4. The contract must include the target achievement or production level.
5. The behavior of all parties should be specified.
6. The contract should provide for frequent reinforcers in small amounts.
7. The reinforcer must be consistently delivered in accordance with the terms of the contract.
8. Reinforcement should be layered.
9. The contract should call for and reinforce accomplishments rather than merely obedience.
10. Students should not be eliminated early from obtaining reinforcement.
11. Behavior should be reinforced after it occurs.
12. The contract must be fair to all parties.
13. The terms of the contract must be clear.
14. The contract must be honest.
15. The contract must be positive.
16. The contract must include the date for review and renegotiation.

Reasons Behavioral Contracts Work

Behavioral contracts are time consuming to develop, and we might wonder whether they are worth the effort to develop. They are, simply because they work, and well-behaved students make for academically engaged students and pleasant classrooms. There are several reasons these contracts work (Cooper, Heron, & Heward, 1987).

First, behavioral contracts focus on rule-governed behavior. During the process of developing a contract, all involved parties—including students—verbalize rules in which specified behaviors result in specified consequences. These statements help students develop self-management skills. In essence, their behavior comes to be under their own control. As a result, contracts can specify reinforcers that are administered several days or even a week later.

Second, the effectiveness of the contracts may not be due to the reinforcers themselves, but rather because the contracts are made public. These contracts are typically displayed in a prominent place. Therefore, students and teachers may adhere to contracts merely to avoid feelings of shame at performing poorly. Another beneficial by-product of making contracts public documents is that something students did not originally find reinforcing may take on reinforcing properties. For example, a student may not initially have found it reinforcing to earn 10 minutes of listening to music at the end of class. But when this same privilege is incorporated into a public document, it attains reinforcing value.

Third, contracts work because students are equal participants in the process. They are involved in generating and negotiating target behaviors, criteria for acceptable performance on the target behavior, and reinforcers earned for meeting the stipulations in the contract. Students are more likely to assume ownership of contracts when they are active participants in the process.

Fourth, contracts work because the behaviors of everyone—not just students but also teachers—are specified. For example, if the student's behavior is to be on time to class, the teacher's behavior may be to let him leave 5 minutes early to get a can of soda. In this sense, both students and teachers are equal participants in the process. Students are more likely to perform the target behavior when they believe that the teacher also has to engage in certain behavior.

Components of a Behavioral Contract

Cooper, Heron, and Heward (1987) listed three components that should be included in every behavioral contract: (1) a description of the task, (2) a description of the reward, and (3) a task record. It may be helpful to refer to the sample contract shown in Figure 9.4 while reading the description of these

Contract

Task

Who: Dalva, principal, teachers, and Dalva's mother

What: Dalva will be in her seat when the bell rings. Her teachers will mark her task record. Her mother will fill up the car with gas.

When: Monday through Friday

How Well: Dalva will be on time 6 out of 7 classes per day four out of five days.

Reward

Who: Dalva's teachers, principal, and her mother

What: Dalva's teachers will give her 10 minutes of free time. Her principal will take her to lunch. Her mother will let her use the family car or have a friend spend the night.

When: Saturday night

How Much: Dalva can use the car Saturday night from 6:00 p.m. to midnight. Mother will see that the car has sufficient amount of gas. Dalva can have a friend spend the night.

Bonus Rewards: (1) For each **class** that Dalva is on time and brings materials and assignments, she can leave the class for the last 10 minutes and visit a friend. (2) For each **day** Dalva is on time to every class, she can select a teacher to give her a ride home instead of taking the bus. (3) For each **week** Dalva is on time to each class five consecutive days, the principal will take her out to lunch the following Monday or her mother will rent a video and buy her a pizza to share with a friend who spends the night on Saturday.

Signature: _____
            Dalva   Date

Signature: _____
            Mother   Date

Signature: _____
            Principal   Date

Signature: _____
            Ms. Jones   Date

Signature: _____
            Ms. Wilson   Date

Signature: _____
            Mr. Filipo   Date

Signature: _____
            Ms. Cole   Date

Signature: _____
            Mr. Rury   Date

Task Record

M	T	W	TH	F	M	T	W	TH	F
★		★	★	★	★	★	★	★	★

★	★	★	★	★	★		★	★	★

FIGURE 9.4

Sample Behavioral Contract

From *Sign here: A contracting book for children and their parents* (2nd ed., p. 31) by J. C. Dardig & W. L. Heward, 1981, Worthington, OH. Copyright 1981 by J. C. Dardig & W. L. Heward. Adapted with permission.

components. Of course, not all contracts require a format as elaborate as the one in Figure 9.4, and teachers can develop their own contract formats.

The Task   The task component of a behavioral contract describes the specific behaviors that each participant will perform. Typically, it is the student's behavior that is specified. However, the behavior of adults involved in the contract (e.g., those monitoring the student's progress or writing notes to parents) may also be specified. A contract may include several pages—one page for the student's behavior and others for the behavior of involved adults.

As Figure 9.4 shows, the task component has four parts: who, what, when, and how well:

1. *Who* initially refers to the individuals who will be performing the task and earning the reward. As mentioned previously, however, the behavior of everyone involved in the contract should be specified. Therefore, "who" could conceivably also include the general education teacher, special education teacher, principal, and parents.
2. *What* refers to the task or behavior the student, as well as any other persons involved in the contract, must perform. For example, a student's behavior may involve being on time to math period in the general education classroom. The general education teacher's task may be to initial the contract each time the student is on time. The special education teacher's task may be to call the student's parents to report that he successfully made it to math class on time.
3. *When* identifies the time that the task or behavior must be performed.
4. *How well* refers to the criterion for acceptable performance (CAP), or the task standard. It involves the specifics of the task. It is helpful to list any skills necessary to perform the task so that the student can use the contract itself as a checklist of what must be done. Any exceptions should be noted here. For example, a contract may specify that a student must be on time to five out of six classes. However, if the social studies class is canceled because a teacher suddenly falls ill, then the student will be unable, due to no fault of his own, to complete the behavior. This exception should be included. Finally, it is important not to set the task standard so high that the student cannot earn the reward. For example, it may be unrealistic for a student who never is on time to class to have the standard state "Be on time seven out of seven class periods a day." If the student is late to second period, the reward is lost, and he has little motivation to be on time for the rest of his classes.

The Reward   The reward component of a behavioral contract includes the same four parts as the task side—with one exception. Instead of stating "how well," which appears on the task side, "how much" is described on the reward side. Technically, the term *reward* is incorrect, because students are actually earning reinforcers. However, the term *reward* is used in contracts because students typically are more familiar with it than the word *reinforcement.*

Just as with the task side of a contract, the reward side should be written objectively and specifically. Reward statements such as "Can have some free time" or "Will take to lunch when I get a chance" are not specific and so are unfair to the student attempting to complete the task. If adults are responsible for disseminating the reward, their behaviors should also be specified on this side of the contract. Specifically, the reward component includes the following:

1. *Who* refers to the persons judging task completion and disseminating the reward. In the contract shown in Figure 9.4, several of the student's teachers, the principal, and her mother will be delivering some aspect of the reward.

2. *What* is simply the reward. In Figure 9.4, the student can earn the reward of using her mother's car on Saturday night and having a friend sleep over. In addition, she has the opportunity to earn bonus rewards. The task standards should not be set so high that a student might be eliminated early on from being able to earn the reward. In Figure 9.4, the student has to be on time for six out of seven classes per day for 4 out of 5 days. However, the ultimate goal is to have the student attend all her classes. Therefore, a bonus reward is included for attending all classes on time and being prepared.

3. *When* specifies the time that the reward will be received by the student. It is crucial that the reward be administered only after the student successfully completes the task. Many rewards cannot be delivered immediately, such as certain activities or outings. Some rewards also have a built-in limited availability—they can be delivered only at certain times. For example, it is impossible to take a student to a weekend ball game on a Tuesday.

4. *How much* refers to the amount of reward a student can earn by completing the task. Bonus rewards can be stated here or in a separate section, as in Figure 9.4. This process often involves layering rewards. For example, a contract may specify that a student must be on time to class 4 out of 5 days in order to go out to lunch on Friday with a friend of her choice. A contract can also include an end-of-the-day reward if the student is on time six out of seven periods. Finally, the contract might specify that the student can earn 5 minutes of free time at the end of every class period for which she is on time. In this way, a smaller reward can potentially be delivered at the end of each period and the end of each day, and a big reward at the end of the week.

Task Record   It is important to include a place on the contract where the student's progress can be recorded. Cooper, Heron, and Heward (1987) stated that a **task record** serves two purposes:

1. Recording task completion and reward delivery on the contract sets the occasion for both parties to look at and be reminded of the contract regularly.
2. If a certain number of task completions are required to earn the reward (e.g., if a child must dress herself each morning before school for 5 days in a row), a checkmark, smiling face, or star can be placed on the task record each time the task is completed successfully. Marking the contract in this manner can help the individual remain on task until the assignment is completed and the reward is earned. (p. 468)

A task record functions as a kind of token because it can bridge the gap between performing a behavior and obtaining reinforcement. The stars appearing on the task record in Figure 9.4 indicate to the student how close she is to receiving the end-of-the-week reward. The stars also indicate that the student received the end-of-the-day reward. In this case, the student received a star every day except for 2 days out of the 20 that the contract was in effect.

Guidelines for Successful Contracting

DeRisi and Butz (1975) offered the following guidelines for successful contracting:

1. Select one or two behaviors that you want to work on first.
2. Describe those behaviors so that they may be observed and counted.
3. Identify rewards that will help provide motivation to do well.
4. Locate people who can help you keep track of the behaviors being performed and who can perhaps give out the rewards.
5. Write the contract so that everyone can understand it.
6. Collect data.
7. Troubleshoot the system if the data do not show improvement.
8. Rewrite the contract (whether or not the data show improvement).
9. Continue to monitor, troubleshoot, and rewrite until there is improvement in the behaviors that were troublesome.
10. Select another behavior to work on. (p. 7)

Cooper, Heron, and Heward (1987) suggested three additional rules that deserve elaboration.

> Contracts are front-end heavy—that is, they require a lot of work to get written. However, the work done up front is paid back in multiples because an effective contract can maintain students' appropriate behaviors for long periods of time.

Rule 1: Contracts Must Be Fair   A fair contract is one in which the type and amount of reward equal the type and amount of behavior the student is required to perform. For example, a contract requiring a student to turn in his math assignments every day to get a piece of bubble gum at the end of the week is unfair, because the task is much greater than the potential reward. A contract may be equally unfair if a student is required to turn in his math assignments every day to earn a trip to Disney World. In this instance, the reward is too large and impractical.

Fairness can be promoted by having the student list his five favorite things and then rate them on a scale from 1 to 10, with 10 being the most favorite. A list of five tasks or behaviors can be generated by all involved parties and rated according to their difficulty or importance using the same scale. In this way, tasks and rewards can be selected that are perceived to have equal value.

Rule 2: Contracts Must Be Clear   One of the most time-consuming aspects of developing behavioral contracts is clearly specifying individuals' behaviors and expectations. Clear contracts include behaviors of students and participating adults that pass the stranger test and have task standards. Rewards should be stated in equally specific terms. The payoff is that this specificity automatically improves everyone's performance—both students' and adults' (Cooper, Heron, & Heward, 1987). In many instances, students are more willing to be specific than adults, who perhaps enjoy the privilege of being able to change their minds (Cooper, Heron, & Heward, 1987).

Rule 3: Contracts Must Be Honest   A contract is honest if the reward is delivered at the specified time and in the specified amount after the student completes the task or behavior. Cooper, Heron, and Heward (1987) suggested that the honesty rule is broken more often than the fairness or clarity rules. In many instances, it is broken by adults who fail to anticipate unexpected circumstances. For example, a reward on a contract might involve having the student eat lunch with her favorite teacher. However, if the teacher is out ill, the contract is dishonest. This problem can be avoided by having the contract list a second teacher with whom the student wants to have lunch if the primary teacher is sick.

The Contract Negotiation Process

Successful contracts are those that have been freely negotiated by all involved parties. Negotiation should be conducted in a systematic and precise fashion. Four tasks must be completed to ensure a successful negotiation session: (1) the system of contracting explained and discussed, (2) the contract written, (3) the contract signed by all participants, and (4) the contract posted in a visible place (Walker & Shea, 1995).

A properly conducted negotiation contract is a time-consuming process. However, this effort pays great dividends in the form of better-behaved students. Walker and Shea (1995) recommended that teachers who are new at developing contracts use the following negotiation procedures:

1. Teacher establishes and maintains rapport with the child.
2. Teacher explains the purpose of the meeting by saying something such as, "I know you've been working hard on your schoolwork [reading, writing, spelling, arithmetic], and I'd like to help you."
3. Teacher gives a simple definition of a contract, explaining that a contract is an agreement between two people.
   a. Teacher gives an example of a contract such as: "When your mother takes your TV to the repair shop, the clerk gives her a ticket. The ticket is a contract between your mother and the repairman. He will repair and return the TV, and your mother will pay him."
   b. Teacher asks the child to give an example of a contract.
   c. If child cannot respond, the teacher gives another example and repeats 3b.
4. Teacher explains to the child that they are going to write a contract.
5. Teacher and child discuss tasks.
   a. Child suggests tasks for the contract.
   b. Teacher suggests tasks for the contract.
   c. Child and teacher discuss and agree on the specific task.
6. Teacher and child discuss reinforcers.
   a. Teacher asks the child which activities the child enjoys doing and which things he or she likes. The teacher may also suggest reinforcers.
   b. Teacher writes a reinforcer menu of child-suggested reinforcers.
   c. Child selects reinforcers for which he or she would like to work.
   d. Teacher and child rank the reinforcers in the child's order of preference.
7. Teacher and child negotiate the ratio of task to reinforcer.
8. Teacher and child agree on the time to be allotted for the child to perform the task; for example, the child works 10 addition problems in 15 minutes to receive the reinforcer, or the child completes a unit of science and does the laboratory experiments in 2 weeks to receive an A.
9. Teacher and child identify the criteria for achievement; that is, the child will work the 10 addition problems in 15 minutes with at least 80% accuracy.
10. Teacher and child discuss evaluation procedures.
    a. Teacher discusses various types of evaluations with the child.
    b. Teacher and child agree on a method of evaluation.
    c. Teacher asks the child to explain the method of evaluation. If the child appears confused, the teacher clarifies the evaluation procedure.
11. Teacher and child negotiate delivery of the reinforcer.
12. Teacher and child agree on a date for renegotiation of the contract.
13. Teacher or child writes the contract. If feasible, the child should be encouraged to write it. Teacher gives a copy of the contract to the child.
14. Teacher reads the contract to the child as the child follows on his or her own copy.
15. Teacher elicits the child's verbal affirmation of the contract terms and gives affirmation.
16. Child and teacher sign the contract.
17. Teacher congratulates the child for making the contract and wishes the child success. (pp. 143–144)

Home-School Contract for Homework Completion

This is an agreement between the following teachers, parents, and student which begins on _____ and ends on _____. The contract will be reviewed on _____.
       Date   Date   Date

We, the undersigned parties, agree to perform the following behaviors:

The student will _____

_____

The parents will _____

_____

Each teacher will _____

_____

Reward _____

_____

Bonus _____

_____

Teachers' Signatures   Parents' Signatures   Student's Signature

_____   _____   _____

_____   _____

_____

_____

_____

FIGURE 9.5

Home–School Contract

From *Behavior management: A practical approach for educators* (6th ed.) (p. 375) by J. E. Walker & T. M. Shea, 1995, New York: Macmillan. Copyright 1995 by Macmillan. Adapted with permission.

The Home–School Contract

One of the major advantages of behavior contracts is that they give students access to reinforcers not readily available at school, such as having a friend spend the night or using their parent's car. Offering these types of reinforcers requires developing a home–school contract. This contract can be used for students who have difficulty bringing home, completing, and returning homework assignments. A relatively simple home–school contract that addresses this problem can be developed by the student and his or her teachers and parents. The contract in Figure 9.5 includes blanks to write the responsibilities of student, parents, and teachers, and to specify the reward and any bonus reward the student can earn. An assignment sheet can be attached to the contract, like

	No homework assignment tonight _____
	Tonight's homework assignment is _____
	_____
	Today's homework assignment was handed in
	No homework assignment was due for today

FIGURE 9.6

Home–School Assignment Sheet

TABLE 9.8   RESPONSIBILITIES FOR HOMEWORK COMPLETION CONTRACT

Individual	Responsibilities
Student	1. Bring assignment sheet home. 2. Show assignment sheet to parents. 3. Complete homework assignments. 4. Bring homework sheet to each class.
Teacher	1. Ask student for assignment sheet. 2. Write down the homework assignment for that night. 3. Write down whether the child turned in the homework assignment for that day. 4. Write down if there is no homework assignment for the next day. 5. Administer a reward for homework turned in and completed that day.
Parent	1. Review homework assignment sheet. 2. Set time for homework. 3. Review homework to ensure it was completed. 4. Administer a reward for homework completed for that day.

Home–school contracts also are an effective tool for increasing parental involvement by including their behavior in a contract for the student.

the one shown in Figure 9.6. This sheet has a place for the teacher to place his or her initials in any of four categories. The responsibilities of each involved party must also be specified, as listed in Table 9.8.

GROUP-ORIENTED CONTINGENCIES

Peer attention can be a major source of reinforcement for students' inappropriate behavior. In addition, the inappropriate behavior of one student may spread to other students until the entire class is being disruptive. A group-oriented contingency may be used to address these problems (Kauffman, Pullen, & Akers, 1986). According to Cooper, Heron, and Heward (1987), a group-oriented contingency "is one in which the presentation, or loss, of a reinforcer is contingent upon the behavior of an individual within the group, a segment of the group, or the group as a whole" (p. 500).

Group-oriented contingencies make positive use of peer pressure and attention. All teachers recognize the existence of peer pressure in their classrooms although they rarely use it to their advantage. Peer pressure typically is viewed as a negative occurrence that teachers are constantly battling. Although this may be true, it is possible to develop a group-oriented contingency that minimizes the effects of negative peer attention and maximizes the influence of positive peer pressure to promote achievement and appropriate behavior (Kauffman, Pullen, & Akers, 1986).

There are perhaps no more powerful reinforcers for students than attention they receive from peers. Instead of trying to eliminate peer attention, teachers should use this attention to make positive changes in students' behaviors.

Types of Group-Oriented Contingencies

The three most common group-oriented contingencies are dependent, independent, or interdependent (Litow & Pumroy, 1975). Each type of contingency is easy to administer, has built-in incentives to prevent group members from reinforcing individual students' inappropriate behaviors, and promotes prosocial behaviors of group members (Sarafino, 1996). However, not all types of group-oriented contingencies make use of peer pressure to the same degree.

Dependent Group-Oriented Contingencies   Dependent group-oriented contingencies are those under which consequences for a group of students depend on the performance of one member, or perhaps a small subsection, of the group (Kauffman, Pullen, & Akers, 1986). This approach is often called the **hero procedure** because it is hoped that peers will view the student who earns the class reinforcement as the hero.

To implement a dependent group-oriented contingency, we first select an individual or small subgroup. Next, we specify the target behavior and criterion for acceptable performance (CAP), or task standard. If the selected student's or subgroup's performance reaches the specified criterion, the entire class earns a reinforcer. For example, we may have a student who makes animal noises in class. We could tell the class that if the target student makes fewer than five animal noises during the next 30 minutes then everyone will earn an additional 10 minutes of recess. Our goal is for peers to give the student positive attention and encouragement to earn the reinforcer for everyone.

Gresham (1983) developed an effective dependent group-oriented contingency for an 8-year-old boy who was setting fires and destroying furniture at home. When the boy refrained from engaging in destructive behavior, his parents wrote a note that was delivered to his teacher. Whenever his teacher received five notes from home, the boy got to host for a party the entire class.

The major advantage of a dependent group-oriented contingency is that it encourages classmates to "root for" or provide the target student with positive attention for either refraining from performing inappropriate behavior or engaging in appropriate behavior. The major disadvantage is that it can easily be mismanaged by teachers who neither monitor individual students' performance nor conduct functional assessment on the student whose performance determines whether the group earns reinforcement. When this unfortunate situation occurs, peers are more likely to threaten, criticize, or harass the target student or subgroup for not performing adequately (Kauffman, Pullen, & Akers, 1986).

Independent Group-Oriented Contingencies Independent group-oriented contingencies are those in effect for individual students regardless of the performance of the group. They are group oriented only in the sense that the same reinforcer is presented to the entire class or group. However, only students whose behavior reaches the CAP receive the reinforcer.

Elementary school teachers often use this type of arrangement to teach spelling. A test on the weekly spelling words is given every day. Students who spell every word correctly on Monday have free time during the spelling period for the rest of the week. Students who miss any words have time to practice them on Tuesday. Before the spelling period ends on Tuesday, they take another test. Students who then get all the words correct have free time for the rest of the week, and so on for Wednesday through Friday. Some teachers prefer to have the contingency apply only through Thursday and to give everyone a final spelling test on Friday. In either case, it is an independent group-oriented contingency because opportunity for reinforcement (free time during spelling period) is presented to the entire class, but only students who meet the CAP (100 percent correct on the spelling test) have access to it.

An advantage of an independent group-oriented contingency is that no student is penalized for the poor performance or behavior of other students. Each student is reinforced depending on whether his or her performance reaches the CAP—all students have access to the reinforcer under exactly the same terms. Therefore, reinforcement is under students' own control instead of being contingent on peers' performances. A disadvantage is that it does not make use of peer pressure to influence the behavior of individual students. Therefore, peers have less incentive to ignore the inappropriate behavior of students or to provide them with attention for appropriate behavior.

Interdependent Group-Oriented Contingencies Interdependent group-oriented contingencies are those in which the performance of all group members must meet the CAP before any group member can receive reinforcement. Group members must work together to earn a reinforcer that they will share equally (Kauffman, Pullen, & Akers, 1986).

The **good behavior game,** developed by Barrish, Saunders, and Wolf (1969), is an example of an interdependent group-oriented contingency. The good behavior game originally involved a teacher dividing a class into two groups. The teacher made a tally mark on the chalkboard for each group every time all members of a group were performing an appropriate behavior. The group with the most tally marks won free time and privileges at the end of the day. The advantage of this arrangement was that group members cooperated among themselves to outperform the other team.

IMPLEMENTATION STEPS   The good behavior game provides us with a valuable technique for managing group behavior. To implement this technique, do the following:

1. Write three appropriate behaviors (e.g., eyes on teacher, feet on floor, talk only after raising hand) on the board.
2. Above the appropriate behaviors, write the words "3 points." Figure 9.7 shows how this arrangement would appear.
3. Obtain a large glass jar (like the ones used to make sun tea), a good supply of marbles, and a tape recorder.
4. Make an hour-long tape with random beeps sounding at intervals ranging from 20 seconds to 180 seconds (3 minutes).
   a. Write the numbers of every possible interval length (depending on the desired tape length) on pieces of paper (e.g., 10 through 90 for a 15-minute tape and 20 through 180 for a 30- to 50-minute tape) and place them in a container.
   b. Draw a slip of paper out of the container and write the number on a piece of lined paper.
   c. Place the slip of paper back in the container so that each number has an equal chance of being drawn each time.
   d. Repeat this process until 30 to 60 numbers have been written.
   e. Obtain a tape recorder, tape, mechanism for making tones (e.g., a child's electronic toy), and a clock with a second hand.
   f. Find a quiet room and let the tape run for the number of seconds indicated by the first number on the list. At the end of this time, make the signal tone and let the tape recorder run for the number of seconds

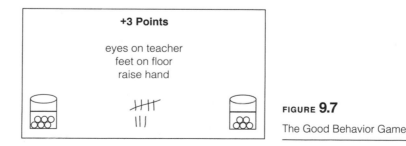

FIGURE 9.7

The Good Behavior Game

Steps 4a–4f, which are used to make a beep tape, are the same steps that are used to make a self-monitoring cuing tape, as described in Chapter 12.

indicated by the second number on the interval list. It is helpful to check off each interval on the random interval list after it has been recorded or to use a ruler to keep place on the list. Repeat this process until the tape ends.

5. Tell the students that whenever the tape "beeps," if everyone is performing one of the three appropriate behaviors, three marbles will be placed in the jar.
6. Inform the students that, if the jar is completely filled with marbles, everyone gets to select one of several free-time privileges in which to engage during the last 10 minutes of class.

CONSIDERATIONS   For the good behavior game to be effective, it is essential that we initially set up students for success so that they will buy into the process. We want to ensure that the jar is full of marbles by the end of the first day, so that students are able to obtain the reinforcer. Here is an approach for setting an attainable initial criterion. If there are 30 beeps on a tape, the most marbles the class can earn is 90 ($30 \times 3 = 90$). We can set the initial criterion at 70 percent of 90, or 63 marbles ($.70 \times 90 = 63$). (This criterion may be raised once students have experienced success.) We then place the 63 marbles in the jar, wrap a piece of black electrical tape around the jar even with the top level of the marbles, and remove the marbles from the jar. We let students know that if they can accumulate enough marbles to reach the black line by the end of the day they earn a reinforcer.

MODIFICATIONS   We can undertake a variety of modifications when implementing the good behavior game, some of which are listed here:

1. Instead of marbles, use candy. Therefore, at the end of the class, if the jar is filled, distribute the candy equally to everyone in class. As an added incentive, designate the last 5 minutes of class as a time when students can trade candy with each other.
2. Instead of using a jar and marbles (or candy), keep track of the number of points the class earns on the chalkboard by making tally marks (see Figure 9.7). As with marbles or candy in a jar, establish a predetermined number of points the class must accumulate to earn reinforcement.
3. Create two to four groups of students, each with its own jar. When the beep sounds, place the marbles (or candy) in the jars of the groups whose members are all engaging in one of the appropriate behaviors. Groups that fill their jar, or that have the most marbles, by the last 10 minutes of class earn reinforcement.
4. Write each student's name on a slip of paper and place the slips in a bag. Pull one name out of the bag (without telling students whose name was drawn). When the beep sounds, place three marbles (or pieces of candy)

in the jar if the student whose name was pulled is performing one of the appropriate behaviors. Either announce the student's name after each beep or keep the name anonymous.

5. List three inappropriate behaviors on the chalkboard with a −1 over them. If any student is performing one of the inappropriate behaviors when the beep sounds, remove one point, marble, or piece of candy. However, use this adaptation cautiously, because if students lose more points than they have earned, they have no motivation to behave appropriately.

There are two common methods for setting a CAP for a group to receive reinforcement using interdependent group-oriented contingencies. First, every member of the group must reach the stated CAP. For example, the class receives 10 minutes of free time if each student gets 90 percent correct on a math quiz. Second, the average performance of the entire class reaches a set CAP. For example, an entire class can earn 10 extra minutes of recess if their average score on the math quiz is 90 percent.

The major advantage of interdependent group-oriented contingencies is that we can plan the use of positive peer pressure and competition to promote individual students' appropriate behaviors. However, unless skillfully applied, the potential exists for peers to threaten others whom they perceive are not performing adequately. Another problem is that high-achieving students may resent peers who do not meet the CAP for the class to receive reinforcement. These disadvantages can be minimized by carefully implementing the contingency and monitoring students' progress.

Ethical Considerations When Using Group-Oriented Contingencies

There are many advantages of group-oriented contingencies (Cooper, Heron, & Heward, 1987). They save us time and reduce our workload because we can address the behavior of an entire class with one intervention. They are useful in situations in which individual interventions are impractical, especially for substitute teachers who are not familiar with students and their behaviors. They can help resolve problems quickly when used during a lesson that demands high levels of student engagement. They capitalize on using peer influence positively, thereby facilitating prosocial interactions between students. However, several ethical issues should be addressed to ensure that group-oriented contingencies are practical, effective, and economical (Cooper, Heron, & Heward, 1987).

Harmful Peer Pressure on Students Who Fail to Improve   A major advantage of a group-oriented contingency over individual interventions is that peers can provide students with positive reinforcement for performing a desired behavior. However, if we are not careful, some students may be victims

The advantages and disadvantages of group-oriented contingencies must be carefully weighed. These interventions have the potential to be powerful in both positive and negative ways.

TABLE 9.9	STRATEGIES FOR REDUCING SCAPEGOATING
Strategy	**Description**
Have the target child's name remain anonymous.	The names of students should be placed in a bag. The behavior or performance of the student whose name is drawn is used to determine whether the group earns the reward. The student can remain anonymous.
Adjust the criteria for the group-oriented contingency.	The criteria should be set at a level such that one student's performance will not prevent the group from receiving the reward. A criterion of an 80 percent average for the group will allow some students to score below this average without jeopardizing the reward.
Increase the criteria for students who are scapegoating.	Students who scapegoat others should have a higher criterion. For example, students who scapegoat may be required to obtain a score of 95 percent correct on an assignment while other students only need to get 85 percent correct. The group can only earn the reward if the child who is scapegoating gets 95 percent correct.
Reinforce students who do not engage in scapegoating.	Students who refrain from scapegoating can earn one point, which is added to their score. If their name is selected, they have more leeway to obtain a lower score and still earn a reward for the class. Or individual students who refrain from scapegoating can earn several minutes more free time than is specified in the original group reward.
Implement a response cost for students who are scapegoating.	Students can lose 1 minute of group participation in the reward for every incident of scapegoating behavior in which they engage gage while the contingency is in effect.

of scapegoating by peers. **Scapegoating** occurs when unpopular students are unfairly blamed by peers for all types of negative classroom outcomes and behaviors. Table 9.9 provides some strategies for reducing scapegoating. In addition to implementing these strategies, we should directly observe and monitor students to identify those whose performance may be below standard and who therefore are potential targets of scapegoating.

The Issue of Anonymity   A second ethical concern is whether to announce students' names publicly, as with the hero procedure. Peers may engage in scapegoating if the target student's behavior does not improve and the reinforcer is not earned. A strategy appearing in Table 9.9 that addresses this concern is to have students' remain anonymous. For example, a hero procedure can be used in which the performance of a student whose name is pulled from a bag determines whether the entire group obtains the reinforcer. All students have to try to obtain a score at the designated criterion level because there is an equal chance that their names will be drawn. If the student whose name is drawn does not perform up to the criterion, then he or she remains anonymous. We simply announce that the class did not earn the reinforcer today. But if the student's performance meets the criterion, we can state his or her name so that peers provide him or her with positive attention. However, we may want to keep the student's name anonymous either way if he or she might be embarrassed by peer attention, even if it is positive.

Misleading Improvement of the Group   One of the strategies for reducing scapegoating listed in Table 9.9 involves averaging the performance of the class as the criterion for reinforcement. However, this can become a liability because it may mask the performance of individual students. Therefore, we should monitor individual students' performance to determine who is and is not learning the skills. In this case, two criteria can be used: (1) The group average must be 85 percent, and (2) an individual student's performance, randomly selected, must reach 80 percent. Regardless of the modification, a group-oriented contingency should not be used if we are unable to monitor individual students' performance.

Students Unable to Complete the Specified Behaviors   There is no greater disservice to students than including them in a group-oriented contingency when they are unable to complete the specified behaviors. The easiest way to avoid this problem is to assess individual students' performance on the behaviors targeted for the group-oriented contingency. We can then set the initial criterion for the group at the level of the lowest performance of any student in the group. In this way, we are guaranteeing success for all students. When all students "win" the reinforcer, there is no one to blame. However, students are adept at identifying the low-achieving and unpopular students. Therefore, if the group initially does not receive the reinforcer, members may scapegoat specific students. As individual students' performance improves, the CAP for the group can be set higher.

Students Who Enjoy Sabotaging the Contingency   The last ethical consideration represents one of the biggest threats to the success of a group-oriented contingency. Some students may find it more reinforcing to sabotage the group-oriented contingency than to receive the reinforcer because of the power/control they obtain or the attention (albeit negative) they receive from others. We have two options with students who are sabotaging the contingency. We can try to find a more powerful reinforcer than the power/control and attention the student receives—a truly daunting task. Or we can eliminate the offending student from the group-oriented contingency by having her or him watch but not participate. If we choose this second option, we want to place the student on an individual behavior management intervention such as a token economy or behavioral contract. Otherwise, the student will engage in disruptive behavior while the rest of the class participates in the group-oriented contingency.

NOVEL APPLICATIONS OF POSITIVE REINFORCEMENT

Students sometimes satiate on traditional reinforcement programs. For example, students may initially find participating in a token economy to be a novel and enjoyable experience. However, the novelty may quickly wear off even when the backup activities and privileges are still reinforcing. The same problem can occur when teachers use behavioral contracts, group-oriented contingencies, or any other techniques for delivering reinforcement. Therefore, the more novelty in the method of positive reinforcement, the less likely students are to experience satiation. Six of the techniques Rhode, Jenson, and Reavis (1992) developed are described here, along with some modifications.

It is a simple process to combine various novel approaches for using positive reinforcement to make a behavior management program even more desirable to students.

Chart Moves

A "chart move" is a modification of a token economy. In this technique, students connect two of the dots in a dot-to-dot picture when they perform a target behavior. Figure 9.8 provides an example of a completed dot-to-dot chart.

There are a variety of ways to administer reinforcement using chart moves. First, we can have students select one from several available dot-to-dot pictures and then earn chances to connect the dots by performing the target behavior. Second, we can have students select reinforcers—either trinkets or slips of paper with privileges written on them—from a bag once the dot-to-dot picture is completed. In this case, the dots provide students with a visual representation of how close they are to earning the reinforcer. Third, special dots can be created by circling them. Interspersing these "special dots," throughout the picture provides more frequent access to reinforcement. When students connect to one of the special dots, they receive small reinforcers. And at the end, they receive a bigger one.

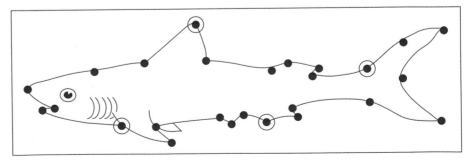

FIGURE 9.8

Completed Dot-to-Dot Chart Picture Using the Chart Moves Approach

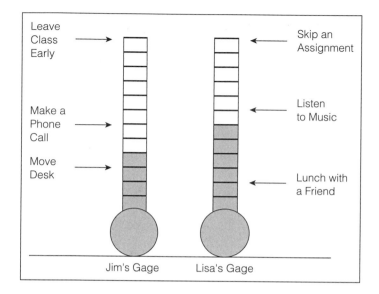

FIGURE 9.9

Temperature Gages Used in Chart Moves

Middle and high school students may find dot-to-dot pictures too "baby-ish." We can have these students create temperature gages like those appear-ing in Figure 9.9. Students shade in one increment each time they engage in the requested behavior. When they reach a designated level, they earn the specified reinforcer. This approach can also be modified two ways. First, we can require students to perform a specified amount of some behavior before shading in one increment. This modification makes use of a fixed-ratio sched-ule of reinforcement. Second, we can let students select a reinforcer from a menu or grab bag when they reach a designated level.

Spinners

We can modify a spinner from a board game or make one out of cardboard. In either case, we divide the spinner into five or more sections, as shown in Fig-ure 9.10. In each section, we draw a picture of the reinforcer or write its name. When students perform a target behavior, they take a spin. Whichever section the arrow lands on is the reinforcer that is obtained.

A variation of this approach is to write the numbers 1 through 5 on the sec-tions of the spinner, as shown in Figure 9.11. When students perform the tar-get behavior, they earn a spin. A grab bag can be made for each number and

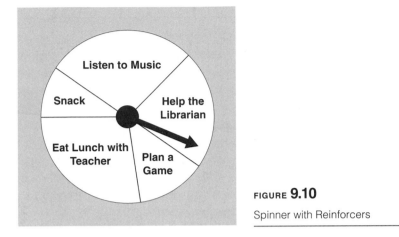

FIGURE **9.10**

Spinner with Reinforcers

then filled with trinkets or slips of paper with privileges written on them. When the spinner lands on a number, the student randomly draws from the grab bag that corresponds to the number.

Numerous other variations can be devised using spinners. Students can earn tokens when they engage in the target behavior. The number of tokens represents the number of times students can spin the spinner. This adds novelty to the intervention and makes use of intermittent reinforcement. Some teachers get even more elaborate. The numbers on the spinner can represent points that students can accumulate (e.g., a student who spins a 3, receives three points). Students can then exchange points at a designated time for privileges and activities. In another variation, students get to spin and earn points only when they perform the targeted behavior. After reaching a specified number of points can they select a reinforcer from a grab bag.

Raffles and Lotteries

With a raffle, we distribute tickets to students when they perform a target behavior. The students write their names on the tickets and place them in a jar. At the end of the class, day, or week (depending on how intermittently students can tolerate receiving reinforcement), we pull one ticket, and that student wins a reinforcer. The more tickets students earn, the greater the chance that they will win a reinforcer. An alternative approach is to write students' names on a poster board and make tally marks every time one or more of them performs the target behavior. We then let students purchase raffle tickets for a set number of points (e.g., one raffle ticket costs 10 points). This approach makes use of a fixed-ratio schedule of reinforcement.

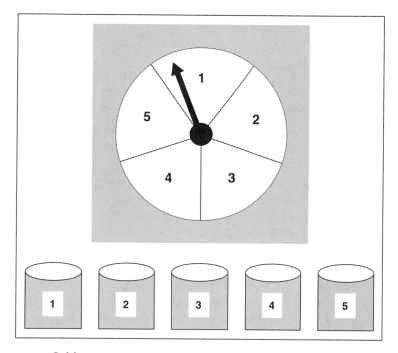

FIGURE 9.11

Numbered Spinner with Accompanying Grab Bags of Reinforcers

With a lottery, the winning ticket is secretly predetermined or determined in a chance drawing. This technique is implemented in a fashion similar to the way state lotteries operate. We obtain (or make) a roll of tickets, write a number (1 through 20 or higher if necessary) on each one, and place them in a jar. We prepare another roll of tickets with the same numbers on them to give to students when they perform the target behavior. At a designated time, such as each Friday afternoon, we pull a ticket out of the jar and announce the number. The student with the winning number gets a reinforcer. As with a raffle, the more tickets students earn, the greater the chance that they will hold the winning number. Reinforcement will be more intermittent if we initially place more tickets in the jar.

100-Square Charts

The 100-square chart is a method that combines intermittent reinforcement with a group-oriented contingency. We create a 100-square chart by dividing two poster boards into 100 squares (10 by 10) of equal size using a ruler and per-

1	2	3	4	5	6	7	8	9	10
11	12	13	14	15	16	17	18	19	20
21	22	23	24	25	26	27	28	29	30
31	32	33	34	35	36	37	38	39	40
41	42	43	44	45	46	47	48	49	50
51	52	53	54	55	56	57	58	59	60
61	62	63	64	65	66	67	68	69	70
71	72	73	74	75	76	77	78	79	80
81	82	83	84	85	86	87	88	89	90
91	92	93	94	95	96	97	98	99	100

FIGURE **9.12**

100-Square Chart

manent marker, as in Figure 9.12. We laminate one of the poster boards—this will be the 100-square chart. We then cut out the squares on the other board and fasten them to the top of each square on the chart with velcro fasteners or masking tape so that they can be peeled off to reveal the square below.

The next step is to randomly mark an "X" in many of the boxes throughout the chart and to apply the square covers. When students perform the target behavior, they earn the privilege of removing a cover to see if an "X" is designated below. If an "X" appears, then the entire group wins a reinforcer, such as a popcorn party or video viewing.

The number of "X's" that appear on the chart can be decreased over time so that students are working to earn a chance at a relatively obscure reinforcer.

However, it is important not to decrease the number of "X's" too quickly; otherwise, students will not find this program reinforcing.

We can also administer the 100-square chart so that the reinforcer is won by an individual student instead of the group. In either case, there are two variations to consider. We can establish that students need to earn a specific number of points in order to obtain the privilege of removing a cover. For example, we might set the criterion at 10 points. When students earn 10 points, they uncover one of the squares. Alternatively, we can determine a specific number of squares with "X's" that must be uncovered before a student or group earns the reinforcer. For example, a criterion of five "X's" could be required before a reinforcer is earned. In this variation, students who perform the target behavior either take a turn uncovering a square or are required to earn a certain number of points before they can uncover a square. In either arrangement, a certain number of "X's" must be uncovered before a student or group earns access to the reinforcer.

Mystery Motivators

The first step in using mystery motivators is to generate a list of positive reinforcers with input from students. Each reinforcer is written down on a slip of paper and placed in its own envelope. We can display the envelopes in a prominent place for all students to see or have students decorate the sealed envelopes and place them inside a shoe box. We then obtain a calendar and place pieces of opaque tape or small Post-It notes over each school day on the calendar for the entire year. As students perform target behaviors, they earn the right to uncover that day on the calendar. If an "X" appears, the students can open a mystery motivator envelope and obtain the reinforcer. The number of "X's" we write on the calendar determines the frequency with which students receive reinforcement.

The Compliance Matrix

The compliance matrix is a variation of bingo—a popular game in which players use matrix cards to win prizes. The word *matrix* refers to a square composed of several equal-sized cells. The following materials are needed to implement the compliance matrix:

- Several matrices with numbered cells, such as those appearing in Figure 9.13.
- Cardboard key tags, available from office supply stores, or small pink erasers, poker chips, checkers, or slips of paper. Label each object with a number from the matrix. Include one marked "Wild Card."
- An opaque container to hold the numbered objects.

Matrix X

1	2	3	4
5	6	7	8
9	10	11	12
13	14	15	16

Matrix Y

1	2	3	4	5
6	7	8	9	10
11	12	13	14	15
16	17	18	19	20
21	22	23	24	25

Matrix Z

1	2	3	4	5	6
7	8	9	10	11	12
13	14	15	16	17	18
19	20	21	22	23	24
25	26	27	28	29	30
31	32	33	34	35	36

FIGURE **9.13**

Sample Compliance Matrices

To implement this technique, we post a matrix (see Figure 9.13) or draw it on the chalkboard in an area visible to students. The numbered objects (e.g., key tags) are placed in the opaque container. When students comply with a direction, follow classroom rules, or are on task, they get to draw an object. When an object is drawn, the corresponding number on the matrix is marked with an "X." If students draw the wild card, they can pick any number to be marked off on the matrix.

Students earn a preselected reinforcer after any row, column, or diagonal is completed on the matrix. We then erase the matrix board, and the game starts over. Matrix Y is introduced after students are responding to our instructions at a high rate, and matrix Z is introduced when a high rate of compliance is achieved with matrix Y.

Rather than targeting one student, the compliance matrix can be used to promote compliance with groups of students. With either a single student or groups, we place the matrix, reinforcers, and opaque container in the front of the room. We also post the predetermined reinforcer, or mystery motivator, next to the matrix to build class expectations. Students who follow a direction are randomly chosen to select one of the numbered objects. When a row, column, or diagonal is completed, the entire class receives the reinforcer.

The number of cells in a matrix can be decreased (e.g., 9) or increased (e.g., 49) depending on how intermittent students can tolerate reinforcement.

The second modification for groups involves splitting the class into several teams. We assign each team a color, which can be marked in the matrix cell of the drawn number whenever a team member complies with our request. Several teams can occupy the same cell if they randomly draw that cell's number. This approach encourages teams to compete at being compliant and to follow classroom rules. Any number of teams can win by reaching the set criterion. And a student who tries to sabotage his or her team's effort can be made a one-person team.

SUMMARY

Methods for delivering reinforcement are often referred to as interventions. A token economy involves giving students some type of token (e.g., tally marks, hole punches in cards, or funny money) when they perform certain specified target behaviors. They can then exchange the tokens at a later time for backup reinforcers.

A behavioral contract is a written document specifying a contingent relation between two or more people. Students are equal participants in determining the task, criteria for successful performance, and reinforcers. This method works well with older students, who may find a token economy "babyish." It also works well when parents are involved because they can deliver reinforcers not available at school (e.g., a friend spending the night).

Group-oriented contingencies also can be used to increase behavior. The dependent group-oriented contingency (i.e., hero procedure) helps peers give students positive attention. The independent group-oriented contingency does not make use of peer pressure, and students can earn reinforcers regardless of how their peers behave. The interdependent group-oriented contingency has the highest amount of peer pressure built in because everyone has to perform at a certain level before anyone can get a reinforcer. Six novel approaches for delivering reinforcement provide ways to prevent students from satiating on any one program.

ACTIVITIES

1. Get together with several friends and list as many real-life examples of a token economy as possible (e.g., punch cards at clothing stores).
2. Using a form like the one in Figure 9.4, develop a contract for a student with whom you work. You may also want to list ways contracts are used in everyday life.
3. Write down three situations in classrooms in which you might use a group-oriented contingency. What type of contingency would you use, and why?
4. Write down an additional modification that could be made for each of the following techniques: chart moves, spinners, 100-square chart, and compliance matrix.

REVIEW QUESTIONS

1. Why are token economies effective?
2. Describe the procedures for establishing a token economy.
3. What are the four reasons behavioral contracts work?
4. What are the three components of behavioral contracts?
5. What are the guidelines for successful behavioral contracting?
6. Describe the contract negotiation process.
7. Describe how to implement a home–school behavioral contract.
8. Describe three types of group-oriented contingencies, and provide an example for each.
9. What are the advantages of using group-oriented contingencies?
10. Describe several strategies for reducing scapegoating.
11. What ethical issues should be considered before implementing a group-oriented contingency?

12. Describe the novel applications of positive reinforcement and several ways these techniques can be modified.

REFERENCES

Alberto, P. A., & Troutman, A. C. (1999). *Applied behavior analysis for teachers* (5th ed.). Columbus, OH: Merrill.

Barkley, R. A. (1998). *Attention-deficit hyperactivity disorder* (2nd ed.). New York: Guilford.

Barrish, H. H., Saunders, M., & Wolf, M. M. (1969). Good behavior game: Effects of individual contingencies for group consequences on disruptive behavior in a classroom. *Journal of Applied Behavior Analysis, 2,* 119–124.

Cooper, J. O., Heron, T. E., & Heward, W. L. (1987). *Applied behavior analysis.* Columbus, OH: Merrill.

DeRisi, W. J., & Butz, G. (1975). *Writing behavioral contracts: A case simulation practice manual.* Champaign, IL: Research Press.

DuPaul, G. J., & Stoner, G. (1994). *ADHD in the schools: Assessment and intervention strategies.* New York: Guilford.

Gresham, F. M. (1983). Use of a home-based dependent group contingency system in controlling destructive behavior: A case study. *School Psychology Review, 12,* 195–199.

Kauffman, J. M., Pullen, P. L., & Akers, E. (1986). Classroom management: Teacher-child-peer relationships. *Focus on Exceptional Children, 19*(1), 1–10.

Kazdin, A. E. (1985). The token economy. In R. M. Turner & L. M. Ascher (Eds.), *Evaluating behavior therapy outcome* (pp. 225–253). New York: Springer.

Litow, L., & Pumroy, D. K. (1975). A brief review of classroom group-oriented contingencies. *Journal of Applied Behavior Analysis, 3,* 341–347.

Martin, G., & Pear, J. (1996). *Behavior modification: What it is and how to do it* (5th ed.). Englewood Cliffs, NJ: Prentice-Hall.

Rhode, G., Jenson, W. R., & Reavis, H. K. (1992). *The tough kid book: Practical classroom management strategies* (5th ed.). Longmont, CO: Sopris West.

Sarafino, E. P. (1996). *Principles of behavior change: Understanding behavior modification techniques.* New York: Wiley.

Walker, J. E., & Shea, T. M. (1995). *Behavior management: A practical approach for educators* (6th ed.). New York: Macmillan.

DIFFERENTIAL REINFORCEMENT FOR DECREASING BEHAVIOR

CHAPTER OVERVIEW

- Types of Differential Reinforcement
- Schedules of DRO and DRL
- Considerations When Using Differential Reinforcement

CHAPTER OBJECTIVES

After completing this chapter, you will be able to do the following:

1. Explain how differential reinforcement can be used to decrease inappropriate behavior.

2. Describe the four types of differential reinforcement: DRI, DRA, DRO, and DRL.

3. Describe the four schedules on which DRO can be implemented.

4. Describe the two schedules on which DRL can be implemented.

5. Identify considerations when using differential reinforcement.

In the previous chapter, several intervention techniques based on principles of positive reinforcement were described for increasing students' appropriate behaviors. Recall also from Chapter 5 the fair pair: When students are reinforced for behaving appropriately, we reduce the likelihood of misbehavior occurring. For example, it is difficult for a student to repeatedly tap his pencil when he is reinforced for writing answers. However, in some situations, simply reinforcing an appropriate behavior may not automatically decrease an inappropriate behavior. For example, it is possible for a student to use a polite tone of voice and still punctuate her speech with curses. When this situation occurs, we may be tempted to punish her to decrease swearing. However, reinforcement does not automatically have to be abandoned in favor of punishment.

Several techniques exist for reducing inappropriate behavior. Based on principles of differential reinforcement, these techniques rely on presenting rather than withdrawing reinforcement to eliminate inappropriate behavior (Cooper, Heron, & Heward, 1987). Specifically, reinforcement is delivered (1) when a behavior is topographically incompatible with the behavior targeted for reduction, (2) when a more appropriate form of the behavior is performed, (3) when the target behavior is not emitted for a specified period, or (4) when the number of responses in a specified period is less than an established criterion. These approaches, respectively, correspond to differential reinforcement of incompatible behavior (DRI), differential reinforcement of alternative behavior (DRA), differential reinforcement of other behavior (DRO), and differential reinforcement of low rates of behavior (DRL). These techniques may eliminate as much as 95 percent of students' inappropriate behaviors with minimal or no use of punishment.

The concept of differential reinforcement was defined in Chapter 4.

In this chapter, four types of differential reinforcement are briefly described. In addition, several specific schedules of reinforcement for using DRO and DRL are discussed in detail. The reason for elaborating on these schedules is that we have already become familiar with the fair pair and with replacement behavior—concepts that form the basis for understanding DRI and DRA, respectively. Finally, some considerations in using these schedules of differential reinforcement are described.

DRI and DRA make use of the fair pair and replacement behavior, which were discussed in Chapters 5 and 7, respectively.

TYPES OF DIFFERENTIAL REINFORCEMENT

The various types of differential reinforcement have certain properties in common (Sulzer-Azaroff & Mayer, 1977):

- A target behavior is reinforced when it is performed in the presence of a stimulus.
- A target behavior is not reinforced (i.e., is extinguished) if it is performed in the absence of a stimulus.

As the behavior is repeatedly reinforced in the presence of some stimuli but not others, stimulus control is established. That is, a stimulus begins to prompt the occurrence of the behavior even if it does not follow reinforcement every time. Differential reinforcement of incompatible behavior (DRI) and differential reinforcement of alternative behavior (DRA) are discussed together because they both involve reinforcing a more appropriate behavior that replaces the inappropriate behavior.

Differential Reinforcement of Incompatible and Alternative Behavior

Differential reinforcement of incompatible behavior (DRI) involves selecting and reinforcing behaviors that are topographically incompatible with the inappropriate behavior. DRI is synonymous with the fair pair. Regardless of the terminology, the approach is the same: A behavior is selected and reinforced that cannot coexist with the inappropriate behavior. For example, if we target "pencil tapping" to decrease, then we reinforce writing answers because a student cannot perform both behaviors simultaneously. However, DRI has a major limitation: Just because a behavior is topographically incompatible does not guarantee that it accomplishes the same purpose as the inappropriate behavior. For example, a student may repeatedly tap a pencil to get the attention of a peer. "Writing answers" is unlikely to accomplish that same outcome and so may not be easily promoted in place of the inappropriate behavior.

Differential reinforcement of alternative behavior (DRA) is similar to DRI in that alternatives to the inappropriate behavior are reinforced. However, unlike with DRI, the alternative behavior is not topographically incompatible with the inappropriate behavior. Instead, we are reinforcing students for performing some replacement behavior. By conducting a functional assessment to determine the intent of the inappropriate behavior, we can select a replacement behavior that accomplishes the same outcome in a more appropriate fashion. In the previous example, "pencil tapping" may be a way for the student to get the attention of a peer. Therefore, a replacement behavior for differential reinforcement may be "student and peer working together on appropriate task." In this way, we can still reinforce the student for writing answers rather than tapping a pencil. This process represents the goal of DRA.

Differential Reinforcement of Other Behavior

Differential reinforcement of other behavior (DRO) involves reinforcing students for not engaging in inappropriate behavior for a specified time. For example, a student can earn 1 minute of extra free time for every 5 minutes in which she does not make any animal noises. A drawback of this approach is that the student may be reinforced for the absence of the inappropriate behavior even if other problem behaviors occur during the same time. Therefore, if the student swears but does not make animal noises, she still receives extra free time.

Alberto and Troutman (1999) described three important factors that should be considered before implementing a DRO procedure. First, because reinforcement is delivered if students do not perform the target behavior, we run the risk of positively reinforcing a variety of other inappropriate behaviors. Some students quickly figure out this contingency and manipulate it to their own benefit. For example, a student may refrain from poking his peers so as to obtain the reinforcer, but knock books off their desks. Technically, he will still be reinforced. Second, we may create a "behavioral vacuum" for students who do not possess a large repertoire of appropriate behaviors, because DRO reinforces the *absence* of behavior. Unless we identify an appropriate replacement behavior, some students may fill the vacuum by performing other inappropriate behaviors. Third, DRO is effective only if the reinforcer is as powerful as the one students naturally obtain from performing the inappropriate behavior. For example, earning free time for not making animal noises may not be as reinforcing as the attention from peers the student receives for performing the maladaptive behavior.

> The problems associated with DRO can be minimized if teachers conduct a functional assessment prior to implementing this form of differential reinforcement.

Differential Reinforcement of Low Rates of Behavior

Differential reinforcement of low rates of behavior (DRL) involves reinforcing students when the target behavior is at a tolerable or desirable level. Thus, we provide reinforcement either after a response that follows a specified interval or after a specified interval if the frequency of the behavior is below some established criterion.

DRL is sometimes used to reduce behaviors that occur so frequently that using a DRO schedule would be difficult. For example, suppose a student leaves his seat an average of 30 times per day. A DRO schedule would require too many reinforcement intervals for his teacher to manage in order for the behavior to not occur at all. Therefore, his teacher uses a DRL procedure to reinforce him each hour in which there are five or fewer occurrences of the behavior. The criterion number of occurrences is gradually reduced until the rate is low enough for a DRO procedure to be feasible.

In other instances, DRL is an effective method for reducing, but not eliminating, behaviors that otherwise would occur at an unacceptably high rate. For example, suppose a student politely asks for the teacher's help 20 times per day during independent seat-work assignments. Although the teacher is glad to lend assistance, the student is capable of completing most of the assignments independently. Therefore, her teacher uses a DRL procedure to reduce her requests for help to an average of one or two per seat-work assignment.

The important consideration in each of these examples is that reinforcement is delivered if the behavior occurs at a rate below some predetermined criterion. As with DRO, the students can engage in other inappropriate behaviors and still obtain reinforcement.

SCHEDULES OF DRO AND DRL

As previously noted, the major advantage of DRI and DRA is that they provide students with reinforcement for performing appropriate behaviors. The major disadvantage is that inappropriate behavior may persist even when alternative behaviors are reinforced. Some experts believe that for DRI or DRA to be effective they must be paired with punishment (e.g., Luiselli, 1980; Stokes & Kennedy, 1980). However, an alternative to punishment in these situations is to use a schedule of DRO and DRL, which can reduce and even eliminate behaviors that occur frequently. One of the best features of DRO and DRL is that they can be combined with other procedures, such as a token economy. For example, a student may receive a token for every five math problems completed accurately during an independent seat-work assignment. Although this reinforcement may increase his rate of accurate completion of assignments, he may continue to get out of his seat. A DRO schedule can be combined with the token economy so that he receives one token for every 5 minutes in which he refrains from getting out of his seat. Therefore, he can earn tokens for completing math problems correctly *and* for staying in his seat.

The schedules of DRO and DRL are based on information provided by Donnellan et al. (1988).

Schedules of DRO

There are four schedules upon which DRO can be programmed: (1) DRO reset schedule, (2) DRO fixed-interval schedule, (3) DRO increasing-interval schedule, and (4) DRO progressive schedule (Donnellan, Negri-Shoultz, Fassbender, & LaVigna, 1988). With all of these schedules, we have to determine an appropriate time interval in which the target behavior cannot occur in order for students to receive reinforcement. For some behaviors, one full day may be an appropriate time interval. For example, a student may hit her peers or destroy property three times during the day. Although these behaviors occur infrequently, they are extremely disruptive and damaging. Therefore, one day might be an appropriate length of time that must pass in which she does not engage in these behaviors. In other instances, 50 minutes may be an appropriate interval because this time represents the length of most classes. In still

The use of interresponse time virtually ensures that any type of schedule of differential reinforcement will be successful. If the desired results are not obtained, a shorter interresponse time can be implemented. The idea is to "set up" the student for success.

other instances, a shorter interval of time is desirable, such as 15 minutes during a seat-work activity. The key is to start with short-enough intervals to "set up" students for success.

One way to ensure an appropriate interval length is by determining **interresponse time (IRT)**—the time that passes between occurrences of the inappropriate behavior. This period (or one slightly longer) becomes the initial interval that must pass without the student engaging in the inappropriate behavior in order to obtain reinforcement.

IRT is easy to calculate: The number of times the behavior occurs is divided by the total time a DRO schedule is to be in effect. For example, suppose a student whistles 14 times during a 50-minute math lesson. His teacher wants to completely eliminate this behavior using a DRO schedule. First, she needs to determine an appropriate interval of time in which he has to refrain from whistling in order for him to obtain reinforcement. Dividing 14 into 50 yields 3.6, the average number of minutes that pass between incidents of whistling. Therefore, she sets an initial interval length of 4 minutes in which he must refrain from whistling in order to obtain reinforcement.

The other aspect of DRO schedules to keep in mind is that reinforcement is delivered not only after the absence of the inappropriate behavior but also after any display of an appropriate behavior. Otherwise, we run the risk of reinforcing the occurrence of another inappropriate behavior. In the previous example, after 4 minutes pass in which the student doesn't whistle, he is reinforced after performing any type of appropriate behavior, such as writing answers, asking questions, or reading a book.

The DRO Reset Schedule

In the **DRO reset schedule,** the interval is reset every time the inappropriate target behavior occurs. This schedule can be used for a student who repeatedly gets out of her seat. To eliminate this behavior, her teacher establishes an interval length of 15 minutes. This means that the student obtains reinforcement for every 15 minutes in which she does not get out of her seat. Figure 10.1 shows the DRO reset schedule partially filled out for her morning schedule on this arrangement. As the figure shows, she did not get out of her seat between 8:00 and 8:15, so she received reinforcement at 8:15. Similarly, she did not get out of her seat between 8:15 and 8:30 or between 8:30 and 8:45, so reinforcement also was delivered at 8:30 and 8:45. Thus, if she refrains from getting out of her seat during the entire morning, she is reinforced every 15 minutes.

Whenever she gets out of her seat, regardless of what time it is, her teacher resets the timer, and a new 15-minute interval starts. Figure 10.2 illustrates this arrangement. On this particular day, at 8:17, she got out of her seat. As a result, she did not get her reinforcer at 8:30, and the 15-minute interval was reset to begin at 8:17. After another 15 minutes, she had not gotten out of her seat, so

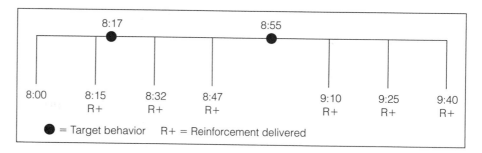

FIGURE **10.1**

Partial DRO Reset Schedule

From *Progress without punishment: Effective approaches for learners with behavior problems* (p. 72), by A. M. Donnellan, N. Negri-Schoultz, L. L. Fassbender, & G. W. LaVigna, 1988, New York: Teachers College Press. Copyright 1988 by Teachers College, Columbia University. All rights reserved. Adapted with permission.

FIGURE **10.2**

DRO Reset Schedule When Misbehavior Occurs

From *Progress without punishment: Effective approaches for learners with behavior problems* (p. 73), by A. M. Donnellan, N. Negri-Schoultz, L. L. Fassbender, & G. W. LaVigna, 1988, New York: Teachers College Press. Copyright 1988 by Teachers College, Columbia University. All rights reserved. Adapted with permission.

at 8:32, reinforcement was delivered, and again at 8:47. But when she got out of her seat at 8:55, she missed her 9:02 reinforcer, and the 15-minute interval was reset to begin at 8:55. She had the opportunity to receive up to seven reinforcers. However, because the interval was reset twice after she behaved inappropriately, she earned only six.

The DRO Fixed-Interval Schedule   In the **DRO fixed-interval schedule,** the interval length is fixed, and reinforcement is delivered at the end of each interval during which the behavior does not occur. The procedure differs from the reset schedule in that the interval time is not reset with each occurrence of target behavior. For example, suppose a student frequently scribbles on his worksheet, books, or other materials. His teacher uses this schedule for

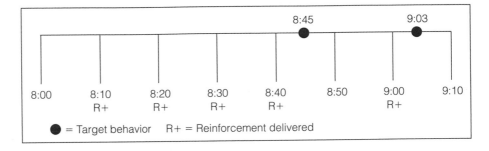

FIGURE 10.3

Results of a DRO Fixed-Interval Schedule

From *Progress without punishment: Effective approaches for learners with behavior problems* (p. 74), by A. M. Donnellan, N. Negri-Schoultz, L. L. Fassbender, & G. W. LaVigna, 1988, New York: Teachers College Press. Copyright 1988 by Teachers College, Columbia University. All rights reserved. Adapted with permission.

the target behavior of "scribbles," with a specified interval of 10 minutes. That is, reinforcement is presented every 10 minutes in which no scribbling occurs.

The results of this program for one morning are shown in Figure 10.3. As can be seen, the student did not scribble on any materials between 8:00 and 8:45, so reinforcement was given at 8:10, 8:20, 8:30, and 8:40. But at 8:45, he scribbled, which meant that at 8:50 no reinforcement was delivered. He did not scribble between 8:50 and 9:00, so at 9:00 reinforcement was delivered. But he scribbled again between 9:00 and 9:10, so there was no reinforcement at 9:10. Notice that with a fixed interval like this, because the clock is not reset, one scribble may force the student to wait almost 20 minutes without reinforcement if the inappropriate behavior occurs soon after reinforcement for the previous interval is delivered. The advantage of this arrangement is that the student may be motivated to refrain from scribbling so that he doesn't have to wait more than 10 minutes to receive reinforcement. In addition, it is a fairly easy schedule to implement because the teacher does not have to regularly stop what she is doing to reset an interval. At the same time, however, if the student scribbles immediately after he receives reinforcement for the previous interval, he may decide to continue scribbling because he must now wait almost twice as long before he can receive reinforcement again for not scribbling.

The disadvantages of the DRO fixed-interval schedule can be offset by using very small intervals. In this way, students do not have time to figure how much they can misbehave during an interval in which they will not receive reinforcement.

The DRO Increasing-Interval Schedule   A **DRO increasing-interval schedule** is one way of "fading" reinforcement by gradually increasing the length of the interval. As with the previous two DRO schedules, reinforcement is delivered for every interval that a student can refrain from performing the target behavior. However, with the DRO increasing-interval schedule, if a specified number of consecutive intervals passes without the target behavior occurring, reinforcement is delivered, but the next interval length can be

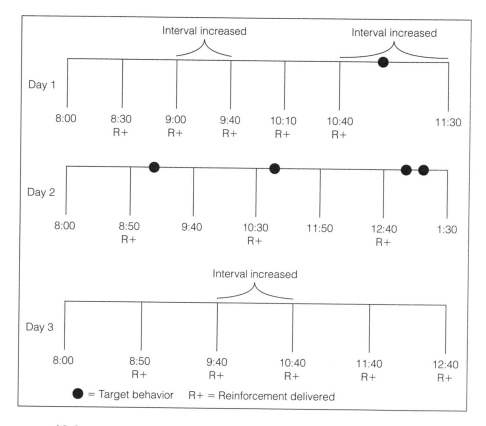

FIGURE **10.4**

DRO Increasing-Interval Schedule

From *Progress without punishment: Effective approaches for learners with behavior problems* (p. 75), by A. M. Donnellan, N. Negri-Schoultz, L. L. Fassbender, & G. W. LaVigna, 1988, New York: Teachers College Press. Copyright 1988 by Teachers College, Columbia University. All rights reserved. Adapted with permission.

increased. If the behavior occurs before the interval is over, the interval length is not increased.

Figure 10.4 illustrates this arrangement for a student who pinches other students during morning classes. Two consecutive intervals refraining from the target behavior was the criterion for an interval to be increased by 10 minutes. As the figure shows, on day 1, the student was able to refrain from engaging in the target behavior from 8:00 to 8:30 and from 8:30 to 9:00, so reinforcement was delivered at the end of these two intervals, and the interval length was increased by 10 minutes. She did not engage in the target behavior for the next three 40-minute intervals, so reinforcement was delivered at 9:40, 10:10, and 10:40. The interval length was then increased to 50 minutes. However, because she misbehaved at 11:00, no reinforcement was delivered. At the beginning of

The number of intervals that must pass before increasing the interval length may depend on the initial length of the intervals. Teachers may require more consecutive intervals to pass before increasing an interval with a relatively short initial duration.

day 2, the interval length remained at 50 minutes. She obtained reinforcement for not engaging in the target behavior from 8:00 to 8:50. However, at 9:15, she misbehaved, and so no reinforcement was delivered at 9:40. Because she was unable to go two consecutive intervals without misbehaving, the interval length remained at 50 minutes for the remainder of day 2. On day 3, she received reinforcement at 8:50 and 9:40, and so the interval length was increased to 60 minutes. She refrained from performing the target behavior from 10:40 to 11:40 and from 11:40 to 12:40, so she was reinforced at 11:40 and 12:40.

With this DRO schedule, as the interval size is increased, the amount of reinforcement that can be earned for each successful interval should remain the same as that obtained for the first interval length. Otherwise, students will be penalized for being able to go longer periods without engaging in the target behavior. For example, if our student pincher receives three tokens for every 30 minutes of not pinching classmates, then she should receive four tokens for going 40 minutes without engaging in the inappropriate behavior.

The DRO Progressive Schedule In a **DRO progressive (DROP) schedule,** the interval length remains the same, but the amount of reinforcement increases as students refrain from performing the inappropriate behavior for more and more consecutive intervals. For example, suppose a student can earn stickers when he does not burp in class. He can exchange the stickers for backup reinforcers at the end of the morning. Thus, he might earn one sticker for the first 10-minute interval of not burping in class, two stickers for the second consecutive 10-minute interval, three for the third consecutive 10-minute interval, and three stickers thereafter for every consecutive 10-minute interval with no occurrence of burping. However, if he burps, he receives no stickers for that 10-minute interval, and in the following interval, he is "recycled"; that is, he starts over at one sticker per 10-minute interval. This reinforcement schedule is depicted in Figure 10.5. No burping occurred between 8:00 and 8:40, so he progressed to the maximum reinforcement. When burping occurred between 8:40 and 8:50, he received no stickers at 8:50. No burping occurred between 8:50 and 9:00, so he began again by receiving one sticker at 9:00 and two stickers at 9:10.

A never-ending progression of increasing reinforcers is unrealistic because satiation will quickly occur. Furthermore, students who receive stickers as part of a token economy that can subsequently be exchanged for backup reinforcers may accumulate enough stickers early in the morning to purchase backup reinforcers and continue to engage in the inappropriate behavior. Therefore, limits must be set on the amount of reinforcement that can be earned by applying the free-access rule. Recall that the free-access rule involves determining how much students might want of a particular reinforcement if there are no limits on its availability. For example, a student might want to consume a maximum

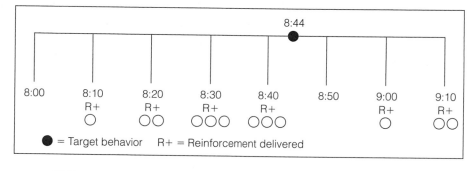

FIGURE 10.5

Reinforcement Schedule for DROP

From *Progress without punishment: Effective approaches for learners with behavior problems* (p. 76), by A. M. Donnellan, N. Negri-Schoultz, L. L. Fassbender, & G. W. LaVigna, 1988, New York: Teachers College Press. Copyright 1988 by Teachers College, Columbia University. All rights reserved. Adapted with permission.

of one 10-piece package of Star Bursts candy per day. Therefore, the number of Star Bursts that this student can earn in a day should not exceed 10; otherwise, satiation will occur.

Schedules of DRL

DRL schedules require students to decrease, but not completely eliminate, the occurrence of the inappropriate target behavior. There are two reasons for this arrangement. First, an inappropriate behavior may occur at such a high rate that initially using a DRO schedule may require such short intervals as to be impractical. Second, some behaviors are appropriate (e.g., asking for help or sharpening a pencil) but occur too frequently. There are two variations of DRL schedules: (1) DRL-IRT schedule and (2) DRL-below-criterion schedule. As was the case with DRO schedules, with both DRL-IRT and DRL-below-criterion schedules, we need to determine the interval length in order for students to receive reinforcement using interresponse time (IRT).

A word of caution: The information on the two schedules of DRL is sometimes more confusing than that presented for schedules based on DRO. The key distinction between the two DRL schedules is that with the DRL-IRT the student sets the interval length based on interresponse time whereas with the DRL-below-criterion the teacher sets the interval length and then observes whether the student performs the target behavior less than the computed average for a given time period.

The DRL-IRT Schedule   In a **DRL-IRT schedule,** the target behavior is reinforced following a specified interval since the previous episode. The inter-

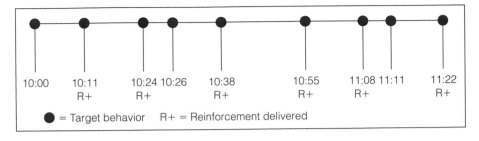

FIGURE **10.6**

Sequence of Reinforcement for DRL-IRT Schedule

val is determined by calculating interresponse time as described previously. The interval length then is gradually increased until the target behavior occurs only after longer periods have passed; thus, the procedure is called DRL-IRT.

For example, suppose a student asks for help from her teacher an average of six times per hour. However, her teacher believes that the student possesses the requisite skills to complete the assignments accurately and will finish more work if she asks for help less frequently. Therefore, with an average of six requests for help per hour, her teacher calculates that the interresponse time (IRT) for this behavior is 10 minutes (60 minutes/6 occurrences). Armed with this information, the teacher tells the student that she will get assistance and receive praise for good work only when she asks for help after at least 10 minutes (the identified IRT) have elapsed since the previous request. If she asks for help before 10 minutes have passed, the teacher, in a matter-of-fact manner, redirects her to continue working. Gradually, the length of the interval is increased until the student's requests for help decrease to a more reasonable rate.

Figure 10.6 shows how the sequence of reinforcement might initially look. The first occurrence of the target behavior was at 10:00. Eleven minutes passed before the next request for help; therefore, the student received reinforcement. The next request occurred at 10:24, 13 minutes after the previous request, so, again, reinforcement was delivered. The next request, however, came 2 minutes later, at 10:26, so no reinforcement was delivered. Instead, her teacher, in a matter-of-fact way, directed her to return to work. Because the next request came at 10:38 (12 minutes later), reinforcement was again delivered; and so forth. Notice that the chart does not have predetermined intervals. The interval times were marked down based on how long the student went without making a request. The only requirement was that she refrain

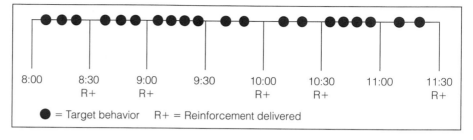

FIGURE **10.7**

Sequence of Reinforcement for DRL-Below-Criterion Schedule

From *Progress without punishment: Effective approaches for learners with behavior problems* (p. 87), by A. M. Donnellan, N. Negri-Schoultz, L. L. Fassbender, & G. W. LaVigna, 1988, New York: Teachers College Press. Copyright 1988 by Teachers College, Columbia University. All rights reserved. Adapted with permission.

> DRL-IRT is used when we want to increase the time that passes between incidents of some behavior. DRL-below-criterion is used when we don't care how much time has passed between occurrences, but rather want to see its total occurrence decrease.

from making requests for help less than 10 minutes apart. As the requests become more infrequent, a new IRT can be computed, and that time can be used as the standard for receiving reinforcement.

The DRL-Below-Criterion Schedule The **DRL-below-criterion schedule** involves determining the average number of times the target behavior is typically exhibited during a certain interval of time. Reinforcement is delivered if the frequency of the behavior is below this baseline rate during the specified interval, thus reinforcing lower rates of responding. In this arrangement, the teacher determines and sets the interval length.

This procedure differs from DRL-IRT in that reinforcement occurs for each interval of time (e.g., after every 30 minutes, class activity, or school day) during which the target behavior occurs at a lower rate—say, three or fewer times for the activity. DRL-below-criterion is used when we are interested not in how much time elapses between incidents of the target behavior, but in how many times it occurs. For example, suppose a student asks for help on average four times per 30 minutes. His teacher does not care if he asks for help three times back-to-back. Rather, she does not want him to ask for help more than three times during a 30-minute period because she knows he can do the work. Figure 10.7 illustrates a possible sequence for this schedule. The behavior occurred only three times between 8:00 and 8:30 and only three times between 8:30 and 9:00. Because the rate was below the baseline (i.e., four times per 30 minutes), the student received reinforcement at 8:30 and 9:00. However, between 9:00 and 9:30, he knocked materials off the table four times (the baseline rate), so at 9:30, no reinforcement was delivered. Between 9:30 and 10:30, the behavior occurred only twice, so reinforcement was again delivered at 10:00 and 10:30.

Schedules of DRO and DRL are probably underused compared to DRI and DRA because the latter two also focus on reinforcing positive behaviors. However, schedules of DRO and DRL can be quite effective as an alternative to punishment for suppressing inappropriate behavior.

CONSIDERATIONS WHEN USING DIFFERENTIAL REINFORCEMENT

Cooper, Heron, and Heward (1987) raised several considerations in selecting a differential reinforcement schedule. The schedule selected depends on (1) the type of target behavior (e.g., a behavior to eliminate versus one to decrease) and (2) the type of situation (e.g., independent seat-work activities versus group instruction).

First, DRI and DRA are used to increase appropriate behaviors. They correspond to the fair pair and replacement behaviors, respectively. These two approaches should be tried before using other schedules of differential reinforcement because they promote students' educational and social development.

Second, DRO does not specify what behaviors will be reinforced, thereby creating the potential for the "behavioral vacuum," as described previously. However, on the positive side, when DRO is used, the first occurrence of any appropriate behavior after a specified time in which the target behavior does not occur is reinforced. For example, the target behavior in a DRO schedule may be "animal noises." After a specified interval during which a student refrains from making animal noises, he is reinforced for the next appropriate behavior he performs, such as asking questions, talking politely, or writing answers. In this situation, many appropriate behaviors can be reinforced. The drawback is that, unlike with DRI and DRA, the teacher is not controlling which appropriate behaviors will be reinforced.

Third, DRL is the only type of differential reinforcement technique that does not require the target behavior to be completely eliminated for students to receive reinforcement. This arrangement lets students know that their behavior is acceptable although they should strive to reduce its occurrence. There is one major drawback to DRL, which Martin and Pear (1996) illustrated with the case of a student who begins doing well in school by giving correct answers to questions:

> At first the teacher is quite impressed and enthusiastically reinforces the behavior. But as the rate of the behavior increases, the teacher gradually becomes less impressed. This is "obviously a bright child," and so one expects a high rate of good behavior from her. Thus, the reinforcement gradually decreases, perhaps to zero, as the rate of the behavior increases. Eventually, the child learns that she obtains more reinforcement if she performs at a low rate, because the teacher is more impressed with good behavior when it occurs infrequently than when it occurs frequently. Many kids breeze through school showing only occasional "flashes of brilliance" instead of developing to their full potential. (pp. 98–99)

This problem can be reduced when teachers operationally define the target behavior they want to maintain at a high rate and reinforce its occurrence.

Fourth, DRI, DRA, and DRL usually produce a *gradual* change in behavior, which may not be desirable for behaviors that are dangerous to self or others, such as aggression or self-injury. In these instances, Cooper, Heron, and Heward (1987) recommended that the DRI, DRA, or DRL schedule be combined with some type of mild punishment procedure, such as those described in the next chapter.

Fifth, DRO may be the technique of choice when the behavior is dangerous to self or others because it can reduce and even eliminate inappropriate behaviors quickly. Even when using DRI or DRA, the inappropriate behavior may still occur. Sometimes it is impossible to find an incompatible behavior to reinforce using DRI. In the case of DRA, an alternative behavior may accomplish the same outcome but not be as highly reinforcing to the student as performing the inappropriate behavior. DRO is one way to avoid these problems.

SUMMARY

Differential reinforcement involves techniques and schedules aimed at reducing or eliminating inappropriate behaviors by extinguishing them and reinforcing alternative behaviors. This approach is reflected in the use of DRI and DRA. DRI involves reinforcing an incompatible behavior and is synonymous with the fair pair; DRA involves reinforcing a functional alternative (i.e., replacement) behavior.

With both DRO and DRL, students are reinforced for not performing inappropriate behavior or for performing it less frequently. Schedule of DRO involve resetting the interval, keeping the interval constant, increasing the interval, and increasing the reinforcement for students who go longer periods of time without performing the inappropriate behavior. Schedules of DRL involve reinforcing students for going a longer time without engaging in the target behavior and for displaying the target behavior less often. Determining interresponse time is an important consideration in using DRO and DRL schedules effectively.

ACTIVITIES

1. Think of five typical student behaviors that make it difficult for teachers to manage classrooms effectively. For each of these behaviors, come up with a fair pair that could be targeted using DRI.
2. List five behaviors that are appropriate for students to engage in but that may become inappropriate if they occur too frequently. Design a DRL schedule to decrease, but not eliminate, them.

3. Visit a classroom and note the number of times the teacher verbally reprimands for students' misbehaviors versus praising students for not engaging in inappropriate behavior. As a teacher, what might you do to reduce the number of verbal reprimands and increase the frequency of praise?

REVIEW QUESTIONS

1. How does DRI makes use of the fair pair?
2. How does DRA focus on behavioral intent and replacement behavior?
3. What is the purpose of calculating interresponse time (IRT)?
4. What is the purpose of DRO, and what are the steps for using this procedure?
5. What is the purpose of DRL, and what are the three guidelines for using this procedure?
6. Describe the four schedules of DRO and provide an example for each.
7. Describe the two schedules of DRL and provide an example for each.
8. What are the key considerations when using differential reinforcement?

REFERENCES

Alberto, P. A., & Troutman, A. C. (1995). *Applied behavior analysis for teachers* (4th ed.). Columbus, OH: Merrill.

Cooper, J. O., Heron, T. E., & Heward, W. L. (1987). *Applied behavior analysis.* Columbus, OH: Merrill.

Donnellan, A. M., Negri-Schoultz, N., Fassbender, L. L., & LaVigna, G. W. (1988). *Progress without punishment: Effective approaches for learners with behavior problems.* New York: Teachers College Press.

Luiselli, J. K. (1980). Controlling disruptive behaviors of an autistic child: Parent-mediated contingency management in the home setting. *Education and Treatment of Children, 3*, 195–203.

Martin, G., & Pear, J. (1996). *Behavior modification: What it is and how to do it* (5th ed.). Englewood Cliffs, NJ: Prentice-Hall.

Stokes, T. F., & Kennedy, S. H. (1980). Reducing child uncooperative behavior during dental treatment through modeling and reinforcement. *Journal of Applied Behavior Analysis, 13*, 41–49.

Sulzer-Azaroff, B., & Mayer, G. R. (1977). *Applying behavior-analysis procedures with children and youth.* New York: Holt, Rinehart & Winston.

PUNISHMENT

CHAPTER OVERVIEW

- Undesirable Side Effects of Punishment
- Limitations of Punishment
- Types of Punishment

CHAPTER OBJECTIVES

After completing this chapter, you will be able to do the following:

1. Identify the effects punishment has on behavior.

2. Describe the undesirable side effects and limitations of punishment.

3. Describe the desirable aspects of response cost and ways to implement response cost effectively.

4. Explain how time-out works, what the various types of time-out are, how time-out is commonly abused, and how time-out can be used effectively.

5. Identify different overcorrection procedures.

6. Describe reductive techniques similar to overcorrection.

Punishment is the most often used, misused, and abused behavior management technique. The word *punishment* comes from the same root (Latin, *poena*) as do the words *penalty* and *pain* (Maurer, 1974). As a behavior management technique, it refers to either the administration or the removal of a stimulus after a behavior occurs in order to decrease the future occurrence of the behavior. Punishment has a broad appeal to teachers, parents, and society in general. Almost all our societal norms and laws are enforced through punishment, and not reinforcement. For example, a speeding ticket represents contingent withdrawal of a positive reinforcer—money.

It is easy to understand the widespread use of punishment, given that it may indeed suppress inappropriate behavior. For many students, mild forms of punishment, such as receiving a verbal reprimand or being sent out of the room, are effective in managing their behavior. Less frequently, some students may be sent to the principal's office or have their parents called as a consequence of engaging in inappropriate behavior. The reason these actions are taken is that they are effective for many students.

A problem arises, however, when these forms of punishment are ineffective, as is the case for students who repeatedly misbehave. Unfortunately, punishment is the only behavior management technique many teachers know. Therefore, when students misbehave, these teachers punish them. If the students continue to misbehave, they continue to be punished, and herein lies the problem: If punishment is effective, teachers should be using it *less* rather than *more* often because, by definition, it suppresses behavior.

Ethical and legal considerations may limit the use of some forms of punishment in schools, such as corporal punishment and time-out. Based on a legal analysis of the relevant literature, Yell (1990) recommended that schools follow five principles when using punishment:

1. Do not violate the due process rights of students with and without disabilities.
2. Be sure punishment serves a legitimate educational function.
3. Follow punishment procedures that are reasonable and not excessive.
4. Begin punishment with the least intrusive intervention, and advance to more intrusive interventions only after less intrusive ones have failed.
5. Keep extensive records on the use of punishment.

Over 23 national organizations have come out in opposition to the use of certain types of punishment such as corporal punishment (Walker & Shea, 1995). For example, the Association for Persons with Severe Handicaps and the American Association on Mental Retardation have advocated nonaversive "behavioral support" in which the use of punishment techniques is eliminated and the use of other aversive methods is severely curtailed (Butterfield, 1990; Horner et al., 1990).

In this chapter, the undesirable side effects and limitations of punishment are presented first and second, respectively. This information is important not only because it highlights many of the ethical and legal problems associated with punishment but also because it points out the difficulties that can be encountered when using certain types of punishment. This chapter also discusses various types of punishment, from least to most intrusive. A key theme is that punishment techniques should be used only in combination with positive reinforcement and differential reinforcement, and never in isolation.

This description of punishment refers to types I and II, as described in Chapter 4.

UNDESIRABLE SIDE EFFECTS OF PUNISHMENT

Newsom, Flavel, and Rincover (1983) categorized the effects of punishment along four dimensions: primary, physical, social, and secondary. The primary effect of punishment is to suppress behavior. The physical effect is usually the result of contingent stimulation punishment—for example, the pain associated with slapping or spanking, or the fatigue associated with most forms of overcorrection and contingent exercise. The social effects refer to the reactions individuals have to the person being punished. Finally, secondary effects of punishment refer to undesirable side effects and are the focus of the first part of this section.

It is important to keep in mind the following characteristics of the research into these side effects:

- Most studies focused on individuals with severe and profound developmental disabilities.
- The most frequently used forms of punishment were slapping, brief contingent electric shock, and overcorrection. Most students are not exposed to the first two types of punishment.
- Many of the subjects received treatment in residential facilities that were much more highly structured than public school classrooms.
- The results were based on subjects ranging from preschoolers to middle-aged adults.
- The behaviors targeted to receive punishment often involved severe levels of self-injury (e.g., head banging and biting) or self-stimulation (e.g., hand flapping and object mouthing).

It is important to remember that many of the undesirable side effects have been researched for individuals with developmental disabilities. Undesirable side effects have often been cited by opponents of corporal punishment in schools. However, it is probably somewhat erroneous to conflate these data and the debate over corporal punishment.

These characteristics necessarily limit our ability to generalize the findings to students in public school classrooms. Nevertheless, the literature on the undesirable side effects of punishment provides important cautions and ethical considerations in using these techniques with any students. In addition, this information will help us more fully understand the limitations of punishment, as described in the next section.

Escape and Avoidance

Most students try to escape or avoid punishment because it represents an aversive consequence. However, it is difficult for us to provide students with opportunities to receive reinforcement when they are trying to escape our punishment. Furthermore, students may come to view us as a conditioned punisher because our presence has been paired with some punisher.

When students cannot escape or avoid punishment, they may experience **learned helplessness**—a hypothesized cause of depression in humans (Abramson, Seligman, & Teasdale, 1978; Seligman & Peterson, 1986). In laboratory experiments, dogs subjected to repeated experiences of painful, unpredictable, and inescapable shock lost their ability to learn a simple escape routine—they simply sat there and "took it." Seligman and his colleagues inferred from this that human depression is a reaction to the inability to escape or avoid negative consequences.

Although the theory of learned helplessness as applied to humans is intriguing, there is little conclusive evidence indicating its role in certain behavior problems.

Emotional Reaction

Students who cannot escape or avoid punishment may have an emotional reaction to it. These reactions can include overt behaviors such as crying or frowning and internal states such as fear or anxiety.

In a study Maag, Rutherford, Wolchik, and Parks (1986) conducted using overcorrection to suppress self-stimulation, the student initially screamed when the punishment was administered, and his facial expression changed from a smile to a frown. These effects were short-lived and did not generalize to other settings once the punishment was discontinued. However, if the aversive stimuli are strong enough, students may experience levels of anxiety and fear that interfere with learning.

Aggression

Like wounded animals that cannot avoid or escape an unpleasant interaction, individuals who are punished may respond by lashing out at the punisher or someone else. For example, a student may attack his teacher after being deprived of something positive. Sometimes, if students lack the power to attack the one who punished them, they may attack someone weaker. Many younger siblings can attest to the aggression they experienced at the hands of older brothers and sisters who had been punished by a parent.

Sometimes students who are punished (e.g., by spanking) or who observe others being punished will subsequently engage in aggression as a way to control others' behaviors. It has been well established that children not only imitate the aggressive behaviors of models but also imitate punishment

Imitative aggression pro-
vides another example
of the powerful effect of
social learning on human
behavior.

procedures they have experienced (Bandura, Ross, & Ross, 1961, 1963; Bandura & Walters, 1959). Rutherford and Neel (1978) suggested that punishment teaches that individuals with strength and power can punish and control others.

Response Substitution

Response substitution occurs when one inappropriate behavior is suppressed and another inappropriate behavior occurs. This undesirable side effect is likely to occur when we fail to identify and reinforce students for performing a replacement behavior. For example, we may successfully suppress animal noises a student makes only to have him begin poking his peers in the arm. The reason for this response substitution is that making animal noises is a way for the student to get attention from peers. When making animal noises no longer earn him peer attention, he switches to another inappropriate behavior—poking peers—to obtain attention. But if we give this student opportunities to interact with peers appropriately, then the likelihood of his engaging in another inappropriate behavior to get attention is decreased. Thus, we might conduct lessons using a cooperative learning format in which groups of students work together. Group interaction gives the student an appropriate way (i.e., replacement behavior) to obtain peer attention.

Response Facilitation

Ironically, the occurrence of some behaviors increases rather than decreases after the application of an aversive stimulus—a phenomenon known as **response facilitation.** There are several reasons an undesirable behavior may increase rather than decrease.

First, the aversive stimulus may be relatively weak (e.g., a verbal reprimand) but function as a powerful reinforcer for students—gaining attention, albeit negative. After all, negative attention is better than no attention.

Second, a punishment may be a way for students to escape or avoid a more aversive situation. For example, a student may not like staying in from recess as a punishment for talking out in class. However, she may dislike even more the teasing she receives from peers on the playground. When presented with two potential punishers, she will opt for the milder of the two. Moreover, students will actively place themselves in a position to be punished if it means that, in so doing, they avoid a more severe punisher.

Third, the punisher may serve as a discriminative stimulus that positive reinforcement will be forthcoming. For example, a student may be doodling instead of completing a math assignment. As punishment, we require him to stay after school to complete the assignment. After school, we first verbally repri-

The association of reinforcement with punishment is a thorny issue. Most teachers would agree that it is important to "process" with students the reason for being punished. The problem is how long to wait before processing. In beginning too soon, we run the risk of reinforcing the misbehavior; in waiting too long, we run the risk of having students not make the connection between the processing and the misbehavior.

mand him and then provide assistance, which the student finds to be reinforcing. In essence, we have created a stimulus–response chain: Misbehavior becomes a cue that punishment will be delivered, which, in turn, becomes the antecedent stimulus that reinforcement will be forthcoming. Although it may be unavoidable, it is important for us to understand that if reinforcement is associated with punishment then the punishment becomes a cue for students that they will then be reinforced.

Generalized Suppression

Recall from Chapter 4 that stimulus generalization occurs when students respond in a similar manner to different stimuli. Therefore, when a behavior is suppressed by being punished in the presence of one stimulus, it may similarly be suppressed in other situations. In one respect, stimulus generalization can be a positive side effect of punishment. For example, if a student is punished for yelling in math class and similarly refrains from yelling in science class, then stimulus generalization is considered desirable. However, if the student is punished for yelling during math class, she may not yell in situations in which it is appropriate to do so, such as playing a game at recess.

Punishment also can result in **response generalization**—a phenomenon that occurs when an inappropriate behavior is suppressed and, as a result, certain appropriate behaviors are also suppressed. To understand this phenomenon, recall the concept of a response class—a set of behaviors that share some common characteristic. For example, the response class for obtaining teacher attention may include yelling, making animal noises, raising hands, and approaching the teacher's desk. Response generalization occurs if punishment for yelling and making animal noises also results in the suppression of raising hands and approaching the teacher's desk.

Punishment Contrast

Punishment contrast occurs when a behavior that is suppressed through punishment in one situation increases in another situation in which punishment was not administered. For example, a student's yelling may be successfully suppressed during math class only to have it occur at a higher level during physical education. Punishment contrast results when the inappropriate behavior served an appropriate function—either obtaining attention from others or escaping a perceived aversive stimulus. Therefore, in the absence of teaching and reinforcing the student for performing a replacement behavior, he may engage in more frequent and intense yelling during P.E., where punishment did not occur to make up for the lost attention during math class, when he could not yell.

LIMITATIONS OF PUNISHMENT

There are several limitations of punishment besides those posed by the negative side effects discussed previously. In some instances, these limitations can be successfully avoided. For example, when we punish an inappropriate behavior, we can ensure that the student is taught a replacement behavior and reinforced for performing it. However, it is impossible to ethically justify administering punishment initially at maximum intensity even if this practice will be most effective.

Punishment Does Not Teach Appropriate Behaviors

Just because an inappropriate behavior is suppressed with punishment does not automatically mean that students will then perform an appropriate behavior. Teachers who use punishment often leave the development of desirable behavior to chance (Rutherford & Neel, 1978). Some teachers mistakenly believe that through punishment students are learning how to behave appropriately. Ironically, before punishing them, these teachers may tell students that they are going to teach them a lesson. The lesson is taught when we reinforce students for performing replacement behaviors.

Punishment Does Not Eliminate Reinforcement

Punishing students for behaving inappropriately does not automatically mean that the reinforcer that maintained the inappropriate behavior has been eliminated. For example, as a consequence of a student making animal noises in class, a teacher may institute several punishment procedures including a verbal reprimand, loss of privileges, time-out in the hallway, a trip to the principal's office, and a phone call to his parents. However, these forms of punishment do not eliminate the reinforcement in the form of the peer attention the student receives for misbehaving. Peers may respond by saying "Here he goes again," "Gross, you pig, why don't you shut up," or "Hey, can't you think of a new animal noise to make?" Or peers may look at the student when he makes animal noises and giggle. Peer attention—even if it is negative—can be a powerful reinforcer.

It is poor professional practice for teachers to use punishment without identifying and eliminating the reinforcers that are maintaining students' inappropriate behaviors. In most cases, reinforcement will win out over punishment. Therefore, students may find it a desirable trade-off to be punished because the reinforcement (i.e., peer attention) is more powerful. We can avoid this problem by conducting functional assessment.

Punishment Becomes Reinforcing

In the short run, if the aversive stimulus is sufficiently intense, punishment may quickly and easily suppress students' inappropriate behavior (Rutherford & Neel, 1978). Although the effect of punishment is often temporary, many teachers nevertheless find its easy, quick, and effective results to be highly negatively reinforcing. Most teachers view students' inappropriate behavior as aversive. By suppressing an inappropriate behavior, teachers are negatively reinforced—that is, the aversiveness of the inappropriate behavior is terminated. Therefore, teachers are more likely to punish students in the future because doing so terminates the aversiveness of their inappropriate behavior.

The negative reinforcement trap described in Chapter 4 illustrates how some teachers administer frequent punishments to students.

Punishment May Affect Peers' Behavior

The effects of vicarious punishment are frequently cited as a positive attribute of punishment (Rutherford & Neel, 1978). Recall that vicarious punishment is the process whereby students who are punished serve as models for other students, who may now refrain from misbehaving to avoid the established consequences. Many teachers want to "make an example" of certain students in the hope that the effect of the punishment will "spill over" into peers' behaviors. If students observe a classmate receiving punishment for a given response, they may be less likely to engage in similar inappropriate behaviors.

What most teachers do not realize, however, is that this desirable effect may be offset by the undesirable side effect of generalized suppression. For example, a punishment may be effective in eliminating a student's habit of shouting out answers. However, other students may be less likely to raise their hands to answer questions because this desirable behavior is in the same response class as shouting out answers. Therefore, caution should be used when punishing students in an attempt to set an example for peers. An unintended result may be the suppression of certain desirable classroom behaviors.

Punishment Should Be Intense

The sudden introduction of intense punishment appears to result in a much larger reduction in the punished responses than if the punishment intensity is increased gradually (Schmidt, 1982). The initial effectiveness of an intense punishment may be due to the fact that it constitutes a dramatic change from the prior environmental conditions. In fact, there is evidence that the sudden introduction of any novel stimulus will reduce responding. However, a gradual increase in the intensity of the aversive stimulus allows students to adapt to the punishment. This phenomenon is similar to what happens when we go swim-

> Punishment is like a drug—teachers become addicted to its initial effects and administer it in increasing intensities, much like the drug addict who needs ever-larger doses to obtain a high.

ming in a lake. Because the water near the shore is shallower than the water in the middle of the lake, it also tends to be warmer. Some of us adapt to the colder water by wading in the shallows before venturing out into the deeper, colder water.

The fact that punishment is most effective when initially delivered at maximum intensity points out an ethically unacceptable limitation. For many years, the doctrine of beginning with the least severe punishment has been accepted practice (Skiba & Deno, 1991; Wood & Braaten, 1983). Imagine a situation in which a student turns to a peer to say something, and the teacher abruptly grabs him by the arm and escorts him to the principal's office, where he promptly receives a 2-day suspension. We want the punishment fit the crime. A just punishment is one that is neither too lenient nor too punitive. Unfortunately, this practice may result in students adapting to the punishment. Administering an initial punishment at maximum intensity may reflect results of research but nevertheless be ethically unacceptable.

Punishment Should Be Immediate

Punishment is most effective when it is delivered immediately after the inappropriate behavior occurs. The longer the delay between the start of a misbehavior and the punishment, the less positive the results (Schmidt, 1982). For example, it is better to verbally reprimand a student before she finishes misbehaving than to wait until she is finished misbehaving.

Although this recommendation is solidly rooted in research and is ethically desirable, it rarely is implemented in schools. Most schools' disciplinary codes call for punishments (e.g., keeping students after school, sending them to a detention room before school, or suspending or expelling them) to be administered well after the misbehavior occurs. In essence, they are too delayed to be effective suppressants. Ironically, reinforcement methods such as token economies and behavioral contracts have built-in mechanisms for dealing with the issue of delayed reinforcement. Punishment procedures have no such mechanism.

Punishment Should Be Continuous

Unlike reinforcement, which is most effective when delivered on an intermittent basis, punishment is most effective when delivered on a continuous basis. When punishment is delivered intermittently, students may come to believe that they can "get away" with misbehaving because "the teacher might not punish anyone today."

The irony here is that some teachers complain about not having enough time to reinforce students every time they behave appropriately. Yet it takes a

An irony is that it takes more teacher time to catch students being bad and punish them than it takes to catch them being good and reinforce them intermittently.

lot more time and effort to watch students continuously to catch them misbehaving and then administer punishment than to occasionally "catch them being good."

TYPES OF PUNISHMENT

There are a variety of punishment techniques based on either contingent application of an aversive stimulus or contingent withdrawal of a positive reinforcer. In this section, four types of punishment are discussed, from least to most intrusive: (1) response cost, (2) time-out, (3) overcorrection, and (4) reductive techniques similar to overcorrection.

It is important to consider the undesirable side effects and limitations of punishment, as well as the characteristics of effective punishment, as the various types of punishment are presented. Unlike techniques based on positive reinforcement, punishment is not always easy, practical, or ethical. In addition, punishment should not be administered in a cavalier fashion, because it has many potential negative side effects that can adversely affect students' interpersonal functioning.

Response Cost

The concept of a response cost was introduced in Chapter 9 as a way to reduce the effect of scapegoating during the implementation of group-oriented contingencies. A response cost involves removing a certain amount of reinforcement when students misbehave. There are many real-life examples of the uses of response costs, such as receiving a ticket for speeding. Teachers routinely use a response cost in revoking privileges when students misbehave. Smith and Rivera (1993) provided the following example:

> A class was allowed to earn a free period each week when all of their homework assignments were turned in daily and they entered the class without disruption each period change. One day, the teacher was ill and a substitute teacher replaced her. Unfortunately, the class was not cooperative with the substitute. They were excessively noisy, refused to do the assignments she gave them, and in several instances were rude to her. Although the class had met the criterion for earning a free period that week, the class was fined because of their misconduct with the substitute. They did not receive the free period that week. (p. 81)

A response cost procedure is based on contingent withdrawal of a positive reinforcer.

A response cost represents a relatively mild form of punishment. As such, it has several advantages over other, more severe, punishment techniques (Cooper Heron, & Heward, 1987), including the following:

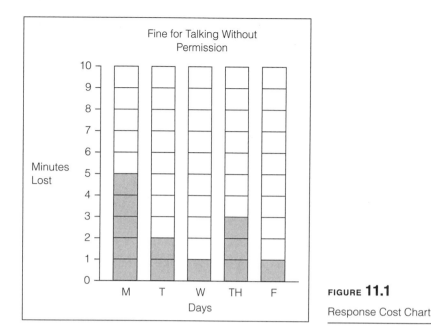

FIGURE 11.1

Response Cost Chart

- Response costs result in a fairly quick decrease in inappropriate behavior. The suppressive effects of a given response cost should be easy to determine within 3 to 5 days.
- Response costs are convenient to use in the classroom. For example, teachers can minimize classroom disruptions by listing the number of minutes of recess that will be lost when students engage in a specified inappropriate behavior.
- Teachers can avoid direct confrontation with students when using response costs. Teachers can make a response cost chart with the specified rule infraction that results in a fine; Figure 11.1 gives an example. When students engage in the inappropriate behavior, the teacher simply adds a fine to the chart, without having to constantly reprimand students.
- Response costs can be combined with other behavior management procedures such as a token economy or group-oriented contingency. For example, in defining what inappropriate behaviors will result in the loss of a specific number of points, a teacher can add a fining system to a token economy.

Implementing a Response Cost Procedure   It is relatively easy to implement response cost procedures. Cooper, Heron, and Heward (1987) offered seven guidelines. First, inappropriate behaviors that will result in fines should be operationally defined. Operational definitions ensure that students and teachers are on the same wavelength, preventing ambiguity that may cause some students to try to manipulate an intervention.

Second, the magnitude of the fines should be clearly specified. A typical procedure is for students to lose 1 point each time they misbehave. The fine should be commensurate with the misbehavior—the greater the infraction, the larger the fine. However, a never-ending increase in fines is not effective. For example, Sajwaj (1968) reported that fines that increased from the loss of 1 point to up to 5 points resulted in greater reductions in behavior, but no further reductions were noted when losses were greater than 5 points.

Third, as with any type of punishment, fines should be imposed immediately after each occurrence of the inappropriate behavior. In fact, points should be removed as soon as the inappropriate behavior commences, and not when it ends.

Fourth, students should not lose more points than they earn. As a general rule, students should earn 3 to 5 points for behaving appropriately for every 1 point they lose for displaying inappropriate behavior. It is possible to precisely calculate the ratio of appropriate-to-inappropriate behavior. If baseline observations indicate that the inappropriate target behavior occurs frequently, then a large number of points should be available to remove. The availability of reinforcement should be increased 25 percent over the baseline occurrence of inappropriate behavior (Walker, 1983). For example, if a student makes animal noises 16 times during the baseline (16 x 0.25 = 4), then a total of 20 points should be available for him to earn for behaving appropriately (16 + 4 = 20).

Fifth, records should be kept on the occurrence of inappropriate behaviors and the number of points students lose. This information should be collected daily and graphed in order to assess the effectiveness of the response cost. The target behavior should decrease quickly if the response cost is effective. If the rate of behavior remains high, then peers may be reinforcing students for engaging in the inappropriate behavior. Any source of unintended reinforcement maintaining students' inappropriate behaviors must be eliminated before a response cost can be effective.

Sixth, we should be aware of two potential unexpected outcomes (Cooper, Heron, & Heward, 1987). First, the process of fining students may actually serve to reinforce, rather than punish, the misbehavior. For example, a student may find the attention she receives from a teacher taking away points to be reinforcing. In this instance, the response cost should be abandoned and the student taught a replacement behavior for obtaining attention appropriately. Second, students may refuse to relinquish the positive reinforcers they have earned. Cooper, Heron, and Heward (1987) described four steps that can be taken when this situation occurs:

1. Impose an additional fine for not giving up points.
2. Reimburse students with some small portion of the fine for relinquishing points immediately.
3. Allow students who owe substantial fines to repay them in installments.
4. Make sure that an adequate supply of backup reinforcers are available so that students will not want to lose points.

Seventh, response costs should not be overused. Because the use of all forms of punishment can negatively reinforce teachers, there is a tendency to overuse them. Consequently, teachers run the risk of focusing exclusively on inappropriate behaviors and failing to positively reinforce students for performing appropriate behaviors.

Implementing a Response Cost Lottery   A novel application of fining systems is the **response cost lottery** (Rhode, Jenson, & Reavis, 1995). This procedure works well with students who have mild or occasional behavior problems. However, it should be avoided with students with emotional or behavioral disorders, who may become upset at losing reinforcers.

To use this procedure, we tape an envelope to each student's desk. We then place five or more tickets in each envelope with the student's name written on each ticket. Students lose a ticket every time they engage in one of three inappropriate behaviors we have written on the chalkboard. At the end of a specified time, the remaining tickets are placed in a grab bag and mixed up. We draw three or four tickets, and the students whose names appear on the tickets win a reward. Students quickly learn that the less they misbehave, the more tickets they will have in the bag, which, in turn, increases their chances of winning a reward.

Rhode, Jenson, and Reavis (1995) also described how the response cost lottery can be combined with an interdependent group-oriented contingency. In this arrangement, the class is divided into two or three teams, each of which has an envelope. Whenever any member of a team misbehaves, a ticket is removed from its envelope. Losing tickets reduces the likelihood of a team having one of its tickets drawn and winning a reward.

A final modification Rhode, Jenson, and Reavis (1995) described is to place a wild card ticket in the grab bag. If this ticket is drawn, any team that has a ticket in the grab bag wins a reward. The wild card ticket helps motivate teams with only a few tickets to behave appropriately. Even if a team has only one ticket, it can still win the reward if the wild card ticket is drawn. However, a team with no tickets to place in the grab bag cannot receive the reward with the wild card ticket.

Using a Bonus Response Cost   A **bonus response cost** is an innovative and mild form of punishment that can be used in isolation or incorporated into

The good behavior game, described in Chapter 9, often makes use of a response cost.

10	10	10	10	10	10	10	10	10	10

Hall Pass

20	20	20	20	20	20	20	20	20	20

FIGURE 11.2

Hall Pass

a variety of reinforcement programs. In this arrangement, we make additional reinforcers available that students do not have to earn. When they misbehave, we remove a specified amount of the bonus reinforcement. For example, we may provide a student with 10 additional minutes of recess. Every time he makes an animal noise prior to recess, he loses 1 minute of the extra recess time. We do not remove any of the normally scheduled recess time, but any bonus time the student earns depends on his not making animal noises.

Cooper, Heron, and Heward (1987) described two advantages of a bonus response cost. First, students can add to the reinforcement they earn by refraining from engaging in the inappropriate behavior. For example, in a token economy, a student may receive 1 token for every five math problems she completes correctly. In addition, she may have a reserve of 10 bonus tokens that are removed when she leaves her seat without permission. The number of bonus tokens remaining after a specified period of time is added to the tokens she earns for completing math problems. Second, a bonus response cost eliminates the need to remove existing tokens students have earned for engaging in appropriate behaviors.

Bonus response costs can be implemented in a variety of ways. A middle school teacher devised a novel and highly effective bonus response cost system for reducing two common problem behaviors of junior high students: (1) coming to class late and (2) asking to leave the classroom either to get a drink of water, use the bathroom, or go to a locker.

The teacher laminated orange cards for every student that said "Hall Pass" on one side, with each student's name and teacher's signature on the other side. There were 10 squares across the top and the bottom of the cards. The top squares contained the number "10," and the bottom squares the number "20." Figure 11.2 shows a sample hall pass.

Students' cards were kept in a shoe box—one shoe box for each class period. Any time students were tardy, they went over to the shoe box for that class period, removed their card, punched a hole in one of the 10-point squares, and left the card on the teacher's desk. Any time students wanted to leave the classroom for any reason, they got their hall pass, punched out one of the 20-point squares, and left. In this way, students did not disrupt the teacher's lesson by having to ask for permission to leave the classroom. Similarly, the teacher did not have to disrupt the lesson to verbally reprimand students for being tardy or wanting to leave the classroom. It was important that students placed their "passes" on the teacher's desk after punching the appropriate squares so that the accuracy of the punches could be checked.

If students used up all the points on the card, they could not use the hall pass for the remainder of the 6-week grading period. However, any unused points on the hall pass were added to students' 6-week grade point total. We can include the stipulation that a certain number of homework assignments must be completed or that students must be minimally passing the class as prerequisites for having bonus points added to the 6-week grade point total. In this way, students are discouraged from not doing homework assignments in the hope that they will have enough bonus points to "pull them through" to a passing grade.

A number of variations on the "hall pass" bonus response cost procedure are possible. For example, we can give students a "talking and moving" card with the number "1" appearing in the boxes across the top and bottom of the card (any number will suffice depending on the desired ratio of behaviors to reinforcement). This technique can be used in conjunction with a token economy. With this system, students are free to talk and move around the classroom. However, every time they engage in these behaviors for a set period of time, one of the squares is punched out, thereby indicating the loss of 1 bonus point. The number of points remaining on the card after a specified amount of time are added to the student's point earnings for purchasing backup reinforcers.

Time-Out

Perhaps no other behavior management technique has so permeated our society as has time-out. Time-out has been used for over 100 years. A 19th-century example is Itard's use of it with Victor, the so-called Wild Boy of Aveyron in France (Lane, 1976). Time-out became a popular form of behavior management among special educators and, consequently, made its way into the public schools in the 1970s. Today, time-out has become such an integral part of our vernacular that preschool children are familiar with the term.

Time-out typically refers to the removal of students from the environment in which they are misbehaving. A common example is requiring a student to sit

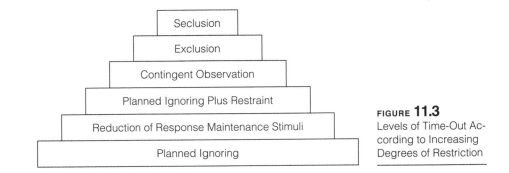

FIGURE **11.3**
Levels of Time-Out According to Increasing Degrees of Restriction

in the hallway. Although this is an accurate example, time-out is actually based on the behavioral principle of extinction—that is, of withholding reinforcement. The technical term is "time-out from positive reinforcement." Unfortunately, time-out, as it is commonly called, is rarely employed in this fashion. Instead, the punishment aspect is emphasized even though a number of behavioral principles are in effect.

Contingent withdrawal of a positive reinforcer (type II punishment) may be in effect because students are placed back in the environment in which reinforcement existed prior to the misbehavior. In contrast, if students find the time-out area to be aversive, it may be considered an application of contingent stimulation (type I punishment). Time-out can also be negatively reinforcing to students and teachers. Students may enjoy time-out as a way to escape the aversiveness of a lesson, and teachers may enjoy sending students to time-out because doing so terminates the aversiveness of the misbehavior.

A variety of behavior principles can be used to explain the function of time-out.

Levels of Time-Out   Although time-out is most often conceptualized in terms of removing students from the "time-in environment," various applications of this approach are possible. The most extensive, and arguably still the best, description of different levels of time-out was provided by Nelson and Rutherford (1983). Figure 11.3 illustrates the six levels of time-out they described, arranged in a sequence from least to most restrictive.

Before describing these applications in detail, it is helpful to understand the legal ramifications of using time-out. Although some schools may prohibit the use of certain techniques such as planned ignoring plus restraint or seclusion, time-out is, according to the courts, legal (Yell, 1990). Under certain circumstances, contingent observation, exclusion, and seclusion may be used. However, time-out cannot be used indiscriminately, nor can students be placed in time-out for indeterminate lengths of time. Yell (1990) provided six guidelines to ensure that time-out is used in accordance with court rulings:

1. Provide clearly specified written procedures for using time-out, and make sure students understand beforehand what behaviors will lead to time-out.
2. Never place students in time-out without a legitimate reason.
3. Maintain adequate time-out facilities.
4. Keep the time spent in time-out relatively brief.
5. Be sure the time spent in time-out is not unduly harsh or disproportionate in relation to the offense.
6. Recognize that prolonged and/or uninterrupted periods in time-out with no educational provisions made are a violation of students' rights.

Ignoring is an effective technique as long as teachers catch students being good. Unfortunately, this technique is not often thought of as a form of time-out.

Planned ignoring is the mildest form of time-out because it applies the behavioral principle of extinction. By ignoring, we seek to withhold positive reinforcement by refraining from any physical, verbal, or visual interaction with students who misbehave. As with any form of ignoring, all other reinforcers must also be removed—including peer attention. Otherwise, planned ignoring will not be effective.

Reduction of response maintenance stimuli is based on the principle of differential reinforcement and the fair pair. Environmental stimuli (e.g., peer attention) that are maintaining inappropriate behavior are extinguished. These stimuli (e.g., peer attention) are reintroduced (i.e., differential reinforcement) when students perform appropriate behaviors (i.e., fair pair). An application of this form of time-out is the time-out ribbon developed by Foxx and Shapiro (1978) for five students with mental retardation. The students wore a ribbon on their wrists when they behaved appropriately. These ribbons were a cue for teachers and other students to deliver high levels of social reinforcement. When one of the students misbehaved, the ribbon was removed and reinforcement was withheld for 3 minutes (extinction). On the next occurrence of appropriate behavior, the ribbon was replaced, and the students again received high levels of social reinforcement from teachers and peers (differential reinforcement).

Reduction of response maintenance stimuli can be used in conjunction with group-oriented contingencies.

Planned ignoring plus restraint involves physically holding students while simultaneously withholding all other reinforcers (extinction). It typically is used with students who are tantruming and is designed to control the behavior without providing additional reinforcement. In the past, many schools did not permit this approach because of potential injuries to both students and teachers. Recently, more schools are not only permitting teachers to restrain students but are providing them with guidance on its proper use (e.g., Mandt, 1990). Unfortunately, there are several problems associated with this approach besides the obvious potential for injuries. First, physical contact may be a powerful reinforcer to some students. Second, a teacher may try to talk a student into calming down—a form of social reinforcement that may maintain the inappropriate behavior. Third, if the teacher is unable to restrain the student, the physical interaction may be highly reinforcing to the student and aversive to the teacher, and present an undesirable model to other students.

Contingent observation involves moving students who misbehave away from the activity in which the misbehavior occurs to a place where they can observe but not participate in the activity. All reinforcement is withheld during this time. The success of this procedure depends upon the teacher's ability to withhold all reinforcement (including that from other students) and to teach the misbehaving student appropriate time-out behavior (e.g., sit quietly or put materials away). The irony is that if teachers can teach and reinforce students for performing appropriate time-out behaviors, they can just as easily teach and reinforce students for performing appropriate behaviors that eliminate the need for time-out.

Exclusion involves physically removing students from the time-in setting. Examples of exclusion time-out include having students sit in the hallway, placing them in a chair behind a portable chalkboard, and requiring them to sit at a study carrel. Although the students are removed, they are not physically restrained from the activities in the time-in setting. There are three problems with this approach. First, it is important that students not receive reinforcement in time-out—a difficult task when they are sitting in a hallway with other students and teachers passing by. Second, it is not always possible, or sometimes takes much effort, to keep students in the time-out area and prevent them from engaging in undesirable behaviors (e.g., scribbling on walls or making animals noises). Third, the length of time students are excluded should be monitored. Some students may ask if their time is up as a way to return to the classroom; others, however, may remain silent and run the risk that teachers may forget they are in time-out—a distinct possibility given how highly negatively reinforcing the use of time-out is for teachers.

Seclusion, the most restrictive time-out procedure, involves placing students in a specially constructed room that often has a locked door. The typical behaviors for which a time-out room is used include aggression—both physical and verbal—and destruction of property. Although seclusion time-out may be effective, it is easily misused. The problems mentioned in conjunction with exclusion apply to seclusion as well. In addition, many states regulate the use of seclusion time-out.

Most teachers think of time-out in terms of exclusion and seclusion—perhaps because time-out is often conceptualized as a "place" rather than a procedure.

Common Misuses of Time-Out   Although various levels of time-out have been demonstrated to be effective in certain circumstances, time-out is also frequently misused because it is negatively reinforcing to teachers. An irony is that, because time-out is designed to reduce behavior, teachers should be using it less rather than more often. If time-out increases, then it is being misused. Nelson and Rutherford (1983) described four common abuses of time-out that are still relevant today.

First, some teachers fail to understand that time-out is most effective if the level of positive reinforcement is very high in the time-in setting. Time-in settings lack positive reinforcement when students are understimulated or unchallenged, do not understand the material, or have mostly negative interactions with the teacher. Behaviors that allow students to escape from a minimally reinforcing environment will be negatively reinforced.

Second, time-out is often teachers' first intervention of choice, instead of techniques based on positive reinforcement and differential reinforcement. Consequently, mildly inappropriate behaviors (e.g., talking out) may be penalized with time-out. If more severe undesirable behavior occurs, teachers often increase the duration of time-out or verbally reprimand students before and after time-out. In other instances, teachers may wait too long and try and send students to time-out when they are already "out of control" (e.g., having a tantrum or being physically aggressive).

Third, teachers may be unable to enforce the time-out contingency because they have not gained stimulus control over students' behavior. Or they may be unable to physically handle larger, more powerful, or more aggressive students. Either situation may lead to a power struggle and to reinforcement for noncompliance. Nelson and Rutherford (1983) suggested that these problems can be avoided by teaching students how to take a time-out appropriately. Specifically, they provided the following four strategies:

1. The teacher schedules training sessions at times other than when time-out intervention is required. This permits the teacher to reinforce approximations to the terminal objective (e.g., putting materials away, moving to the time-out area) and increases the probability of student compliance.
2. Specific components of the terminal behavior should be shaped, using a continuous reinforcement schedule.
3. When it is possible to begin using time-out, the teacher can reinforce compliance using such reinforcers as earlier release or verbal or token reinforcement after release; however, the teacher must be careful that time-out does not become a discriminative stimulus for a richer schedule of reinforcement.
4. Noncompliance can be punished through response cost (e.g., a token fine). (p. 64)

Fourth, the effectiveness of time-out often is not evaluated. Levels of time-out, except for seclusion and exclusion, are difficult to monitor because they are applied while teachers are performing other activities such as delivering instruction. It is extremely important, if only in the interest of professional self-protection, to monitor the use of time-out. Nelson and Rutherford (1983) suggested that daily records of time-out should include the following information:

1. The student's name.
2. A description of the episode leading to time-out.
3. The time of day the student was placed in time-out and the time released.
4. The total duration of each time-out.
5. The type of time-out employed.
6. A description of the student's behavior in time-out. (p. 64)

Recommendations for Using Time-Out   As with most interventions described in this book, it is important for us to conduct functional assessment on a continuous basis to determine factors maintaining inappropriate behaviors and preventing appropriate behaviors from being performed. Most importantly, time-out should only be used in conjunction with positive reinforcement techniques. We should remember that mild forms of time-out are effective only if the time-in environment is highly reinforcing. Nelson and Rutherford (1983) provided the following recommendations for using time-out:

1. Use planned ignoring during one-to-one instruction. This is the only instructional setting where the teacher can be reasonably sure she or he controls reinforcement contingencies well enough to ensure that withdrawing her/his attention will constitute a behavior reduction procedure. Planned ignoring is likely to be more effective with younger or lower functioning pupils (i.e., those for whom teacher attention is a more powerful reinforcer).
2. Planned ignoring plus physical restraint should be avoided as a general intervention. It may be appropriate for specific pupils, but if employed its effects on target behaviors should be carefully monitored.
3. Contingent observation, a widely-applicable type of time-out, may be used in a variety of settings. However, students require specific instruction in how to take time-out in the instructional setting. There also should be back-up intervention for pupils who fail to take contingent observation time-out properly.
4. Adaptive behaviors should be differentially reinforced. If time-out appears not to be working, the teacher may attempt to enrich the time-in environment for the student by providing a richer schedule of reinforcement and using more powerful or more varied reinforcers.
5. Exclusionary levels of time-out (i.e., exclusion and seclusion) should be used only after careful planning and consideration. Students should not routinely be sent out into the hall or to the principal's office. These levels of time-out require additional policy safeguards. (p. 65)

Overcorrection

Overcorrection typically is considered a form of punishment because the end result is the reduction of students' inappropriate behaviors. However, it is much more than a simple punishment technique because it focuses on training students in the use of appropriate behaviors. The goal of an overcorrection procedure is to teach students to take responsibility for their actions. Through repetition and exaggeration, students engage in an appropriate behavior. In this way, they experience the inconvenience suffered by other people who must otherwise correct the problems caused by their own inappropriate behavior. Most authors have described overcorrection as consisting of two main approaches: (1) restitutional overcorrection and/or (2) positive practice overcorrection (Foxx & Azrin, 1972; Foxx & Bechtel, 1983). Alberto and Troutman (1999) summarized the necessary characteristics of any overcorrection procedure:

1. The consequences (behavior) required of the student should be directly related to the misbehavior. This should reduce the likelihood of use in a punitive or arbitrary fashion and should prevent the inappropriate response from occurring.
2. The student should directly experience the effort normally required of others to correct the results of the misbehavior.
3. Overcorrection should be instituted immediately following the misbehavior.
4. The student performing the overcorrection should act rapidly so that consequences constitute an inhibitory effort requirement.
5. The student is instructed and manually guided through the required acts, with the amount of guidance adjusted on a moment-to-moment basis according to the degree to which he/she is voluntarily performing the act. (pp. 331–332)

Because of its emphasis on teaching appropriate behaviors, overcorrection is often viewed not in terms of a single intervention but as a program or package.

Restitutional Overcorrection

Restitutional overcorrection is a technique in which students are required to correct the effects of inappropriate behavior by restoring the environment to a state superior to that which existed before the misbehavior occurred. For example, a student who throws food in the cafeteria might be required to pick up not only the food she threw but also any other food or garbage in the cafeteria. When using this form of overcorrection, it is important not to reinforce students in any way for engaging in the restituting behavior, because that may have the effect of increasing, rather than decreasing, the initial inappropriate behavior that prompted intervention (Martin & Pear, 1996). Smith and Rivera (1993) described several guidelines for effectively implementing restitutional overcorrection:

Restitution overcorrection is commonly used by teachers and parents to deal with children's misbehaviors.

1. The student who is receiving a restitution intervention should be the one who performed the disruptive behavior as observed by the teacher.
2. The restitution consequence should match the infraction.
3. The student should be expected to perform the restitution even if teacher prompts are necessary.
4. Restitution should not be an activity that the student enjoys. If the student is enjoying the restitution activity, then another intervention is necessary. (p. 132)

Positive Practice Overcorrection

Positive practice overcorrection requires that students repeatedly practice an appropriate behavior that is topographically related to the misbehavior. This exaggerated and prolonged practice performing an incompatible behavior presumably represents an educative component. For example, Maag, Parks, and Rutherford (1984) described a study in which a child with mental retardation who habitually pulled out her hair (trichotillomania) was required to repeatedly brush her hair.

It is often easy to confuse restitutional and positive practice overcorrection. In restitutional overcorrection, students are restoring the environment to a state superior to that which existed before the misbehavior; with positive practice, students repeatedly engage in a topographically similar appropriate behavior. For example, when a student throws paper on the floor, a restitutional overcorrection procedure might be to require him to pick up all the paper. A positive practice procedure might be to require him to take the piece of paper he threw on the floor and repeatedly place it in the trash can.

Cooper, Heron, and Heward (1987) described a variation of positive practice called **habit reversal,** which involves having students practice behavior that is incompatible with the inappropriate behavior. Habit reversal is similar to the concept of the fair pair described in Chapter 5 except that students repeatedly perform the appropriate behavior. For example, habit reversal takes place if we require a student who yelled to repeatedly whisper.

Considerations When Using Overcorrection   The major consideration when using overcorrection is how to get students to engage in restitution or positive practice. We do not want to reinforce students for complying—a practice that may increase rather than decrease the inappropriate behavior. Yet we are asking students to engage voluntarily in behaviors that are unpleasant. Azrin and Foxx (1971) suggested that a minimum amount of physical guidance be used to get students to overcorrect. Ideally, students overcorrect after receiving verbal instructions to do so. If verbal instructions are insufficient, then gestural or environmental prompts can be tried; physical prompts are a last resort. However, there are two problems associated with physical prompts: (1) Students may find physical contact reinforcing, and (2) it may be impossible to physically force students to overcorrect. For example, it is unlikely that a 120-pound female teacher can physically guide a 180-pound adolescent male who refuses to overcorrect.

Procedures Resembling Overcorrection

Several procedures are often confused with overcorrection, including simple correction, contingent exercise, quiet training, negative practice, and stimulus satiation (Alberto & Troutman, 1999; Cooper, Heron, & Heward, 1987). The confusion can occur because, as with overcorrection, these procedures result in a decrease in behavior. Consequently, they all are classified as forms of punishment.

Procedures resembling overcorrection have the same problem of how to get noncompliant students to engage in the punitive, or corrective, activities.

Simple Correction   With **simple correction,** students are required to restore the environment to its original state prior to the misbehavior. For example, a simple correction procedure for a student who throws paper on the floor is to have her pick it up and place it in the trash can. Simple correction generally is used with students who neither deliberately nor frequently engage in inappropriate behavior or behavior that does not interfere with other students' well-being (Azrin & Besalel, 1980). Cooper, Heron, and Heward (1987) described two situations in which simple correction should be avoided. First, it should not be used if the inappropriate behavior produces an irreversible effect. For example, it is impossible for a student who rips up a peer's assignment to replace it. Second, simple correction should not be used if the behavior involved in correcting the situation is impossible for students to perform. For example, a student probably does not have the financial resources to replace a window that he broke.

Contingent Exercise   With **contingent exercise,** students perform behavior that is not topographically related to the misbehavior. For example, a student who swears at a teacher may be required to do 20 push-ups, and a student who hits peers may be required to run laps. In both examples, contingent exercise may indeed suppress the inappropriate behaviors, yet it is not a form of overcorrection because the exercises do not provide students with positive practice in an appropriate behavior related to the misbehavior. As with overcorrection procedures, the problem of getting students to comply with the exercise is always present. In addition, some school districts prohibit the use of contingent exercise.

Quiet Training   **Quiet training** is most often used in response to verbally or physically aggressive behaviors or in situations in which students are extremely agitated. When these forms of inappropriate behavior occur, the offending students are required to lie face down (or face up) until all forms of disruptive behavior have subsided for a specified time. Quiet training seems to be based on the behavioral principle of extinction because reinforcers maintaining the inappropriate behavior are eliminated by restricting offending students' access to them—either physically or visually. For example, visual screening is a technique in which a towel or an adult's hand is placed over the eyes of a misbehaving student (McGonigle, Duncan, Cordisco, & Barrett, 1982). The intent is to extinguish any visual reinforcers maintaining the inappropriate behavior. The problems with quiet training procedures are the same as those with overcorrection and contingent exercise: (1) It may be impossible to "force" students to be quiet, (2) students may find it reinforcing to receive physical contact from an adult performing the restraint, and (3) some schools do not allow teachers to become physically involved with students.

Negative Practice   With **negative practice,** students repeatedly engage in the problem behavior. This technique is based on the assumption that students will become fatigued or satiated by repeatedly performing the inappropriate behavior. For example, a student who spits on a peer may be instructed to spend 10 minutes after school spitting into an empty coffee can. This approach has been used for decades under several guises. In the early 1930s, Dunlap (1930) argued that it is possible to break habits by repeatedly performing the inappropriate, or unwanted, behavior. Several decades later, Frankl (1959) promoted **paradoxical intention**—a technique that originally required people who were phobic to "intend to" that which they feared; that is, they were required to purposely engage in the behavior causing them distress. More recently, Hally (1984) described **ordeal therapy,** in which the therapist's task is to impose an ordeal more severe than the problem behavior targeted for change.

Negative practice shares many of the same problems described previously. But there are additional problems specific to negative practice. First, although it can reduce inappropriate behavior, it is not as effective as procedures that include an educative component such as habit reversal (e.g., Azrin, Nunn, & Frantz, 1980). Second, some professionals object to the use of negative practice on the grounds that students should be taught appropriate behaviors and that negative practice only serves to focus undo attention on the misbehavior.

Stimulus Satiation   **Stimulus satiation** is sometimes confused with negative practice. Whereas negative practice involves repeatedly performing the inappropriate behavior, stimulus satiation focuses on repeatedly exposing students to the antecedents of their misbehavior. For example, a student who continuously doodles on worksheets might be given an increasing number of worksheets every week. The worksheets represent the antecedent stimulus to doodling. The student is likely to experience satiation on the stimulus of receiving an increasing number of worksheets.

Over four decades ago, Ayllon (1963) used stimulus satiation to treat a hospitalized female psychiatric patient who hoarded and stored large numbers of towels in her room. The treatment consisted of having the nurses go into the patient's room and, without comment, hand her an ever-increasing number of towels. The first week nurses handed her an average of 7 towels; the number was increased to 60 towels by the third week. After accumulating over 600 towels, the patient began taking a few out of her room. At that point, no more towels were handed to her. Over the course of a year, the average number of towels in her room decreased to 1 to 5 per week, as compared with 13 to 29 before intervention was implemented. This study illustrates how the context surrounding the antecedents can be changed.

SUMMARY

The effect of punishment is to reduce or eliminate students' maladaptive behaviors. Punishment techniques should be used only as a last resort when positive reinforcement and differential reinforcement have failed. Even then, positive reinforcement should always be used in conjunction with punishment to increase appropriate behaviors. There are numerous negative side effects of punishment, many of which occur because teachers fail to consider the functions the inappropriate behavior serves. Consequently, punished behavior may result in students' engaging in a different maladaptive behavior that accomplishes the same purpose. In addition to these negative side effects, punishment also has many limitations. For example, it is unethical to administer punishment at maximum intensities for a first offense.

A response cost, when paired with positive reinforcement, is the mildest, and arguably the most effective, form of punishment—especially the bonus response cost. Time-out is a form of extinction although it can function as positive and negative reinforcement as well. Overcorrection techniques include restitutional and positive practice. The main problem with time-out, overcorrection, and techniques similar to overcorrection is that it may be impossible to force students to comply.

ACTIVITIES

1. Go to a public place such as a restaurant or playground and identify the types of consequences parents or caregivers administer to children who misbehave. Did those consequences result in a decrease in the behavior?
2. Think about your interactions with significant others in your life (e.g., roommate, spouse, boyfriend/girlfriend, siblings), and identify a situation in which that person behaved in a way you did not like. How did you respond? Did your response have the effect of decreasing, maintaining, or increasing that person's behavior? Provide reasons for the effect you observed.

REVIEW QUESTIONS

1. Why might the side effects of punishment not generalize to students with mild disabilities?
2. What are the undesirable side effects of punishment?

3. What are the limitations of punishment?
4. Provide several examples of how recommendations for improving the effectiveness of punishment also reflect severe limitations.
5. What is a response cost, and why is it a desirable punishment procedure?
6. What are the advantages of using a bonus response cost?
7. What are the steps for implementing a response cost?
8. What are the four behavioral principles under which time-out may operate?
9. Describe the various levels of time-out, and provide an example for each.
10. What are the common abuses of time-out?
11. What are some recommendations for using time-out effectively?
12. Describe restitutional and positive practice overcorrection, and provide an example for each type.
13. Describe the five procedures resembling overcorrection.

REFERENCES

Abramson, L. Y., Seligman, M. E. P., & Teasdale, J. D. (1978). Learned helplessness in humans: Critique and reformulation. *Journal of Abnormal Psychology, 87,* 49–74.

Alberto, P. A., & Troutman, A. C. (1999). *Applied behavior analysis for teachers* (5th ed.). Columbus, OH: Merrill.

Ayllon, T. (1963). Intensive treatment of psychotic behavior by stimulus satiation and food reinforcement. *Behavior Research and Therapy, 1,* 53–61.

Azrin, N. H., & Besalel, V. A. (1980). *How to use overcorrection.* Austin, TX: Pro-Ed.

Azrin, N. H., & Foxx, R. M. (1971). A rapid method of toilet training the institutionalized retarded. *Journal of Applied Behavior Analysis, 4,* 89–99.

Azrin, N. H., Nunn, R. G., & Frantz, S. E. (1980). Habit reversal vs. negative practice treatment of nervous tics. *Behavior Therapy, 11,* 169–178.

Bandura, A., Ross, D., & Ross, S. A. (1961). Transmission of aggression through imitation of aggressive models. *Journal of Abnormal and Social Psychology, 63,* 575–582.

Bandura, A., Ross, D., & Ross, S. A. (1963). Imitation of film-mediated aggressive models. *Journal of Abnormal and Social Psychology, 66,* 3–11.

Bandura, A., & Walters, R. H. (1959). *Adolescent aggression.* New York: Ronald Press.

Butterfield, E. C. (1990). The compassion of distinguishing punishing behavioral treatment from aversive treatment. *American Journal on Mental Retardation, 95,* 137–141.

Cooper, J. O., Heron, T. E., & Heward, W. L. (1987). *Applied behavior analysis.* Columbus, OH: Merrill.

Dunlap, K. (1930). Repetition in breaking of habits. *The Scientific Monthly, 30,* 66–70.

Foxx, R. M., & Azrin, N. H. (1972). Restitution: A method of eliminating aggressive-disruptive behavior of retarded and brain damaged patients. *Behavior Research and Therapy, 10,* 15–27.

Foxx, R. M., & Bechtel, D. R. (1983). Overcorrection: A review and analysis. In S. Axelrod & J. Apsche (Eds.), *The effects of punishment on human behavior* (pp. 133–220). New York: Academic Press.

Foxx, R. M., & Shapiro, S. T. (1978). The timeout ribbon: A non-exclusionary timeout procedure. *Journal of Applied Behavior Analysis, 11,* 125–136.

Frankl, V. W. (1959). *Man's search for meaning.* New York: Simon & Schuster.

Haley, J. (1984). *Ordeal therapy.* San Francisco: Jossey-Bass.

Horner, R. H., Dunlap, G., Koegel, R. L., Carr, E. G., Sailor, W., Anderson, J., Albin, R. W., & O'Neill, R. E. (1990). Toward a technology of "nonaversive" behavioral support. *Journal of the Association for Persons with Severe Handicaps, 15,* 125–132.

Lane, H. (1976). *The wild boy of Aveyron.* Cambridge, MA: Harvard University Press.

Maag, J. W., Parks, B. T., & Rutherford, R. B., Jr. (1984). Assessment and treatment of self-stimulation in severely behaviorally disordered children. In R. B. Rutherford, Jr., & C. M. Nelson (Eds.), *Severe behavior disorders of children and youth* (Vol. 7, pp. 27–39). Reston, VA: Council for Children with Behavioral Disorders.

Maag, J. W., Rutherford, R. B., Jr., Wolchik, S. A., & Parks, B. T. (1986). Comparison of two short overcorrection procedures on the stereotypic behavior of autistic children. *Journal of Autism and Developmental Disorders, 16,* 83–87.

Mandt, D. (1990). *The Mandt system: Managing non-aggressive and aggressive people.* Richardson, TX: Author.

Martin, G., & Pear, J. (1996). *Behavior modification: What it is and how to do it* (5th ed.). Englewood Cliffs, NJ: Prentice-Hall.

Maurer, A. (1974). Corporal punishment. *American Psychologist, 29,* 614–626.

McGonigle, J. J., Duncan, D., Cordisco, L., & Barrett, R. T. (1982). Visual screening: An alternative method for reducing stereotypic behaviors. *Journal of Applied Behavior Analysis, 15,* 461–467.

Nelson, C. M., & Rutherford, R. B., Jr. (1983). Timeout revisited: Guidelines for its use in special education. *Exceptional Education Quarterly, 3*(4), 56–67.

Newsom, C., Flavell, J. E., & Rincover, A. (1983). The side effects of punishment. In S. Axelrod & J. Apsche (Eds.), *The effects of punishment on human behavior* (pp. 285–316). New York: Academic Press.

Rhode, G., Jenson, W. R., & Reavis, H. K. (1995). *The tough kid book: Practical classroom management strategies.* Longmont, CO: Sopris West.

Rutherford, R. B., Jr., & Neel, R. S. (1978). The role of punishment with behaviorally disordered children. In R. B. Rutherford, Jr., & A. G. Prieto (Eds.), *Severe behavior disorders of children and youth* (Vol. 1, pp. 69–76). Reston, VA: Council for Children with Behavioral Disorders.

Sajwaj, T. (1968). *Some parameters of point loss.* Unpublished doctoral dissertation, University of Kansas, Lawrence.

Schmidt, J. J. (1982). Understanding punishment and encouraging positive discipline. *Journal of Humanistic Education and Development, 21,* 43–48.

Seligman, M. E. P., & Peterson, C. (1986). A learned helplessness perspective on childhood depression: Theory and research. In M. Rutter, C. E. Izard, & P. B. Read (Eds.), *Depression in young people: Developmental and clinical perspectives* (pp. 223–249). New York: Guilford.

Skiba, R. J., & Deno, S. L. (1991). Terminology and behavior reduction: The case against "punishment." *Exceptional Children, 57,* 298–313.

Smith, D. D., & Rivera, D. M. (1993). *Effective discipline* (2nd ed.). Austin, TX: Pro-Ed.

Walker, H. M. (1983). Application of response cost in school settings: Outcomes, issues and recommendations. *Exceptional Education Quarterly, 3*(4), 46–55.

Walker, J. E., & Shea, T. M. (1995). *Behavior management: A practical approach for educators* (6th ed.). Columbus, OH: Merrill.

Wood, F. H., & Braaten, S. (1983). Developing guidelines for the use of punishing interventions in the schools. *Exceptional Education Quarterly, 3*(4), 68–75.

Yell, M. L. (1990). The use of corporal punishment, suspension, expulsion, and timeout with behaviorally disordered students in public schools: Legal considerations. *Behavioral Disorders, 15,* 100–109.

CHAPTER

12

TEACHING SELF-MANAGEMENT

CHAPTER OVERVIEW

- Theoretical Underpinnings of Self-Management
- Self-Monitoring
- Self-Evaluation
- Self-Reinforcement

CHAPTER OBJECTIVES

After completing this chapter, you will be able to do the following:

1. Explain the difference between self-control and self-management.

2. Describe the operant and cognitive models of self-management.

3. Describe how self-monitoring of attention and performance can be implemented.

4. Explain areas of concern when implementing self-monitoring interventions.

5. Identify techniques for promoting self-evaluation.

6. Identify techniques for promoting self-reinforcement.

Many teacher-applied techniques for managing students' behaviors require considerable time and effort to develop, implement, and monitor. For example, although techniques such as token economies and behavioral contracts can be highly effective, they may produce changes in students' behaviors only while they are in effect or only in the setting in which they are implemented. One of the reasons is that certain elements in the training environment, such as teachers themselves, becomes antecedents cuing students that reinforcement will occur after they perform a target behavior. Cues for engaging in appropriate behavior and receiving reinforcement may not exist across all school settings and with all teachers. However, students who are taught self-management carry with them cues for engaging in appropriate behaviors and techniques for reinforcing themselves when they perform the behaviors (Baer & Fowler, 1984).

There are several reasons to teach self-management. First, it provides a means for us to spend more time teaching and less time trying to control students' undesirable behaviors. Second, it increases the likelihood that appropriate behaviors will endure and be performed in various settings. Third, it provides students with a sense of ownership for their behavior because they are active participants in developing, implementing, and monitoring interventions. Fourth, self-management is congruent with a key goal of education—to develop self-sufficient adults who contribute to society and behave in a way that respects the rights of others without requiring the supervision of others.

This chapter provides a theoretical overview of self-management and describes techniques for teaching students how to monitor, evaluate, and reinforce their own behavior. These techniques help students become aware of their behavior, set goals, evaluate their performance, and reinforce their successes.

THEORETICAL UNDERPINNINGS OF SELF-MANAGEMENT

It is not easy to pinpoint the exact mechanisms that lead to our developing self-management skills. Many of the principles of social learning theory discussed in Chapter 3 probably are at work, as are developmental considerations. An argument could be made that it is irrelevant what processes are at work as long as techniques for teaching students self-management are effective. However, understanding the theoretical underpinnings of self-management may help us select appropriate techniques for promoting it. Therefore, this section begins with a discussion of the usefulness of the terms *self-control* and *self-management,* and then examines two major theories accounting for self-management: the operant conditioning and cognitive models.

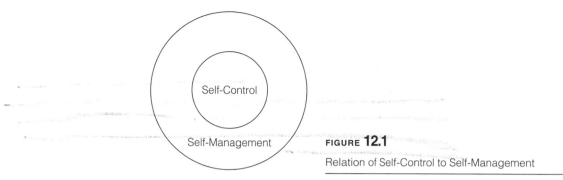

FIGURE **12.1**

Relation of Self-Control to Self-Management

It is easy to blur the distinction between the terms *self-control* and *self-management.* Rather than trying to "split hairs," the key is to focus on the intervention—external, internal, or both.

Self-Control or Self-Management?

It may seem irrelevant, or at best trivial, to discuss whether to use the term *self-control* or *self-management*. However, it should become clear that *self-management* is the more desirable term in terms of intervention.

Self-control involves two responses: (1) the target behavior to be controlled or changed (e.g., eating, completing math problems, or tantruming) and (2) the behavior displayed to control or change the target behavior (e.g., recording everything eaten, or the number of math problems completed correctly, or the number of temper tantrums per day) (Skinner, 1953). The main problem with this conceptualization is that it is very difficult to determine what behavior controls the behavior to be controlled. For example, if the goal in writing Post-It notes is to control (i.e., increase) the behavior of studying for a test, then what will control (i.e., cue) the behavior of writing the Post-It notes? If we answer that students will control their own controlling behavior, then there appears to be no reason to write the Post-It notes—the students will simply remember to study. However, it is of little help to tell students that they can control their own behavior simply by willing it (Skinner, 1953).

The advantage of using the term *self-management* is that it helps us avoid circular reasoning and enables us to embrace techniques considered to be both internal (i.e., self-control) and external (i.e., environmental). Consequently, **self-management** generally refers to the range of activities, both overt and covert, in which students may engage that increase or decrease the probability of appropriate behaviors occurring (Mace, Brown, & West, 1987). Internal activities may involve cognitive prompts such as repeating instructions to oneself. External strategies may involve manipulating the environment to establish stimulus control. Therefore, self-control is part of self-management, as Figure 12.1 shows.

The Operant Conditioning Model of Self-Management

The operant conditioning model of self-management is based on B. F. Skinner's (1953) work on the functional relation between behavior and consequences, as described in Chapter 3. From the operant conditioning perspective, the key issue in teaching students self-management is to take delayed consequences and turn them into more immediate consequences. Many of the problems students experience occur because their behaviors are controlled by short-term rather than long-term consequences. For example, hitting a peer may result in the negative long-term consequence of being suspended or expelled from school. However, the short-term consequence of getting the peer to stop teasing is more reinforcing than the long-term consequence is punishing. Similarly, for some students, end-of-semester grades have little effect over their study behavior because the consequences (i.e., grades) are too far removed from the present. Playing instead of studying is more immediate and reinforcing, and so controls the behavior. Short-term consequences are typically more reinforcing than long-term consequences.

Although the operant conditioning model of self-management focuses on the impact of short-term versus long-term consequences, antecedents also play a role. When students are taught to arrange antecedents to prompt certain behaviors, they are engaging in self-management. Cooper, Heron, and Heward (1987) described several antecedent manipulation techniques for self-management. First, students can provide extra cues in the environment. For example, the student who writes a Post-It note reminding himself to study for a test is using this technique. Second, the environment can be altered to make the undesirable behavior less likely to occur. For example, a student may purposely sit away from her friends in order to talk out less in class. Third, the antecedent cues for engaging in an inappropriate behavior can be restricted. For example, a student who wants to decrease the number of times he criticizes peers may criticize only at a certain time or in a certain location.

The Cognitive Model of Self-Management

As discussed in Chapter 7, cognition refers to an interactive process in which individuals generate, code, transform, or manipulate information from the environment.

From a cognitive perspective, self-management occurs when students attach self-statements to a situation to give that situation meaning. There are three steps in self-management: (1) self-monitoring, (2) self-evaluation, and (3) self-reinforcement.

Self-monitoring involves having students become aware of their behavior (self-observation) and then make a tangible mark to keep track of it (self-recording). For example, a student may keep track of the number of multiplication problems she gets correct. Self-monitoring may lead to **self-evaluation**—comparing the performance to some standard—when students are able to accurately judge their behavior. For students who do not possess this skill, having them place self-monitored data on a graph and set a performance goal helps promote self-evaluation. **Self-reinforcement** may occur when students meet or exceed their performance standard. Each of these three mechanisms are operationalized into specific interventions described for teaching students self-management.

SELF-MONITORING

Self-monitoring has been used with students with and without disabilities ranging in age from 4 years old to adolescence, in a variety of settings including psychiatric hospitals, residential facilities, and special and general education classrooms (Lloyd & Landrum, 1990). In school settings, self-monitoring has been used to improve students' academic achievement in reading, spelling, and mathematics and to decrease inappropriate social behaviors such as aggression and noncompliance (Reid, 1996; Snider, 1987; Webber, Scheuermann, McCall, & Coleman, 1993). In a review of research on self-monitoring, Reid (1996) concluded that it is an intervention repeatedly proved to be effective by any objective standard and easily incorporated into existing classroom structures and activities.

Self-monitoring originated as an assessment technique used primarily by psychotherapists (Mace & Kratochwill, 1988). Many problems for which individuals might see a therapist, such as treating depression, gaining anger control skills, becoming more assertive, or desiring to lose weight or stop smoking, are amenable to self-monitoring. Typically, the therapist has clients keep a diary describing the situation in which they felt depressed or got angry, or recording the number of cigarettes smoked or the amount of food ingested. The purpose is to help the therapist obtain assessment information about how frequently the target behavior occurs and how different situations may affect its occurrence. Amazingly, on their next visit to the therapist, many clients report that the symptoms or behaviors have improved. This phenomenon, known as **reactivity** or the **reactive effect,** refers to a person's behavior changing when that person observes and records its occurrence.

Reactivity seems to operate on the principle of negative reinforcement. When individuals monitor their behavior, they are more likely to be aware of whether it is performed at either an acceptable or an unacceptable level. If they judge that their behavior is at an unacceptable level—something they may not have been aware of previously—they may feel guilty. Guilt feels bad—it's aversive. Therefore, the guilt can only be assuaged through better performance. For example, it is easy for a smoker to rationalize this habit when she is

Make a mark beside each day every time you raise your hand and wait to be called on before asking or answering a question.

Monday	///
Tuesday	////
Wednesday	//// ////
Thursday	//// //
Friday	//// //// //

Name: <u>Brad DeSandro</u>

Week: <u>April 8–April 11</u>

FIGURE 12.2

Sample Frequency Self-Recording Card

From *Teaching behavioral self-control to students* (2nd ed.) (p. 39) by E. A. Workman & A. M. Katz, 1995, Austin, TX: Pro-Ed. Copyright 1995 by Pro-Ed. Adapted with permission.

unaware of how many cigarettes she smokes a day. However, keeping track of the number of cigarettes smoked daily forces her to confront the reality of her habit, thus creating guilt that may be eliminated only by smoking fewer cigarettes. Consequently, this **guilt-control** is nothing more than negative reinforcement in action.

Two types of self-monitoring interventions will be described shortly. However, regardless of the type, all self-monitoring interventions should include the following components:

- *Self-observation.* This occurs when students become aware of their own target behavior. Accurate discriminations are enhanced by operationally defining the target behavior.
- *Self-recording.* This requires students to record the frequency or duration of a target behavior or the situations in which the behavior occurs. Most often, these recordings are based on physically tangible data. Students can use a variety of self-recording cards; Figure 12.2 shows one example.
- *Self-graphing.* This involves having students take the data from their self-recording cards and chart them on graphs. Either a line or bar graph can be used for this purpose although bar graphs provide students with a clear visual representation of their behavior. Figure 12.3 shows an example of a bar graph with the hypothetical data from the self-monitoring recording card appearing in Figure 12.2.

In addition to describing two techniques for self-monitoring, areas of concern are discussed in this section.

The self-recording card shown in Figure 12.2 requires students to simply make tally marks. More or even less sophisticated self-recording cards can be employed depending on the task, the type of self-monitoring technique used, and students' cognitive levels.

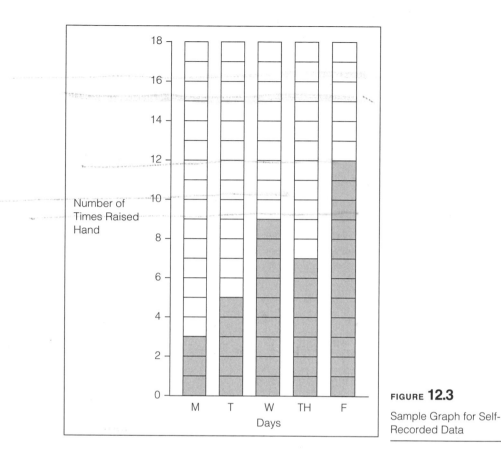

FIGURE 12.3

Sample Graph for Self-Recorded Data

Self-Monitoring Attention

Self-monitoring attention (SMA) involves instructing students to observe their own behavior and determine whether they were paying attention and recording the results when cued through the use of randomly presented tones from a tape recorder. This procedure, developed by Hallahan, Lloyd, and Stoller (1982), has four main parts:

1. Tape recorded tones to cue students to self-monitor
2. A self-questioning strategy for students to use when self-monitoring
3. A recording form for students to mark their answers to the self-monitoring questions
4. A graph for students to chart their progress

Materials needed for implementing self-monitoring attention in the classroom are a self-monitoring tape, a self-monitoring card, and a sheet of paper containing a bar graph. Students should be engaging in academic tasks while self-monitoring.

Self-Monitoring Tape   Tape-recorded tones serve as auditory cues for students to self-observe and self-record their behavior. A variety of techniques can be used to produce the auditory tone, including tapping a wine glass with a spoon, striking a piano key, and pushing a button on a phone. There are also many children's toys that emit tones.

Tones should be recorded at random intervals so that students do not perform the on-task behaviors only just prior to some regular tone being emitted. For a typical independent work period of 15 to 20 minutes, intertone intervals should average 45 seconds and range from 10 to 90 seconds. These figures may be doubled for work periods lasting 30 to 40 minutes. When the average intertone intervals and ranges have been decided, we can generate a list of random intervals as follows:

1. Write the numbers of every possible interval length on slips of paper (10 through 90 for a tape averaging tones every 45 seconds and 20 through 180 for a tape averaging tones every 90 seconds), and place them in a container.
2. Draw a slip of paper out of the container and write its number on a piece of paper.
3. Place the slip of paper back in the container so that each number has an equal chance of being drawn each time.
4. Repeat this process until 20 to 40 numbers have been listed.

The next step is to make the self-monitoring tape. This process requires the list of random numbers, a tape recorder and tape, the mechanism for making the tone, and a clock with a second hand. With these materials in hand, find a quiet room and let the tape run on "record" for the number of seconds indicated by the first number on the list. At the end of this time, make the signal tone, pause the tape, and cross off that number. Then restart the tape recorder and let it run for the number of seconds indicated by the second number on the interval list, repeating the process described previously for this and subsequent numbers until the tape ends.

The steps for making a self-monitoring attention tape are similar to the steps involved in making taped tones for the good behavior game described in Chapter 9.

Self-Monitoring Card   The simple self-monitoring card shown in Figure 12.2 required students to tally the number of time they raised their hand. The self-monitoring card appearing in Figure 12.4 was specifically designed for use in SMA. It has a place for the student's name and date, a description of the behaviors defining "paying attention," and squares where the student can indicate whether he or she was paying attention. Younger students may benefit from pictures of a happy and sad face or a "thumbs up" and "thumbs down" image instead of the words "yes" or "no" in each column.

Name _____   Date _____

WAS I PAYING ATTENTION?

When you hear the beep, ask yourself if you are:

- writing answers to problems
- watching the teacher
- sitting in your seat

If the answer is yes to any of these, place a check in the **"Yes"** column. If the answer is no, place a check in the **"No"** column.

	YES	NO			YES	NO
1				13		
2				14		
3				15		
4				16		
5				17		
6				18		
7				19		
8				20		
9				21		
10				22		
11				23		
12				24		

FIGURE 12.4

Self-Monitoring Card for Paying Attention

Self-Monitoring Graph Researchers have found that self-graphing increases the reactivity of self-monitoring (DiGangi, Maag, & Rutherford, 1991). It allows students to compare their performance from day to day or session to session and is a prerequisite for self-evaluation and self-reinforcement. At the end of the session, students tally the number of marks in the "yes" columns on the self-monitoring card and graph these data, as shown in Figure 12.5.

Self-Monitoring Activities Students can engage in a variety of activities while self-monitoring attention, including arithmetic, reading, spelling, and handwriting, during both group lessons and independent practice activities.

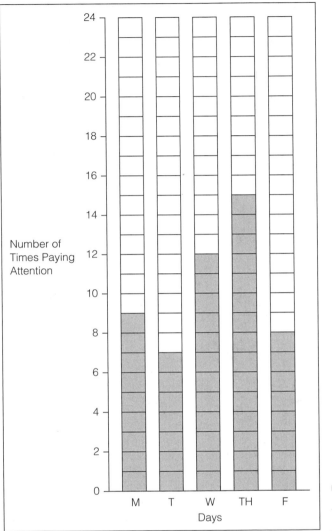

FIGURE **12.5**

Sample Bar Graph for
Self-Monitoring Attention

The types of activities in which students might be engaged while self-monitoring attention are potentially limitless.

Self-Monitoring Procedures   There are several procedures for implementing SMA. Students can be trained in these steps in about 15 to 20 minutes, depending on their age and cognitive ability.

1. Provide students with a rationale for self-monitoring (e.g., it will help them get their work done quicker).
2. Get a commitment from students to try self-monitoring.

3. Present the self-monitoring materials to students (card, recorder, and graph).
4. Define the specific behaviors of paying attention, and model instances and noninstances of them.
5. Explain that the tape to be played has tones on it.
6. Tell students they have to ask themselves if they are paying attention when the tone sounds. If the answer is "yes," they should make a mark in the "yes" column; if the answer is "no," then they should make a mark in the "no" column.
7. Tell students they will be graphing the number of "yes" marks at the end of each session.
8. Have students paraphrase back to you how the procedure works.
9. Demonstrate how the procedure works, instructing students to watch to make sure you self-monitor correctly.
10. While demonstrating the procedure, make some incorrect marks and see if students catch them.
11. Have students practice the procedure while you give them feedback. Continue this process until they can perform self-monitoring attention independently.

Self-Monitoring Performance

The process of self-monitoring academic variables is often referred to as **self-monitoring performance (SMP),** because students monitor some aspect of academic performance and record the results. There is much more variability in the procedures for SMP than for SMA. For example, SMP may involve having students self-monitor productivity (e.g., the number of math problems attempted), accuracy (e.g., the number of math problems completed correctly), or strategy use (e.g., whether the steps in the division algorithm were performed) (Reid, 1996). SMP typically does not involve the use of a cuing device although there are some exceptions (e.g., Maag, Reid, & DiGangi, 1993). In this section, the steps Reid and Harris (1989) developed for teaching students how to self-monitor their academic performance are described.

Define a Target Behavior As with any intervention, it is necessary to operationally define the target behaviors students are to self-monitor. The definition should be specific but simply stated so that students can understand it. "Improved math performance" may be a desirable goal, but it does not pass the stranger test. Therefore, more specifically defined behaviors could include "correctly answering reading comprehension questions," "correctly writing answers to multiplication problems," "correctly spelling words," and "correctly pronouncing vocabulary words." These definitions are specific enough for students to accurately observe and record their behavior on the selected task.

Collect Baseline Data   Reasons for collecting baseline data were presented in Chapters 5 and 6. There are two additional reasons to collect baseline for SMP. First, it provides students with a rationale for participating in the intervention. For example, showing a student that he completed only five multiplication problems correctly and that he may have to miss recess to complete the rest of the assignment can provide motivation for him to try self-monitoring. Second, students can visually track their performance before and during self-monitoring, which may prompt self-evaluation.

Meet with the Student   After collecting baseline data, we want to meet with students to enlist their participation. Therefore, it is helpful to have graphs of their performance during baseline. We begin by explaining the purpose and benefits they will derive from self-monitoring. For example, we might say, "I would like to teach you how you can improve the number of multiplication problems you get correct on your assignments and to get a higher score on your quizzes." It is helpful to use concrete examples and simple explanations with younger students. With older students, a more detailed elaboration may be helpful, as may be responding to questions. However, we should avoid making blanket promises about the benefits students will obtain from self-monitoring.

Teachers should be optimistic but honest when communicating with students regarding the importance of self-monitoring performance.

Provide Instruction in the Procedures   Once students' cooperation has been enlisted, we are ready to instruct them in the procedures involved in SMP. This process takes about 15 to 20 minutes. It is important that students clearly understand the procedures because they will be running the intervention.

First, we provide students with answers to the following questions about SMP:

1. What will be self-monitored (e.g., the number of multiplication problems done correctly)?
2. What criteria are necessary for success (e.g., must show all steps in the multiplication problem and arrive at the correct answer)?
3. How will the results be counted (the number correct can be tallied for each assignment using a recording form similar to the one shown in Figure 12.6)?
4. How will the results be graphed (the number of correct problems must be recorded accurately using a graph like the one shown in Figure 12.7)?
5. When is the self-monitoring performance procedure to be performed (e.g., after a math independent practice session Monday through Friday)?

Second, we model these steps for students while verbalizing what they should be doing at each step. Third, we model the process again but have students verbalize what they should be doing at each step. Fourth, we have students model

Multiplication Completion Form

Student's Name _____ Date _____

Circle the number of multiplication problems you solved correctly on each daily assignment. Use the answer key to score your assignments.

Monday	1	2	3	4	5	6	7	8	9	10
	11	12	13	14	15	16	17	18	19	20
	21	22	23	24	25	26	27	28	29	30
Tuesday	1	2	3	4	5	6	7	8	9	10
	11	12	13	14	15	16	17	18	19	20
	21	22	23	24	25	26	27	28	29	30
Wednesday	1	2	3	4	5	6	7	8	9	10
	11	12	13	14	15	16	17	18	19	20
	21	22	23	24	25	26	27	28	29	30
Thursday	1	2	3	4	5	6	7	8	9	10
	11	12	13	14	15	16	17	18	19	20
	21	22	23	24	25	26	27	28	29	30
Friday	1	2	3	4	5	6	7	8	9	10
	11	12	13	14	15	16	17	18	19	20
	21	22	23	24	25	26	27	28	29	30

FIGURE 12.6

Self-Recording Sheet for Multiplication

From *Teaching behavioral self-control to students* (2nd ed.) (p. 65) by E. A. Workman & A. M. Katz, 1995, Austin, TX: Pro-Ed. Copyright 1995 by Pro-Ed. Adapted with permission.

and verbalize the steps independently. We can always provide feedback any time they are either modeling or verbalizing incorrectly. Students should self-monitor several instances of the target behavior while we observe that they can perform the steps properly. If we detect any confusion or problems, we can schedule a short booster session to review or reteach parts of the process. Some students may benefit from having a card listing the steps as a visual cue. Table 12.1 summarizes the steps for teaching self-monitoring.

For maximum benefit, students should self-monitor performance on a regular basis.

Specific Areas of Concern in Self-Monitoring

Reid (1993) noted several areas of specific concern, in the form of questions, that we may encounter when implementing self-monitoring interventions. Although the following concerns are not exhaustive, they are questions that

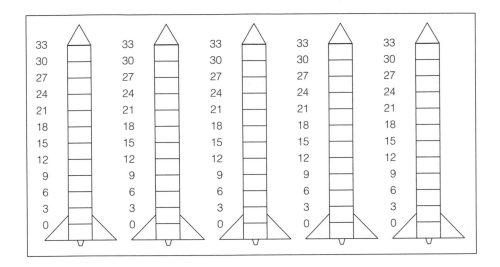

FIGURE **12.7**

Multiplication Missiles Graph

From "Self-monitoring performance" by R. Reid & K. R. Harris, 1989, *LD Forum, 15*(1), p. 40. Copyright 1989 by the Council for Learning Disabilities.

TABLE **12.1** **STEPS FOR TEACHING SELF-MONITORING**

Step	Description
Explain the procedures.	Provide students with written or pictorial instructions describing the self-monitoring procedure. Specify performance criteria for self-monitoring accuracy where applicable. Use an upwardly changing criterion for students who are slow to acquire the self-monitoring skills.
Model performance while verbalizing the steps.	Demonstrate the self-monitoring procedure using actual recording forms and devices. Label each step as it is completed. Ask students if they have any questions about what is to be done.
Have students verbalize the steps as you perform them.	Have students paraphrase the target definitions and self-monitoring instructions while you actually engage in the self-monitoring intervention.
Have students verbalize and perform the steps.	Have students identify the target behavior and provide examples and nonexamples. They should paraphrase the instructions while engaging in the self-monitoring intervention. Students should attain a high degree of mastery at this stage. After they are able to model and verbalize the procedures correctly, provide a brief period of guided practice. Test students' acquisition of self-monitoring skills by conducting several assessment trials in an analogue (role-play) situation.

commonly crop up in classroom practice. Knowing the answers to these questions will help us implement more effective self-monitoring interventions.

How Accurate Should Self-Monitoring Be? It is not necessary for students to be highly accurate using self-monitoring procedures in order for reactivity to occur. For example, a student may average 10 multiplication problems correct per assignment during the baseline. The student begins self-monitoring, but inaccurately, as follows:

- On Monday, he records 16 problems correct when he actually got 14 correct.
- On Tuesday, he records 17 problems correct when he actually got 18 correct.
- On Wednesday, he records 20 problems correct when he actually got 18 correct.
- On Thursday, he records 13 problems correct when he actually got 16 correct.
- On Friday, he records 15 problems correct when he actually got 17 correct.

The average number of problems he actually got correct for the week is a little over 16. Therefore, although he was self-monitoring inaccurately, his performance improved on average from 10 to 16 problems completed correctly.

Sometimes improving the accuracy of self-monitoring can improve reactivity. In general, however, meaningful improvements in the target behavior have been noted when self-monitoring accuracy was quite low (Lloyd & Landrum, 1990). Remember that the goal of self-monitoring is to improve behavior, and not to provide accurate self-recording. If reactivity is occurring, it is wise to simply ignore any inaccuracies.

What Should I Do If Reactivity Does Not Occur? If reactivity is not occurring, we should take action. A good first step is to determine if students can accurately assess whether the target behavior is adequate. Accurate discriminations are enhanced when the target behavior is precisely defined and when it does not occur so automatically that students are unaware of performing the behavior. For example, if a student has impulsively shouted out answers for years, it will be better to target the behavior "raising hand." This behavior will be easier for her to discern because it entails an obvious physical motion. Cuing devices also help students become aware that they are performing the target behavior.

If discrimination is adequate, the next step is to determine whether students are using the self-monitoring procedures consistently and properly. Some students have difficulty accurately counting up work or properly graphing their data. In these situations, aids such as paper with numbered lines and simplified graphs can be helpful. Another technique is to reinforce students for properly and consistently using self-monitoring procedures. For example, in using SMA, we can tell the student that when the tape-recorded tone sounds we will observe him and make a mark on a self-recording form identical to the one he is using to record his own behavior. We can then tell him that every mark for which we both agree will earn him 1 minute of free time. This approach may help increase his motivation to self-monitor accurately in situations in which reactivity is not occurring.

What Is the Best Target Variable to Self-Monitor?   There is no "best" target behavior for students to self-monitor. There is little difference between self-monitoring attention to and academic variables in students' on-task behaviors. However, in terms of the effects on academic performance, self-monitoring productivity or accuracy is superior (Maag, Reid, & DiGangi, 1993). A good approach is to expose students to different types of self-monitoring, collect data to see which is more effective with the target behavior, and ask them which one they want to continue using.

Should Students Self-Monitor the Positive or Negative Aspects of a Behavior?   There is some evidence to suggest that self-monitoring the positive aspects of a behavior increases these responses, and that self-monitoring the negative aspects of a behavior decreases the frequency of that behavior (Cormier & Cormier, 1998). However, self-monitoring negative responses may have a counterproductive effect. For example, it is unwise to have a student who is aggressive self-monitor the number of times she hits peers. But there may be times when having students self-monitor the negative aspects of a behavior can increase their awareness of that behavior, thereby bringing it from an unconscious to a conscious level (Maag, 1993). In the long run, because reactivity is affected by the value assigned to a behavior, it may be beneficial to have students monitor the behaviors that they care most about changing.

It may be wise to self-monitor the positive aspect of behavior. If students want to self-monitor the negative aspect of a behavior, we should quickly encourage them to move to self-monitoring the positive aspect. This approach is more consistent with the goals of behavior management—to increase appropriate behavior.

How Long Should the Self-Monitoring Intervention Last?   There does not appear to be an upper limit to the amount of time self-monitoring interventions can be used effectively. After all, how many of us actually stop self-monitoring our behavior? It is a life-long process. However, because the goal of self-monitoring interventions is self-management, we may wish to ultimately have students function at desirable levels without the use of overt self-monitoring procedures. We may ask students to self-observe without self-recording the results. Taped cues can be eliminated, and students can be instructed to self-observe when they think of it. Self-reinforcement may also be used during the fading process.

SELF-EVALUATION

With self-evaluation, students compare their performance against some criteria (Mace, Brown, & West, 1987). Self-monitoring is a necessary prerequisite, because students must have some data (from self-monitoring) to evaluate their performance. For example, if a student sees that he completed 10 more math problems correctly after self-monitoring his performance, he is more likely to evaluate his performance positively and to set a higher standard for subsequent assignments. In essence, we want students to examine the degree to which a match exists between their behavior and some self-selected standard. This process often results in students making judgments as to whether their behavior has reached or exceeded a desired level. If the behavior meets the criterion, they may engage in self-reinforcing verbalizations. Also, many students will adjust their self-evaluative standards upward when they view their progress as satisfactory. Conversely, when students fall short of a desired behavior, they either engage in self-statements aimed at increasing their performance or lower their standards.

Several techniques for teaching students to self-evaluate their performance are described next. Regardless of the technique employed, it is important that students develop the evaluative criteria—although they may require our assistance in setting realistic standards. When students develop their own evaluative criteria, they are more likely to take responsibility for their behavior (Glasser, 1992). In addition, it provides information to students on the amount of work necessary to earn reinforcement and prompts awareness of goals. The two major, and related, ways to promote self-evaluation are through the use of rating systems and goal setting.

Self-evaluation techniques can easily be tied to the process of self-monitoring.

Developing a Rating System

One of the simplest ways to promote self-evaluation is to include a rating scale at the bottom of a self-recording card or sheet. Rating scales may have a range from 0 to 2, 0 to 3, 0 to 4, or 0 to 5 depending on the age of the students. For younger students, a scale of 0 to 2 is desirable because it requires them to make less complex discriminations. It is important to clearly define each point on the rating scale. Figure 12.8 includes a rating scale at the bottom of the self-recording sheet that first appeared in Figure 12.4. Sometimes it is helpful to operationally define ratings to a greater degree. For example, a student could be told to give himself a 1 if he had 0 to 4 marks in the "yes" column, a 2 if he had 5 to 8 marks in the "yes" column, a 3 if he had 9 to 15 marks in the "yes" column, or a 4 if he had 16 to 20 marks in the "yes" column.

Name _____   Date _____

WAS I PAYING ATTENTION?

When you hear the beep, ask yourself if you are:

- writing answers to problems
- watching the teacher
- sitting in your seat

If the answer is yes to any of these, place a check in the **"Yes"** column. If the answer is no, place a check in the **"No"** column.

	YES	NO		YES	NO
1			13		
2			14		
3			15		
4			16		
5			17		
6			18		
7			19		
8			20		
9			21		
10			22		
11			23		
12			24		

Rate how well you paid attention today

1	2	3	4
Poor	Fair	Good	Excellent

FIGURE **12.8**

Self-Recording Form with Rating Scale

The advantage of a rating scale at the bottom of a self-recording form is that it gives students immediate feedback about their performance. The disadvantage is that it is more difficult for students to visualize their performance before the self-recording data are placed on a graph. Therefore, an alternative approach is to use a rating scale at the bottom of the weekly graph, such as the

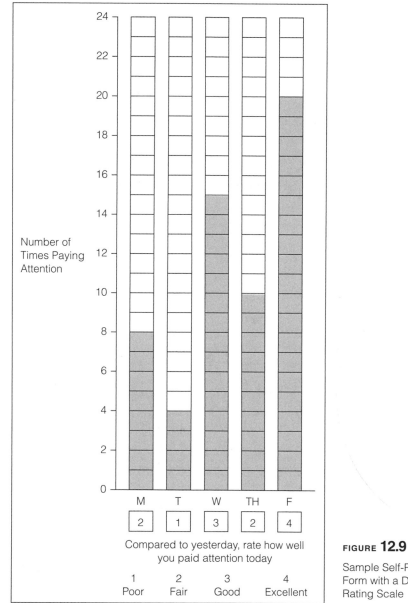

FIGURE **12.9**

Sample Self-Reporting
Form with a Daily
Rating Scale

one shown in Figure 12.9. This technique can be used in isolation or in conjunction with the rating scale appearing at the bottom of the self-monitoring form. With this arrangement, we have students rate their performance after graphing their self-recording data and place their rating in the box underneath the column containing the self-recording data for that day. This approach

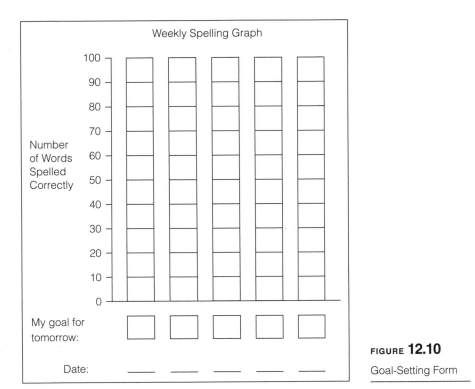

FIGURE **12.10**

Goal-Setting Form

Rating scales can be incorporated into self-monitoring in an endless number of ways. The key to making these rating scales work is for students to be able to visually trace their progress.

represents a way to "layer" self-evaluation procedures into the self-monitoring process. In Figure 12.9, the following self-rating criteria were used: 1 (poor) = 0–4 times paying attention, 2 (fair) = 5–8 times paying attention, 3 (good) = 9–15 times paying attention, and 4 (excellent) = 16–20 times paying attention.

Setting a Daily Goal

Goal setting has been used in industry and business for many years, and has resulted in improvements in such areas as truck loading, safety behavior, keypunching, customer service, and typing (Locke & Latham, 1990). Goal setting also has been used by athletes to improve the number of laps completed in track; foul shots made in basketball; first serves in, tennis; and accuracy in archery (Locke & Latham, 1985). A **goal** describes a level of performance toward which students should work (Martin & Pear, 1996).

An easy and effective way to promote self-evaluation is to have students set daily goals for their performance, which they can self-monitor. Figure 12.10 shows a form that can be used in incorporating goal setting into a program for self-monitoring—in this case, the number of words students spell correctly. In this approach, a list of words is generated that individual students spelled incorrectly during the pretest, which usually is given on a Monday. Students self-record the number of words they spelled correctly during subsequent daily practice sessions and then graph the data. Based on the number of words spelled correctly, students set individual goals for the number of words they want to try to write correctly the following day. In this way, setting goals promotes self-evaluation, higher standards, and self-reinforcement—the topic of the next section.

Martin and Pear (1996) discussed a number of conditions that should be met to ensure that goal setting is effective. Each of these conditions is described below.

Set Specific Goals   As with other aspects of behavior management, specificity is always better than vagueness in setting goals. For example, rather than "doing better in spelling," a student might agree to write the words she misspelled 50 times correctly. This recommendation has commonsense appeal. After all, which of the following goals would help you save money: "Put some money in bank" or "Put 10 percent of my monthly paycheck in bank"?

Set Realistic and Challenging Goals   Realistic and challenging goals are more effective than "do your best" goals, which are usually too vague. Also, Locke and Latham (1990) suggested that students who set "do your best" goals are employing relatively easy standards that do not result in high levels of performance. We don't want goals to be either too easy or too unreachable—in each case, they will have minimal impact on students' behaviors. One way to help students set realistic and challenging goals is to consider their current level of performance and the range of performance on similar tasks by other students of similar ability (Martin & Pear, 1996).

Make Goals Public   Goals that are posted in a public place, such as on a bulletin board, are more likely to be achieved. The rationale is the same as that described in Chapter 9 for making behavioral contracts public. It sets the occasion for students to look at their goals. In other words, the goal serves as an antecedent stimulus to prompt the occurrence of the target behavior. Although public goals are more effective than private goals, we should ensure that peers provide encouragement and gentle reminders to students rather than engaging in put-downs (Martin & Pear, 1996).

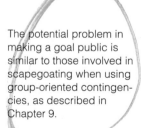

The potential problem in making a goal public is similar to those involved in scapegoating when using group-oriented contingencies, as described in Chapter 9.

Include Deadlines   Most of us have been reinforced in some way when we met a deadline and possibly encountered some type of aversive stimulus when the deadline was not met. Therefore, we should have students recall positive experiences that they have had in meeting a deadline. Deadlines help students avoid procrastinating and increases the likelihood that they will attain the goal.

Provide Feedback   Goal setting is more effective when it includes a daily feedback component than when used in isolation (Martin & Pear, 1996). Using a graph such as the one shown in Figure 12.10 is one way to incorporate feedback into the goal-setting process. A graph provides students with a daily record of their progress. Another way to ensure that students receive feedback is to break long-term goals into short-term ones. Short-term goals are more likely to be reached, which, in turn, encourages students to set higher goals.

SELF-REINFORCEMENT

Self-reinforcement, as the name implies, provides students with ways to reinforce themselves. It can be either external or internal. **External self-reinforcement** occurs when students arrange the environment to receive reinforcement after meeting or exceeding a goal. **Internal self-reinforcement** occurs when students tell themselves something positive about their performance.

Self-monitoring and self-evaluation are prerequisites for teaching students to self-reinforce. Students must have positively evaluated their performance on the target behavior in order to engage in self-reinforcement. To engage in self-evaluation, students need data obtained from self-monitoring their behavior. The key to getting students to use self-reinforcement, and to maintaining its effectiveness, is to ensure that they have developed personal standards (i.e., goals) for appropriate behavior. Once students have set realistic standards or goals, we can decide whether to use external or internal self-reinforcement.

External Self-Reinforcement

External self-reinforcement is similar to the reinforcers we deliver to students who are on a token economy or behavioral contract. However, instead of our delivering the reinforcer, students perform this task. A prerequisite step is for students to generate a list of potential reinforcers. According to Bandura (1997), there are several necessary conditions for students to engage in external self-reinforcement:

- The student (rather than the teacher) must determine the evaluative criteria.
- The student (rather than the teacher) must control access to reinforcement.
- The student (rather than the teacher) must administer reinforcement.

For example, suppose a student selects a computer game as the preferred reinforcer (self-determination) for completing 25 division problems correctly (self-evaluation). He keeps the game in a pocket of his math folder until he completes the 25 problems (self-access). He then inserts the game into the computer and plays it for a specified time (self-administration).

External self-reinforcement is often used to wean students off a token economy. This process begins by having students give themselves the number of points or tokens we specify. The students then set a goal for how many tokens they will earn. Finally, they select the desired reinforcers. Another application of external self-reinforcement is when students generate the reinforcer to be included in a behavioral contract. Regardless of the application, it is absolutely essential that students determine, have access to, and administer the reinforcer if self-reinforcement is to be effective.

There are three recommendations for increasing the effectiveness of external self-reinforcement. First, elaborate self-reinforcement contingencies should be avoided. As a general rule, the least complicated intervention should be employed, because adding complicated procedures makes it more difficult to teach students self-reinforcement. Second, the identified reinforcers should be readily accessible for immediate delivery. This consideration is met when students, rather than the teacher, control access to the reinforcers. Third, bootleg or unintended reinforcers must be eliminated. As when using any type of reinforcement, students should be able to reinforce themselves only after performing the target behavior at the designated criterion level.

Internal Self-Reinforcement

Internal self-reinforcement occurs when students engage in covert self-statements—praising themselves for good performance. In this respect, making covert self-statements is no different than our providing students with verbal praise except that students take on this responsibility. It is important that students develop positive self-statements using colloquialisms appropriate to their age and cultural background. In this way, the statements have more relevance, are less gimmicky and so are more likely to be used. Figure 12.11 provides an example of how covert self-reinforcement can be incorporated into a self-monitoring sheet. The self-reinforcement component is preceded by a self-evaluative rating scale. Also, students can either complete the self-reinforcement item (number 6) by selecting positive self-statements from a prepared list or generate positive self-statements based on the situation.

Sometimes students prefer to visualize images rather than repeat self-statements. These images can be either real or imagined. Students' fantasies have been used as a form of covert self-reinforcement to improve their behav-

---

Frustration-Action Sheet

1. Today I was frustrated when:

2. What I wanted was:

3. I reacted by:

4. This did/did not satisfy me because:

5. Rate how well you handled this situation.

    1   2   3   4
    Poor   Fair   Good   Excellent

6. Based on a rating of 3 or 4, write down what you told yourself that was good about how well you handled the situation.

FIGURE 12.11

Form for Incorporating Covert Self-Reinforcement into Self-Monitoring

ior (Workman & Dickinson, 1980)—an approach known as covert positive reinforcement. Workman and Katz (1995) described this technique as requiring students to imagine the following two things:

1. Being in a situation where a certain appropriate behavior is needed, like when the teacher gives an in-class math assignment.
2. Engaging in the appropriate behavior, and experiencing a highly positive/pleasurable scene. (p. 70)

The purpose of this process is to get students to view the pleasurable scene as a positive reinforcer for successfully performing the target behavior.

Workman and Katz (1995) stated that implementing covert positive reinforcement first requires that students identify several reinforcers to use in the positive scenes. The most effective scenes are those that represent reinforcers we cannot implement, such as a walk on the white, sandy beaches of an island in the Bahamas. Sometimes students need help generating reinforcing positive scenes. We can ask students to list the 10 most exciting things they can think of to do. It may be necessary to prompt students by offering several examples such as seeing their favorite group in concert. Workman and Katz (1995) recommended that this approach be used with groups of students by selecting at least five activities that are liked by all students and then following three steps:

1. Tell your students to imagine themselves in the situation where you want their behavior to improve. For example, you might say, "I want everyone to close your eyes and imagine yourself in this class. Now imagine that I am telling you to take out your reading workbooks to do the assignment."
2. Then, have your students imagine themselves successfully engaging in a behavior that is appropriate to the above classroom situation. For example, "Now imagine yourselves taking out your workbook and really working hard on the reading assignment. Be sure that you keep your eyes closed and imagine this as clearly as possible."

It is probably best to teach students to self-reinforce using both external and internal techniques. After the target behavior comes under the control of students, we can help them fade the external self-reinforcement and rely more heavily on internal self-reinforcement.

3. During the final step, instruct your students to imagine one of the highly positive events from their lists. For example, "Now, imagine yourself getting to meet all the stars of your favorite television show. Imagine that you're really excited, and the stars are all talking with you and being friendly." (p. 71)

These steps should be followed in the order in which they appear, and each should take about 20 seconds for the procedure to be effective. Students can use a physical gesture (e.g., raising a finger) to cue the teacher that they are clearly visualizing the image. Workman and Katz (1995) recommended taking students through the three steps 5 to 10 times per day. However, images should be alternated when giving the instructions for step 3 so that students do not become satiated on a single reinforcement image. Once students begin experiencing success with the three steps, the frequency of practice can be reduced to two or three sessions 3 days per week.

SUMMARY

Self-management involves the use of both internal and external strategies students can use to come into contact with reinforcing contingencies. The main advantage of teaching students self-management is that they, rather than us, are in charge of the intervention. This enables us to devote more time to teaching instead of managing students' inappropriate behaviors. Three interrelated techniques can be used to teach students self-management. Self-monitoring involves teaching students to be aware of their behavior, record whether a given behavior occurred, and graph the results. Self-monitoring techniques have been developed for increasing attention to task, academic performance, and recollection of strategies for performing tasks. Self-monitoring is a prerequisite for students to engage in self-evaluation. Self-evaluation involves students setting goals and determining if they are met. Self-evaluation can be promoted by including a variety of rating scales at the bottom of self-monitoring sheets and graphs. It is a prerequisite for students being able to engage in self-reinforcement. Self-reinforcement can be either external or internal. External self-reinforcement requires students to select, have access to, and deliver a positive reinforcer such as receiving extra time shooting a basketball. Internal self-reinforcement involves teaching students either to give themselves positive self-statements or to visualize positive images.

ACTIVITIES

1. There are many examples of self-monitoring in everyday life. A golfer who keeps track of how many strokes it takes to put the ball in each hole

is one example. Come up with three additional everyday examples of people using self-monitoring to control their performance.

2. Ask three students if they would prefer to evaluate their own performance or have their teachers do it for them. Ask three teachers the same question. What type of answers did you get? What conclusions can you draw?

3. List five tasks you regularly perform. Do you self-reinforce after completing each task? If so, what reinforcers do you use. If not, come up with a reinforcer for completing each task. Did having the reinforcer help improve your performance?

REVIEW QUESTIONS

1. What are the advantages of teaching students self-management?
2. What is the difference between self-control and self-management?
3. How does the operant conditioning model differ from the cognitive model of self-management?
4. What are the three components of self-monitoring?
5. How can teachers implement self-monitoring of attention (SMA)?
6. How can teachers implement self-monitoring of performance (SMP)?
7. What are the specific areas of concern for self-monitoring?
8. What are the benefits of having students set their own evaluative criteria?
9. How can teachers develop a rating system for promoting self-evaluation?
10. What is the purpose of having students set daily goals?
11. Describe the conditions for effective goal setting.
12. What are the differences between external and internal self-reinforcement, and how can each be taught?

REFERENCES

Baer, D. M., & Fowler, S. A. (1984). How should we measure the potential of self-control procedures for generalized educational outcomes? In W. L. Heward, T. E. Heron, D. S. Hill, & J. Trap-Porter (Eds.), *Focus on behavior analysis in education* (pp. 145–161). Columbus, OH: Merrill.

Bandura, A. (1997). *Self-efficacy: The exercise of control.* New York: Freeman.

Cooper, J. O., Heron, T. E., & Heward, W. L. (1987). *Applied behavior analysis.* Columbus, OH: Merrill.

Cormier, W. H., & Cormier, L. S. (1998). *Interviewing strategies for helpers: Fundamental skills and cognitive behavioral interventions* (4th ed.). Monterey, CA: Brooks/Cole.

DiGangi, S. A., Maag, J. W., & Rutherford, R. B., Jr. (1991). Self-graphing of on-task behavior: Enhancing the reactive effects of self-monitoring on on-task behavior and academic performance. *Learning Disability Quarterly, 14,* 221–230.

Glasser, W. (1992). *The quality school* (2nd ed.). New York: HarperCollins.

Hallahan, D. P., Lloyd, J. W., & Stoller, L. (1982). *Improving attention with self-monitoring.* Charlottesville: University of Virginia Learning Disabilities Research Institute.

Lloyd, J. W., & Landrum. T. J. (1990). Self-recording of attending to task: Treatment components and generalization of effects. In T. E. Scruggs & B. Y. L. Wong (Eds.), *Intervention research in learning disabilities* (pp. 235–262). New York: Springer-Verlag.

Locke, E. A., & Latham, G. P. (1985). The application of goal setting to sports. *Journal of Sport Psychology, 7,* 205–222.

Locke, E. A., & Latham, G. P. (1990). *A theory of goal setting and task performance.* Englewood Cliffs, NJ: Prentice-Hall.

Maag, J. W. (1993). Cognitive-behavioral strategies for depressed students. *Journal of Emotional and Behavioral Problems, 2*(2), 48–53.

Maag, J. W., Reid, R., & DiGangi, S. A. (1993). Differential effects of self-monitoring attention, accuracy, and productivity. *Journal of Applied Behavior Analysis, 26,* 329–344.

Mace, F. C., Brown, D. K., & West, B. J. (1987). Behavioral self-management in education. In C. A. Maher & J. E. Zins (Eds.), *Psychoeducational interventions in the schools* (pp. 160–176). New York: Pergamon.

Mace, F. C., & Kratochwill, T. R. (1988). Self-monitoring. In J. C. Witt, S. N. Elliott, & F. M. Gresham (Eds.), *Handbook of behavior therapy in education* (pp. 489–522). New York: Plenum.

Martin, G., & Pear, J. (1996). *Behavior modification: What it is and how to do it* (5th ed.). Englewood Cliffs, NJ: Prentice-Hall.

Reid, R. (1993). Implementing self-monitoring interventions in the classroom: Lessons from research. In R. B. Rutherford, Jr., & S. R. Mathur (Eds.), *Severe behavior disorders of children and youth* (Vol. 16, pp. 43–54). Reston, VA: Council for Children with Behavioral Disorders.

Reid, R. (1996). Research in self-monitoring with students with learning disabilities: The present, the prospects, the pitfalls. *Journal of Learning Disabilities, 29,* 317–331.

Reid, R., & Harris, K. R. (1989). Self-monitoring performance. *LD Forum, 15*(1), 39–42.

Skinner, B. F. (1953). *Science and human behavior.* New York: Macmillan.

Snider, V. (1987). Use of self-monitoring of attention with LD students: Research and application. *Learning Disability Quarterly, 10,* 139–151.

Webber, J., Scheuermann, B., McCall, C., & Coleman, M. (1993). Research on self-monitoring as a behavior management technique in special education classrooms: A descriptive review. *Remedial and Special Education, 14*(2), 38–56.

Workman, E. A., & Dickinson, D. (1980). The use of covert conditioning with children: Three empirical case studies. *Education and Treatment of Children, 2,* 24–36.

Workman, E. A. & Katz, A. M. (1995). *Teaching behavioral self-control to students* (2nd ed.) Austin, TX: Pro-Ed.

COGNITIVE-BEHAVIOR MODIFICATION

CHAPTER OVERVIEW

- An Overview of Cognitive-Behavior Modification
- Methods of Cognitive-Behavioral Assessment
- Cognitive-Behavior Modification Intervention Techniques

CHAPTER OBJECTIVES

After completing this chapter, you will be able to do the following:

1. Describe the cognitive A-B-C model and historical factors contributing to the development of cognitive-behavior modification.
2. Identify methods of cognitive-behavioral assessment.
3. Describe how to implement self-instruction training.
4. Explain the purpose of attribution retraining.
5. Identify the steps in thought stopping.
6. Describe the components of problem-solving training.
7. Explain the differences and similarities between rational-emotive therapy and cognitive therapy.

This book has presented a number of principles and techniques based on applied behavior analysis. The focus has been on rearranging antecedents and consequences to promote the acquisition and performance of appropriate behaviors while decreasing the occurrence of inappropriate behaviors. However, as noted in Chapter 7, there are various reasons students may not perform replacement behaviors. For example, they may lack cognitive problem-solving skills or interpret situations incorrectly. In either case, the result may be that they access and perform behaviors inappropriate to the situation. From a cognitive standpoint, the solution to this problem is to teach the students cognitive problem-solving skills and help them interpret situations more accurately, so that they access and perform behaviors appropriate to situations. Therefore, this chapter provides an overview of cognitive-behavior modification, describes methods of cognitive assessment, and presents common cognitive-behavioral intervention techniques.

Before proceeding, it may be helpful to define **cognitive-behavior modification.** Most definitions focus on preserving the demonstrated effectiveness of behavior modification while incorporating the cognitive activities of students to produce changes in behavior (Kendall & Hollon, 1979). A cognitive approach is based on three assumptions: (1) Cognitive activity affects behavior, (2) cognitive activity may be monitored and altered, and (3) desired behavior changes may be effected through cognitive changes (Dobson & Block, 1988). The first assumption is illustrative of the basic tenet of cognitive mediation—that one's cognitive interpretation of a situation affects the behavior one selects and performs in a given situation. The second assumption is based on the belief that cognitions are accessible and that identifying them is a prerequisite for altering cognitive processes. The third assumption is rooted in the idea that cognitive activity precedes and mediates behavior. Accordingly, behavior can be modified by altering how one interprets or processes an event.

The term *cognitive-behavior modification* is more inclusive than *cognitive therapy,* embracing as it does components such as modeling, role-playing, and behavioral contingencies.

AN OVERVIEW OF COGNITIVE-BEHAVIOR MODIFICATION

The history of cognitive-behavior modification is rich and diverse, and many interrelated factors have contributed to its growth. However, before describing these factors, it will be helpful to discuss the cognitive version of the A-B-C model that appears in Figure 13.1.

The Cognitive A-B-C Model

There are several differences between the model shown in Figure 13.1 and the A-B-C model shown in Figure 1.1. The obvious difference is that in the applied behavior analysis model "B" stands for behavior whereas in the cognitive model

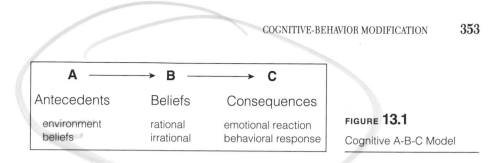

FIGURE **13.1**

Cognitive A-B-C Model

"B" stands for belief. However, there are other differences in how both the "A" and "C" stages are conceptualized.

First, in addition to environmental factors, the cognitive A-B-C model considers students' beliefs to be antecedents or activating events (Dryden & DiGiuseppe, 1990). An example of an antecedent belief may be when a student thinks teammates will criticize his basketball abilities. This activating belief may trigger another belief that influences his ability to select and perform a behavior appropriate to the situation. For example, if he thinks teammates will criticize his performance, he may tell himself that he has to make every shot to impress them. This belief results in his feeling anxious and either missing open shots or hogging the ball.

Second, in the cognitive model, beliefs are assumed to precede and to mediate behavior. Beliefs can be either rigid or flexible. When beliefs are rigid, they are irrational and take the form of "musts," "shoulds," "have tos," and "got tos." When individuals hold rigid beliefs, they tend to reach irrational conclusions. Dryden and DiGiuseppe (1990) described the following four forms that irrational conclusions can take:

> Several procedures for combating irrational beliefs are described later in this chapter.

1. *Awfulizing.* Individuals express a belief that a situation is more than 100% bad, worse than it absolutely should be.
2. *I-can't-stand-it-it's* (low frustration tolerance). Individuals say they cannot envision being able to endure situations or having any happiness at all if what they demand must not exist actually exists.
3. *Damnation.* Individuals tend to be excessively critical of self, others, and/or life conditions.
4. *Always-and-never thinking.* Individuals will insist on absolutes (e.g., that they will always fail or never be approved of by significant others). (p. 4)

Third, the "C" in the cognitive A-B-C model stands for the emotional and behavioral consequences of the beliefs used to interpret or attach meaning to activating events or antecedent situations. According to the cognitive model, we always get the emotional reaction and, consequently, the behavioral response that is appropriate to our belief. However, what is not always accurate is our belief about a situation. In the cognitive A-B-C model, the belief represents the focal point for changing behavior. Stated another way, people behave not according to environmental antecedents, but according to their interpretation of what those events mean.

TABLE 13.1   EXAMPLE OF THE COGNITIVE A-B-C MODEL TO ANALYZE BEHAVIOR

Antecedents	Belief	Consequences
Teacher asks a question.	"I know the answer!"	*Emotion:* joy *Behavior:* raises hand
Billy calls Jimmy a jerk.	"If I let him talk to me that way, I'm a sissy."	*Emotion:* hurt *Behavior:* hits Billy
Teacher gives a spelling test.	"I'm lousy at spelling."	*Emotion:* feeling of inadequacy *Behavior:* complains of stomachache

As discussed in Chapter 1, the applied behavior analysis A-B-C model can be used to analyze behavior (see Table 1.1). Likewise, the cognitive A-B-C model can be used to determine cognitive factors that influence the behaviors students perform when confronted with certain antecedents or situations. Note that the antecedents in Table 13.1 are similar to those appearing in Table 1.1. However, Table 13.1 includes the beliefs students hold about the antecedents, and the consequences refer to students' emotional reactions and behavioral responses.

Factors Contributing to Cognitive-Behavior Modification

Several factors represent important trends in the development of cognitive-behavior modification: (1) a dissatisfaction with behavior modification, (2) the impact of reciprocal determinism, and (3) the development of cognitive psychology. Even though these factors have shaped cognitive-behavior modification, they should not be taken as reasons to abandon the tenets of applied behavior analysis. Rather, they add to our arsenal of methods to help students perform appropriate behaviors.

Dissatisfaction with Behavior Modification   A major trend in the development of cognitive-behavior modification was a growing dissatisfaction with Skinner's operant conditioning approach to behavior modification. The traditional applied behavior analysis explanation was viewed by some as not inclusive enough to account for all human behavior (Mahoney, 1974). Although a large body of research has accumulated demonstrating the effectiveness of many applied behavior analysis techniques, such techniques have sometimes been criticized for not transferring to nontraining settings or for not maintaining behavior after intervention is terminated. Therefore, cognitive techniques have been suggested to augment behavioral interventions to help promote generalization and maintenance of treatment effects.

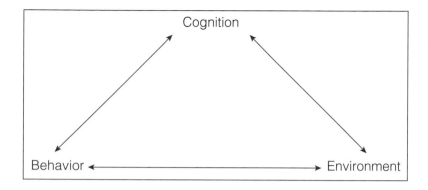

FIGURE 13.2

Model of Reciprocal Determinism

From "The self system in reciprocal determinism" by A. Bandura, 1978, *American Psychologist, 33*, p. 345. Copyright 1978 by the American Psychological Association.

The Impact of Reciprocal Determinism   Bandura's social learning theory, presented in Chapter 3, arguably has been most responsible for advances in both applied behavior analysis and cognitive-behavior modification. However, Bandura's greatest contribution to cognitive-behavior modification was his conceptualization of reciprocal determinism—a model that views the relation between environment, behavior, and cognition as interdependent. This model is presented in Figure 13.2.

As noted in Chapter 3, social learning theory has had a tremendous impact on human functioning—both behavioral and cognitive.

According to Bandura (1978), our behavior is affected by our cognitive interpretations of environmental events. Cognition also plays a part in what environmental events we perceive, whether they have a lasting impact on us, how this information is stored, and under what circumstances it will be retrieved and activated in the future. An example is when two people see the same movie (environmental event) and yet respond to it quite differently. The different responses may be attributed to the different cognitive interpretations each person has of this environmental event. Environmental antecedents and consequences, in turn, affect behavior. For example, a child may be afraid to jump off a diving board. The cognitive interpretation may be "If I jump I will injure myself." However, after engaging in the behavior of plunging into the water and surfacing uninjured, her belief about diving may be positively modified.

The relative influences exerted by cognitive, behavioral, and environmental factors will vary in different individuals and in different situations. Under some circumstances, environmental factors exercise such powerful constraints on behavior that they emerge as the overriding determinant. For example, many of us may have found ourselves stopped at a red light late at night. Even though there is no other traffic in sight, we do not run the light. In this case, the environmental antecedent (i.e., the red light) is so powerful that it affects both our behavior and our belief about the situation.

In other situations, cognitive factors exert a predominant influence. For example, suppose a man likes Steven Seagal action-type movies but avoids movies heavy in dialogue because he believes they will be boring. Therefore, when his spouse suggests that they see *Steel Magnolias,* he thinks it will be boring because it doesn't have enough action. Yet he is pleasantly surprised and enjoys the movie. Sometime later, his spouse wants to see *Fried Green Tomatoes.* Even though he had a positive experience seeing *Steel Magnolias,* his belief system is so ingrained that he is convinced this movie will be high on dialogue, low on action, and, consequently, boring. Again, however, he enjoys the movie. Yet when he is asked to see *Driving Miss Daisy,* his belief is the same as for the previous two movies. In this instance, his cognition, or belief, results in consistent behavior even though the environment (i.e., the movies) results in a positive, pleasurable experience.

In other situations, the three factors develop and are activated in a highly interdependent manner. Bandura (1978) provided the following example of television viewing:

> Personal preferences influence when and which programs, from among the available alternatives, individuals choose to watch on television. Although the potential televised environment is identical for all viewers, the actual televised environment that impinges on given individuals depends on what they select to watch. Through their viewing behavior, they partly shape the nature of the future televised environment. Because production costs and commercial requirements also determine what people are shown, the options provided in the televised environment partly shape the viewers' preferences. (p. 346)

In this example, all three factors reciprocally influence each other. Viewer preferences refer to individuals' cognitive interpretations of the entertainment value of watching certain shows over others. Viewer behavior shapes what the networks place on television and so represents a way to alter the environment. Yet television offerings represent the environment from which individuals must activate cognitive interpretations and behavior.

The Development of Cognitive Psychology   Much of the momentum for the development of cognitive psychology can be traced to Luria's (1961) and Vygotsky's (1962) developmental theories of the functional relation between language and behavior. Luria examined the developmental changes in children's abilities to regulate their behaviors, first through adult verbalizations and then through their own self-verbalizations. Vygotsky described a developmental progression in language control over behavior from talking aloud, to internalized talking, to silence. Several years later, Neisser (1967) wrote *Cognitive Psychology,* which represented the first extensive treatment of cognitive processes such as memory, attributions, problem solving, and self-referent

Reciprocal determinism is not as complicated as it may first appear. The model simply focuses on identifying which factor(s) seem prominent for individuals in a given situation. Those factors can be determined using the techniques for identifying skill deficits in Chapter 7 and the assessment techniques presented in this chapter.

speech. Research on these topics led to the development of a variety of cognitive therapies.

Most cognitive approaches can be organized under three major categories: (1) coping-skills therapies, (2) problem-solving therapies, and (3) cognitive restructuring methods (Dobson & Block, 1988). Coping-skills approaches focus on helping students lessen the impact of negative environmental events as a way to decrease anxiety. Problem-solving interventions focus on helping students generate and select appropriate behaviors when confronted with a problem situation. Cognitive restructuring methods focus on helping students interpret events in less dysfunctional and more logical ways so that their emotional reaction and behavioral responses are appropriate to a given situation.

These approaches have been used extensively to treat a variety of emotional and behavioral problems including, but not limited to, social anxiety, test anxiety, school phobia, depression, impulsivity and hyperactivity, and aggression (Hughes, 1988). Cognitive approaches also have been used to improve a variety of intellectual and academic skills including memory, metacognition, reading comprehension, handwriting, and arithmetic (Harris, 1982).

METHODS OF COGNITIVE-BEHAVIORAL ASSESSMENT

It is not easy to assess students' cognition, given that cognitive activity is covert and so is not subject to direct observation. Therefore, we must infer the presence of cognitive difficulties from observing students' behaviors—not an uncommon practice in education. For example, every time we give a test, we are making an inference, based on students' grades, regarding whether learning has occurred. Similarly, the concept of "intelligence" cannot be measured directly. Therefore, intelligence tests have been developed to make inferences about students' cognitive capabilities by sampling their behavior on various tasks. For example, we might assess a student's discrimination skills by asking her which shape is different after presenting her with two triangles and one square.

Although teachers and school psychologists both formally and informally assess students' cognitions on an ongoing basis, the process is not always easy. This section discusses several dangers in using cognitive assessment and presents some of the most common cognitive assessment techniques.

It takes several years of supervised training to become proficient in cognitive assessment. Yet it is important for teachers to understand these techniques as many teachers apply them informally.

Dangers Associated with Cognitive Assessment

The first danger associated with cognitive assessment is that the behaviors students display may not always correspond with the cognitions they hold in a given situation. For example, we might incorrectly assume that because a student who is playing baseball at recess hits a double that his self-talk will be positive—after all, hitting a double places a runner in scoring position. However, he may actually engage in critical self-talk because he didn't hit a home run.

This problem leads to the second danger: Just because students engage in negative self-talk does not mean that their beliefs are dysfunctional. Another baseball example can illustrates this problem. At the beginning of the season, many players are impatient in their first several at-bats, often swinging at pitches out of the strike zone. Their self-talk may sound like this: "Get a grip, jerk—you're swinging at terrible pitches." These words seem negative, yet they have a facilitative effect—players subsequently wait for better pitches to hit.

The third problem is that, whenever we make inferences about cognition based on students' behavior, error is introduced into the process. Error is inevitable when conducting any type of psychological or educational measurement. However, the greater the inference, the more error that is introduced and the less valid the results.

The final problem is that asking students what they are thinking does not necessarily yield more valid information than making inferences from their behaviors. Students automatically access beliefs about situations that they have encountered in the past. The reason is that through repetition thoughts become habitual, automatic, and so unconscious. Therefore, we may not be aware of the steps involved in performing a task, such as driving a car. The less access we have to cognitive material, the greater the subjectivity of our reports and the more biased the results.

Cognitive Assessment Techniques

Table 13.2 summarizes of the most common types of cognitive assessment techniques. According to Segal and Shaw (1988), cognitive assessment techniques can be organized along two dimensions: (1) temporality and (2) degree of structure.

Temporality refers to the time the thoughts were assessed relative to when they actually occurred. For example, sampling a student's verbalizations as he completes division problems represents **concurrent assessment** because information is being collected at the same time that the actual thoughts are being generated. In contrast, asking a student on Monday to describe what she was thinking when she got into a fight last Friday represents a **retrospective assessment,** because a considerable amount of time has passed between the actual incident and the collection of assessment information.

The second dimension, **degree of structure,** refers to the level of limits or format that the assessment technique imposes on students. For example, self-statement inventories require us to rate the occurrence of certain thoughts

TABLE 13.2	COMMON COGNITIVE ASSESSMENT TECHNIQUES
Procedure	**Description**
Recording of spontaneous private speech	Can be taken unobtrusively or following specific instructions. These recordings represent verbal behavior that can then be transcribed and coded into categories. In this method, the practitioner is limited to the person's verbalizations and can never be fully certain that silences are synonymous with the lack of cognitive processing.
Free association	As used in psychoanalysis, involves asking individuals to verbalize their thoughts as they experience them throughout the therapy session.
Thinking aloud	Requires individuals to provide a continuous monologue of their thoughts during the performance of a specific task.
Random sampling of thoughts	Requires individuals to record their current thoughts when cued (either in person or by a portable mechanical device) at random intervals. This procedure enables the gathering of data over relatively long periods of time.
Self-monitoring	Has individuals record the occurrence of specific thoughts in a particular stimulus situation or at a particular time.
Videotape thought reconstruction	Allows individuals to reconstruct their train of thought by reviewing a videotape of an actual or role-played problematic situation. Individuals may be asked to think aloud while watching themselves or to record the occurrence of specific cognitive events.
Self-statement inventory	Contains a predetermined set of thoughts that individuals are asked to rate with respect to whether they experienced the specific thought and its frequency of occurrence.
Thought listing	Has individuals report on their thoughts while in a particular situation. This procedure is more constrained than think-aloud methods because the assessment takes place once individuals are out of the situation. This method can be likened to videotaped thought reconstruction without the videotape.
Clinical interview	Can be used as a retrospective cognitive assessment tool, in which case the therapist asks clients to recall recently upsetting situations and then recount what they were thinking and feeling at the time.

that appear on the form. Here are four self-statements that appear on the Automatic Thoughts Questionnaire (ATQ), which is an instrument for assessing the extent of negative thoughts related to depression (Hollon & Kendall, 1980):

1. I feel like I'm up against the world.
2. I'm no good.
3. Why can't I ever succeed?
4. No one ever understands me.

We rate how often we experience each thought in terms of "not at all," "sometimes," "moderately often," "often," or "all the time." The obvious disadvantage of this approach is that any thoughts we may have that do not appear on the instrument go unreported. The advantages are that structured techniques are

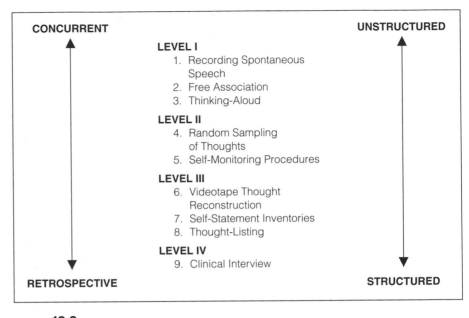

FIGURE 13.3

Relation Between Cognitive Assessments, Temporality, and Degree of Structure

From "Cognitive assessment: Issues and methods" by Z. V. Segal & B. F. Shaw, 1988, In K. S. Dobson (Ed.). *Handbook of cognitive-behavioral therapies* (p. 42). New York: Guilford Press. Copyright 1988 by Guilford Press. Reprinted with permission.

easy to administer and score and have greater potential for standardization (Segal & Shaw, 1988).

Figure 13.3, which was developed by Segal and Shaw (1988), shows the relation between assessment techniques and the degree of temporality (concurrent versus retrospective) and of structure. The most concurrent assessment techniques are also the most unstructured. Structure increases as we employ more retrospective techniques. According to Segal and Shaw (1988), unstructured (concurrent) techniques have the advantage of minimizing reactivity, demands, and inference effects. However, information is obtained only on what students report, and this information may be difficult to code and analyze. Structured (retrospective) methods may stimulate students' awareness and provide more information than unstructured techniques but still restrict their responses based on the directions of the assessment instrument.

Regardless of the technique, Segal and Shaw (1988) described four ways to minimize the subjectivity inherent in all cognitive assessments. First, we should collect verbal reports as soon as possible. Students tend to distort their experiences with the passage of time, which means that their recollections become biased. Second, we should minimize our probing. Probing may provide

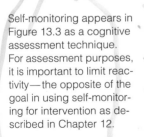

Self-monitoring appears in Figure 13.3 as a cognitive assessment technique. For assessment purposes, it is important to limit reactivity—the opposite of the goal in using self-monitoring for intervention as described in Chapter 12.

us with more information, but students may simply give the answers they think we are looking for. Third, we should ask for verbal descriptions of behavior, and not reasons for it. Asking for reasons only results in excuses and rationalizations. Fourth, we should provide explicit directions so that students do not deviate from the assessment format.

COGNITIVE-BEHAVIOR MODIFICATION INTERVENTION TECHNIQUES

Cognitive-behavior modification intervention techniques include a variety of strategies and procedures. Although the emphasis on "cognitive" versus "behavior" may vary, all these approaches focus on the importance of addressing cognition as a way to obtain positive changes in behavior. In this section, five of the most common cognitive-behavior modification techniques are described.

Self-Instruction Training

Self-instruction training was developed by Meichenbaum and Goodman (1971) for use with students who were impulsive. Their goal was to teach the students to talk to themselves as a method of gaining self-control. They hypothesized that these students had not developed the self-talk skills necessary to solve the problems they confronted. Their hypothesis was based on Luria's (1961) developmental theory that language can be used to develop, modify, or maintain certain behaviors among students with behavior problems (Harris, 1982). Consequently, their self-instruction program focused on providing students with their own verbal prompts for performing certain behaviors.

Aspects of Self-Instruction Training Meichenbaum and Goodman (1971) developed a five-step self-instruction training program for students who were hyperactive:

1. *Cognitive modeling.* The teacher performs a task while talking aloud, and the student observes.
2. *Overt external guidance.* The student and teacher both perform the task while talking aloud together.
3. *Overt self-guidance.* The student performs the task using the same verbalizations as the teacher.
4. *Faded self-guidance.* The student whispers the instructions (often in an abbreviated form) while going through the task.
5. *Covert self-guidance.* The student performs the task, guided by covert self-speech.

These five steps were used to train students to think before they acted. Harris (1982) suggested six types of self-statements that can be taught to, and rehearsed by, students:

1. *Problem identification.* "What is it I have to do?"
2. *Focusing of attention.* "I have to concentrate, think only about my work."
3. *Planning and response guidance.* "Be careful . . . look at one at a time."
4. *Self-reinforcement.* "Good—I got it!"
5. *Self-evaluation.* "Am I following my plan . . . did I look at each one?"
6. *Coping and error-correcting option.* "That's OK . . . even if I make an error I can back up and go slowly." (p. 6)

The decision as to which type of self-statement to use should be based on the nature of the problem and the goal we are trying to accomplish.

Harris (1982) divided self-statements into two levels: (1) task-approach statements and (2) task-specific statements. **Task-approach statements** refer to general strategies that can be used across a variety of related tasks. They focus on either general task characteristics or students' characteristics. For example, problem identification statements such as "What am I supposed to do here? "and" What is my first step?" focus on task characteristics. In contrast, statements like "I must remember to go slow and think first," "It's up to me how well I do," and "What's important is that I do my best" are aimed at student characteristics such as reducing impulsivity. **Task-specific statements** refer to strategies that are specific to the task at hand. An example of a problem identification task-specific statement is "I have to finish the addition problems . . . . First, I have to turn to the correct page . . . . Then I have to remember that the answer will be greater than any of the numbers in the problem."

Harris (1982) described several steps to improve the effectiveness of self-instruction training. First, we should help students identify any negative, maladaptive, or ineffective self-statements (i.e., strategies) that occur while working on a task. Second, we should engage students in "Socratic," question-and-answer dialogues. For example, we may first ask a student how she should do the task and then provide feedback and build on her recommendations. Third, we should discuss collaboratively the purpose of the task, the types of strategies, and ways to implement them effectively. Fourth, we should reduce our support as training progresses so that students are spontaneously generating and answering the questions on their own. During this step, we may sporadically omit the use of correct verbalizations and strategies in order to allow students to catch the errors.

Factors Influencing the Effectiveness of Self-Instructions

Although teaching students self-instructions is fairly easy, it is much more difficult to get them to use the instructions independently. Because self-statements are covert, we have few reliable ways of knowing whether they are actually used.

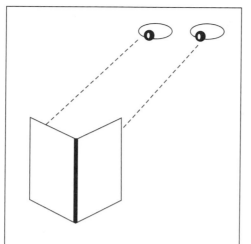

FIGURE 13.4

Self-Instruction Picture to Keep Eyes on Book

Self-instruction training has been used extensively to improve the academic skills of students with learning disabilities.

Self-statements will have no effect on behavior if students fail to use them. Several factors can enhance students' effectiveness in using self-statements (Braswell & Kendall, 1988; Harris, 1982; Kendall, 1977).

First, if students have successfully used self-instructions in the past, they are more likely to use them again. Of course, this brings us to the issue of how to get students to use self-instructions in the first place. One strategy is to ensure that the self-instruction is limited to a few words, a phrase, or perhaps a short sentence. Another strategy is to have students generate the exact wording of self-statements. For example, if the purpose of the self-statement is to help a student stay calm and handle an anxiety-producing situation, then she may come up with the simple statement "Chill out." She is more likely to use this statement because it makes use of her own vernacular.

Second, the effectiveness of self-instructions is affected by students' cognitive ability. Students who are very young or who have mental retardation will have difficulty learning and using self-instructions. In this case, we want to ensure that the self-statement is no more than two words long. An alternative method is to draw a picture, like the one in Figure 13.4, or help students form visual pictures in their minds rather than trying to remember certain words.

Third, students are more likely to use self-instructions when they focus on specific behaviors to increase or decrease. For example, we may want to help a student resist talking to a friend during class. However, having the student say to himself "Work on my assignment" may be ineffective because it does not focus on the specific target behavior to be reduced—talking to a friend. Using the self-instruction "Don't talk to my friend" will be more effective because it specifically addresses the target behavior.

Fourth, like any behavior management technique, self-instructions do not teach students skills—teachers teach skills. Self-instructions only help students display skills they already possess but are not performing regularly. For example, teaching a student to ask for help by having her repeat the self-instruction "When I need help, raise my hand" requires her to know when she needs help.

Fifth, students should be reinforced for using self-instructions, thereby increasing the likelihood that they will use them again. There are several ways to determine whether students are using self-instructions so that they can be reinforced. For example, a student can be required to repeat the instruction aloud while performing the target behavior. If he is too embarrassed to do this, he can whisper it or move his lips. This behavior is necessary for us to determine whether he is saying the instruction and so can receive reinforcement. This procedure also gives the student practice using the self-instruction.

Finally, a **mediation essay** can be used to help students practice self-instructions (Morrow & Morrow, 1985). This procedure requires us to write brief paragraphs answering the following questions regarding a student's behavior:

1. What did the student do wrong?
2. Why shouldn't the student do this?
3. What should the student do?
4. What will happen if the student . . . ?

For the first question, we write a paragraph describing the specific behavior the student performed. We then write a paragraph specifying why the behavior is inappropriate. Next, we write a paragraph specifying the appropriate behavior that should have been performed. Finally, we write a concise description of the consequences for performing the appropriate behavior. We give the student a copy of the mediation essay, which he or she must copy during free time or recess, or before or after school. Morrow and Morrow (1985) described the following potential advantages of using a mediation essay:

> It includes provisions of alternative ways of behaving in current and similar situations, ease of development and implementation, wide applicability to various situations and environments—including the home—in which maladaptive behaviors are displayed, and the highlighting of specific inappropriate behaviors. Also, the level of language utilized can be easily adjusted by the teacher to accommodate the students' functioning level. (p. 24)

Attribution Retraining

Attribution retraining is based on the theory that students' explanations for why they are performing well or poorly has implications for their behavioral persistence, expectancies for future performance, and emotional reactions to success and failure (Braswell & Kendall, 1988). Recall from Chapter 11 the discussion of learned helplessness as a hypothesized cause of depression. The way in which students attribute the causes of aversive experiences determines whether they become helpless and, consequently, depressed. Students who are depressed attribute success to external, unstable, and specific factors, and failure to internal, stable, and global factors (Hughes, 1988). Dweck and colleagues found that the attributional style of students who were depressed was similar to that of students experiencing helplessness (Diener & Dweck, 1978; Dweck, 1975; Dweck & Reppucci, 1973). Students who experienced helplessness gave up after failing and attributed their failure to a lack of ability more often than did proficient students. And the performance of students who experienced helplessness declined sharply after failure. Finally, these students were less likely to attribute success to their ability, expected to do poorly in the future, and believed that peers performed better than they actually did (Hughes, 1988).

Most attribution retraining interventions focus on creating an atmosphere in which students learn to take more personal credit for their accomplishments as a way to promote empowerment and positive control (Braswell & Kendall, 1988). The goal of attribution retraining is to increase students' behavioral persistence while performing tasks. The classic study in attribution retraining was conducted by Dweck (1975). She treated a sample of elementary school students who were prone to expect, and were debilitated by, failure. When these students experienced failure during daily sessions to solve math problems, they were told by an experimenter, "Failure means you should try harder." These students persisted longer on the math problems than students in a success-only condition in which problems were presented that were within their ability and that would ensure success.

Licht and Kistner (1986) described two phases of attribution retraining. In phase 1, students are set up to experience some degree of failure. The failure is not severe and might consist of a few problems among a set that are too difficult for them to solve. In phase 2, they are taught to make statements that attribute the failures to insufficient effort. Zirpoli and Melloy (1997) described the following considerations in the successful application of attribution retraining:

- Teachers should tell students that increased effort leads to success, rather than suggesting that they are not trying hard enough.
- Students should experience some success in order to increase the effectiveness of the self-statement "Increased effort will lead to increased success."
- Teachers should convey to students that the self-statement will contribute to future success.

Attribution retraining, in which students are subjected to failure-producing situations, is designed to enhance psychological resilience, which refers to people's ability to bounce back from adversity.

There are two additional factors to consider before implementing attribution retraining. First, to be effective, attributional statements should be accompanied by specific behavioral efforts. For example, Short and Ryan (1984) found that attribution retraining was ineffective when students made effort-oriented statements prior to reading a passage rather than after having had difficulty with the passage. Second, attribution retraining is most effective for students who are not using skills they already possess, but it is not an appropriate technique for students who have specific skill deficits (Fincham, 1983; Schunk, 1983).

Thought Stopping

Thought stopping was developed by Taylor (1963) and elaborated on by several others (Lazarus, 1971; Wolpe, 1982). However, it was Rimm and Masters (1979) who described the specific steps involved in teaching thought stopping. The goal of this intervention is to help students control negative or self-defeating thoughts and images by suppressing them. Cormier and Cormier (1985) listed the following individuals for whom thought stopping will be most helpful:

1. Persons who ruminate about a past event that cannot be changed ("crying over spilled milk").
2. Persons who ruminate about an event that is unlikely to occur.
3. Persons who engage in repetitive, unproductive, negative thinking or repetitive anxiety-producing or self-defeating images. (pp. 385–387)

There are several situations in which thought stopping should be avoided. First, it may not be appropriate for students who have intense and uncontrollable thoughts, such as those characterized by schizophrenia (Olin, 1976). Second, thought stopping seems to be more effective for students with intermittent rather than continuous self-defeating thoughts (Cormier & Cormier, 1985). Third, thought stopping should not be used for students with vague, counterproductive thoughts (Wolpe, 1971). There are six stages in implementing thought stopping (Cormier & Cormier, 1985; Rimm & Masters, 1974).

Treatment Rationale   The first stage is to explain the rationale for thought stopping to students. Before moving on to the next stage, they should be aware of how their self-defeating thoughts or images create anxiety and interfere with their performing desirable behaviors. We may want to point out how they will be better off not being plagued by such thoughts or images. Here is an example of how the rationale behind thought stopping might be explained:

> "You told me how you are bothered by thoughts that you will not make the basketball team. These thoughts are unnecessary and create a lot of stress that could really affect your performance. You'd feel much better if you weren't constantly

Thought stopping is often used by cognitive therapists. This makes sense—stop the unwanted thoughts until the person has the psychological resources to replace negative thoughts with positive ones.

thinking about this or picturing the basketball team playing without you. This approach can help you learn to break this habit of thinking. How does this sound to you?"

If the student agrees to try thought stopping, we should avoid describing how the procedure works because the element of surprise increases its effectiveness. Therefore, before proceeding to the next stage, we may tell him:

> "I'm going to have you sit back, relax, and tell me the thoughts that come to your mind. When I hear a thought related to not making the basketball team, I will interrupt you. Then I will teach you how to stop the thought whenever it pops into your head."

Teacher-Directed Thought Stopping: Overt Interruption   During the second phase, the student verbalizes all thoughts and images aloud that relate to the problem situation. These verbalizations enable us to determine the exact moment when he begins engaging in negative thinking. We interrupt the negative thoughts by saying a loud "Stop!" that can be accompanied by a noise such as a hand clap or a ruler hitting a desk. We point out how the unexpected and startling interruption terminated the negative thoughts. We should also stress to the student that he, too, can learn use the same technique to control his thoughts.

After this sequence, we direct the student to run the same thoughts through his mind but to raise his finger when he reaches the negative thought that we previously stopped. When he signals the onset of the negative thought or image, we repeat the interruption with a loud "Stop!" and hand clap.

Student-Directed Thought Stopping: Overt Interruption   The student assumes responsibility for the interruption now that he has learned to control negative thoughts in response to our overt interruption. This phase is implemented using the same format as the previous stage, except that the student performs the interruption. He begins by overtly verbalizing his thoughts and images, as in the previous stage. However, when the negative thoughts are verbalized, he says a loud "Stop!" and claps his hands.

As in the second part of the previous stage, the student then thinks about the situation covertly. When he gets to the negative thought or image, he says a loud "Stop!" and claps his hands. The loud "Stop!" and hand clap take the place of the hand signal used in the previous stage.

Student-Directed Thought Stopping: Covert Interruption   There is a major disadvantage to having the student interrupt himself overtly: He draws considerable attention to himself by suddenly saying a loud "Stop!" and clapping his hands in the middle of an activity. Therefore, the next stage of thought stopping requires the student to substitute a covert interruption for the overt one.

The sequence performed during the two previous stages is repeated here: (1) The student verbalizes all thoughts and images aloud that relate to the problem situation, and then (2) he thinks of the situation covertly. However, during each sequence, the student says "Stop!" to himself while visualizing a big stop sign inches away from his face. It is helpful to have the student raise his finger when he reaches the negative self-statement and lower it when the thought is terminated. In this way, we know that he actually employed the covert stop process.

Shift to Assertive, Positive, or Neutral Thoughts   It is fairly easy to startle students into forgetting negative thoughts, but unless they are given more productive thoughts to take their place, the negative ones will quickly resurface. To maintain the effects of the initial thought interruption, students should be taught to verbalize assertive or positive thoughts. Because assertive behavior inhibits anxiety, assertive thoughts will also inhibit any anxiety or arousal that may occur after students have learned to suppress the undesired thoughts (Arrick, Voss, & Rimm, 1981). Assertiveness is not always easy for students to learn and use—especially those at the elementary level. Therefore, students can be asked to focus on a pleasurable or reinforcing scene. The five steps of self-instruction training can be used at this point to teach students assertive or positive thoughts.

Homework and Follow-Up   Once students have mastered the phases of thought stopping, they are ready to use it outside the training setting. At first, students should be instructed to practice the thought-stopping stages several times each day. We can use a self-monitoring worksheet for students to record their performance on each phase while involved in an anxiety-producing situation. In addition to daily practice, students can initiate thought stopping whenever they notice that they are engaging in negative or self-defeating thinking (Cormier & Cormier, 1985).

Problem-Solving Training

Some type of **problem-solving training** is incorporated into almost every cognitive-behavior modification intervention (Braswell & Kendall, 1988). This training covers a variety of skills that can be used to resolve conflicts requiring either initiation of action or reaction to the responses of others (Gesten, Weissberg, Amish, & Smith, 1987). Hughes (1988) described four problem-solving thinking skills:

1. *Problem identification.* Component skills involve problem sensitivity or the ability to "sense" the presence of a problem by identifying "uncomfortable" feelings; also included are skills for identifying major problem issues as well as

maintaining a general problem-solving orientation or "set" versus a tendency to deny, avoid, or act impulsively in dealing with the problem.

2. *Alternative thinking.* The ability to generate multiple alternative solutions to a given interpersonal problem situation.

3. *Consequential thinking.* The ability to foresee the immediate and more long-range consequences of a particular alternative and to use this information in the decision-making process.

4. *Means–ends thinking.* The ability to elaborate or plan a series of specific actions (a means) to attain a given goal, to recognize and devise ways around potential obstacles, and to use a realistic time framework in implementing steps toward the goal. (p. 144)

Zirpoli and Melloy (1997) proposed **perspective taking** as an additional problem-solving thinking skill. This skill refers to the ability of students to identify and take into consideration the fact that others have different motives and may display different behaviors.

D'Zurilla (1988) described a problem-solving model we can use to teach students:

1. *Provide a problem orientation.* Students learn a set of facilitative cognitions (beliefs) to recognize problems and know how to deal with them in appropriate ways.

2. *Define the problem.* Students assemble pertinent and factual information about the problem, clarifying the nature of the problems, setting a realistic problem-solving goal, and reappraising the significance of the problem.

3. *Generate alternative solutions.* Students produce as many solution alternatives as possible in order to increase the chance that the best solution will be considered.

4. *Make a decision.* Students evaluate the available solution alternatives and select the best one(s) to use.

5. *Implement the solution and verify the results.* Students assess the solution outcome and verify the effectiveness of the chosen solution in the real-life situation.

Meichenbaum (1985) provided the following steps for putting into practice the phases of problem solving just described:

1. Define the stressor or stress reactions as a problem-to-be-solved.
2. Set realistic goals as concretely as possible by stating the problem in behavioral terms and by delineating steps necessary to reach each goal.
3. Generate a wide range of possible alternative courses of action.
4. Imagine and consider how others might respond if asked to deal with a similar stress problem.
5. Evaluate the pros and cons of each proposed solution and rank order the solutions from least to most practical and desirable.

Problem-solving training interventions are sometimes difficult to implement because there is no singular procedure for doing so, as is the case for self-instruction training and thought stopping.

TABLE 13.3	PROBLEM-SOLVING STEPS AND QUESTIONS
Step	**Question/Action**
Identify the problem.	What is the concern?
Select a goal.	What do I want?
Generate alternatives.	What can I do?
Consider consequences.	What might happen?
Make a decision.	What is my decision?
Implement the decision.	Now do it!
Evaluate.	Did it work?

6. Rehearse strategies and behaviors by means of imagery, behavioral rehearsal, and graduated practice.
7. Try out the most acceptable and feasible solution.
8. Reconsider the original problem in light of the attempt at problem solving. (p. 67)

Wasik (cited in Meichenbaum, 1985) translated these problem-solving steps into questions that students can ask themselves; these questions appear in Table 13.3.

A variety of interpersonal problem-solving training programs for elementary and secondary students have been developed based on the information previously described (Shure & Spivack, 1974; Siegel & Spivack, 1973). In addition, several well-designed training programs in social skills embed problem-solving skills (Goldstein, 1988; Kendall & Braswell, 1985; Michelson, Sugai, Wood, & Kazdin, 1983).

One of the earliest, and most often cited, problem-solving interventions is the **turtle technique** developed by Robin, Schneider, and Dolnick (1976) as a way to help students be less aggressive or impulsive by developing alternative responses. The turtle technique consists of three phases: (1) turtle response, (2) relaxation, and (3) problem solving.

In phase 1, the teacher introduces the turtle response by telling students the following story:

Little Turtle was a handsome young turtle very upset about going to school. He always got in trouble at school because he got into fights. Other kids would tease, bump, or hit him; he would get very angry and start big fights. The teacher would have to punish him. Then one day he met the big old tortoise, who told him that his shell was the secret answer to all his problems. The tortoise told Little Turtle to withdraw into his shell when he felt angry and rest until he was no longer angry. So he tried it the next day and it worked. The teacher now smiled at him and he no longer got into big fights. (Robin, Schneider, & Dolnick, 1976, p. 450)

The teacher models the turtle response and requires students to practice responding quickly when cued by the word "turtle" interspersed unexpectedly throughout normal class activities. The teacher then explains the four situations in which it is appropriate for students to display the turtle response: (1) A student believes that an aggressive interaction with a peer is about to occur, (2) a student becomes frustrated or angry and is about to throw a tantrum, (3) the teacher calls out "turtle," and (4) a peer calls out "turtle." Students are reinforced for role-playing these four situations and the turtle response.

Students are taught muscle relaxation exercises during phase 2 of the turtle technique in order to further diffuse negative emotional reactions resulting from the original situation. Specifically, they are taught to alternately tense and relax various muscle groups of their bodies independently and then while doing the turtle response. The goal is to pair the turtle response and relaxation.

In phase 3, problem solving is introduced through the use of role playing and discussion. Students are taught to generate alternative strategies for coping with the problem situations that initially resulted in their displaying the turtle response and examining the consequences of their choices. Specifically, the teacher presents incomplete stories of typical problem situations and requires students to role-play alternative endings. The teacher reminds students of their choices during normal class activities whenever they display a turtle response.

Gesten and colleagues (1987) described several factors that may guide the selection of problem-solving curricula depending on students' age. First, the ability to generate multiple solutions, regardless of quality, is most effective for preschool and primary-grade students. Second, the quality of solutions (i.e., their assertiveness and effectiveness), rather than quantity, is most effective for middle school students. The emphasis here is on teaching the consequences associated with each solution choice. Finally, secondary students appear to require less training in solution generation or consequential thinking than in the means—ends thinking that is required to overcome obstacles and to implement successfully the chosen solutions.

Cognitive Restructuring

Think of the times we have told ourselves things such as "I never do things right," "I'm such a fool," and "I always make mistakes." These self-statements are irrational because we do some things right. These all-or-nothing types of self-statements may be accompanied by a variety of negative emotions such as anxiety, depression, inadequacy, and guilt. One approach to correct such faulty thinking is through the use of **cognitive restructuring**—a global term referring to techniques that focus on identifying and altering students' irrational

Cognitive therapy and rational-emotive therapy are similar in that they both focus on identifying irrational beliefs and replacing them with more adaptive ones. One difference is that rational-emotive therapy can be used for a variety of problems whereas cognitive therapy was developed specifically as a treatment for depression.

beliefs and negative self-statements. Its roots can be traced to Ellis's (1962) rational-emotive therapy (RET) and Beck's (1967) cognitive therapy of depression. Both therapies basically teach students to reduce irrational thoughts through the use of logical analysis and abstract thinking (Hughes, 1988).

Rational-Emotive Therapy (RET)   Albert Ellis (1962), the originator of **rational-emotive therapy (RET),** based this approach on the premise that most everyday emotional problems and behaviors stem from irrational self-statements we make when events in our lives do not turn out the way we want them to. Ellis described different types of irrational thinking styles—some of which were introduced at the beginning of this chapter. When things don't go well for us, we tend to tell ourselves that the event shouldn't have happened—a irrational thinking style known as demandingness. We then tend to blow the significance of the situation out of proportion (i.e., awfulizing or catastrophizing). When an event is viewed as "awful" or "catastrophic," we tend to tell ourselves that we can't stand it. This belief, in turn, leads us to condemn and damn either ourselves, others, or the world. For example, we may walk out to our car after work and discover that the windshield is smashed in. Because most of us will find this situation to be undesirable, we tell ourselves that it shouldn't be smashed, it's awful that it is, and someone has to be condemned and damned. These types of irrational beliefs lead to our overreacting emotionally and engaging in counterproductive behavior.

Ellis's therapeutic approach is to teach individuals to counteract such irrational beliefs with more positive and realistic statements. Take, for example, the use of demanding words such as *should/shouldn't, have to,* and *must.* Ellis challenges us to use those words factually. Therefore, if our windshield is smashed in, Ellis encourages us to tell ourselves, "My windshield should be smashed in." This sentence uses "should" factually. Why should our windshield be smashed in? Because it is, and no amount of saying "shouldn't" will reverse that fact. The only thing that saying "shouldn't" does is elevate our emotional state to the point at which we may engage in counterproductive behavior. The difficulty we have in using "should" correctly results from confusion about the words *acceptance* and *approval.* We have a tendency not to accept the reality of an event if we don't approve of it. But we are striving for acceptance when using "should" to describe reality. We don't have to approve of an event to accept its reality. The level of disapproval is irrationally expressed when we blow things out of proportion. One way to combat the tendency to awfulize is to ask ourselves "How bad is it?" by comparing the event to some hierarchy of physical injury. For example, would we be willing to incur a broken nose in order for our windshield to not be smashed in? Telling ourselves that we can't stand it is a fallacy, because we are living proof that we've stood everything that has ever happened to us.

Cognitive Therapy   Although cognitive therapy for depression was developed independently by Aaron T. Beck (1967), it has much in common with Ellis's RET. Like Ellis, Beck and colleagues described several dysfunctional thinking styles:

1. Arbitrary inference refers to the process of drawing a specific conclusion in the absence of evidence to support the conclusion or when the evidence is contrary to the conclusion.
2. Selective abstraction consists of focusing on a detail taken out of context, ignoring other more salient features of the situation and conceptualizing the whole experience on the basis of this fragment.
3. Overgeneralization refers to the pattern of drawing a general rule or conclusion on the basis of one or more isolated incidents and applying the concept across the board to related and unrelated situations.
4. Magnification and minimization are reflected in errors in evaluating the significance or magnitude of an event that are so gross as to constitute a distortion.
5. Personalization refers to the patient's proclivity to relate external events to himself when there is no basis for making such a connection.
6. Absolutistic, dichotomous thinking is manifested in the tendency to place all experiences in one of two opposite categories; for example, flawless or defective, immaculate or filthy, saint or sinner. (Beck, Rush, Shaw, & Emery, 1979, p. 14)

The first step in Beck's approach is to have students identify dysfunctional thoughts and maladaptive assumptions that may be causing unpleasant emotions. To accomplish this goal, we may instruct students to recall or imagine situations that elicited such emotions and to focus on the thoughts experienced in those situations.

Next, Beck recommended the use of several techniques to counteract the debilitating thoughts or dysfunctional assumptions contributing to the emotional distress. One popular technique is reality checking or hypothesis testing. After students have identified the debilitating beliefs or thoughts and have learned to distinguish them as hypotheses rather than as reality, they are in a position to test them experimentally (Martin & Pear, 1996). For example, if a student believes that everyone who smiles is teasing her, then we might help her devise a system for reading context and judging peers' facial expressions and body language so that she can determine objectively if the thoughts related to her problem are indeed accurate.

The third step is to assign students homework assignments that require practicing appropriate behaviors. For example, some students who are depressed rarely engage in pleasurable activities such as visiting friends or going to the movies. Others frequently avoid performing everyday chores such as showering, bed making, or housecleaning. Homework assignments might focus on having these students reestablish these behaviors. Homework *general steps*

TABLE 13.4	STEPS IN COGNITIVE RESTRUCTURING
Step	**Description**
Introduce treatment rationale.	Attempt to instill the belief that self-talk can influence performance and that negative self-statements result in emotional distress and counterproductive behavior.
Identify client thoughts in problem situations.	Analyze the client's thoughts during anxiety-provoking or distressing situations using interviewing and client and therapist modeling.
Introduce and practice coping thoughts.	Shift away from negative thoughts and toward coping statements. An explanation and examples of coping thoughts are provided before clients generate their own coping thoughts and practice them.
Shift from self-defeating to coping thoughts.	Move from self-defeating to coping thoughts during problematic situations. Practice helps clients use self-defeating thoughts as a cue for an immediate shift to coping thoughts.
Introduce and practice reinforcing self-statements.	Teach clients how to reinforce themselves for having copies. The therapist models and clients practice positive or reinforcing self-statements.
Do homework and follow-up.	Instruct clients to use cognitive restructuring during real-life situations. The therapist provides homework log sheets containing written directions on how to practice learned skills.

Source: Cormier & Cormier (1985).

assignments could also involve role-playing. For example, a student who is fearful of social interaction may role-play carrying on a conversation with peers after school.

Steps in Cognitive Restructuring   Martin and Pear (1996) pointed out some obvious similarities between Beck's cognitive therapy and Ellis's RET. First, both assume that emotional distress and inappropriate behavior are caused by irrational or illogical interpretations of events. Second, both focus on eliminating irrational thinking. Third, both use homework assignments that focus on having students perform appropriate behaviors. Martin and Pear also pointed out two differences between the approaches. First, Ellis focused much more heavily on clients' tendency to awfulize or catastrophize than did Beck. Second, in therapy sessions, Ellis was much more confrontational with clients than Beck as a way to help them change irrational beliefs.

Although the therapies of Ellis and Beck are the most popular forms of cognitive restructuring, others have developed programs based on the idea of identifying and changing irrational beliefs. For example, Baker, Thomas, and Munson (1983) developed a primary prevention unit titled "Cleaning Up

Our Thinking" for junior and senior high students. Forman (1980) used cognitive restructuring to modify the aggressive behavior of elementary students. Although the specific interventions and populations may vary, Cormier and Cormier (1985) described six general steps for conducting cognitive restructuring that are summarized in Table 13.4.

SUMMARY

Cognitive-behavior modification represents an extension of traditional applied behavior analysis techniques. The rationale for the use of cognitive-behavior modification is that cognition affects behavior. Therefore, changing the way students interpret situations will result in positive changes in their behavior. Cognitive-behavior modification was heavily influenced by the concept of reciprocal determinism. It is not easy to assess cognition because this activity is covert. Therefore, we must infer cognition through observation of behavior and through self-reports.

Cognitive assessment techniques vary in their degree of structure and in terms of when information was collected relative to the occurrence of a thought. Cognitive-behavior modification interventions vary as well. Self-instruction and attribution retraining are the most frequently used with students and are easy to implement. Thought stopping is more of a clinical technique that helps students stop making irrational self-statements that lead to emotional distress. Problem-solving training is the goal of all cognitive-behavior modification interventions. Problem-solving training can be implemented in a variety of ways with preschool, elementary, middle, and secondary students. The cognitive restructuring techniques of Ellis and Beck are designed to help students interpret situations more factually.

ACTIVITIES

1. Keep a log of the number of positive and negative self-statements you make during the course of the day. Which ones occurred most often, and why?

2. List 10 physical injuries starting with the most minor (e.g., a mosquito bite) and ending with the worst (e.g., death). Keep this list in your car. The next time someone else's bad driving bothers you, ask yourself "How bad is it?" In other words, how much physical pain are you willing to endure to have the other driver not cut in front of you? By framing events in terms of physical pain, you should be able to reduce the level of your emotional arousal.

3. List five common student problems for which you think some type of cognitive-behavior modification technique might be effective. Then list five common student problems for which you think cognitive-behavior modification techniques would not be effective. What are the differences in the types of behaviors?

REVIEW QUESTIONS

1. How does the cognitive A-B-C model differ from the applied behavior analysis A-B-C model?
2. How have past trends in cognitive therapy contributed to current cognitive-behavior modification techniques?
3. What are the dangers in assessing cognition through the inference of behavior?
4. How do temporality and degree of structure affect information obtained from cognitive assessment techniques?
5. Describe the nine types of cognitive assessment techniques.
6. What are the steps in self-instruction training?
7. What are the factors that can influence the effectiveness of self-instructions?
8. What are the two phases of attribution retraining?
9. What factors should be considered before implementing attribution retraining?
10. What factors should be examined when considering the use of thought stopping?
11. What are the steps for implementing thought stopping?
12. What are the four problem-solving skills?
13. What are the five components for teaching problem solving?
14. How are rational-emotive therapy and cognitive therapy similar and different?

REFERENCES

Arrick, M., Voss, J. R., & Rimm, D. C. (1981). The relative efficacy of thought-stopping and covert assertion. *Behaviour Research and Therapy, 19*, 17–24.

Baker, S. B., Thomas, R. N., & Munson, W. W. (1983). Effects of cognitive restructuring and structured group discussion as primary prevention strategies. *School Counselor, 31*, 26–33.

Bandura, A. (1978). The self system in reciprocal determinism. *American Psychologist, 33,* 344–358.

Beck, A. T. (1967). *Depression: Causes and treatment.* Philadelphia: University of Pennsylvania Press.

Beck, A. T., Rush, A. J., Shaw, B. F., & Emery, G. (1979). *Cognitive therapy of depression.* New York: Guilford.

Braswell, L., & Kendall, P. C. (1988). Cognitive-behavioral methods with children. In K. S. Dobson (Ed.), *Handbook of cognitive-behavioral therapies* (pp. 167–213). New York: Guilford.

Cormier, W. H., & Cormier, L. S. (1985). *Interviewing strategies for helpers: Fundamental skills and cognitive behavioral interventions* (2nd ed.). Monterey, CA: Brooks/Cole.

Diener, C. I., & Dweck, C. S. (1978). An analysis of learned helplessness: Continuous changes in performance, strategy, and achievement cognitions following failure. *Journal of Personality and Social Psychology, 36,* 451–462.

Dobson, K. S., & Block, L. (1988). Historical and philosophical bases of the cognitive-behavioral therapies. In K. S. Dobson (Ed.), *Handbook of cognitive-behavioral therapies* (pp. 3–38). New York: Guilford.

Dryden, W., & DiGiuseppe, R. (1990). *A primer on rational-emotive therapy.* Champaign, IL: Research Press.

Dweck, C. S. (1975). The role of expectations and attributions in the alteration of learned helplessness. *Journal of Personality and Social Psychology, 25,* 109–116.

Dweck, C. S., & Reppucci, D. (1973). Learned helplessness and reinforcement responsibility in children. *Journal of Personality and Social Psychology, 25,* 109–116.

D'Zurilla, T. J. (1988). Problem-solving therapies. In K. S. Dobson (Ed.), *Handbook of cognitive-behavioral therapies* (pp. 85–135). New York: Guilford.

Ellis, A. (1962). *Reason and emotion in psychotherapy.* New York: Stuart.

Forman, S. G. (1980). A comparison of cognitive training and response cost procedures in modifying aggressive behavior of elementary school children. *Behavior Therapy, 11,* 594–600.

Gesten, E. L., Weissberg, R. P., Amish, P. L., & Smith, J. K. (1987). Social problem-solving training: A skills-based approach to prevention and treatment. In C. A. Maher & J. E. Zins (Eds.), *Psychoeducational interventions in the schools* (pp. 26–45). New York: Pergamon.

Goldstein, A. P. (1988). *The prepare curriculum.* Champaign, IL: Research Press.

Harris, K. R. (1982). Cognitive-behavior modification: Applications with exceptional students. *Focus on Exceptional Children, 15*(2), 1–16.

Hollon, S. D., & Kendall, P. C. (1980). Cognitive self-statements in depression: Development of an automatic thoughts questionnaire. *Cognitive Therapy and Research, 4,* 383–395.

Hughes, J. N. (1988). *Cognitive behavior therapy with children in schools.* New York: Pergamon.

Kendall, P. C. (1977). On the efficacious use of verbal self-instructional procedures with children. *Cognitive Therapy and Research, 1,* 331–341.

Kendall, P. C., & Braswell, L. (1985). Cognitive-behavioral self-control therapy for children: A component analysis. *Journal of Consulting and Clinical Psychology, 50,* 672–689.

Kendall, P. C., & Hollon, S. D. (1979). Cognitive-behavioral interventions: Overview and current status. In P. C. Kendall & S. D. Hollon (Eds.), *Cognitive-behavioral interventions: Theory, research and procedures* (pp. 1–9). New York: Academic Press.

Lazarus, A. A. (1971). *Behavior therapy and beyond.* New York: McGraw-Hill.

Licht, B. G., & Kistner, J. A. (1986). Motivational problems of learning disabled children: Individual differences and their implications for treatment. In J. K. Torgeson & B. Y. L. Wong (Eds.), *Psychological and educational perspectives on learning disabilities* (pp. 225–249). New York: Academic Press.

Luria, A. R. (1961). *The role of speech in the regulation of normal and abnormal behaviors.* New York: Liverwright.

Mahoney, M. J. (1974). *Cognition and behavior modification.* Cambridge, MA: Ballinger.

Martin, G., & Pear, J. (1996). *Behavior modification: What it is and how to do it* (5th ed.). Upper Saddle River, NJ: Prentice-Hall.

Meichenbaum, D. (1985). *Stress inoculation training.* New York: Pergamon.

Meichenbaum, D., & Goodman, J. (1971). Training impulsive children to talk to themselves: A means of developing self-control. *Journal of Abnormal Psychology, 77,* 115–126.

Michelson, L. Sugai, D., Wood, R., & Kazdin, A. (1983). *Social skills assessment and training with children.* New York: Plenum.

Morrow, L. W., & Morrow, S. A. (1985). Use of verbal mediation procedures to reduce talking-out behaviors. In M. K. Zabel (Ed.), *TEACHING: Behaviorally disordered youth* (Vol. 1, pp. 23–28). Reston, VA: Council for Children with Behavioral Disorders.

Neisser, U. (1967). *Cognitive psychology.* New York: Appleton-Century-Crofts.

Olin, R. J. (1976). Thought stopping: Some cautionary observations. *Behavior Therapy, 7,* 706–707.

Rimm, D. C., & Masters, J. C. (1979). *Behavior therapy: Techniques and empirical findings* (2nd ed.). New York: Academic Press.

Robin, A., Schneider, M., & Dolnick, M. (1976). The turtle technique: An extended case study of self-control in the classroom. *Psychology in the Schools, 13,* 449–453.

Schunk, P. H. (1983). Ability versus effort attributional feedback: Differential effects on self-efficacy and achievement. *Journal of Educational Psychology, 75,* 848–856.

Segal, Z. V., & Shaw, B. F. (1988). Cognitive assessment: Issues and methods. In K. S. Dobson (Ed.), *Handbook of cognitive-behavioral therapies* (pp. 39–81). New York: Guilford.

Short, E. J., & Ryan, E. B. (1984). Metacognitive differences between skilled and less skilled readers: Remediating deficits through story grammar and attribution training. *Journal of Educational Psychology, 76,* 225–235.

Shure, M. B., & Spivack, G. (1974). *Interpersonal cognitive problem-solving (ICPS): A mental health program for kindergarten and first-grade children: Training script.* Philadelphia: Hahnemann University, Department of Mental Health Sciences.

Siegel, J. M., & Spivak, G. (1973). *Problem-solving therapy* (Research Report 23). Philadelphia: Hahnemann Medical College.

Taylor, J. G. (1963). A behavioral interpretation of obsessive-compulsive neurosis. *Behaviour Research and Therapy, 1,* 237–244.

Vygotsky, L. (1962). *Thought and language.* New York: Wiley.

Wolpe, J. (1971). Dealing with resistance to thought-stopping: A transcript. *Journal of Behavior Therapy and Experimental Psychiatry, 2,* 121–125.

Wolpe, J. (1982). *The practice of behavior therapy* (3rd ed.). New York: Pergamon.

Zirpoli, T. J., & Melloy, K. J. (1997). *Behavior management: Applications for teachers and parents* (2nd ed.). Columbus, OH: Merrill.

PROMOTING GENERALIZATION

CHAPTER OVERVIEW

- An Overview of Generalization

- Tactics for Promoting Generalization

- Recommendations for Applying Generalization Tactics

- Issues in Promoting Generalization

CHAPTER OBJECTIVES

After completing this chapter, you will be able to do the following:

1. Describe the different types of and approaches to generalization.

2. Identify methods of promoting generalization.

3. Describe recommendations for applying generalization strategies.

4. Explain issues in promoting generalization.

An important goal of any behavior management technique is to promote **generality of behavior change.** One of the first comprehensive discussions on this topic was provided by Baer, Wolf, and Risley (1968), who stated that "a behavior change may be said to have generality if it proves durable over time, if it appears in a wide variety of possible environments, or if it spreads to a wide variety of related behaviors" (p. 96). The word **generalization** is most often used in the applied literature to describe behavior changes that occur in nontraining conditions (Cooper, Heron, & Heward, 1987).

Many of the cognitive and self-management techniques described in the two previous chapters may be used to promote generalization because they are internal; thus, once learned, students can use them regardless of the setting or time. In addition, behaviorally oriented strategies for promoting generalization have been around since the publication of the seminal article on the topic by Stokes and Baer (1977). Nevertheless, these techniques are rarely incorporated into interventions. For example, of the 5300 behavioral treatment studies with children and adolescents reviewed by Rutherford and Nelson (1988), less than 2 percent addressed generalization and maintenance. The reasons for this omission will soon become clear.

This chapter provides information on and techniques for promoting generalization. To accomplish this purpose, several topics are covered. First, an overview of generalization is given, including a description of the different types of generalization. Second, several tactics for promoting generalization are described. Third, some recommendations for applying generalization strategies are presented. Fourth, issues in promoting generalization are discussed. The main emphasis of this chapter is on programming strategies for promoting generalization into any intervention from its inception. Rarely will generalization occur simply by training and hoping (Stokes & Baer, 1977).

> The lack of generalization programming may be partially due to the belief that generalization is the final step of an intervention to be addressed. However, generalization should be built into interventions from their inception.

AN OVERVIEW OF GENERALIZATION

During the 1960s and 1970s, a large body of literature accumulated that described the effectiveness of interventions based on applied behavior analysis (ABA). However, much of this research failed to address the issue of generalization. The problem of generalization was of central concern to special educators, who were able to teach students with disabilities a variety of skills in highly structured settings only to have them fail to perform the skills outside of training environments. Several different types of generalization and approaches to generalization are important to educators.

TABLE 14.1 TERMS ASSOCIATED WITH GENERALIZATION

Term	Description
Stimulus generalization, transfer of training	Refers to generality across settings, people, and conditions
Response generalization, concomitant behavior change	Refers to development of related behaviors not directly trained
Response maintenance, resistance to extinction, behavioral persistence, durability	Refers to behavior changes that persist over time

Types of Generalization

Stokes and Baer (1977) defined generalization as the "occurrence of relevant behavior under different non-training conditions (i.e., across subjects, settings, people, behaviors, and/or time) without the scheduling of the same events in those conditions as had been scheduled in the training condition" (p. 350). Although this definition is sensible, it does not specify environmental factors that contribute to the occurrence of generalization. In addition, a variety of terms are often used interchangeably to refer to generalization. These terms are summarized in Table 14.1 and discussed in more detail in the following paragraphs. Sulzer-Azaroff and Mayer (1977) suggested that the first two types of generalization—stimulus generalization and response generalization—are most important in teaching students appropriate behaviors.

It may be helpful to review the definitions of the terms *stimulus control, stimulus discrimination,* and *stimulus generalization* in Chapter 4.

Stimulus Generalization Stimulus generalization occurs when students perform behaviors in settings or in the presence of stimuli other than those in which an intervention took place (Rutherford & Nelson, 1988). For example, a student might learn to raise her hand before asking a question in one teacher's class and perform this behavior in another teacher's class. Or a student might learn to say "Excuse me" when he burps and also say "Excuse me" when he bumps into another person or wants to get the attention of a teacher who is talking to another student.

Response Generalization Response generalization occurs when students perform behaviors that were not specifically targeted for intervention. These behaviors are usually members of the same response class as the one targeted for intervention but have not received the intervention. For example, a student who was taught to raise his hand to get assistance may also call out the teacher's name. Or a student who learned a strategy for organizing a mathematics word problem may develop her own strategy for organizing a science formula.

TABLE 14.2   CATEGORIES RELATED TO A TECHNOLOGY OF GENERALIZATION

Category	Description
Natural maintaining contingencies	Uses trapping manipulations, in which responses are introduced to natural reinforcement communities, which refine and maintain target skills without additional intervention
Training sufficient exemplars	Involves learning sufficient exemplars of stimulus conditions or responses
Training loosely	Is conducted with relatively little control over the antecedents and behaviors involved
Indiscriminable contingencies	Deliberately makes antecedent conditions and contingencies less predictable so that it becomes difficult to discriminate reinforcement occasions from nonreinforcement occasions
Common stimuli	Incorporates into training settings social and physical stimuli that appear in generalization settings
Mediated generalization	Establishes a response as part of new learning that can be used for other problems and in other situations
Training "to generalize"	Reinforces generalization as if it were a target behavior

Response Maintenance   When students perform behaviors after an intervention has been terminated, **response maintenance** is said to occur. For example, a student may be taught a conflict avoidance strategy for 2 weeks at the beginning of the school year. Response maintenance has occurred if the student is still using the strategy at the end of the semester or year. This type of generalization is extremely important to educators. The full-inclusion movement and shrinking resources often result in school personnel having limited time to do interventions with students. Therefore, it is important that interventions produce changes in behaviors that are maintained after the intervention is discontinued.

Approaches to Generalization

Since the term "train and hope" was coined, it has become a catchphrase for the failures of studies to obtain generalization. Even cognitive techniques have not automatically led to generalization—it must be programmed.

Baer, Wolf, and Risley (1968) first discussed the notion that generalization must be specifically planned and rarely occurs spontaneously. Stokes and Baer (1977) later coined the phrase "train and hope" to describe how many teachers approach generalization. They presented seven categories related to a technology of generalization, which are summarized in Table 14.2. They also offered seven specific strategies that can be subsumed under the list of categories in Table 14.2:

1. Look for a response that enters a natural community; in particular, teach subjects to cue their potential natural communities to reinforce their desirable behaviors.

2. Keep training more exemplars; in particular, diversify them.
3. Loosen experimental control over the stimuli and responses involved in training; in particular, train different examples concurrently, and vary instructions, S^Ds, social reinforcers, and backup reinforcers.
4. Make unclear the limits of training contingencies; in particular, conceal, when possible, the point at which those contingencies stop operating, possibly by delayed reinforcement.
5. Use stimuli that are likely to be found in generalization settings in training settings as well; in particular, use peers as tutors.
6. Reinforce accurate self-reports of desirable behavior; apply self-recording and self-reinforcement techniques whenever possible.
7. When generalizations occur, reinforce at least some of them at least sometimes, as if "to generalize" were an operant response class. (p. 364)

An S^D is simply a discriminative stimulus.

A variety of instructional programs have been developed to teach these strategies. For example, Lenz, Schumaker, Alley, and Deshler (1981) created a two-stage program to promote generalization of learning strategy interventions in students with learning disabilities. The first stage involves the use of modeling, verbal rehearsal, feedback, and practice with materials while students are being taught the learning strategy. The second stage places less emphasis on variables that the teacher controls and more emphasis on those variables that students control (e.g., motivation, awareness of need for the strategy, and conditions of generalization). Group brainstorming of possible strategy use, planned attempts at strategy use with student reports, and a maintenance procedure featuring goal setting, student reports, and reports from various teachers are used in this stage.

Given the variety of approaches, components, and strategies, it is hardly surprising that promoting generalization is a detailed and tedious process. The following case study illustrates the complexity involved in what at first glance may appear to be a straightforward approach to promote a student's use of socially appropriate behavior.

This case study should point out the importance of using a comprehensive and integrated approach to promoting generalization.

A Case Study in Generalization

Todd was a 12-year-old boy with a learning disability who had been receiving special education services since he was in third grade. His teachers reported that he frequently was disruptive, inattentive, and noncompliant in their classrooms. Therefore, the school psychologist and his special education teacher developed an intervention to decrease these behaviors.

The first step was to interview Todd's teachers to determine the exact nature and extent of the problems. All his teachers reported problems from the first week of class, indicating that perhaps he was having a difficult time adjusting to the increased academic and behavioral expectations he encountered in middle school. His teachers were then asked to specifically describe what they meant by the labels "disruptive," "inattentive," and "noncompliant." The common behaviors the teachers reported for "disruptive" were making animal noises and laughing. "Inattentive" was defined as looking out the window and not knowing the answers to questions. Todd's refusal to follow directions was endorsed by all his teachers as indicative of his being "noncompliant."

His teachers were then asked how they responded to each of these behaviors. Some teachers ignored them until they became too disruptive to other students and then administered verbal reprimands. Other teachers either sent Todd to the principal's office or kept him after school. All the teachers said that these behaviors were worse toward the end of the week, but they were also less likely to punish him at this time because it wasn't viewed as being worth the effort. After obtaining this information, the psychologist and special education teacher arranged to observe Todd in several classes in order to form hypotheses regarding the function these behaviors served.

Functional Assessment   The school psychologist and special education teacher were ready to analyze the behaviors to determine the function of each. This analysis was conducted relative to the teacher–student interactions, task demands of each class, classroom structure, and types of activities employed (e.g., lecture, small group, or individual seat-work).

The "disruptive" behaviors occurred mostly during lecture and large-group activities. Therefore, it was hypothesized that these behaviors resulted in increased attention from peers and teachers. The "inattentive" behaviors also occurred during lecture and large-group activities. They were believed to serve the function of escape and avoidance because Todd did not always understand the material being presented. The "noncompliant" behaviors occurred at various points in a given class but resulted in the largest number of teacher reprimands. Therefore, it was hypothesized that refusal to follow directions served the function of attention. It was agreed that the "disruptive" and "noncompliant" behaviors resulted in Todd's receiving positive reinforcement from peers and teachers. Todd probably was negatively reinforced for engaging in the "inattentive" behaviors.

Intervention   Following the functional assessment, the school psychologist and special education teacher first designed an intervention to reduce the positive and negative reinforcement Todd was obtaining for engaging in the inappropriate behaviors. Specifically, his teachers were told to ignore his inappropriate behavior and provide him with praise when he was sitting in his seat, maintaining eye contact with the teacher, or working on an assignment. His teachers were also instructed to provide reinforcement to students who ignored Todd when he made animal noises or laughed. To avoid power struggles resulting from Todd's refusal to follow directions, the teachers were taught to use the compliance matrix, as described in Chapter 9. For his part, Todd was taught several replacement behaviors that accomplished the same outcome as the inappropriate behaviors. Specifically, he was taught how to appropriately obtain the attention of teachers and peers through the use of questions and comments relevant to course content. He also was taught the requisite skills for completing assignments as a way to eliminate the desire to escape and avoid the tasks. And he was taught the behavior of asking for a short break as an appropriate way to escape task demands. In addition, the teachers were asked to let Todd set some of the criteria for homework assignments as another way for him to obtain power/control.

Analysis   Given this summary of a functional assessment and treatment plan, how effective are these interventions likely to be in facilitating generalized behavior change? How many of the characteristics described in Table 14.2 were employed in the interventions? What additional techniques could have been employed to promote generalization? These questions can be answered based on the discussion of tactics for promoting generalization presented next.

TACTICS FOR PROMOTING GENERALIZATION

Tactics for promoting generalization are based on three general principles described by Stokes and Osnes (1986). The first principle involves **taking advantage of natural communities of reinforcement.** Generalization is more likely to occur when peers reinforce target students for performing appropriate behaviors. The second principle, **training diversely,** emphasizes the importance of maintaining the minimum training control necessary. This principle ensures that the diversity of natural settings is incorporated into training as much as possible. The third principle involves **incorporating functional mediators.** This principle simply makes use of as many discriminative stimuli as possible in the training environment. In this way, students learn that a variety of stimuli can serve as cues to engage in appropriate behavior. There are 11 generalization tactics based on these three assumptions.

Taking Advantage of Natural Communities of Reinforcement

There are three specific tactics in this category: (1) teach relevant behaviors, (2) modify environments supporting maladaptive behaviors, and (3) recruit natural communities of reinforcement.

Teach Relevant Behaviors   Relevant behaviors are those that are likely to be reinforced in natural settings. For example, we are more likely to respond positively to students who maintain eye contact and raise their hands before talking than to students who doodle and blurt out answers. Similarly, peers are

Targeting socially valid behaviors before intervention represents one way generalization can be programmed into an intervention from its inception.

more likely to reinforce students who smile and tell funny stories than those who pick their noses or start fights. Therefore, our goal is to maximize the performance of appropriate behaviors that can be reinforced by us and by peers.

The concept of social validity provides a basis for identifying relevant behaviors. Recall that social validity refers to whether the behaviors targeted for intervention enhance the quality of students' lives (Wolf, 1978). The quality of students' lives is enhanced if learning and using new behaviors results in stronger friendships with peers, better grades and attendance in school, and improved relationships with significant adults. Sometimes behaviors are targeted for intervention without considering whether they are socially relevant. For example, teaching an adolescent to be assertive in a classroom setting may benefit us by reducing aggressive interactions, but the behavior might not be reinforced by peers at a party. In this case, assertion will not generalize to other settings.

Sheldon, Sherman, Schumaker, and Hazel (1984) developed a multimethod procedure for identifying socially valid behaviors. They began by compiling a list of behavioral deficits from a review of research literature. They also had students and teachers list the social situations and specific social skill problems of students. Information from this survey and the list of social skills derived from the literature review were condensed into social skill clusters. Experts then judged the social importance of each skill and the situations in which the skills were to be used.

We can use a similar procedure in the classroom. First, we identify socially competent students using peer or our own nominations. Next, we observe their behaviors to determine which ones they use during various social situations. Then we instruct students to list appropriate behaviors for interacting with others. Finally, we target behaviors appearing in both categories for intervention.

Modify Environments Supporting Maladaptive Behaviors Consequences follow all behaviors and can either maintain, increase, or decrease them. Sometimes consequences may function to either reinforce inappropriate behavior or punish appropriate behavior. For example, a student may obtain a teacher's attention by making animal noises. This behavior will likely persist, even if the student is given an acceptable replacement behavior for obtaining the teacher's attention, if the peer group provides him with attention for making animal noises. Sometimes peers will punish students for performing appropriate replacement behaviors. For example, a student who asks the teacher polite questions may be ridiculed by her peers for trying to "suck up" to the teacher or for being the "teacher's pet." In this case, the target behavior is not likely to generalize or be maintained after intervention is terminated because the student will be punished by her peer group.

Techniques such as a token economy, behavioral contracting, and group-oriented contingencies can be used with peers to reduce negative attention and increase positive attention for the target student's appropriate behaviors. Specifically, in a token economy, peers can earn points every time they ignore the target student's inappropriate behavior. Students can then exchange points for the opportunity to engage in preferred activities at the end of class or the day. A behavioral contract can be used if there is one particularly troublesome peer who constantly provides the target student with reinforcement for engaging in inappropriate behavior. A dependent group-oriented contingency can also be used with this peer. Or an interdependent group-oriented contingency can be used in which everyone has to ignore the target student when he engages in inappropriate behavior before anyone in the class can have access to a reinforcer.

Recruit Natural Communities of Reinforcement   Sometimes a natural community of reinforcement does not exist to "entrap" the target behavior. **Entrapment** occurs when peers reinforce students for performing socially appropriate behavior (McConnell, 1987). For example, a student may ask a peer to join in a game of jump rope. If this offer results in a positive response from the peer, it is likely to be repeated in the future. In other instances, a natural community of reinforcement may exist but be dormant. For example, if the peer who is asked to jump rope is already playing hopscotch and so ignores the offer, then asking to participate may be extinguished.

Our goal in recruiting natural communities of reinforcement is twofold. First, we must teach students socially valid behaviors so that they will be naturally reinforced by peers. Second, we want to restructure existing reinforcement contingencies in peer groups so that newly acquired behaviors will become entrapped. We can promote entrapment by ensuring that students in peer groups are socially competent and friendly and by identifying peers' behaviors that target students will find reinforcing (McConnell, 1987).

The impact of recruiting natural communities of reinforcement illustrates the importance of focusing intervention on the peer group and the target student.

Training Diversely

There are five tactics for training diversely: (1) use sufficient stimulus exemplars, (2) use sufficient response exemplars, (3) train loosely, (4) use indiscriminable contingencies, and (5) reinforce unprompted generalization. The focus of these tactics is to employ a range of antecedents and consequences to expose students to the diversity they will encounter in natural environments.

Use Sufficient Stimulus Exemplars   Stimuli that remain unchanged during intervention are the only ones that cue students' behaviors in nontraining settings. Therefore, generalization is enhanced when a variety of stimulus

The goal of stimulus exemplars is to have them attain stimulus control over targeted behaviors.

exemplars are incorporated into training. **Exemplars** refer to stimuli that are typical or representative of those found in the settings in which generalization is desired. They serve as a pattern or guide for cuing behavior.

Stokes and Osnes (1986) recommended that a variety of stimulus exemplars be introduced gradually into training. It is beneficial to initially have only a few well-defined stimuli cue the performance of the target behaviors. Once the target behavior is performed consistently in response to a few stimuli, a diversity of exemplars can be included in the stimulus conditions. It is better to have too many than too few related exemplars. This process does not have to be burdensome. For example, Stokes, Baer, and Jackson (1974) taught children who were mentally retarded to generalize the behavior of "greeting others" to over 20 staff members simply by using 2 staff members during intervention.

For this tactic to be effective, we need to specify the extent of generalization desired. If generalization across people and settings is desired, then we should identify the type of people the target student will encounter and the setting events, and incorporate this information into the training. For example, if the goal is to have a high school student learn to raise his hand to answer questions in all his classes, then intervention should be conducted in various classrooms with different teachers, textbooks, and materials. The idea is to present the student with multiple stimuli that cue the performance of the target behavior. This recommendation is not as burdensome to implement as it first may appear.

Use Sufficient Response Exemplars   The use of many response exemplars is a tactic for promoting generalization across behaviors because the target behavior may belong to several different response classes. Therefore, it is helpful to incorporate into training several examples of similar behaviors that belong to the same response class. For example, a student may be trained to raise her hand to ask for assistance from a teacher. Other appropriate members of this response class may include walking up to the teacher's desk and calling out the teacher's name politely. These latter two behaviors need to be incorporated into training if generalization is to occur. For example, if a teacher is busy grading papers at her desk, she may not see a student's raised hand. In this case, the ability to obtain teacher assistance rests on the student's ability to select a similarly appropriate behavior such as approaching her desk or calling out her name.

Train Loosely   Training loosely incorporates aspects of sufficient stimulus and response exemplars into the intervention. Stokes and Osnes (1986) stated that "a little controlled chaos is more advantageous than carefully controlled order" (p. 425). The idea is to ensure that distractions occur sometimes, but not always, in the training setting. This tactic is the opposite of the typical approach of teaching students skills in highly structured settings in which all extraneous and distracting stimuli are minimized. Although this latter approach may result in students' quickly acquiring the target behavior, little generalization is likely to occur. The reason is that real-world environments seldom have constant and controlled structures. Therefore, students who have not been exposed to a variety of stimulus and response conditions during training will not know how to behave when confronted with the diversity most environments contain.

Neel (1988) described two strategies for teaching social skills that reflect nicely the idea of training loosely. First, he emphasized the importance of setting up a place for students to work together. Some teachers design classrooms to minimize interaction as a way to reduce students' feeding into each others' negative behavior. Although this approach may promote appropriate behavior in training settings, it is unlikely to promote generalization. An alternative approach is to rearrange the classroom to encourage interaction, put certain students in charge of different sets of supplies and services, and create more work tables. Second, Neel suggested developing management programs that promote social interaction. Often, we want students to interact appropriately but set up behavior management systems that reinforce students for sitting quietly in their seats and talking only when they raise their hands. This approach to behavior management does not promote entrapment, nor does it incorporate enough diversity to produce generalization.

The approach of training loosely may be incorporated into an intervention from its inception or gradually incorporated later on. The advantage of training loosely when the intervention is first implemented is that students are quickly exposed to various stimulus and response exemplars that exist in natural environments. If students do not respond favorably to these cues, they can become a focus of future training. A disadvantage is that it may take students longer to learn and perform target behaviors when they are inundated with exemplars during training. Therefore, loose training may gradually be incorporated into the intervention after students begin performing the target behavior on a regular basis. This approach is analogous to starting students on a continuous schedule of reinforcement to get a new behavior performed regularly and then moving to a more intermittent schedule.

Use Indiscriminable Contingencies   Predictable consequences help students determine what behaviors will be followed by either reinforcement or punishment. Although this approach initially helps students acquire and perform target behaviors, it may be counterproductive in the long run because it will be difficult for them to adapt to the variability in consequences that exist from teacher to teacher. Therefore, to enhance generalizability, consequences should be made progressively less discriminable. This approach is the consequence equivalent of training loosely (Stokes & Osnes, 1986).

The easiest way to introduce indiscriminable contingencies is to use intermittent schedules of reinforcement as soon as students are regularly performing a new behavior. In addition, we can occasionally present a reinforcer used in training noncontingently in nontraining environments, after intervention had been terminated, to enhance maintenance. The reason is that reinforcers may serve as a cue for students to perform the target behavior. For example, the reinforcer for a student's being taught to ask for help may be our approaching him and, while smiling, offering assistance. In nontraining settings, we approach the student and offer assistance in a noncontingent and unpredictable manner.

The presence of vicarious reinforcement is another example of indiscriminable contingencies. As we learned in Chapter 3, when students see a model responded to positively, they want to remember what the model did so that they can maximize their own reinforcement by performing the same behavior. An application of vicarious reinforcement is to occasionally reinforce peers for performing the behaviors taught to the target student during intervention.

Reinforce Unprompted Generalization   Occasionally, generalization will occur on its own. When this happens, we want to immediately reinforce the generalization performance. In this approach—sometimes called "training to generalize"—generalization itself is a target behavior to be reinforced. Stokes and Osnes (1986) described a variation of this tactic in which target skills are reinforced in novel situations or untrained behaviors belonging to the same response class as the target behavior are reinforced in training settings.

> Reinforcing unprompted generalizations forces teachers to catch students being good rather than simply expecting appropriate behavior and reacting to inappropriate behavior.

Incorporating Functional Mediators

Generalization that incorporates functional mediators features three tactics: (1) Use common physical stimuli, (2) use common social stimuli, and (3) use self-mediated stimuli. These three tactics focus on providing students with various antecedent stimuli that will prompt the use of target behaviors in different settings.

Use Common Physical Stimuli   One of the guiding principles for selecting discriminative stimuli is that they must be salient. Physically salient stimuli are those that are obvious to students, such as tables, chairs, lights, books, toys, adults, and peers. It is important that salient stimuli be incorporated into training and also be present in nontraining settings in order for them to promote generalization.

Not all physical stimuli serve equally well as discriminative stimuli. Stokes and Osnes (1986) recommended that physical stimuli be tested to determine which ones are most likely to function as discriminative stimuli. We want to make obvious a variety of physical stimuli during intervention and see which ones are most likely to prompt the occurrence of the target behavior. These physical stimuli are then incorporated into nontraining settings. For example, we may determine that a certain placement of our desk is most likely to prompt the occurrence of the target behavior. Therefore, the placement of the desk should remain constant in nontraining settings. In addition, the target behavior should be reinforced in the presence of the physical stimulus but not in its absence. After the target behavior has come under control of the discriminative stimulus, the placement of the desk can gradually be changed across settings.

Use Common Social Stimuli   Certain social stimuli such as peers, parents, siblings, and teachers may become discriminative stimuli for students performing learned behaviors. Peers may be particularly potent social stimuli because they exist in all classrooms and often participate during interventions. For example, when teaching a student social skills, peers frequently participate in role-plays in the training sessions. These peers also may be present in nontraining sessions and serve as a discriminative stimulus for a student to perform target behaviors. Therefore, peers should be introduced into the training setting so that they acquire a discriminative function (Stokes & Osnes, 1986).

Although there is no guarantee that peers will automatically become discriminative stimuli, their presence in the training setting may help promote generalization. For example, certain peers with whom a student has social interaction problems can be incorporated into training by having them participate in modeling, rehearsal, role-playing, and reinforcement. They can also be present in nontraining settings as a way to prompt the target student to use the newly acquired social skills. As is the case with common physical stimuli, peers are more likely to acquire a discriminative function if a student is reinforced for performing the target behaviors in their presence.

Use Self-Mediated Stimuli   Self-mediated stimuli involve internal rather than external control of students. In essence, the target student and the discriminative stimuli are one and the same. For example, teacher instructions are external stimuli that may assume a discriminative function for a student to engage in some behavior. A self-mediated version of this example involves a student who gives herself a self-instruction to engage in a target behavior. Many of the self-management and cognitive-behavior modification techniques presented in Chapters 12 and 13 are examples of self-mediated stimuli.

Although the process of transferring control from external to internal stimuli may appear to be straightforward, actual implementation can be difficult. There is no guarantee that students will automatically use self-management and verbal mediation (e.g., self-instruction or problem-solving) techniques in nontraining settings. When these techniques do not work, the two most common reasons are that they did not truly function as discriminative stimuli or that they were simply not used by target students. Although the self-mediated techniques associated with cognitive-behavior modification may be important components for promoting generalization, they should not be viewed as a panacea. Programming for generalization requires attention to a variety of factors and should not rely on only one type of tactic.

RECOMMENDATIONS FOR APPLYING GENERALIZATION TACTICS

The generalization tactics described previously should not be implemented after intervention has been terminated. Rather, generalization tactics should be carefully programmed into any intervention from its inception. The programming of generalization tactics into an intervention before it is implemented can be accomplished by following three steps that were described by Baer (1981) and adapted by Cooper, Heron, and Heward (1987).

The first step in incorporating generalization tactics into an intervention is to list all the requisite skills to perform the target behavior and the members of the response class to which the behavior belongs. An intervention will not be effective, nor will generalization occur, if students do not possess the requisite skills for performing the target behavior. Determining whether students possess these skills is a fairly straightforward process, as described in Chapter 7. For example, a student cannot "join a peer group conversation" without possessing the requisite skills listed in Table 7.3.

We should also generate a list of behaviors that are members of the same response class as the target behavior. For example, if the target behavior is having a student raise his hand for assistance, then the other acceptable members of the response class (e.g., calling the teacher's name and approaching the teacher's desk) should also be identified. In this way, we can make decisions as to which behaviors will be taught and which ones will be addressed through generalization tactics.

The second step is to list all the situations, settings, and places in which students will perform the target behavior. For example, for the student joining in a peer group conversation, we should determine what situations will be desirable for doing so—for instance, working with a cooperative learning group, painting scenes for a school play, selecting team members for a basketball game, or participating in an activity at recess. Cooper, Heron, and Heward (1987) suggested that this type of analysis may add more behaviors to the list developed in the previous step.

All identified situations, settings, and places should be prioritized in terms of the most important and the most likely opportunities for students to perform the target behavior. Further A-B-C analyses should be conducted on the prioritized environments in order to identify discriminative stimuli that cue the performance of the target behavior in each situation and setting. The A-B-C analyses will also help us determine what types and schedules of reinforcement exist in nontraining settings. We can then incorporate this antecedent and consequent information into training.

From the discussion of the use of common social stimuli, we know that other people (e.g., peers and adults) are involved in programming for generalization. Baer (1981) suggested grouping these people according to two classifications:

1. A tolerance list that identifies behaviors that must be performed by those who have to merely tolerate the student's behavior
2. An active support list that includes behaviors that must be performed by those who actively support the new behavior by providing cues, opportunities to respond, and reinforcement

In the example of joining in a peer group conversation, a tolerance list might include teachers who will allow the student to join in peer group conversations. Teachers will also have to tolerate the behavior of peers talking during class in order to provide the target student with opportunities to perform the desired behaviors. An active support list might include several key peers who will reinforce the behaviors of the target student. In addition, the specific behaviors of peers should be specified, such as looking and smiling at the target student as he approaches to join in their conversation. Other active support variables may include instructing the peer group to engage in several topics of conversation in which the target student is well versed.

ISSUES IN PROMOTING GENERALIZATION

There is no reason promoting generalization cannot be established in a fashion similar to any other behavior management technique. Stokes and Osnes (1988) discussed several issues relevant to incorporating generalization into an intervention from its inception. These issues are predicated on the belief that developing effective generalization tactics is not easy and the process cannot be learned overnight. It requires time, practice, and, whenever possible, supervision by a professional with experience in promoting generalization. Nevertheless, we have an obligation to our students to incorporate generalization tactics into every intervention.

Generalizing Teacher Repertoire

Besides promoting the generalization of students' behaviors, we should strive to generalize our own repertoires. However, when we are confronted with the

As these steps show, programming generalization is not easy. Yet generalization should be the goal of all educators. Knowledge is useless to students unless they can apply it in a larger context than a classroom.

Because programming for generalization can be such a daunting task, it is important for teachers to "think small" and identify a short period during which the target behavior is performed in a nontraining setting.

challenges of promoting generalization, the tendency is to revert to techniques we have used in the past, even when they did not lead to generalization.

We should strive to be comprehensive and unrestricting in our thinking. This mentality is not easy to put into practice because we tend to follow a very careful routine without realizing we are restricting our behavior. Fisch, Weakland, and Segal (1982) suggested that when we limit our options students' misbehaviors becomes more severe because the initial problem was mishandled and remains unresolved. Consequently, we often apply linear interventions (Watzlawick, Weakland, & Fisch, 1974). For example, if a student is kept after school for misbehaving, the problem is presumed to have been addressed by the punishment. But what if the student misbehaves again? The linear solution is to keep the student after school for 2 days, then 3, and so forth. This type of solution, called "more of the same," seldom works. Stokes and Osnes (1988) recommended breaking this pattern by relating successful generalization tactics to principles of behavior and using them as mediators in planning for generalization changes.

Using Functional Contingencies

Conducting functional assessment improves the effectiveness of generalization tactics. The reason is that results of functional assessment help us develop contextual, curricular, and replacement behavior strategies. Manipulating contextual variables provides students with common physical and social stimuli necessary for successful generalization. Curricular modifications help students view learning tasks as something within their grasp rather than as a cue to misbehave. Replacement behavior training is perhaps the most important aspect of promoting generalization. The reason is that, once students have an acceptable replacement behavior in their repertoire, they can use it in any situation or setting to obtain a desired outcome. Functional assessment should always proceed systematically in order to generate socially valid contextual, curricular, and functional hypotheses.

Providing Sufficient Detail

Although it is time consuming to provide sufficient detail, it is impossible to effectively implement interventions without it. The same principle holds for generalization programming. A specific plan for promoting generalization should be formulated at the same time the initial intervention is being developed. Through direct observation and feedback from others, we may modify the generalization plan. This approach is time intensive at the front end but results in positive outcomes for students and less work for us in the long run.

A generalization plan should contain information relevant to the functional assessment, including an operational definition of the target behavior and data on its frequency, duration, intensity, and setting. The plan should also contain antecedent and consequent information including factors related to teacher, student, and environmental variables. In addition, the plan, should include information related to the hypothesized behavioral intent. Finally, the plan should provide information on the types of contextual modifications, curricular accommodations, and replacement behavior strategies that will be implemented.

Many teachers do not conduct outcome assessment because they believe they "know" when an intervention is effective. This may be true in some cases, but it is not a good way to go about obtaining information relevant to promoting generalization.

Conducting Outcome Assessment

The outcomes of generalization programming should be evaluated throughout the initial intervention and on a regular basis thereafter. Outcome assessment information will help us make modifications in the intervention and generalization tactics as needed.

Outcome assessment requires collecting information from both impact- and specifying-level measures. **Impact measures** tell us whether the intervention produced improvements in socially important outcomes. Impact assessment procedures include sociometric techniques, teacher ratings of social competence, and measures of academic performance. **Specifying assessment** helps us determine whether the intervention resulted in targeted behaviors being performed in nontraining settings. The two most common specifying procedures are naturalistic observation and role-play assessment.

There are several recommendations for conducting outcome assessment (Hughes & Sullivan, 1988). First, it is important that the observation system used to measure performance in nontraining settings correspond to that used during intervention. For example, if we use a time sample recording technique to measure a student's level of giving compliments during baseline and intervention, then we should also use it to assess generalization and maintenance. Second, outcome measures should reflect pretreatment skill deficiencies. For example, if a student possesses the skills to perform a behavior but irrational beliefs interfere with her selecting the correct behavior, then some type of cognitive-behavior modification intervention may be needed. Therefore, outcome evaluation requires the use of some type of cognitive assessment. Third, outcome assessment should be conducted over an extended time. For example, Bierman, Miller, and Stabb (1987) found that the performance of boys trained in specific social skills in real-life settings did not result in improved peer acceptance when assessed several weeks after intervention. Apparently, a time span of more than several weeks was necessary for peers to change their perceptions of students receiving training.

SUMMARY

Promoting generalization is necessary for ensuring that the results of intervention transfer to other settings and are maintained. Types of generalization include stimulus generalization, response generalization, and response maintenance. Even when the best practices for behavior management are used, generalization may not follow. The reason is that generalization tactics must be built into any intervention from its inception. Various tactics for programming generalization can be classified according to three principles: take advantage of natural communities of reinforcement, train diversely, and incorporate functional mediators. Steps for incorporating these tactics into interventions include listing all desired behavior changes; listing all situations, settings, and places where, and person with whom, the desired behavior changes should occur; and listing all the behaviors that must be performed by everyone else involved in or affected by the behavior change.

ACTIVITIES

1. Think of a new skill you've learned. List the steps you went through to see that the skill generalized to other areas.
2. Observe a student who behaves well in one classroom or for one teacher but not in another classroom or for another teacher. What factors account for these differences?
3. Interview three teachers, asking several questions. First, do they believe it is important for students to use learned skills outside of the classroom? Second, what tactics do they use to ensure that students can use skills outside of the classroom? Third, what barriers do they encounter that prevents generalization?

REVIEW QUESTIONS

1. What is the definition of "generality of behavior change"?
2. Describe the three types of generalization.
3. What are the categories related to a technology of generalization?
4. What are the key components in the case study on generalization, and what important information is missing?
5. What are the three tactics for promoting generalization that take advantage of natural communities of reinforcement?

6. What are the five tactics for promoting generalization that focus on training diversely?
7. What are the three tactics for promoting generalization that incorporate functional mediators?
8. Describe the three steps for applying generalization tactics.
9. What issues should be considered in promoting generalization?

REFERENCES

Baer, D. M. (1981). *How to plan for generalization.* Austin, TX: Pro-Ed.

Baer, D. M., Wolf, M. M., & Risley, T. (1968). Current dimensions of applied behavior analysis. *Journal of Applied Behavior Analysis, 1,* 91–97.

Bierman, K. L., Miller, C. L., & Stabb, S. D. (1987). Improving the social behavior and peer acceptance of rejected boys: Effects of social skill training with instructions and prohibitions. *Journal of Consulting and Clinical Psychology, 55,* 194–200.

Cooper, J. O., Heron, T. E., & Heward, W. L. (1987). *Applied behavior analysis.* Columbus, OH: Merrill.

Fisch, R., Weakland, J., & Segal, L. (1982). *The tactics of change: Doing therapy briefly.* San Francisco: Jossey-Bass.

Hughes, J. N., & Sullivan, K. A. (1988). Outcome assessment in social skills training with children. *Journal of School Psychology, 26,* 167–183.

Lenz, B. K., Schumaker, J. B., Alley, G. R., & Deshler, D. D. (1981). *Promoting generalization of learning strategies.* Unpublished manuscript. Lawrence: University of Kansas, Institute for Research in Learning Disabilities.

McConnell, S. R. (1987). Entrapment effects and the generalization and maintenance of social skills training for elementary school students with behavioral disorders. *Behavioral Disorders, 12,* 252–263.

Neel, R. S. (1988). Classroom conversion kit: A teacher's guide to teaching social competency. In R. B. Rutherford, Jr., & J. W. Maag (Eds.), *Severe behavior disorders of children and youth* (Vol. 11, pp. 25–31). Reston, VA: Council for Children with Behavioral Disorders.

Rutherford, R. B., Jr., & Nelson, C. M. (1988). Generalization and maintenance of treatment effects. In J. C. Witt, S. W. Elliott, & F. M. Gresham (Eds.), *Handbook of behavior therapy in education* (pp. 277–324). New York: Plenum.

Sheldon, J., Sherman, J. A., Schumaker, J. B., & Hazel, J. S. (1984). Developing a social skills curriculum for mildly handicapped adolescents and young adults: Some problems and approaches. In S. Braaten, R. B.

Rutherford, Jr., & C. A. Kardash (Eds.), *Programming for adolescents with behavioral disorders* (Vol. 1, pp. 105–116). Reston, VA: Council for Children with Behavioral Disorders.

Stokes, T. F., & Baer, D. M. (1977). An implicit technology of generalization. *Journal of Applied Behavior Analysis, 10,* 349–367.

Stokes, T. F., Baer, D. M., & Jackson, R. (1974). Programming the generalization of a greeting response in four retarded children. *Journal of Applied Behavior Analysis, 7,* 599–610.

Stokes, T. F., & Osnes, P. G. (1986). Programming the generalization of children's social behavior. In P. S. Strain, M. J. Guralnick, & H. M. Walker (Eds.), *Children's social behavior: Development, assessment, and modification* (pp. 407–443). Orlando, FL: Academic Press.

Stokes, T. F., & Osnes, P. G. (1988). The developing applied technology of generalization and maintenance. In R. H. Horner, G. Dunlap, & R. L. Koegel (Eds.), *Generalization and maintenance* (pp. 5–19). Baltimore: Brookes.

Sulzer-Azaroff, B., & Mayer, G. R. (1977). *Applying behavior-analysis procedures with children and youth.* New York: Holt, Rinehart & Winston.

Watzlawick, P., Weakland, J., & Fisch, R. (1974). *Change: Principles of problem formation and problem resolution.* New York: Norton.

Wolf, M. M. (1978). Social validity: The case for subjective measurement or how applied behavior analysis is finding its heart. *Journal of Applied Behavior Analysis, 11,* 203–214.

Glossary

AB design The most basic method for graphing behavioral observations. The designation *AB* refers to the two phases of the design: (1) the A, or baseline, phase, and (2) the B, or intervention, phase. During the A phase, baseline data are collected and recorded. After a stable baseline trend has been established, a vertical line is drawn, and then the intervention is introduced, which signifies the beginning of the B phase. In this phase, intervention data are collected and recorded. The teacher can evaluate the effectiveness of the intervention by comparing the data trend during the B phase to the behavioral observations collected during the A phase. A problem with this design is that it is impossible to rule out alternative explanations for behavior change during the B phase.

ABAB design A design that involves the temporary removal of the intervention in order to evaluate its effects on a student's behavior. The purpose is to determine whether the effectiveness of the intervention can be replicated. If the effectiveness can be replicated, then a functional relation between the behavior and the intervention is established. If the effectiveness cannot be replicated, then the change in behavior was due to some extraneous variable(s). Commonly referred to as the *reversal* or *withdrawal design.*

A-B-C analysis The process of keeping a log of the antecedents, behavior, and consequences for a particular student in order to pinpoint a problem and the circumstances that elicit and maintain it.

Accuracy A level of proficiency that focuses solely on whether a student can perform a task correctly.

Adaptation An ecological process that occurs when organisms change their behavior so that it better fits the rest of the ecosystem.

Affiliation The process of joining with other people to form groups.

Affirming the consequent A mistake in logic in which a person observes an effect and ascribes to it a cause.

Alien niches An ecological term used to describe deviant categories (i.e., labels), such as emotional disturbance, behavior disorder, or mental illness, that provide society with places or roles in which individuals can function without disturbing the mainstream of society.

Alternating treatments design A method for graphing behavioral observations that permits analysis of the differential effectiveness of more than one intervention on a target behavior. Unlike the changing conditions design, in which interventions are introduced consecutively, one intervention is rapidly substituted for another, sometimes on a session-to-session basis.

Anal stage The second psychosexual stage of development in Freud's theory, which begins during the second year of life. The anal area of the body becomes the principal region for gratification. Two substages are delineated: (1) the anal-expulsive substage, when a child derives much gratification from expelling feces, and (2) the anal-retentive substage, when gratification is obtained by holding in and controlling feces.

Analogue (role-play) assessment An approach used to assess whether a student possesses requisite behavioral skills. An ability to perform the target behavior during staged situations is assessed. Analogue assessment is so-named because the situation under which observation is being conducted is contrived.

Analytic A term used to describe an aspect of applied behavior analysis when a functional relation between the intervention implemented and the target behavior can be demonstrated.

Anecdotal recording A recording technique that makes use of an A-B-C analysis in order to get an initial fix on a problem behavior, including the antecedents that cue its performance and the consequences that maintain it.

Antecedents The circumstances that exist in the environment before a behavior is exhibited. Antecedents may or may not serve as cues to elicit behavior.

Anticipatory set Statements of activities that introduce students to the content of the lesson, help them recognize important points, and offer them motivation for learning the material.

Application of contingent stimulation A type of punishment, sometimes called type I, that involves following a specific behavior with some stimulus. A child who is spanked or a student who receives a verbal reprimand from a teacher are examples of the application of contingent stimulation punishment.

Applied behavior analysis (ABA) A systematic, performance-based, self-evaluative method of changing behavior by applying interventions based on behavioral principles.

Applied A termed used to describe an aspect of applied behavior analysis that is characterized by the social importance of the behavior to be changed.

Assistance cards A nondisruptive way for students to obtain assistance during independent seat-work activities. Assistance cards are taped to students' desks and are used to signal the teacher for help with assigned work.

Attribution retraining A cognitive-behavior modification intervention based on the theory that students' causal explanations for why they are performing well or poorly have implications for their behavioral persistence, expectancies for future performance, and emotional reactions to success and failure. The goal of attribution retraining is to increase students' behavioral persistence while performing tasks.

Automaticity A level of proficiency that refers to being able to perform a task accurately at a high rate within a relevant context.

Average duration A type of duration recording that produces only one number to graph. In this approach, the durations of each episode of a target behavior are added together and divided into the total number of times the behavior occurred.

Avoidance conditioning A response that prevents the occurrence of a punisher. This increases the probability of a low-occurring response and maintains that response at a high level. The principle of avoidance conditioning states that a behavior will increase in frequency if it prevents a punisher from occurring.

Backup reinforcers   The items or activities that can be purchased using the conditioned reinforcer.

Backward chaining   A method for teaching a stimulus–response chain. When backward chaining is used, the reinforcing power of the positive reinforcer (presented at the end of the chain) is transferred "down the line" to each discriminative stimulus as it is added to the chain. This makes for very efficient use of positive reinforcement to establish a strong chain.

Baseline   A term used to describe data collected from behavioral observations of a target behavior before intervention is implemented. Baseline data help teachers determine whether an intervention was effective by comparing the rate at which a behavior occurred before and after the intervention was implemented.

Baseline logic   A level or uniform baseline trend providing the means for teachers to apply inductive reasoning.

Behavior   A term that simply refers to what individuals do—their observable actions. Behavior can be verbal or nonverbal. Behavior is also one of the four components of objectives, representing the actions students undertake to indicate that they have knowledge of the content.

Behavior covariation   A behavioral term used to describe the phenomenon of having an inappropriate behavior displayed when another inappropriate behavior has been previously eliminated.

Behavior modification   A process in which specific behaviors are identified, defined, measured, and changed using interventions based on principles of applied behavior analysis.

Behavior observation chart   An observation form in which various tasks and activities are listed along a vertical axis and certain types of appropriate and inappropriate behaviors appear along the horizontal axis. By marking an "X" in the box that intersects a certain task/activity and behavior, a general pattern emerges of the antecedent conditions that prompt certain behaviors to occur. This observation chart provides teachers with possible variables to manipulate during the hypothesis testing phase of functional assessment.

Behavioral contract   A written document that specifies a contingent relation between the completion of a specified behavior and access to or delivery of a specified reinforcer. Behavioral contracts specify how two or more individuals will behave toward each other. One person's behavior is dependent upon the other person's behavior.

Behavioral intent   A term used to describe the relation between the behaviors students exhibit and the outcomes they desire. When students act, even with behaviors considered to be inappropriate, they do so to achieve a result. The desired result, or outcome, can be viewed as the intent or function of the behavior. In turn, the intent of the behavior will affect the form (i.e., appearance) the behavior takes to achieve a desired outcome.

Behavioral model   The theory that people learn behavior—both appropriate and inappropriate—by receiving either reinforcing or punishing consequences.

Biophysical model   The theory that neurological and biochemical factors, physical defects or malfunctions, and illnesses are responsible for individuals' engaging in inappropriate behavior.

Bonus response cost   A process whereby a teacher makes additional reinforcers available to a student noncontingently. When a student misbehaves, a specified amount of the bonus reinforcement is removed.

Changing conditions design   A method of graphing behavioral observations used to determine the effectiveness of two or more interventions to positively affect a target behavior. *A* refers to the baseline, *B* designates the intervention, and *C* designates the application of a second intervention. In a changing conditions design, different interventions are implemented consecutively without ever returning to baseline conditions. Sometimes called an *ABC design*.

Changing criterion design   A method of graphing behavioral observations used to evaluate a slow and orderly increase or decrease in a student's performance level by changing the criterion for the student to receive an intervention in a stepwise fashion.

Cognitive-behavior modification   A fairly inclusive term that includes both cognitive activities and behavioral components such as modeling, role playing, and behavioral contingencies. Cognitive-behavior modification approaches are based on three assumptions: (1) Cognitive activity affects behavior, (2) cognitive activity may be monitored and altered, and (3) desired behavior change may be affected through cognitive change.

Cognitive deficit   The absence of reflective thinking that governs behavior. For example, a student may fail to maintain a conversation with peers because she has not learned the specific strategies for selecting, from her repertoire, appropriate behaviors.

Cognitive distortion   Maladaptive or dysfunctional thinking patterns that result in the activation of inappropriate emotional reactions and behavioral responses. Cognitions such as jumping to conclusions, viewing events dichotomously (i.e., all-or-nothing thinking), and awfulizing (i.e., making mountains out of molehills) are examples of cognitive distortions.

Cognitive restructuring   A global term used to describe cognitive-behavior modification techniques that focus on identifying and altering individuals' irrational beliefs and negative self-statements or thoughts.

Cognitive therapy   A multistep approach developed for treating individuals with depression. First, individuals identify dysfunctional thoughts and maladaptive assumptions that may be causing unpleasant emotions. Second, several techniques are used to counteract the debilitating thoughts or dysfunctional assumptions contributing to the emotional distress. Third, individuals complete assignments that require practicing appropriate thoughts and behaviors.

Compensatory curriculum   An approach used with high school students in special education classes, although it is being used more in junior high and middle schools. Students with disabilities, who may never catch up to their grade-level peers, are taught a variety of nontraditional skills such as vocational skills, school survival skills, self-management skills, life skills, and self-help skills. The goal is to provide these students with skills to compensate for deficiencies in traditional academic areas.

Competency-based curriculum   A curriculum that focuses on ensuring that students are proficient in a specific piece of content before advancing to more sophisticated content.

Concurrent assessment   A term used to describe cognitive assessment techniques that collect information at the same time that the actual thoughts are being generated.

Conditioned punishers Stimuli such as "No!" and "Stop that!" that assume punishing qualities when followed by type I or type II punishers.

Conditioned reinforcer Any stimulus that is not originally reinforcing but that acquires reinforcing power through association with a stimulus that is reinforcing, such as money.

Conditioning A term that refers to the procedure of introducing a positive reinforcer immediately following a response so that an increased frequency of that response occurs.

Conditions One of the four components of objectives, representing the situation or circumstances under which a behavior will be performed. Conditions are how individuals add context to a task.

Consequences Circumstances that change the environment shortly after a behavior is displayed and that affect the future performance of the behavior by serving to either increase, decrease, or maintain it.

Content One of the four components of objectives, representing the specific subject matter from the curriculum we want students to learn. Specific content statements are derived from task analysis.

Content of different difficulty A term related to how content is sequenced. There are two ways for sequencing content of different difficulty. The first method, functionality, usually is the most desirable. Obviously, if content is of different difficulty, there is some assumption that certain skills will precede others. The second method, developmentally, is based on the idea that children can only learn certain skills once they have attained a certain level of development.

Content of equal difficulty A term related to how content is sequenced. The way chosen to sequence content of equal difficulty may vary from

student to student. It is important to select a method that fits the needs of a particular student. In this way, the student is more likely to view the content as contextually relevant, which, in turn, is likely to reduce inappropriate behavior. There are four ways to sequence content of equal difficulty: logically, chronologically, based on student interest, and based on utility.

Context The situation or circumstances surrounding a behavior. Context is what gives behavior its meaning and is the determinant as to whether behavior is viewed as appropriate or inappropriate.

Contingency A term used to describe the relation between behaviors and their antecedents and consequences.

Contingent exercise A procedure similar to overcorrection that requires a student to perform a behavior that is not topographically related to the misbehavior.

Contingent observation A form of time-out that involves moving students who misbehave away from the activity in which misbehavior occurs to a place where they can observe but not participate in the activity. All reinforcement is withheld during this time.

Contingent withdrawal of positive reinforcer A type of punishment, sometimes called type II, that involves removing a reinforcer following a specific behavior. A student who must stay in from recess or a teenager who cannot use the phone for a week are examples of contingent withdrawal of a positive reinforcer punishment.

Continuous reinforcement A situation in which each response always produces reinforcement. Continuous reinforcement is effective when teaching new behaviors. However, if used too long, continuous reinforcement can result in satiation.

Core curriculum   A curriculum that typically refers to the "3 Rs" of reading, 'riting, and 'rithmetic. These content areas are considered to be core, or essential, to the development of skills in other areas.

Correlation   A statistical concept used to summarize the degree to which two variables relate to each other. Correlations can be either positive or negative.

Criterion   One of the four components of objectives, representing the standards for judging whether students successfully learned the content in the objective.

Criterion-referenced testing   An approach to assessment in which students' performance or behavior is measured and compared to a performance standard.

Curriculum   A structured set of learning outcomes or objectives. The curriculum reflects what school districts decide students need to know and the sequence in which the content will be learned. A complete curriculum includes numerous objectives covering different content areas.

Data   The numbers collected from observing and recording behavior. The word *data* designates the numerical results of intentional, programmed, and controlled observations.

Dead man's test   A way to determine whether behaviors are a fair pair. If a dead man can perform the target behavior, then it is not a fair pair. If a dead man cannot perform the target behavior, then it is a fair pair.

Degree of structure   A dimension of cognitive-behavioral assessment that refers to the level of limits or format that the assessment technique imposes on individuals.

Deprivation   A period of time prior to a training session during which an individual does not experience the reinforcer in order to increase the reinforcers effectiveness.

Differential diagnosis   The process of being able to differentiate one condition or disorder from another through the use of set diagnostic criteria. The term is based on a medical-disease model in which accurate diagnosis is believed to inform the clinician about effective treatments.

Differential reinforcement   The process of reinforcing one response from a response class and neglecting to reinforce all other members of that class.

Differential reinforcement of alternative behavior (DRA)   An approach similar to DRI in that an alternative to the inappropriate behavior is reinforced. However, unlike DRI, an alternative behavior is not topographically incompatible with the inappropriate behavior. DRA focuses on selecting a functional alternative—a more appropriate behavior that replaces and serves the same function or purpose as an inappropriate behavior A functional alternative refers to behavioral intent and replacement behavior.

Differential reinforcement of incompatible behavior (DRI)   An approach that involves selecting and reinforcing a behavior that is topographically incompatible with the inappropriate behavior. DRI is synonymous with the fair pair.

Differential reinforcement of low rates of behavior (DRL)   An approach in which reinforcement is provided either after a response that follows an interval of specific length or after a specified interval if the frequency of the behavior is below some established criterion.

Differential reinforcement of other behavior (DRO)   An approach that involves reinforcing a student for not engaging in the inappropriate behavior for a specified time. In a DRO schedule, only zero responding of the inappropriate behavior targeted to decrease is reinforced.

Direct instruction One of the best research-based methodologies for teaching students with disabilities. A teacher presents subject matter using a review of previously taught information presentation of new concepts or skills, guided practice, feedback and correction, independent practice, and formative evaluation.

Discipline Actions that seek to improve behavior in some way by increasing skills or competence in a given area.

DRL-below-criterion schedule A DRL schedule that involves determining the average number of times the target behavior is typically exhibited during a certain interval of time. Reinforcement is delivered if the frequency of the behavior is below this baseline rate during the specified interval of time, thus reinforcing lower rates of responding.

DRL-IRT schedule A DRL schedule in which the target behavior is reinforced following a specified interval of time since the previous episode. The interval is determined by calculating interresponse time (IRT). The interval length is gradually increased until the target behavior occurs only after longer periods of time have passed.

DRO fixed-interval schedule A DRO schedule that delivers reinforcement at the end of each interval during which the response does not occur. The procedure differs from the reset schedule in that the interval time is not reset with each occurrence of the target behavior.

DRO increasing-interval schedule A DRO schedule that thins or fades the reinforcement by gradually increasing the length of the interval. If the specified interval passes without a target response occurring, reinforcement is delivered, and the next interval can be increased by a certain amount of time. If the response does occur, however, the next interval stays the same.

DRO progressive (DROP) schedule A DRO schedule in which the interval size remains the same. However, the amount or kind of reinforcement increases as the student refrains from performing the inappropriate behavior for more and more consecutive intervals.

DRO reset schedule A DRO schedule that involves resetting the interval every time the inappropriate target behavior occurs.

Duration per occurrence A type of duration recording that involves recording the length of time per episode that a student engages in a target behavior.

Duration recording A recording technique that is used for measuring how long behavior lasts. It is most appropriate for behaviors that occur infrequently but continue for some length of time or for behaviors that occur at a high rate so that one episode blends into the next.

Ecological/sociological model The theory that behaviors are not inherently inappropriate but only acquire meaning when examined in relation to the social and cultural context or situation in which they occur.

Efficacy expectations A term that refers to individuals' beliefs that they can adequately perform a modeled behavior.

Ego The mediating system between the demands of the id and the social constraints of the world according to psychodynamic theory. The ego is the cognitive component that mediates the demands made by the id.

Entrapment A term used to describe the process of restructuring the existing reinforcement contingencies in peer interaction groups so that the new contingencies reinforce the appropriate to-be-performed behaviors of the target student.

Environment   The conglomerate of surroundings in which individuals reside and behave at any given point in time.

Exclusion   The second-most-restrictive type of time-out, in which students are removed physically from the time-in setting. Examples of exclusion time-out include having a student sit in the hallway, placing a student in a chair behind a portable chalkboard, and requiring a student to sit at a study carrel.

Exemplars   Stimuli that are typical or representative of those found in the settings in which generalization is desired. They serve as a pattern or guide for cuing behavior.

Expectations   A cognitive term used to describe the anticipation of certain consequences.

External self-reinforcement   A type of reinforcement paralleling that administered by a teacher. However, instead of the teacher delivering the reinforcer, the student performs this task.

Extinction   The process of withholding reinforcement for a conditioned response. Extinction has two parts: (1) If, in a given situation, somebody emits a previously reinforced response and the response is not followed by the usual reinforcing consequence, (2) then that person is less likely to do the same thing again when he or she next encounters a similar situation.

Extinction curve   A process that occurs during extinction in which the behavior may increase before it begins to decrease.

Fading   The gradual change of the stimulus controlling a response, such that the response eventually occurs to a partially changed or completely new antecedent stimulus.

Fair pair   A way to avoid symptom substitution or behavior covariation. The term *fair pair* refers to a maladaptive behavior intended to decrease and an incompatible, or competing, target behavior intended to increase in its place.

Fixed-duration (FD) schedule of reinforcement   A schedule of reinforcement that occurs after the behavior has been engaged in for a certain continuous period of time.

Fixed-interval (FI) schedule of reinforcement   The first instance of a particular behavior after a fixed period of time (measured from some event such as the previous reinforcement or the beginning of a trial) being reinforced. All that is required for reinforcement to occur is that the individual engage in the behavior after the reinforcement has become available due to the passage of time.

Fixed-ratio (FR) schedule of reinforcement   Reinforcement that occurs each time a set number of responses of a particular type are emitted.

Fluency   A level of proficiency that refers to the ability to perform a task correctly and quickly. Sometimes called *mastery*.

Forgetting   A decrease in a response as a result of not being able to emit it over time. Forgetting involves preventing a response from occurring for some period after it has been conditioned.

Formative evaluation   An approach used for instructional purposes. These techniques help capture not only students' performance but, more importantly, their progress through the curriculum. Formative approaches involve collecting information on a regular basis throughout the school year.

Free-access rule   A rule stating that the maximum amount of a reinforcer available to students should be less than that which they will seek if they have free access to it. This rule helps teachers avoid having students experience satiation on a reinforcer.

Frequency (event) recording A recording technique that involves tallying or counting the number of times a target behavior occurs. It is the most commonly used technique and the most advantageous in that it is fairly easy to do, produces a number that can be graphed, and applies to many disruptive behaviors in the classroom.

Functional assessment A technology for identifying environmental factors that affect the performance of a behavior and the desired outcome that behavior serves, selecting a replacement behavior that is an appropriate way for students to obtain a desired goal, and ensuring that students possess the requisite skills for performing the replacement behavior.

Functionalism A term used to emphasize that individuals' behavior serves a specific purpose or function.

Generality of behavior change A term that refers to the goal of any intervention—to get a newly acquired behavior to be displayed over time, in other situations, or to get similar behaviors to the target behavior to be displayed.

Generalization The term most often used in the applied literature to describe behavior changes that occur in nontraining conditions.

Generalized conditioned reinforcer A specific type of conditioned reinforcer. Generalized conditioned reinforcers can be exchanged for a virtually limitless amount of items and activities. Money is the prototypic example.

Genital stage The fifth psychosexual stage of development in Freud's theory, which begins with puberty and leads to mature adulthood. During this stage, earlier conflicts of the phallic stage emerge once again. However, sexual interest is external to the family, children seek to bring satisfaction not only to themselves but to the persons of interest, and they have the physiological capability to act out their feelings toward the opposite sex.

Goal A term used to describe a level of performance toward which an individual or group should work, although in everyday use, goals are considered to be motivational.

Good behavior game A type of group-oriented contingency that encourages competition between groups and cooperation within groups. Classroom rules are posted and reviewed, and then the class is divided into two or more groups. The teacher makes a tally mark on the chalkboard whenever she observes a student breaking one of the rules. The team with fewer than five tally marks "wins" free time and other privileges at the end of the day. Both teams can "win" if neither has more than five tally marks.

Grade-level curriculum The curriculum that reflects the content school districts determine students should acquire at different grades.

Group-oriented contingency A set of interventions in which the presentation or loss of a reinforcer is contingent on the behavior of an individual within the group, a segment of the group, or the group as a whole.

Guilt control A term associated with self-management and sometimes behavioral contracting. It is the covert application of negative reinforcement—engaging in a behavior to escape some aversive stimulus. It is partially used to explain why reactivity occurs during self-monitoring.

Habit reversal A variation on positive practice overcorrection that involves having students practice a behavior that is incompatible with the inappropriate behavior.

Hawthorne effect The phenomenon of working harder and producing more as a result of participating in something new and special even when the innovations have no corrective merit.

Hero procedure   A type of dependent group-oriented contingency in which a student, by successfully performing a target behavior, can earn reinforcement for the entire class.

Id   The biological component of personality, present at birth. According to psychodynamic theory, the id supplies the total inherited instinctual energy for the entire personality. The id operates on the pleasure principle—the reduction or elimination of tension.

Imitation   The process of a student performing the behavior of a model. Imitation consists of three environmental manipulations: (1) A model is presented that prompts the same behavior from the student, (2) the student imitates the modeled behavior within a specified time, and (3) the student is reinforced for performing the modeled behavior.

Immediacy   The process of maximizing positive reinforcement by ensuring that it is delivered immediately after a behavior occurs.

Impact measures   An approach associated with outcome assessment that answers the question of whether an intervention produced improvements in socially important outcomes. Impact assessment procedures include sociometric techniques, teacher ratings of social competence, and measures of academic performance.

In vivo (naturalistic) assessment   The most ecologically valid assessment approach, which involves observing behavior in the natural environment. Students are observed performing the target behavior in the natural environment while the practitioner systematically controls or manipulates situational and contextual events as part of functional assessment. The approach is also used to collect baseline and intervention data on a target behavior.

Inclusive   A term referring to how a useful explanation of behavior should be able to account for almost all behavior in which individuals engage.

Incorporating functional mediators   A general principle for promoting generalization that makes use of as many discriminative stimuli as possible in the training environment. In this way, students learn that a variety of stimuli can serve as cues to engage in appropriate behavior.

Inductive reasoning   Reasoning that uses logic originating from a specific situation and progressing to inferences concerning a general case. It is the primary means by which teachers can make generalizations about an intervention from its effects in a specific instance.

Instructions   The act of providing written or verbal explanations in order to elicit a certain behavior. Instructions serve as a discriminative stimulus, or cue, for individuals to engage in a desired behavior.

Instrumental conditioning   A term sometimes used to describe operant conditioning because the organism's behavior is instrumental in its receiving reinforcement.

Intermittent reinforcement   The maintenance of a behavior by reinforcing it only occasionally, rather than every time it occurs. Intermittent reinforcement is effective after a behavior is established and can help avoid satiation. There are several types of intermittent reinforcement including ratio, interval, and duration.

Internal self-reinforcement   The process by which students engage in covert self-statements, the goal being to praise themselves for good performance. Covert self-statements are no different from teachers' providing students with verbal praise—except that students take on this responsibility.

Interobserver agreement An approach for determining how consistently two observers agree on the occurrence or nonoccurrence of a target behavior. There are several ways to compute interobserver agreement. The method used depends on the type of recording technique employed.

Interresponse time (IRT) A term used in conjunction with differential reinforcement schedules. IRT refers to the time that passes between occurrences of the inappropriate behavior. This time period (or one slightly longer) becomes the initial interval that must pass without a student engaging in the inappropriate behavior in order to obtain reinforcement.

Interval recording A behavior recording technique that measures the occurrence or nonoccurrence of behavior within specified time intervals. The total observation time is divided into equal intervals, and the observer records whether the behavior occurs during those intervals.

Latency recording A variation of duration recording in which an observer records how long it takes a student to begin engaging in a behavior after the teacher instructs the student to perform it.

Latency stage The fourth psychosexual stage of development in Freud's theory, which is characterized as a rest period between the turbulent phallic and genital stages. During this period, sexual interest is dormant, the conflicts of the phallic stage are resolved, and identification with the parent of the same sex is accomplished.

Learned helplessness A hypothesized cause of depression in humans. It has been established in laboratory experiments with dogs that, when subjected to repeated experiences of painful, unpredictable, and inescapable shock, these animals lose their ability to learn a simple escape routine—they simply sit there and "take it." Based on this observation, it has been argued that human depression is a reaction to the experience of noncontingency between an individual's behavior and the outcomes of that behavior.

Limited hold A technique used with interval schedules that has a powerful effect on behavior: For a student to receive reinforcement, the behavior must occur within an interval following the first interval. That is, once the initial interval has elapsed and the student has the opportunity to earn reinforcement, its availability is "held" for only a limited time.

Mediation essay A cognitive-behavior modification intervention in which a teacher write briefs paragraphs answering the following questions regarding a student's behavior: (1) What did the student do wrong? (2) Why shouldn't the student do this? (3) What should the student do? and (4) What will happen if the student . . .? The idea is to help students rehearse adaptive strategies to handle situations effectively.

Modeling One of the most powerful techniques for helping students acquire new information. Modeling simply refers to learning by imitation.

Model-lead-test strategy A strategy to ensure that students become actively involved in guided practice. The strategy involves having teachers model and orally present the task, guide students in understanding the process through prompts and practice, and then test for mastery.

Movement cycle The process of ensuring that a behavior has a specific beginning and ending point. A movement cycle increases the specificity of the operational definition of a behavior.

Multiple baseline design A method of graphing behavioral observations that provides a way to evaluate the effectiveness of an intervention when a reversal design is not desirable. A multiple baseline design permits recording and analyzing behavioral observations from three variables: (1) two or more behaviors associated with one student in a single setting, (2) two or more students exhibiting the same behavior in a single setting, and (3) two or more settings in which one student is exhibiting the same behavior.

Multiple-probe technique A method of graphing behavioral observations that is a variation of the multiple baseline design. However, unlike the multiple baseline design, data are not continuously collected on the behaviors, students, or settings for which intervention is being implemented. Instead, one or more observations under baseline conditions are recorded intermittently on the subsequent behaviors.

Negative practice A procedure that is the opposite of positive practice overcorrection. A student is required to repeatedly engage in the problem behavior.

Negative reinforcement The process of removing a stimulus an individual finds to be aversive after that individual performs some behavior in order to increase the future occurrence of that behavior. The bell that sounds when a car is started until the driver performs the behavior of putting on the seat belt is an example of negative reinforcement. Also called *escape conditioning*.

Negative reinforcement trap A term used to explain the coercive relationships that often evolve between parents and children or between teachers and students. Both teachers and students learn to behave in ways that allow them to avoid aversive stimuli. For example, a student may misbehave to avoid completing a boring assignment. The teacher may remove the student from class when he or she misbehaves, which terminates the aversiveness of the student's misbehavior.

Objectives Written descriptions of the anticipated behavioral outcomes resulting from instruction that typically contain a description of the content and the behavior, conditions under which the behavior is to occur, and criteria for acceptable performance (CAP).

Observational learning A social learning theory term used to describe how students can learn new behaviors by watching the actions of important models around them such as their parents, siblings, teachers, and playmates.

Observer drift A phenomenon that results in a different behavior being observed and recorded than the one originally targeted. Observer drive can occur even when a target behavior is operationally defined and solidly passes the stranger test.

Operant conditioning A process in which consequences presented immediately after a behavior is performed either increase or decrease its future likelihood.

Operational definition The process of breaking down a broad concept into its observable and measurable component behaviors. For example, "aggression" becomes "hits peers with hand closed." The purpose of operational definitions is to ensure that all involved parties are conceptualizing, recording, and measuring behaviors similarly.

Oral stage The first psychosexual stage of development in Freud's theory, which begins at birth and usually continues until the child is about 2 years of age. During this stage, the mouth is the center of gratification.

Ordeal therapy A therapeutic approach in which the therapist's task is to impose an ordeal more severe than the problem behavior targeted for change. Like paradoxical injunction, ordeal therapy is designed to change the context surrounding a problematic behavior, which has the effect of changing the meaning and purpose of the behavior, as well as the desire of the individual to engage in it.

Outcome expectations A term that refers to the belief that performing certain behaviors will lead to certain consequences.

Overcorrection A term that encompasses several different techniques and behavioral principles to reduce inappropriate behavior. The objective is to have students practice repeatedly a positive behavior contingent on the performance of an inappropriate behavior.

Pacing A term used to describe the speed at which material is presented. A quickly paced lesson consists of concrete and relevant materials and examples maximizing the number of objectives students reach while minimizing classroom disruptions.

Paradigm A term used to describe a set of rules and regulations that establish boundaries and explain how to solve problems within the given boundaries.

Paradigm paralysis A condition characterized by an inability to see alternative points of view.

Paradoxical intention A technique that originally required people who were phobic to "intend to" that which they feared. That is, they were required to purposely engage in the behavior causing them distress. By doing so, the context surrounding the behavior was changed, which, in turn, changed the meaning, purpose, and desire for the individual to engage in the problematic behavior.

Parsimonious A term meaning that useful explanations of behavior should be the least complicated ones that account for the behavior.

Partial interval recording A type of interval recording in which a target behavior is marked if it occurs at any time during any particular interval.

Performance based A term used to describe an aspect of applied behavior analysis that is concerned with individuals' behavior and the way in which environmental factors affect its expression.

Permanent products recording The process by which many behaviors, particularly academic behaviors, leave a permanent product after a student performs the behavior. These products can be observed, counted, and recorded. The advantage of using permanent products recording is that a teacher does not have to split attention between leading activities and observing students.

Perspective taking A problem-solving skill that refers to the ability of individuals to identify and take into consideration the fact that various people have different motives and may display different behaviors.

Phallic stage The third psychosexual stage of development in Freud's theory, during which the superego emerges and becomes dominant, at about age 4. During this stage, children are preoccupied with the genital area of the body, and conflicts surrounding the Oedipal complex are presented unconsciously.

Placebo effect The process in which individuals' behavior changes as a result of believing they received a treatment when, in reality, they received something that lacked any intrinsic treatment value.

Planned ignoring A mild form of time-out in which a teacher withholds positive reinforcement by refraining from any physical, verbal, or visual interaction with a student who misbehaves.

Planned ignoring plus restraint   A controversial form of time-out that involves physically holding a student while simultaneously withholding all other reinforcers. It typically is used with individuals who are tantruming and is designed to control the behavior without providing additional reinforcement.

Positive practice overcorrection   A type of overcorrection that requires a student to repeatedly practice an appropriate behavior that is topographically related to the misbehavior. This exaggerated and prolonged practice performing an incompatible behavior presumably represents an educative component.

Positive reinforcement   A term that refers to any stimulus, presented after the occurrence of a behavior, that increases the future occurrence of the behavior.

Positive teaching   Not so much a set of techniques as an attitude toward teaching that focuses on manipulating antecedents. The idea behind positive teaching is that, by analyzing and modifying antecedents, inappropriate behavior can be prevented from occurring in the future.

Positivism   A term emphasizing that the only valid knowledge is that which is objectively observable. It is a philosophy responsible for the early manifestations of behavioral thought.

Power/control   An aspect of social influence, such that one person causes another to perform a behavior that is contrary to the latter's desires.

Prediction   The first element of baseline logic, in which speculations can be made on a future outcome by examining current data.

Predictive utility   A term referring to the fact that a useful explanation of behavior should be able to forecast the probability of people's behavior occurring under certain circumstances.

Premack principle   A principle stating that a high-probability behavior is contingent on the occurrence of a low-probability behavior. A high-probability behavior refers to a behavior that individuals have a greater likelihood of engaging in when they have free access to preferred activities. A low-probability behavior refers to a behavior that individuals have a low likelihood of engaging in when they have free access to preferred activities.

Primary reinforcer   Any stimulus that is reinforcing in itself, such as food, drinks, and shelter.

Principles of behavior   Lawful relations between behavior and the environmental variables that affect its occurrence.

Problem-solving training   A cognitive-behavior modification intervention that can be used to resolve conflicts requiring either initiation of action or reaction to the responses of others. Problem-solving training involves teaching children to practice the skills of self-interrogation and self-checking; to analyze tasks, break problems into manageable steps, and proceed through these steps; and to scan strategies to find those that match the demands of a task.

Prompts   An approach for helping students who fail to imitate a modeled behavior. Prompts refer to antecedent stimuli that supplement discriminative stimuli to help students perform a desired behavior.

Psychodynamic theory   The theory that deviant behavior results from disharmony between parts of an individual's personality and unresolved conflicts arising at different stages in her or his development. These conflicts create anxiety, which is displayed in the form of inappropriate behavior.

Punishment Any stimulus, when presented or removed after the occurrence of a behavior, that has the effect of decreasing the future occurrence of that behavior.

Punishment contrast A phenomenon whereby a behavior that is suppressed through punishment in one situation increases in another situation in which punishment was not administered.

Quiet training A procedure most often used for verbally or physically aggressive behavior or situations in which a student is extremely agitated. When these forms of inappropriate behavior occur, the offending student is required to lie face down or face up until all forms of the disruptive behavior have subsided for a specified time.

Ratio strain A condition that occurs when too much responding is required or when the amount of responding required to receive reinforcement is increased too rapidly. In these cases, the pause between responding is so great that little or no subsequent responding occurs.

Rational-emotive therapy A cognitive-behavior modification technique based on the premise that most everyday emotional problems and behaviors stem from irrational self-statements people make when events in their lives do not turn out as they want them to. The focus of intervention is on identifying irrational beliefs and replacing them with more logical ways of interpreting events.

Reactivity A phenomenon that results from the act of self-monitoring. Reactivity is said to occur when a behavior being monitored changes as a result of observing and recording it. Also known as the *reactive effect*.

Reduction of response maintenance stimuli A type of time-out that is based on the principle of differential reinforcement and the fair pair. Environmental stimuli (e.g., peer attention) that are maintaining inappropriate behavior are eliminated. These stimuli are reintroduced when the student is performing appropriate target behaviors.

Reinforcement The term used to describe a specific effect on behavior. Reinforcement occurs when a consequence results in behavior increasing.

Remediation An approach to providing special instruction to students with disabilities, with the goal of eventually "catching them up" in the curriculum.

Replication The third element of baseline logic, which refers to the process of reinstituting the intervention after it has been temporarily discontinued in order to determine its effectiveness.

Respondent conditioning A process in which a neutral stimulus acquires the prompting power of an unconditioned stimulus through repeated pairing of the unconditioned stimulus with the neutral stimulus.

Response class A group of responses (behaviors) that have at least one characteristic in common. For example, a student whose raises his hand, calls for the teacher, makes animal noises, and runs around the class is exhibiting behaviors that are members of the same response class because they result in his obtaining teacher attention.

Response cost An application of contingent withdrawal of a positive reinforcer punishment. A response (or behavior) "costs" the individual something he or she likes, such as money, points, or activities/privileges. Receiving a speeding ticket is an example of a response cost because the behavior of speeding costs individuals something they find reinforcing—money.

Response cost lottery A technique in which every student has an envelope taped to his or her desk. The teacher places five or more tickets in each envelope with the student's name written on each ticket. Students lose a ticket every time they engage in one of three inappropriate behaviors specified by the teacher. At the end of a prespecified time, the remaining tickets are placed in a grab bag and mixed up. The teacher draws three or four tickets, and the students whose names appear on the tickets win a reward.

Response differentiation The point at which individuals are able to recognize that the performance of certain members of a response class will result in reinforcement while others will not.

Response facilitation A phenomenon whereby the occurrence of some behaviors increases rather than decreases after the application of an aversive stimulus.

Response generalization A type of generalization that occurs when behaviors change that were not specifically targeted in the original intervention program. These behaviors are usually members of the same response class as the one targeted for intervention but have not received the intervention.

Response maintenance A type of generalization that occurs when a behavior is performed following the withdrawal of an intervention. It is measured in terms of the strength or durability of learned behaviors once the initial contingencies are removed.

Response substitution A phenomenon whereby one inappropriate behavior is suppressed and another inappropriate behavior occurs.

Restitutional overcorrection A type of overcorrection in which a student is required to correct the effects of inappropriate behavior by re-storing the environment to a state superior to that which existed before the behavior occurred.

Retrospective assessment A term used to describe cognitive assessment techniques that collect information after a considerable amount of time has passed between the original thoughts and the collection of the assessment information.

Reward Something that is given to a person for some accomplishment. Other words for reward are "merit" or "prize." A reward may or may not be a positive reinforcer.

Satiation A process that occurs when an individual has experienced a reinforcer to such an extent that it is no longer reinforcing.

Scapegoating The practice of unfairly blaming unpopular students for all types of negative classroom outcomes and behaviors.

Scatter plot A direct observation approach used in functional assessment in which a school day is divided into units (e.g., class periods) that appear on a vertical axis and the days for several weeks are listed on the horizontal axis. This process results in a grid in which instances (or noninstances) of a behavior can be charted over a period of weeks, thereby making it possible to identify certain patterns.

Seclusion The most restrictive time-out procedure. In this arrangement, the student is removed from the time-in setting and placed in a specially constructed seclusion room contingent upon the occurrence of misbehavior.

Self-control A hypothetical construct referring to "will power" that involves two responses: (1) the target response to be controlled (e.g., eating, completing math problems, or throwing temper tantrums) and (2) the response emitted in order to control the rate of the target behavior (e.g., recording everything eaten, the number of math problems completed correctly, or the number of temper tantrums thrown during the day). Self-control is assumed to reflect an internal process that occurs without the presence of immediate and obvious external contingencies.

Self-evaluation A phase of self-management and intervention that requires students to compare their performance against some criterion. Self-monitoring is a necessary prerequisite. Students must have some form of data (from self-monitoring) to evaluate their performance. The goal is to have students examine the degree to which a match exists between their behavior and some self-selected standard.

Self-instruction training A cognitive-behavior modification technique designed to get students to talk to themselves as a method of gaining self-control, learning or using strategies, or accessing appropriate behaviors in their repertoires.

Self-management A term that generally refers to the range of activities, both overt and covert, in which students may engage that increase or decrease the probability of appropriate behaviors occurring. *Self-management* is a more encompassing term than *self-control* in that it avoids the designation of locus of control. It encompasses techniques considered to be both internal (i.e., self-control) and external (i.e., environmental).

Self-monitoring A phase of self-management and an intervention technique. Self-monitoring involves the process of operationally defining a target behavior and having students observe and record its occurrence or absence while engaging in some activity or task.

Self-monitoring attention (SMA) A type of self-monitoring that involves having students observe their own behavior, determine whether they were paying attention, and record the results when cued through the use of randomly presented tones from a tape recorder.

Self-monitoring performance (SMP) A process in which students are instructed to self-monitor some aspect of academic performance and to self-record the results. There is much more variability in the procedures for self-monitoring performance than exists for self-monitoring attention.

Self-reinforcement A phase of self-management and an intervention technique. The process involves teaching students to either provide themselves with a tangible reinforcer after completing a desired behavior or to engage in positive self-statements. Self-evaluation and self-monitoring are necessary prerequisites.

Shaping The development of a new behavior by the successive reinforcement of closer approximations and the extinguishing of preceding approximations of the behavior.

Simple correction A procedure similar to overcorrection, in which students are required to restore the environment to its original state prior to the infraction. No additional practice is required.

So-what test A method of determining whether a behavior is worth the effort and time involved in analyzing, counting, graphing, and intervening on it. This test simply consists of asking ourselves if there is evidence that students' behavior is presently or potentially harmful to their own or peers' social, physical, emotional, or academic well-being. If the answer is "no," then the behavior should be left alone, and perhaps another behavior should be targeted.

Social learning theory The theory that individuals learn through observation, imitation, and cognitive processes (i.e., perception, beliefs, problem solving).

Social reciprocity   A term used to describe the interactive nature of behavior and mutually reinforcing social exchanges between individuals.

Social validity   A term used to describe both target behaviors and the outcome of intervention. Social validity refers to the extent to which behaviors targeted for intervention and the effects of intervention enhance the quality of students' lives.

Specifying assessment   An approach associated with outcome assessment that helps determine whether intervention resulted in targeted behaviors being performed in nontraining settings.

Spontaneous recovery   A term referring to behavior that is completely suppressed through the use of extinction or punishment but that reappears at the next opportunity. The reappearance of an extinguished behavior following a recess is an example of spontaneous recovery.

Stimulus control   A term referring to antecedent stimuli that have the capability to alter a response. When certain responses occur in the presence of some stimuli and not others, stimulus control has been established.

Stimulus discrimination   The procedure by which individuals learn to emit appropriate behavior in the presence of certain stimuli and not in the presence of other stimuli. Stimulus discrimination involves reinforcing a response in the presence of one stimulus and not reinforcing the response (i.e., extinguishing it) in the presence of other stimuli.

Stimulus generalization   A phenomenon whereby individuals respond in a similar manner to different stimuli. A response conditioned in the presence of one discriminative stimuli tends to occur in the presence of novel stimuli.

Stimulus–response chain   A sequence of discriminative stimuli and responses in which each response produces the discriminative stimuli for the next response. The entire sequence is typically followed by a reinforcer.

Stimulus satiation   A behavior management technique. Sometimes confused with negative practice, stimulus satiation focuses on repeatedly exposing students to the antecedents of their misbehavior in order to reduce or eliminate it.

Stranger test   A test to determine whether a behavior has been sufficiently operationally defined. A stranger not familiar with the student could take the definition of a behavior and accurately determine its occurrence or nonoccurrence at a level commensurate with that of teachers who have daily contact with the student.

Subject-area curriculum   A curriculum that focuses on the skills required to master a particular content area.

Subtasks   The simpler requisite skills individuals must possess in order to competently perform the main task.

Successive approximation   A term used to represent the general logic of shaping. Shaping refers more to the actual actions of the person doing the intervention.

Summative evaluation   An approach to summarize students' performance during the school year. These tests may be appropriate to compare one student's performance to that of other students for the purposes of making classification or placement decisions.

Superego   The social conscience component of personality according to psychodynamic theory. It represents the norms and values of society that are taught to a child by his or her parents and significant others. The superego can be thought of as punishing or controlling (conscience) or as guilt control.

Superstitious behavior   The accidental association of a response and a positive reinforcer. Superstitious behavior contributes greatly to much human behavior. Its effect can be reduced by reinforcing individuals immediately after a desired behavior is performed.

Sure-fire work folders   A technique to reduce teacher involvement with individual students during independent practice activities while also ensuring their success. Sure-fire work folders contain work that students can complete without teacher assistance or instruction.

Taking advantage of natural communities of reinforcement   A general principle for promoting generalization that is based on the belief that generalization is more likely to occur when peers reinforce the target student for performing appropriate behaviors.

Task analysis   The process of breaking down a task into its subtasks, and the strategy necessary for individuals to combine the subtasks into competent performance on the task.

Task-approach statements   A type of self-statement used with self-instruction training that refers to general strategies that can be used across a variety of related tasks. They focus on either components of a task or characteristics of students.

Task record   A place on a behavioral contract where a student's progress can be recorded. A task record enables both parties to look at and be reminded of the contract regularly, and helps the student remain on task until the behavior is completed and the reinforcement earned.

Task-specific statements   A type of self-statement used with self-instruction training that refers to strategies specific to the particular task at hand.

Task strategy   The procedure, strategy, or algorithm that combines subtasks together, leading students to perform competently on a task.

Tasks   That which we want students to master. There are two components to every task: subtasks and task strategy.

Temporality   A term used in conjunction with cognitive-behavioral assessment. The temporal dimension refers to the time the thoughts were assessed relative to when they actually occurred.

Thought stopping   A cognitive-behavior modification intervention designed to help students control unproductive or self-defeating thoughts and images by suppressing or eliminating them through the use of a multistage process.

Three-term contingency   A term used to describe the A-B-C analysis. The three-term contingency is a basic tool for conducting functional assessment as it provides information on the antecedents that prompt inappropriate behavior and the consequences that maintain inappropriate behavior.

Time sampling   A type of interval recording in which a target behavior is recorded only if it occurs at the end of an interval.

Time-delay strategy   A strategy to ensure that students become actively involved in guided practice. Time-delay consists of five steps: (1) The teacher presents the task to students and asks them to respond, (2) the teacher prompts students immediately (zero-second delay) by providing correct answers during several trials, (3) students respond and receive feedback based on their responses, (4) students repeat prior steps while incrementally increasing the amount of time between the presentation of the content and the teacher's providing the correct response, and (5) the teacher fades out assistance so that students can respond quickly and independently.

Time-out   Based on the principle of extinction, the process by which reinforcement is removed from students contingent upon misbehavior. There are various applications and forms of time-out, but it is most often conceptualized as a form of punishment.

Token economy   A program in which students can earn tokens that can be exchanged for a variety of back-up reinforcers.

Tokens   The tangible objects, such as money, trading stamps, or gift certificates, that are exchanged for items or activities.

Total duration   A type of duration recording in which the entire time a student engages in a target behavior during a specified observation period is recorded.

Training diversely   A general principle for promoting generalization that emphasizes the importance of maintaining the minimum training control necessary. This principle ensures that the diversity of natural settings is incorporated into training as much as possible.

Turtle technique   A cognitive-behavior modification intervention that combines elements of problem-solving training, self-instruction training, and relaxation training. It was developed as a way to help students who were emotionally disturbed to inhibit aggression or impulsive responding in social situations and to generate alternative responses. The turtle technique consists of three phases: (1) turtle response, (2) relaxation, and (3) problem solving.

Variable-duration (VD) schedule of reinforcement   A schedule that resembles a fixed-duration schedule except that the amount of continuous time the behavior must be engaged in

to produce reinforcement changes unpredictably from one reinforcement to the next. The amount of time required varies around some mean value.

Variable-interval (VI) schedule of reinforcement   A schedule of reinforcement that resembles a fixed-interval schedule except that the time that must elapse before reinforcement becomes available changes unpredictably from one reinforcement to the next, instead of being constant. The interval varies around some mean value.

Variable-ratio (VR) schedule of reinforcement   A schedule that resembles a fixed-ratio schedule except that the number of responses required to produce reinforcement changes unpredictably from one reinforcement to the next. The number of responses required varies around some mean value.

Verifiable   A term meaning that a useful explanation of behavior should be able to be scientifically tested.

Verification   The second element of baseline logic, which is accomplished by demonstrating that the prior level of baseline responding would have remained unchanged had the intervention not been employed.

Vicarious punishment   The process in which children anticipate receiving punitive consequences by observing others receive the consequence for performing some behavior.

Vicarious reinforcement   The process in which children anticipate receiving reinforcing consequences by observing others receive the consequence for performing some behavior.

Whole interval recording   A type of interval recording in which a target behavior must be displayed for the entire duration of an interval in order to mark the behavior as having occurred.

Index

A

AB design, 132, 133–134
ABAB design, 132, 134–136
A-B-C analysis, 10–12
    cognitive A-B-C model and, 352–354
    contextual hypothesis generation with, 158–159
    generalization tactics and, 394–395
Absolutistic thinking, 373
Academic behavior, 26–27
Acceptance, 156
Accuracy level of proficiency, 210
Acting-out behaviors, 153
Active support list, 395
Adaptation, 57
ADHD. *See* Attention deficit/hyperactivity disorder
Adolescent Reinforcement Survey Schedule (ARSS), 70, 71
Adolescents
    backup reinforcers for, 245, 247
    See also Students
Affiliation, 156, 189–190
Affirming the consequent, 41
Aggression, 298–299
Alcohol abuse, 27–28
Alien niches, 55
Alternating treatments design, 132, 144–147

Alternative thinking, 369
Always-and-never thinking, 353
Analogue assessment, 186
Anal retentive, 42, 44
Anal stage, 44
Analytic system, 16
Anorexia nervosa, 28
Antecedent modeling, 215–216
Antecedents, 9, 155
    cognitive view of, 353
    performance of behavior and, 154, 155
    preventative approaches and, 200
Anticipatory set, 212
Application of contingent stimulation, 83
Applied behavior analysis (ABA), 15–17, 94, 382
Approximations of behavior, 73–74
Arbitrary inference, 373
Ascending baseline trend, 130, 131
Assertive behavior, 368
Assessment
    analogue, 186
    cognitive-behavioral, 357–361
    concurrent, 358
    in vivo, 185–186
    outcome, 397
    retrospective, 358
    See also Functional assessment
Assimilation, 57

Assistance cards, 221–222
Attention deficit/hyperactivity disorder
    (ADHD)
    cross-cultural view of, 26
    medical diagnosis of, 23–24
    motor movement and, 31–32
Attention seeking, 156
Attribution retraining, 364–366
Auditory cues, 330
Automaticity level of proficiency, 211
Automatic Thoughts Questionnaire
    (ATQ), 359
Average duration, 110
Aversion therapy, 49
Avoidance behaviors, 156, 298
Avoidance conditioning, 77
Awfulizing, 353

B

Backup reinforcers, 239, 243–248
Backward chaining, 74
Bandura, Albert, 51–54, 355, 356
Baseline data, 95
    collection of, 130–132, 334
    graphic representations of, 131
    precount data and, 97–98
    reasons for establishing, 130
    self-monitoring performance
        and, 334
Beck, Aaron T., 373
Behavior
    approximations of, 73–74
    behavioral objectives and, 208
    contextual variation in, 27–31
    counting, 94–104
    covert, 5–6
    decreasing, 67, 82–86, 280
    definition of, 4–5
    descriptions of, 6–8
    graphing, 125–149
    identification, 208
    increasing, 66–77, 238
    observing, 164–166
    principles of, 16, 65–92

production, 208
    purposefulness of, 155–157
    recording, 104–120
    relevant, 387–388
    superstitious, 69
    theories of, 37–63
Behavioral contracts, 251–260
    components of, 252–256
    essential features of, 251
    guidelines for, 256–257
    home-school type of, 259–260
    negotiation process for, 257–258
    reasons they work, 252
    sample of, 253
Behavioral intent, 155–157
    classification of, 156
Behavioral model, 39, 45, 47–51
    operant conditioning and, 48, 50–51
    respondent conditioning and, 47–48
Behavioral objectives, 207–210
Behavioral skill deficiencies, 181–184
Behavioral support plans, 175–179
    areas of concern in, 177–178
    general approach described in,
        176–177
    important characteristics of, 175
    monitoring and evaluation of,
        178–179
    summary of findings in, 176
Behavior analysis, 15–17
Behaviorism, 47
Behavior management, 2
    impediments to, 21–36
    terms associated with, 12–15
Behavior modification, 2–4
    attributes of, 2–3
    cognitive, 351–379
    contributions of, 5
    dissatisfaction with, 354
    misconceptions about, 4
Behavior observation charts, 164–165
Behavior problems
    curriculum as antecedent for,
        202–204
    functional assessment of, 151–197

Behavior theories. *See* Theories of behavior
Beliefs, 353, 372
Biophysical model, 39, 40–41
Bonus response cost, 307–309
Bonus rewards, 255
Brea, Joseph, 42

C

Challenging goals, 343
Changing conditions design, 132, 143–144
Changing criterion design, 132, 139–142
Chariot, Jean, 42
Chart moves, 268–269
Children. *See* Students
Chronological curriculum, 205
Classical conditioning, 47–48
    interventions based on, 49
Classrooms
    developing rules for, 225–227
    ecological conditions in, 58
    environmental accommodations in, 223–232
    handling materials in, 228–230
    managing paperwork in, 230–232
    physical arrangement of, 224–225
    transition time in, 227
Clinical interview, 359
Cognitive A-B-C model, 352–354
Cognitive assessment, 357–361
    dangers associated with, 357–358
    techniques of, 358–361
Cognitive-behavior modification, 351–379
    assessment methods, 357–361
    attribution retraining, 364–366
    cognitive A-B-C model, 352–354
    cognitive restructuring, 371–375
    factors contributing to, 354–357
    intervention techniques, 361–375
    overview of, 352–357

problem-solving training, 368–371
review questions/activities on, 375–376
self-instruction training, 361–364
summary of, 375
thought stopping, 366–368
Cognitive deficit, 184
Cognitive distortion, 184–185
Cognitive modeling, 361
Cognitive model of self-management, 326–327
Cognitive problems, 184–185
Cognitive psychology, 356–357
Cognitive restructuring, 357, 371–375
    cognitive therapy, 373–374
    rational-emotive therapy, 372
    steps in, 374
Cognitive therapy, 373–374
Collecting materials, 229–230
Communities of reinforcement, 387–389
Community-based curriculum, 205
Compensatory curriculum, 203
Compliance matrix, 273–275
Comprehension, checking for, 218–219
Concurrent assessment, 358
Conditioned punishers, 84
Conditioned reinforcers, 75, 239
Conditioned response (CR), 47
Conditioned stimulus (CS), 47
Conditioning, 69
    avoidance, 77
    escape, 75–77
    operant, 50–51
    respondent, 47–48
Conditions, 208–209
Consequences, 9–10
    cognitive view of, 353
    functions of, 10, 13
    performance of behavior and, 154, 155
Consequential thinking, 369
Consequent interventions, 177

Content
   behavioral objectives and, 208
   sequencing of, 204–205, 212–213
Context, 27–31
   appreciation of, 29–30
   behavior determined by, 28–29, 155
   social interaction and, 30–31
   sociocultural, 27–28
Contextual hypotheses, 158–159
Contingencies, 8
   functional, 396
   group-oriented, 260–267
   indiscriminable, 391–392
Contingent exercise, 317
Contingent observation, 312, 314
Contingent reinforcement, 69
Contingent withdrawal of a positive
   reinforcer, 83–84, 310
Continuous reinforcement, 74
Control
   concept of, 32–34
   self-, 185, 325
   stimulus, 86–87
   See also Power/control behaviors
Control mentality, 33–34
Coping-skills therapies, 357
Corporal punishment, 296, 297
Correction vs. instruction, 33–34
Counting behavior, 94–104
   direct and continuous, 94–97
   evaluating success via, 99–100
   identifying correct behaviors,
     98–99
   pinpointing target behaviors,
     101–104
   precount data and, 97–98
   questions to consider before, 100
   review questions/activities on,
     120–121
   summary of, 120
   See also Recording behavior
Covert behavior, 5–6
Covert positive reinforcement,
   346–347
Covert self-guidance, 361

Covert self-reinforcement, 345–346
Covert sensitization, 49
Covert thought stopping, 367–368
Criteria for acceptable performance
   (CAP), 207, 243, 261
Criterion, 209
Criterion-referenced testing, 206, 210
Cues, 217
Curricular hypotheses, 159–160
Curriculum, 201–211
   analyzing content knowledge for,
     205–211
   behavior problems and, 202–204
   classroom behaviors and, 201–202
   compensatory, 203
   definition of, 201
   disabled students and, 205
   guidelines for developing, 203
   proficiency levels and, 210–211
   types and sequencing of, 204–205
Curriculum-based measurement
   (CBM), 142

D

Daily school behavior report card, 250
Damnation, 353
Data, 126
   collecting, 130–132, 334
   graphing, 126–147
   precount, 97–98
   See also Baseline data
Data path, 128
Data points, 128
Deadlines, 343–344
Dead man's test, 104
Decreasing behavior, 82–86, 280
   differential reinforcement for,
     279–294
   principles related to, 67, 82–86
   See also Increasing behavior
Defense mechanisms, 42, 45, 46
Deficiencies, 179–185
   behavioral skill, 181–184
   cognitive, 184–185

model for understanding, 180
replacement behaviors and, 179–181
self-control, 185
Degree of structure, 358–359
Delivering information, 213–214
Denial, 46
Dependent group-oriented contingencies, 261–262
Deprivation, 73
Descending baseline trend, 130, 131
Designs for graphing behavior, 132–147
  AB design, 133–134
  ABAB design, 134–136
  alternating treatments design, 144–147
  changing conditions design, 143–144
  changing criterion design, 139–142
  multiple baseline design, 136–139
  summary table of, 132
Determinism, reciprocal, 355–356
Dichotomous thinking, 373
Differential diagnosis, 23–24
Differential reinforcement, 89, 279–294
  considerations for using, 292–293
  review questions/activities on, 293–294
  schedules of, 283–291
  summary of, 293
  types of, 280–283
Differential reinforcement of alternate behavior (DRA), 280, 281, 292–293
Differential reinforcement of incompatible behavior (DRI), 280, 281, 292–293
Differential reinforcement of low rates of behavior (DRL), 280, 282–283, 289–291, 292–293
Differential reinforcement of other behavior (DRO), 280, 281–282, 283–289, 292–293

Differentiation, 89–90
Difficult situations, 178
Direct instruction, 211–223
  comprehension checking and, 218–219
  delivering information in, 213–214
  explaining goals and objectives of, 212
  feedback and, 219, 220
  formative evaluation and, 222–223
  giving clear instructions, 214–215
  guided practice and, 217–218
  independent practice and, 219–222
  modeling behavior in, 215–217
  overview of, 211
  prompts used in, 217
  reviewing requisite skills for, 213
  sequencing content for, 212–213
Disabled students. *See* Students with disabilities
Discipline, 12
Discrimination, 87
Displacement, 46
Display characteristics, 215, 216
Distributing materials, 229–230
Down syndrome, 40, 56
DRL-below-criterion schedule, 291
DRL-IRT schedule, 289–291
DRO fixed-interval schedule, 285–286
DRO increasing-interval schedule, 286–288
DRO progressive (DROP) schedule, 288–289
DRO reset schedule, 284–285
Duration per occurrence, 110
Duration recording, 105, 108–110
  average duration and, 110
  duration per occurrence and, 110
  interobserver reliability and, 118
  latency recording and, 110
  total duration and, 109–110
Duration schedules of reinforcement, 81–82
Dysfunctional thinking styles, 373

E

Eagleton, Thomas, 56
Ecological niche, 57
Ecological/sociological model, 39,
    54–60
    basic tenets of, 56–58
    environmental factors and, 54–56,
        58–60
    labeling process and, 55–56
Ecosystems, 56–57
Efficacy expectations, 53
Ego, 43
Elementary school students
    backup reinforcers for, 245, 246
    independent group-oriented con-
        tingencies for, 262
    See also Students
Ellis, Albert, 372
Emotional disturbance, 55–56
Emotional reaction to punishment, 298
Entrapment, 389
Environment, 8, 27, 223
    interaction between children and,
        54–55
    poorness of fit between behavior
        and, 59–60
Environmental accommodations,
    223–232
    arranging the classroom, 224–225
    establishing classroom rules,
        225–227
    handling classroom materials,
        228–230
    managing paperwork, 230–232
    overview of, 223–224
    transition times and, 227
Environmental disturbances, 58–60
Environmental factors
    ecological/sociological model and,
        54–56, 58–60
    preventative approaches and,
        223–232
    problem behavior and, 58–60,
        388–389

Epilepsy, 41
Equilibrium, 56–57
Error-dependent modeling, 216–217
Escape avoidance behaviors, 156, 298
Escape conditioning, 75–77
Ethical issues
    group-oriented contingencies and,
        265–267
    punishment and, 296–297
    See also Legal issues
Evaluation
    behavioral support plan, 178–179
    formative, 222–223
    self-, 339–344
Event recording, 106–108
Event strategies, 176
Exclusion, 312, 314
Exemplars, 390
Expectations, 52–53
Expression of self, 156
Expulsion, 57
External self-reinforcement, 344–345
Extinction, 84–86
    forgetting compared to, 86
    spontaneous recovery and, 85–86
    time-out based on, 310
Extinction curve, 85

F

Faded self-guidance, 361
Fading, 88, 217
Fair pair, 103, 280
Feedback
    direct instruction and, 219, 220
    goal setting and, 344
First-order respondent conditioning, 47
Fixed-duration (FD) schedules of
    reinforcement, 81–82
Fixed-interval (FI) schedules of
    reinforcement, 79
Fixed-ratio (FR) schedules of
    reinforcement, 78
Fluency level of proficiency, 210–211
Forgetting, 86

Formative evaluation, 222–223
Free-access rule, 73
Free association, 359
Frequency recording, 106–108
    inappropriate use of, 108
    interobserver reliability and, 117–118
Freud, Sigmund, 41–45, 103
Function
    definition of, 154
    task analysis of, 207
Functional assessment, 151–197
    assumptions of, 155–157
    behavioral intent and, 155–157, 187–190
    behavioral support plans and, 175–179
    deficiency areas and, 179–185
    hypotheses of, 157–160
    key issues in, 179–190
    multiply controlled behaviors and, 187
    naturalistic vs. contrived, 185–186
    overview of, 153–154
    process and goal of, 154
    review questions/activities on, 192–193
    stages of, 160–175
    summary of, 191
    transfer of functions and, 187
Functional contingencies, 396
Functional curriculum, 205
Functional hypotheses, 157–158
Functionalism, 45
Functional mediators, 387, 392–394

G

Generality of behavior change, 382
Generalization, 87–88, 381–400
    approaches to, 384–385
    case study in, 385–387
    diverse training and, 389–392
    functional contingencies and, 396
    functional mediators and, 392–394

    issues in promoting, 395–397
    outcome assessment of, 397
    overview of, 382–387
    peer reinforcement and, 387–389
    review questions/activities on, 398–399
    steps for applying tactics of, 394–395
    summary of, 398
    tactics for promoting, 387–394
    teacher repertoire and, 395–396
    types of, 383–384
    unprompted, 392
Generalized conditioned reinforcers, 75
Generalized suppression, 300
Genital stage, 45
Gestural prompts, 218
Goals, 342
    explaining, 212
    setting, 342–344
Goal-setting form, 342
Good behavior game, 262–265
    considerations about, 264
    modifications to, 264–265
    steps for implementing, 263–264
Goodness of fit, 57, 59
Graphing behavior, 125–149
    AB design for, 132, 133–134
    ABAB design for, 132, 134–136
    alternating treatments design for, 132, 144–147
    baseline data for, 130–132
    benefits of, 126–127
    changing conditions design for, 132, 143–144
    changing criterion design for, 132, 139–142
    designs for, 132–147
    elements of graphs and, 128–129
    hypothesis testing and, 172–174
    multiple baseline design for, 132, 136–139
    overview of, 126
    review questions/activities on, 147–148
    summary of, 147

Graphs
    elements of, 128–129
    self-monitoring, 328, 329, 331, 332
Gratification, 156
Group-oriented contingencies,
        260–267
    dependent, 261–262
    ethical considerations about,
        265–267
    explanation of, 260–261
    independent, 262
    interdependent, 262–265
    peer pressure and, 261
    types of, 261–265
Group self-correction, 232
Guided practice, 217–218
Guilt control, 328

H

Habit reversal, 316
Hall pass, 308–309
Hawthorne effect, 115
Hero procedure, 261
Hippocrates, 40
Home-school contracts, 259–260
Homework completion contract, 260
Homme, Lloyd, 70
Horizontal axis, 128
Hunt, Morton, 42
Hyperactivity, 31
Hypoactivity, 31
Hypotheses, 157–160
    contextual, 158–159
    curricular, 159–160
    functional, 157–158
Hypothesis development, 161–170
    defining a target behavior for, 162
    hypothesis generation and, 166–170
    interview stage in, 162–164
    observing behavior for, 164–166
Hypothesis testing, 170–175
    graphing behavior in, 172–174
    steps in, 171–172
Hysteria, 28

I

Id, 43
IDEA (Individuals with Disabilities
        Education Act), 153
Identification behaviors, 208
Ignoring inappropriate behavior, 68,
        311
Imitation, 215
Imitative performance
    cognitive factors in, 52–53
    observational learning and, 51–52
Immediacy
    of punishment, 303
    of reinforcement, 68–69
Impact measures, 397
Improvement, 12
Inclusive theories, 38
Incorporating functional mediators,
        387, 392–394
Increasing behavior, 66–77, 238
    avoidance conditioning for, 77
    negative reinforcement for, 75–77
    positive reinforcement for, 67–75,
        238–276
    See also Decreasing behavior
Independent group-oriented contin-
        gencies, 262
Independent practice, 219–222
Indiscriminable contingencies, 391–
        392
Individual-specific deficiencies, 179–
        185
Individuals with Disabilities Education
        Act (IDEA), 153
Instruction
    correction vs., 33–34
    direct, 211–223
    See also Teaching; Training
Instructional interventions, 176–177
Instructions
    effective use of, 214–215
    providing in SMP procedures,
        334–335
Instrumental conditioning, 48, 50–51

Intelligence, 357
Intelligence tests, 357
Intense punishment, 302–303
Intent, behavioral, 155–157
Interdependent group-oriented con-
    tingencies, 262–265
Interim criteria, 140–141
Intermittent reinforcement, 75
Internal self-reinforcement, 344,
    345–347
Interobserver agreement, 116
Interobserver reliability, 115–120
    duration recording and, 118
    frequency recording and, 117–118
    Hawthorne effect and, 115
    interobserver agreement and, 116
    interval recording and, 119–120
    latency recording and, 118
    observer drift and, 116
    permanent product recording and,
        116–117
    placebo effect and, 115
    time sampling and, 119–120
Interrelatedness, 58
Interresponse time (IRT), 284,
    289–291
Interruption of thoughts, 367–368
Interval recording, 105, 110–113
    advantages/disadvantages of,
        112–113
    interobserver reliability and,
        119–120
    partial, 111
    whole, 112
Interval schedules of reinforcement,
    79–81
Interventions
    consequent, 177
    instructional, 176–177
Interviews
    clinical, 359
    hypothesis development and, 162–
        164
Intrapsychic components, 43
Introjection, 46

In vivo assessment, 185–186
Irrational beliefs, 353, 372

J

Justice/revenge behaviors, 156

K

Key routines, 178
KISS acronym, 225

L

Labeling, 55–56
Latency recording, 105, 110
Latency stage, 44–45
Learned helplessness, 298
Learning
    materials for, 228–230
    observational, 51–52
Learning disabilities, 56
    See also Students with disabilities
Legal issues
    punishment and, 296–297
    time-out procedure and, 310–311
    See also Ethical issues
Legend, 128
Life management curriculum, 205
Limited-hold interval schedules, 80–81
Line graphs, 128–129
Logical curriculum, 204–205
Loose training, 390–391
Lotteries and raffles
    positive reinforcement using,
        270–271
    response cost lottery, 307

M

Magnification, 373
Materials for learning
    developing, 228
    distributing and collecting, 229–230
    storing, 229

McGovern, George, 56
Means-ends thinking, 369
Mediation essay, 364
Mediators, functional, 387, 392–394
Medical model, 23–26
    differential diagnosis and, 23–24
    mental illness and, 24–26
Mental illness, myth of, 24–26
Mental retardation, 56
Minimization, 373
Modeling, 215–217
    antecedent, 215–216
    enhancers, 215, 216
    error-dependent, 216–217
    partial, 217
Model-lead-test strategy, 217
Money, 239
Monitoring
    behavioral support plans, 178–179
    self-, 326, 327–338
    time-outs, 313–314
Motor movement, 31–32
Movement cycle, 102
Multiple baseline design, 136–139
Multiply controlled behaviors, 187
Multipurpose point sheets, 248–251
Muscle relaxation exercises, 371
Mystery motivators, 273
"Myth of Mental Illness, The"
        (Szasz), 24

N

Natural communities of reinforcement,
        387–389
Natural habitat, 57
Naturalistic assessment, 185–186
Natural prompts, 218
Negation, 46
Negative practice, 317–318
Negative punishment, 83–84
Negative reinforcement, 75–77
    avoidance conditioning and, 77
    behavioral intent and, 156
    punishment and, 302
    See also Reinforcement
Negative reinforcement trap, 76–77
Negotiating behavioral contracts,
        257–258
Niche breadth, 57
Nonverbal behavior, 4–5
No trial learning, 52

O

Objectives
    behavioral, 207–210
    explaining, 212
Observational learning, 51
    mechanisms of, 52
    performance and, 51–52
Observer characteristics, 215, 216
Observer drift, 116
Observing behavior, 164–166
Oedipus complex, 44
100-square charts, 271–273
Operant conditioning, 48, 50–51
    model of self-management, 326
Operational definitions, 101
    sample sheet of, 249
    token economies and, 248, 249
Oppositional-defiant disorder
        (ODD), 25
    diagnostic criteria for, 26
Oral stage, 43–44
Ordeal therapy, 318
Outcome assessment, 397
Outcome expectations, 53
Overcorrection, 314–316
    considerations when using, 316
    necessary characteristics of, 315
    positive practice, 315–316
    procedures resembling, 316–318
    restitutional, 315
Overgeneralization, 373
Overt external guidance, 361
Overt self-guidance, 361
Overt thought stopping, 367

P

Pacing, 212
Paperwork management, 230–232
Paradigm, 22
Paradigm paralysis, 39
Paradoxical intention, 318
Parallel curriculum, 205
Parsimonious theories, 38–39
Partial interval recording, 111
Partial modeling, 217
Pavlov, Ivan, 47
Peer pressure, 260–267
    ethics of using, 265–267
    good behavior game and, 262–265
    harmful use of, 265–266
    hero procedure and, 261
Peers
    effect of punishment on, 302
    generalization reinforced by,
        387–389
    group-oriented contingencies and,
        260–267
Performance
    applied behavior analysis and, 16
    observational learning and, 51–52
    self-monitoring, 333–335
Permanent products
    direct measurement of, 104–106
    interobserver reliability and,
        116–117
Permanent products recording,
    104–106
    inappropriate use of, 106
    interobserver reliability and,
        116–117
Personalization, 373
Personal standards, 31–32
Perspective taking, 369
Phallic stage, 44
Phase change lines, 128
Phase/condition labels, 128
Phenylketonuria (PKU), 40
Physical prompts, 218

Physical stimuli, 392–393
Placebo effect, 115
Planned ignoring, 311, 314
    plus restraint, 311–312, 314
Poorness of fit, 59–60
Positive practice overcorrection,
    315–316
Positive punishment, 83
Positive reinforcement, 13–15, 67–75,
    238–276
    behavioral contracts and, 251–260
    chart moves and, 268–269
    compliance matrix and, 273–275
    contingent, 69
    continuous, 74
    covert, 346–347
    criticisms of, 14–15
    deprivation and, 73
    examples of, 14
    group-oriented contingencies and,
        260–267
    guidelines for, 68–75
    immediacy of, 68–69
    intermittent, 75
    mystery motivators and, 273
    novel applications of, 268–275
    100-square charts and, 271–273
    preferences for, 69–72
    raffles and lotteries for, 270–271
    restricting access to, 72–73
    review questions/exercises on, 276
    satiation and, 72–73
    shaping and, 73–74
    spinners and, 269–270, 271
    summary of, 275–276
    token economies and, 239–251
    See also Reinforcement
Positive teaching, 200
Positivism, 45
Positron emission tomography (PET)
    scans, 38
Power/control behaviors, 156, 188–189
Precounting behavior, 97–98
Predictive utility, 38

Preference scales, 70, 71
Premack principle, 70, 72
Preventative approaches, 199–235
    curricular considerations and,
        201–211
    direct instruction and, 211–223
    environmental accommodations
        and, 223–232
    overview of, 200–201
    review questions/activities on, 233
    summary of, 232
Primary reinforcers, 75
Principles of behavior, 16, 65–92
    avoidance conditioning, 77
    differential reinforcement, 89
    extinction, 84–86
    fading, 88
    forgetting, 86
    negative reinforcement, 75–77
    positive reinforcement, 67–75
    punishment, 83–84
    response class, 89
    response differentiation, 89–90
    review questions/activities on, 91
    schedules of reinforcement, 77–82
    stimulus control, 86–87
    stimulus discrimination, 87
    stimulus generalization, 87–88
    summary of, 90
Probes, 210
Problem identification, 368–369
Problem-solving therapies, 357
Problem-solving training, 368–371
    steps and questions, 370
    thinking skills, 368–369
    turtle technique, 370–371
Production behaviors, 208
Proficiency levels, 210–211
Projection, 46
Prompts, 217
    cues vs., 217
    types of, 218
Prosocial skills, 53–54
Protection behaviors, 156
Psychodynamic theory, 39, 41–45

    ego defense mechanisms, 45
    intrapsychic components, 43
    psychosexual stages of development,
        43–45
Psychological resilience, 365
Psychosexual stages of development,
    43–45
Public goals, 343
Punishment, 13, 83–84, 295–322
    conditioned, 84
    contingent exercise, 317
    continuous use of, 303–304
    control and, 33
    immediacy of, 303
    intensity of, 302–303
    limitations of, 301–304
    negative practice, 317–318
    overcorrection, 314–316
    overview of, 296–297
    positive vs. negative, 83–84
    principles for using, 296
    quiet training, 317
    reinforcement and, 301–302
    response cost, 84, 304–309
    review questions/exercises on, 319–
        320
    simple correction, 316–317
    stimulus satiation, 318
    summary of, 319
    time-out, 309–314
    types of, 304–318
    undesirable side effects of, 297–300
    vicarious, 53, 302
Punishment contrast, 300

Q

Quiet training, 317

R

Raffles and lotteries, 270–271
Random sampling of thoughts, 359
Rating system, self-evaluation,
    339–342

Rational-emotive therapy (RET), 372
Ratio of exchange, 248
Ratio schedules of reinforcement, 78
Ratio strain, 78
Reaction formation, 46
Reactive effect, 327
Reactivity, 327, 337–338
Reading decoding, 209
Realistic goals, 343
Reciprocal determinism, 355–356
Recording behavior, 104–120
    duration recording, 108–110
    frequency or event recording,
        106–108
    hypothesis testing and, 172
    interobserver reliability for,
        115–120
    interval recording, 110–113
    latency recording, 110
    overview of techniques for, 105
    permanent products recording,
        104–106
    questions to consider before,
        100–101
    review questions/activities on,
        120–121
    self-recording, 328, 340, 341
    summary of, 120
    time sampling, 113–115
    See also Counting behavior
Recording spontaneous private
    speech, 359
Recruiting natural communities of
    reinforcement, 389
Reduction of response maintenance
    stimuli, 311
Reinforcement, 13
    contingent, 69
    continuous, 74
    control and, 33
    deprivation and, 73
    differential, 89, 279–294
    immediacy of, 68–69
    intermittent, 75
    negative, 75–77

positive, 13–15, 67–75, 238–276
    preferences for, 69–72
    primary and secondary, 75
    punishment and, 301–302
    restricting access to, 72–73
    rewards and, 14–15
    satiation and, 72–73
    schedules of, 77–82
    self-, 327, 344–347
    shaping and, 73–74
    vicarious, 53
Reinforcers
    backup, 239, 243–248
    conditioned, 75, 239
    primary and secondary, 75
    procedure for determining, 238
    selecting for students, 181–182
Relaxation exercises, 371
Relevant behaviors, 387–388
Reliability, interobserver, 115–120
Remediation, 203
Replacement behaviors
    deficiencies and, 179–185
    identification of, 177
    need for teaching, 157
Repression, 46
Resilience, 365
Respondent conditioning, 47–48
    interventions based on, 49
    second-order, 48
Response class, 89
Response cost, 84, 304–309
    advantages of, 304–305
    bonus response cost, 307–309
    example of using, 304
    implementation of, 305–307
    response cost lottery, 307
Response differentiation, 89–90
Response exemplars, 390
Response facilitation, 299–300
Response generalization, 300, 383
Response maintenance, 384
Response substitution, 299
Restitutional overcorrection, 315
Retrospective assessment, 358

Revenge behaviors, 156
Reversal design, 132, 134–136
Reviewing requisite skills, 213
Rewards, 14–15
    behavioral contracts and, 254–255
    See also Reinforcers
Rhodes, William, 55
Ritalin, 24
Role-play, 183–184
    assessment based on, 186
    example script for, 184
    problem solving and, 371
    steps in setting up, 183
Rules, classroom, 225–227
    behavioral contracts and, 252
    steps for establishing, 226
    tips for implementing, 226–227
    token economies and, 243, 244
Russell, Bertrand, 188

S

Satiation, 72
    positive reinforcement and, 72–73
    stimulus, 318
Scapegoating, 266
Scatter plots, 165–166
Schedules of differential reinforce-
        ment, 283–291
    DRL schedules, 289–291
    DRO schedules, 283–289
Schedules of reinforcement, 77–82
    fixed-duration, 81–82
    fixed-interval, 79
    fixed-ratio, 78
    interval with limited hold, 80–81
    variable-duration, 82
    variable-interval, 80
    variable-ratio, 78
SCREAM method, 213–214
Seat-work activities, 219–220
Seclusion, 312, 314
Secondary reinforcers, 75
Second-order respondent condition-
        ing, 48

Selective abstraction, 373
Self-control, 185, 325
Self-correction procedures, 230–232
Self-evaluation, 326–327, 339–344
    rating system for, 339–342
    setting daily goals for, 342–344
Self-expression, 156
Self-graphing, 328, 329
Self-instruction training, 361–364
    aspects of, 361–362
    effectiveness of, 362–364
Self-management, 323–350
    cognitive model of, 326–327
    operant conditioning model
        of, 326
    overview of, 324
    review questions/activities on,
        347–348
    self-control vs., 325
    self-evaluation and, 326–327,
        339–344
    self-monitoring and, 326, 327–338
    self-reinforcement and, 327,
        344–347
    summary of, 347
    theoretical underpinnings of,
        324–327
Self-mediated stimuli, 393–394
Self-monitoring, 326, 327–338
    accuracy of, 337
    attention, 329–333
    cognitive assessment and, 359, 360
    essential components of, 328
    length of process, 338
    overview of, 327–328
    performance, 333–335
    specific areas of concern in,
        335–338
    steps for teaching, 336
    target variables for, 338
Self-monitoring attention (SMA),
        329–333
    activities, 331–332
    card, 330–331
    graph, 331, 332

procedures, 332–333
tape, 330
Self-monitoring performance (SMP),
    333–335
    collecting baseline data, 334
    defining a target behavior, 333
    meeting with the student, 334
    providing instructions for,
        334–335
Self-observation, 328
Self-recording, 328, 340, 341
Self-reinforcement, 327, 344–347
    external, 344–345
    internal, 344, 345–347
Self-statements
    inventory of, 359
    self-instruction training and,
        362–363
Sequencing content, 204–205, 212–
    213
Shaping, 73–74
Simple correction, 316–317
Skinner, B. F., 3, 15, 48, 50, 326
Skinner box, 50
Social behavior
    academic behavior and, 26–27
    personal standards and, 31–32
Social influence, 188
Social interaction, 30–31
Social learning theory, 39, 51–54
    cognitive factors in, 52–53
    implications of, 53–54
    observational learning and, 51–52
Social reciprocity, 30–31
Social skills training, 53–54
Social stimuli, 393
Social validity, 158, 388
Sociocultural context, 27–28
Sociological model. *See* Ecological/
    sociological model
So-what test, 102
Specialized curriculum, 205
Specific goals, 343
Specifying assessment, 397
Spinners, 269–270, 271

Spontaneous recovery, 85–86
Stable baseline trend, 130, 131
Stimulus control, 86–87
Stimulus discrimination, 87
Stimulus exemplars, 389–390
Stimulus generalization, 87–88, 383
Stimulus-response chain, 74
Stimulus satiation, 318
Stranger test, 101
Students
    backup reinforcers for, 243–248
    group-oriented contingencies for,
        261–265
    self-correcting of papers by,
        230–232
    self-instruction training for, 363
    self-monitoring of performance by,
        334–335
    social skills training for, 53–54
    thought stopping directed by,
        367–368
Students with disabilities
    curricula appropriate for, 205
    direct instruction for, 211
    self-instruction training for, 363
Sublimation, 46
Subtasks, 206
Succession, 57
Successive approximations, 73
Superego, 43
Superstitious behavior, 69
Supplementary materials, 228
Suppression, 46, 300
Sure-fire work folders, 220–221
Symptom substitution, 103
Systematic desensitization, 49
Szasz, Thomas, 24

T

Tables of specification, 209
Taking advantage of natural communi-
    ties of reinforcement,
        387–389
Tape-recorded tones, 330

Target behaviors
    factors in pinpointing, 101–104
    hypothesis testing and, 162
    operationally defining, 171–172
    selecting for token economies,
        242–243
    self-monitoring performance and,
        333
Task analysis, 206
    content knowledge and, 208
    observation form for, 182–183
Task-approach statements, 362
Task record, 256
Tasks, 206
    behavioral contracts and, 254
    criterion-referenced tests and, 206
Task-specific statements, 362
Task strategies, 206–207
Teachers
    continuous data collection by, 96–97
    generalizing the repertoire of,
        395–396
    paperwork management and,
        230–232
    supplementary materials developed
        by, 228
    thought stopping directed by, 367
Teaching
    of relevant behaviors, 387–388
    of self-monitoring, 334–335, 336
    See also Training
Temporality, 358, 360
Testing
    criterion-referenced, 206
    hypothesis, 170–179
Theories of behavior, 37–63
    behavioral approaches, 45, 47–51
    biophysical model, 40–41
    ecological/sociological model,
        54–60
    overview of, 39
    psychodynamic theory, 41–45
    requirements for, 38–39
    review questions/activities on,
        60–61

social learning theory, 51–54
    summary of, 60
Thinking aloud, 359
Thought listing, 359
Thought stopping, 366–368
Three-term contingency, 8–10
Time-delay strategy, 217–218
Time-out, 309–314
    appropriate use of, 313
    legal guidelines for, 310–311, 313
    levels of, 310–312
    misuses of, 312–314
    monitoring the use of, 313–314
    overview of, 309–310
    recommendations for using, 314
Time sampling, 105, 113–115
    advantages/disadvantages of,
        114–115
    interobserver reliability and,
        119–120
Token economies, 75, 239–251
    advantages of, 239–240
    chart moves and, 268–269
    key aspects of, 239
    multipurpose point sheets and,
        248–251
    procedures for establishing,
        242–248
    reasons for effectiveness of,
        240–242
    rules for operating, 243, 244
    target behaviors for, 242–243
Tokens, 239, 243
    criteria for selecting, 245
    ratio of exchange for, 248
Tolerance list, 395
Total duration, 109–110
Training
    diversely, 387, 389–392
    loosely, 390–391
    problem-solving, 368–371
    quiet, 317
    self-instruction, 361–364
    social skills, 53–54
    See also Teaching

Transfer of functions, 187
Transition time, 227
Turtle technique, 370–371

U

Unconditioned response (UCR), 47
Unconditioned stimulus (UCS), 47
Undoing, 46
Unprompted generalization, 392
Unstable baseline trend, 130–131
Utility-based curriculum, 205

V

Variable baseline trend, 130–131
Variable-duration (VD) schedules of
    reinforcement, 82

Variable-interval (VI) schedules of
    reinforcement, 80
Variable-ratio (VR) schedules of
    reinforcement, 78
Verbal behavior, 4
Verbal prompts, 218
Verifiable theories, 38
Vertical axis, 128
Vicarious punishment, 53, 302
Vicarious reinforcement, 53
Videotaping thought reconstruc-
    tion, 359

W

Watson, John B., 47–48
Whole interval recording, 112
Withdrawal design, 134–136